THE TRIUMPH OF
MILITANT REPUBLICANISM

A Study of Pennsylvania and Presidential Politics
1860-1872

THE TRIUMPH OF MILITANT REPUBLICANISM

A Study of Pennsylvania and Presidential
Politics 1860-1872

by

Erwin Stanley Bradley

University of Pennsylvania Press
Philadelphia

7409
Printed in the United States of America

To
VIVIAN

Acknowledgements

The writer acknowledges the assistance and many courtesies extended to him by the staffs of the Manuscript Division of the Library of Congress; the Pennsylvania Historical and Museum Commission; the Pennsylvania State University Library; the Historical Society of Pennsylvania; Lancaster Newspapers, Incorporated; Pennsylvania State Library; Blair County Historical Society; and Western Pennsylvania Historical Society. I am especially indebted to Sylvester K. Stevens, Sanford W. Higginbotham, Donald H. Kent, Henry Howard Eddy, and Mrs. Autumn Leonard; all of the Pennsylvania Historical and Museum Commission; and to Bertha L. Jones of the Pennsylvania State Library. The illustrations were made possible through the courtesy of Donald H. Kent and R. N. Williams, 2nd, Director of the Historical Society of Pennsylvania.

Special thanks is due Professor Philip S. Klein of the Pennsylvania State University who first suggested such a work and who gave the manuscript a critical reading. Professor Ira V. Brown of the same institution also contributed help and advice.

Preface

DURING THE PAST twenty-five years, several monographs
dealing with various periods of Pennsylvania's political
history have appeared.* As the number increased it was seen
that there was a good chance of completing a co-operative
history of the Commonwealth. This work represents an
effort to fill one of the uncompleted gaps, the Civil War and
post-bellum era.

The Triumph of Militant Republicanism reviews the
sectional controversy of the 1850's which precipitated
political parties into a state of flux and notes the new align-
ments emerging from it. From the beginning of the Republican Party's national organization, the leaders of the new
party recognized the importance of the Keystone State. The
victories of the Peoples Party in 1858 and 1859 apparently
signified the electorate's condemnation of the policies of
President James Buchanan, the titular head of the
Democracy.

Because Pennsylvania's political history was fashioned
by the issues of the civil conflict, the leaders of the majority

---

* Theodore Thayer, *Pennsylvania Politics and the Growth of
Democracy, 1740-1776* (Harrisburg, 1953) ; Robert L. Brunhouse,
The Counter-Revolution in Pennsylvania, 1776-1790 (Harrisburg,
1942) ; Harry M. Tinkcom, *Republicans and Federalists in Pennsyl-
vania, 1796-1801* (Harrisburg, 1950) ; Sanford W. Higginbotham,
*The Keystone in the Democratic Arch: Pennsylvania Politics, 1800-
1816* (Harrisburg, 1952) ; Philip S. Klein, *Pennsylvania Politics,
1817-1832 ; A Game Without Rules* (Philadelphia, 1940) ; Charles
M. Snyder, *Jacksonian Heritage: Pennsylvania Politics, 1833-1848*
(Harrisburg, 1958).

9

Republican Party found that the state's citizenry was using
them as a medium to attack or sustain the Lincoln Administration. The Democratic opposition, seizing the opportunities presented by the War's exigencies, demanded the return
of cherished Constitutional liberties, and accused the
Unionists of prostituting legitimate restoration of the Union
to the will of the abolitionist-radicals. The War's end found
the defeated Democratic Party suffering from its issues, and
seeking desperately to rehabilitate itself.

Two Republican governors, Andrew G. Curtin and John
White Geary served during the period, 1861-1873. The
former, although at times not in harmony with Lincoln's
policies, used all his tremendous energy to support the war
effort and rightfully earned the popular sobriquet, "the
Soldier's Friend." The latter served during a period generally
prosperous, but one stigmatized by political corruption and
degradation of political office. John White Geary, assuming
leadership of a small coterie of progressive radicals, failed
in his attempt to gain leadership of the Commonwealth's
Republican Party.

The entire narrative is modified by the personal and
political feud between Andrew G. Curtin and Simon
Cameron for control of their party within the State. During
this formative period of the Cameron-Quay political dynasty,
Cameron, through alliances with leaders like Lincoln and
Grant, and powerful business interests, rebuilt a political
hierarchy welded by the spoilsman's philosophy of rewards
and punishments.

In 1872 came the supreme effort to overthrow the forces
of Grantism, which, largely for political purposes, had
determined to maintain a militant policy toward the prostrate
South. In Pennsylvania the Liberal Republican movement,
led by the Curtin faction, and assisted by the Democracy,

represented the final effort to destroy the political machine
of Simon Cameron, now an adjunct of Grantism. The outcome was a victory for the militant conservative wing of the
Republicans who were Radicals only in their continued
acceptance of policies engendered by war hysteria.

Of the several typists who have labored on the manuscript,
I am especially indebted to Kay Privett Deaton and Doris
B. Marsee.

ERWIN STANLEY BRADLEY

Union College
November, 1963

Contents

Illustrations

Abbreviations

The following abbreviations have been used to designate manuscript repositories frequently mentioned in the notes:

DCC   Dauphin County Historical Society Collection, Harrisburg, Pennsylvania.

DCL   Dickinson College Library, Carlisle, Pennsylvania.

HSP   Historical Society of Pennsylvania, Philadelphia, Pennsylvania.

HSWP   Historical Society of Western Pennsylvania, Pittsburgh, Pennsylvania.

LC   Manuscripts Division, Library of Congress, Washington, D.C.

PHMC   Pennsylvania Historical and Museum Commission, Harrisburg, Pennsylvania.

WHGS   Wyoming Historical and Geological Society, Wilkes-Barre, Pennsylvania.

THE TRIUMPH OF
MILITANT REPUBLICANISM

A Study of Pennsylvania and Presidential Politics,
1860-1872

I

The Political Antecedents

THE DECADES before the Civil War witnessed the passing of over a century and a half since the white man had settled in the geographical region now constituting the Commonwealth of Pennsylvania. The aborigines had accomplished little in modifying the physical landscape of a fertile region covered by immense forests and penetrated by innumerable streams. By 1860 the cultural landscape presented an imposing picture illustrating the remarkable advances achieved by a progressive people, engaged primarily in agricultural or related pursuits but whose life was increasingly affected by a fast growing industrialization of the nation's economy.

A traveler of the early 1850's making the trip by rail from Philadelphia to Pittsburgh, a journey of some 360 miles, would upon leaving the state's metropolis, pass the giant city gas works, a mute witness to progress already achieved in processing coal, the Keystone State's leading mineral resource. Along the sixty-mile ride to Lancaster, through the "garden of America," a few decaying inns reminded the tourist of the turnpike era and the colorful Conestoga wagon. The fields of grains, herds of cattle, numerous apple orchards, and the spacious barns of the Pennsylvania German testified to his monotonous routine of physical toil. En route from Lancaster one would pass through Middletown, an old canal intersection, then a lumber and coal distributing center. The first leg of the locomotive tour

21

terminated at the capital, Harrisburg, where Charles Dickens had found the most hospitable landlord in America.[1]

Turning westward the traveler passed over the wide Susquehanna River and followed the gorgelike route of the serpentine Juniata River between innumerable ridges and hills. He would observe much wild picturesque scenery, portions of the state canal in operation, and small towns like Lewistown and Huntingdon which thrived principally because of their location on the chief artery of trade. Excursions from the main line would have revealed a multiplicity of iron forges operated by capitalistic-minded ironmasters. And farther north and west lay the expanse of the great northern forest scarcely penetrated by man. At Hollidaysburg one would view one of the great engineering feats of the age, the canal portage, and at the newborn town of Altoona, the gift of the Pennsylvania Central Railroad, the traveler would leave the cars.[2] But near Conemaugh Station, at the western terminus of the portage, our traveler passing through one of the greatest bituminous coal areas of the nation had easy passage to Pittsburg, the new iron city.

Over half of the state's population of two and one half millions[3] depended upon agriculture for their subsistence. From approximately 9 million acres of improved farmland upon which the value of farm implements and machinery alone was set at $15 million vast crops of grain, hay, tobacco, and other crops were raised. In 1850, a very ordinary year, 15 million bushels of wheat and 20 of corn were harvested.

---

[1] Eli Bowen, *Pictorial Sketch-Book of Pennsylvania* (Philadelphia, 1852), 37-38, 69; Charles Dickens, *American Notes* (Greenwich, Conn., 1961), 107.

[2] At the time of Bowen's description, 1851, the railroad to Pittsburgh had not been completed. The mountain division began operation in 1854.

[3] In 1860 the state's population was 2,906,370, an increase of almost one-half million in a decade.

In pounds, the production of wool and tobacco amounted to almost five million and 900,000 pounds, respectively. Not to be ignored was the forest product of two and one quarter million pounds of maple sugar. The value of the Commonwealth's livestock exceeded $40 million.[4]

But the production of $290 million worth of manufactured goods, second in value only to New York, in 1860, proved the increasing importance of industry in Pennsylvania's economy. The leaders, Philadelphia and Allegheny Counties, together produced 55 per cent of the state's total. In terms of value in millions of dollars the leaders were flour and meal, 30; sheet bar iron, 15; leather, 13; cotton goods, 12.4; pig iron, 12; sawed lumber, 10; and other iron products, 7. To produce these goods over 22,000 establishments representing a capital investment of almost $200 million employed 220,000 laborers including 30,000 women, whose total annual wage amounted to $60 million, or less than $275 per person.[5]

Production figures establish the fact that iron constituted the heart of Pennsylvania's heavy industry in 1860. Her total iron products amounting in value to $35 million annually, easily led all others. The Keystone State was producing over half the iron ore and pig iron of the nation and almost half of the finished manufactured products.[6] The Commonwealth's iron masters like J. K. Moorhead, Thaddeus Stevens, Andrew G. Curtin, and Simon Cameron, some of whom had suffered from the iron depression of the 1830's, joined with economists and journalistic expositors of the type of Henry C. Carey and Morton McMichael to

[4] Figures from the Census of 1850.
[5] United States Census Bureau, *Eighth Census, Manufactures of United States in 1860.*
[6] *Ibid.*

bring about the incorporation of protectionism into the tenets of their political philosophy.

The political system of the independent Commonwealth began with the adoption of the constitution of 1776, the most ultrademocratic document of its kind in the colonies. The conservatives secured a new constitution in 1790 more to their liking, but one still democratic for the age. The governor and legislature were chosen by popular vote and there were no property qualifications to debar the white freeman from voting or holding office.

In 1838 the Commonwealth accepted its third constitution which remained in force until 1874.[7] The chief objections to the constitution of 1790 were the power of the governor over many appointive offices, his eligibility for three consecutive terms, life tenure of judges, limitations on the amending process; and the authority granted to the General Assembly to charter corporations, and to establish state banks empowered to issue currency. The new constitution was the work of farmers and lawyers in a convention evenly divided between the camps of the Democratic Party and that of the opposition Whigs and Anti-Masons.[8]

The lengthy constitution of 1838 consisted of eleven articles subdivided into numerous sections.[9] Article IX, a Declaration of Rights with 26 sections, illustrated the desire of the people to guarantee their private liberties against encroachment from their government. It retained prohibitions against the enforcement of two obsolete memorials to our English heritage—the infamous bill of attainder and its corollary, "corruption of blood." Changes increased the

---

[7] Amendments were adopted in 1850, 1857, 1864.

[8] Charles M. Snyder, *The Jacksonian Heritage: Pennsylvania Politics, 1833-1848* (Harrisburg, 1958), 96, 112.

[9] The complete text of the Constitution of 1838 with amendments is contained in Smull's *Legislative Handbook,* 1873, 35-67.

powers of the electorate and provided for more frequent submission of the names of public servants to the public will. The term of state senator was reduced from four to three years and the governor was limited to two consecutive terms. The General Assembly was empowered to initiate amendments, to elect a state treasurer, and to choose (as required by the Federal Constitution) the United States Senators. The franchise was restricted to "white freemen only"—there being little sentiment for extending the franchise to Negroes.[10]

The democratic elective trend which began with local officers continued when the office of auditor general became subject to popular will in 1850, and the same year a constitutional amendment provided for the election of judges of the state supreme court and of the courts of common pleas.[11]

The legislature underwent few changes under the new constitution. The annually elected House numbered 100, and the Senate, one-third of which was elected each year, consisted of 33 members. New apportionments which established the legislative districts were determined by population changes and feats of gerrymandering steamrolled through the legislature by the majority party. Nominations for legislative office although ostensibly determined in the local party caucus were more often dictated by a leading political figure or a provincial party boss. Legal qualifications for legislative office were simple, including the usual requirements of citizenship, minimum residence, etc. The minimum ages for representatives and senators were 21 and 25, respectively. After 1857, the constitution called for the choosing of state senators "at the same time, in the same

---

[10] Snyder, op. cit., 105.
[11] Smull's *Legislative Handbook*, 1873, 49.

manner, and at the same places where they shall vote for Representatives."[12]

The early state elections held in Pennsylvania on the second Tuesday of October, approximately three weeks prior to the time of the presidential election, elicited much national interest. If a governor were to be elected in a presidential year, the gubernatorial contest in the Commonwealth attracted special attention. With few exceptions the party victorious in the state's October polls also won the November national election. It is little wonder therefore that the outcome of these early elections came to be regarded throughout the nation as an infallible political weathervane for the purpose of predicting the presidential victor. This explains why Pennsylvania's voice was often a commanding one at the national conventions and also why national party committeemen allowed precious campaign funds to be channeled into the state for the purpose of winning the state elections. In addition, the party's premier campaign orators were often found stumping the Keystone State.

Politically, the decade 1850-1860 represented the triumph of sectionalism throughout the nation.[13] At the end of the era no party could claim to be truly national in scope, and even the proud party of Jefferson and Jackson found itself rent in twain. The fruits of manifest destiny which opened vast new areas to territorial organization and final incorpora-

---

[12] Third Amendment of 1857, Article I, Section V.

[13] No satisfactory work on the political history of Pennsylvania has yet appeared for this period but the student can cull much information from the following list: William C. Armor, *Lives of the Governors of Pennsylvania;* Lee F. Crippen, *Simon Cameron: Antebellum Years;* James T. DuBois and Gertrude S. Matthews, *Galusha A. Grow;* Malcolm Eiselen, *Rise of Pennsylvania Protectionism;* Philip Klein, *President James Buchanan;* Charles Going, *David Wilmot;* Alexander K. McClure, *Old Time Notes of Pennsylvania;* James Woodburn, *Life of Thaddeus Stevens.*

tion into the Union rapidly accelerated the growth of the wedges of separation and eventually led to the great civil strife of 1861-1865. The differences between the two sections were multiple and inextricably intertwined. Social, economic, and political factors all contributed to the South's determination to maintain an agrarian civilization calling for supremacy of the whites.[14] The vicious chain of economic ills attendant upon the slave-cotton-plantation system of the South were shouldered largely by Northern financial interests and the many illusory evils of the protective tariffs. The continued existence of slavery on a profitable basis depended upon its ability to expand into greener fields of pasture westward beyond the Mississippi. Politically it was imperative for the slave states to add enough senatorial representation in Congress to ward off unfriendly legislation. The fetish of "states' rights," focusing largely upon the determination of the slavocracy to enter freely into all new territories of the Union, was essentially a movement to guarantee perpetuation of the South's peculiar institutions and civilization; and its drive was engendered in great measure by *fear*—the specter of future hostile action by that aggressive giant, the North.

The issues of slavery had played a very minor role in the earlier political history of the Commonwealth. An antislavery sentiment was present from the beginning because of the influence of the Quakers, and slavery died easily in Pennsylvania. Later the antislavery strength in the state was evidenced through a series of personal liberty laws passed in 1826, 1827, and 1847[15] which were intended to protect free Negroes, to insure justice to fugitive slaves, and

---

[14] Ulrich B. Phillips, *"The Central Theme of Southern History,"* *American Historical Review* (October, 1928), XXXIV, 30.

[15] Stanton Ling Davis, *Pennsylvania Politics: 1860-1863* (Cleveland, 1935), 8. This doctoral thesis discusses in detail the political history of the period.

finally to scotch enforcement of the Federal Fugitive Slave Act within the Commonwealth. Many citizens opposed to slavery on a social or moral basis were not willing to go along with the extreme abolitionist. The abolitionists were divided into two groups: one faction bent on ignoring the laws of man and accepting only those of God (as they interpreted them); the other, the political group who were willing to gain their ends through constitutional channels. The latter faction represented by the Liberty Party in 1844 and the free-soilers in 1848 polled only a small vote in the Commonwealth.[16] General acceptance of the Compromise of 1850 greatly reduced the strength of the free-soilers.

For years Pennsylvania led the nation in the fight for a protective tariff. Although commercial capitalism, centered in Philadelphia, together with the western agrarian interests, were opposed or indifferent to protection, the gradual industrial growth of the Commonwealth, representing the triumph of merchant capitalism, came to consolidate public opinion in its favor. Industrial leaders like Simon Cameron repeatedly represented the protective tariff a boon to the working man and consequently labor, now converted to the apparent benefits of protectionism, was found in the vanguard of its exponents. Pennsylvania's representatives in the Congress, regardless of party affiliation, generally agreed in supporting any measure which afforded protection to the state's peculiar products. In 1844 when the National Democratic Party exhibited no interest in protectionism, the state Democratic Convention resolved that a protective tariff was one of the "cardinal principles of the democratic creed."[17]

---

[16] Edward Stanwood, *History of the Presidency from 1788 to 1897* (Boston and New York, 1898), 243.

[17] Henry Mueller, *Whig Party in Pennsylvania* (New York, 1922), 100, f.n.

The Whigs of the Commonwealth surpassed their party in their devotion to protectionist principles, proclaiming the well-regarded Tariff of 1842 an exclusively Whig measure.

In the two decades preceding the great civil strife of 1861, Pennsylvania's leaders of the several parties were often evaluated before the bar of public opinion on the basis of their stand on the tariff. James Buchanan, the Democratic leader, suffered repeated embarrassment in his native state because of his party's indifference to protection. The free-soiler David Wilmot received more notoriety in his home state over his vote on the Tariff of 1846 than he did with the introduction of his famous "Proviso." He was the only representative from Pennsylvania to vote for the Tariff of 1846—and even Wilmot, who represented agrarian interests, desired protection for his state's products.

Pennsylvania produced the nation's outstanding literary and philosophical apologists for the protective tariff, the Carey family. Matthew Carey (1760-1837), a charter member of the Philadelphia Society for Promotion of National Industry, shared with Alexander Hamilton the distinction of establishing the nationalist school of economic thought. Matthew's son, Henry C. Carey (1793-1879), also a publisher, received wide recognition in the broad sociological field. This Anglophobe, using *laissez-faire* as his guiding principle, argued at first for free trade, and then suffered sudden conversion to the principles of protectionism in the 1840's; yet he still looked upon free trade as a utopia yet unattainable. In spite of his faulty logic and many contradictions (he saw no inconsistency in protectionism and cheap money), Henry C. Carey became a recognized leader of the American school of political economy. He "at one and the same time assured his Northern compatriots that the tariff would ultimately end slavery and addressed Southern planters with the plea that only the tariff could save them. . . ."[18] Carey found the proper political medium for his talents within the new Republican party. He assisted in the organization of the party in Philadelphia in 1856 and was the author of Pennsylvania's tariff plank in the Republican platform of 1860. The Morrill Tariff of 1861 with its amendments represented the fulfillment of Carey's ultraprotectionist dreams.

The leading political organization of the Commonwealth during the first quarter of the nineteenth century had been Jefferson's Democratic-Republican Party. The absence of a two-party system prior to 1832 led to much political confusion in both national and state politics. When battle lines cleared in the early 1830's, two great national parties, Jacksonian Democracy and the National Republican-Whigs had appeared. In addition, a new political monstrosity, Anti-Masonry, brought with it the national presidential convention to succeed "King Caucus."

During the following years the state's Democrats endeavored to follow the traditions of popular Jacksonian Democracy. During the first part of the period, Pennsylvania was the scene of a three-cornered struggle among the Democracy, the Whigs, and Anti-Masonry; at the end the Native Americans had risen to take the place of extinct Anti-Masonry in the political triad. The Democrats were usually able to maintain their supremacy, and only opposition coalitions, particularism, or party schism could unseat them.[19] The latter calamity took place in 1835 when the Democracy, rent by a major schism, ran two gubernatorial

---

[18] Arnold W. Green, *Henry Charles Carey: Nineteenth Century Sociologist* (Philadelphia, 1951), 37.

[19] The Whig–Anti-Masonic victory in 1840 may be attributed largely to the coattails of the popular national Whig hero, William Henry Harrison.

candidates and thus enabled the minority group, the Anti-Masons, to elect Joseph Ritner.

In 1848, Whig strength attained its zenith. An exciting concurrent gubernatorial and presidential race was made possible through the resignation of Democratic Governor Francis R. Shunk, in midsummer. The Whig presidential candidate, Zachary Taylor, was not a strong tariff man like Clay or even General Scott. But interim Governor William Freame Johnston, the Whig gubernatorial candidate,[20] stressing the tariff issue along with a good word for capital, labor, and free-soil principles, won by only 277 votes over his Democratic opponent, Morris Longstreth. Taylor's comfortable state margin of 13,000 over Lewis Cass was reputedly achieved through "gunpowder and the tariff."[21] David Wilmot, now a free-soiler, had campaigned vigorously for his candidate, Martin Van Buren.

The Compromise of 1850, widely hailed as the harbinger of a new era free from sectional strife, actually provided only temporary respite, and in 1854 particularism emerged stronger than ever to debate the merits of the Kansas-Nebraska Bill which would allow the opening of new territorial areas to the slave interests. This intense factional strife, presaging the final wedges of separation to follow in the next decade, was the vital factor in precipitating the Keystone State's political organizations into a state of flux. The Commonwealth's political cauldron, consisting of Pierce Democrats, tariff Democrats, free-soilers, Conscience Whigs, anti-Nebraska men, and Know-Nothings, seethed and stewed for half a decade before party lines again became clearly distinguishable.

---

[20] Johnston had succeeded to the duties of the government by virtue of his position as Speaker of the Senate.

[21] Hendrick B. Wright quoted in Snyder, *Jacksonian Heritage*, 218,

It was the Know-Nothing or American group which furnished the chief political catalytic agent from which new parties could emerge. Within the secret lodges of this new species of nativism there lay the answer to Pennsylvania's mystifying elections of 1854 which produced a Whig governor and a 190,000-majority Democratic canal commissioner. In local elections defeated candidates became acquainted with their successful opponents the day after election. Although Know-Nothing clubs and lodges mushroomed simultaneously in all parts of the state, to Philadelphia goes the dubious honor of fathering and propagating the gospel of "Americanism."[22]

With the anti-Catholic riots of Philadelphia still fresh in the memories of many, fuel was added to the flame through heavy foreign immigration into the country, the announced visit to the United States of a papal nuncio and the entrance of a Catholic into the Pierce Cabinet. Alarmists would not have been surprised to hear that the Vatican, shaken by a terrific national awakening in Italy, was seeking to establish a new demesne in America. However, the view that Americanism was wholly anti-Catholic and anti-foreign is erroneous. There was actual fear that our time-honored democratic institutions were jeopardized because of the influx of an alien people bred in political faiths antagonistic to our beloved republic.[23]

The state Whigs, finding their party in the process of disintegration, mounted the convenient Know-Nothing bandwagon. Allegedly, James Pollock, the successful Whig candidate for governor in 1854, was unaware of his backing by

---

[22] Forney, *Anecdotes of Public Men* (New York, 1874), 135.
[23] Sister M. Theophane Geary, *History of Third Parties in Pennsylvania, 1840-1860* (Washington, 1938). 161,

American lodges.[24] For the bolstered Whigs their victory was
an endorsement of their anti-Nebraska plank.[25] In some cases
the Americans supported Whigs; in others, Democrats; and
occasionally, a regular Know-Nothing candidate. In any case
the Americans held the balance of power; and many political
leaders fearful of this unseen monster protested their belief
in the principles of "Americanism" while at the same time
maintaining nominal affiliation with their old party. Consequently men of opposing political complexion were found
consorting together within the confines of an American
caucus; and many found the means of emerging from the
flux to the ranks of another party without suffering loss of
prestige.

It was because of the foregoing factors that the new legislature of 1855, although ostensibly composed of 61 Whigs,
49 Democrats, and 23 Americans, included enough members
of pro-American sentiments to elect a United States senator
if the various wings and juntos could agree upon a candidate.[26] It was under these peculiar circumstances that two
important state leaders, Simon Cameron and Andrew G.
Curtin, from the opposing Democratic and Whig groups,
found themselves in the same caucus contending for the
senatorial nomination. This senatorial contest marked the
beginning of a political and personal feud which was destined
to color Pennsylvania's political history until 1873, and
which ended in a complete triumph for Simon Cameron.
Special attention must be given to these two men who later
contested for leadership of the Commonwealth's Republican
Party, who were entrusted with carrying out the Lincoln

[24] Alexander K. McClure, *Old Time Notes of Pennsylvania* (two
volumes, Philadelphia), 1905, I, 216.
[25] Harrisburg *Telegraph,* March 18, 1854 quoted in Mueller, *Whig
Party,* 210.
[26] *Whig Almanac,* 1855, 55.

policies during the trying war years, and who were largely responsible for the factional nature of the Republican organization during the war and post-bellum eras.

Simon Cameron was born of mixed Scotch-German ancestry at Maytown, Lancaster County, in 1799. His father's extreme poverty compelled him, at an early age, to be received into the home of a Jewish physician in Sunbury where young Simon made the most of his high cultural surroundings. A brilliant Italian émigré, Lorenzo Da Ponte, was probably the one who influenced young Cameron to try his fortune as a printer. From an apprenticeship he gradually worked his way at the end of a decade to part ownership of the Harrisburg *Pennsylvania Reporter*.

Cameron was initiated into the mysteries of politics under Samuel D. Ingham, a leading factional leader in the Calhoun wing of the Democratic-Republican Party. The election of his friend John Andrew Shulze in 1823 to the governorship stood him in good stead. Before retiring from office Shulze appointed Cameron adjutant general, which explains Cameron's lifetime rank of "General," the title by which he was generally addressed. But the honoree was too busy profiteering from lucrative canal contracts (another example of Shulze's friendship) to remain in office long. His talents in the political field received recognition from Jackson himself when Cameron was chosen on short notice to force Martin Van Buren, Old Hickory's choice of a running mate, upon a recalcitrant Pennsylvania delegation at the 1832 Democratic National Convention. Cameron's efficient execution of this charge was no doubt performed in the expectation of securing a reward from the Little Magician should he succeed Jackson. When the benefice finally came to Cameron in the form of an agency to adjust the claims of the half-breed relatives of the Winnebago Indians in Wisconsin Territory, it boomeranged into the basis for charges against Cameron of corruption and of personal profit in the transaction. Cameron was never able to live down this questionable episode in his early career, and enemy journalists periodically took delight in saluting the "Great Winnebago Chieftain."

Simon Cameron had chosen to hitch his political star to the train of James Buchanan, but now with the stench of the Winnebago notoriety surrounding him, both Buchanan and his journalistic mouthpiece, John W. Forney, ostracized him. Cameron suffered another setback when Francis Shunk, the new governor, contrary to assurance given the Improvement-Muhlenberg faction, proscribed that group now headed by Cameron. When Buchanan failed to sponsor him for the Democratic nomination to succeed retiring United States Senator Daniel Sturgeon, in January, 1845, Cameron determined to strike out for himself. His advocacy of a high tariff, internal improvements, relief for banks, and a check on the growth of slavery all combined to place him closer to the Whig Party than to the Democracy.

Buchanan's retirement from the senatorship and his entrance into the Polk Cabinet provided Cameron with the opening necessary to enable him to catapult himself into the United States Senate and to establish his reputation as a master strategist. A Democratic rump caucus of only 48 party members made the mistake of nominating George W. Woodward, a Shunk man of free-trading inclinations. Playing the role of an opportunist, Cameron made advances to the cautious Whigs who first elicited proper safeguards from him and then proceeded to throw their strength to him. Whig backing, together with a coterie of 16 dissatisfied Democrats which he was able to draw with him, enabled the bolter,

Simon Cameron, to defeat Woodward.[27] John Forney greeted
news of Cameron's election with a "God Save the Commonwealth."[28] But Cameron's status as a party regular was very
questionable and future advancement seemed likely to be
blocked by his new enemy, James Buchanan. In 1849
Cameron's name was not even presented for re-election to
the Senate.

Andrew Gregg Curtin was eighteen years the junior of
Simon Cameron. His father, an Irish immigrant, established
himself in 1800 at the village of Bellefonte, Centre County,
then a remote section of the Commonwealth, and after years
of hard labor became a successful ironmaster. For his second
wife, Roland Curtin chose Jean Gregg. daughter of Andrew
Gregg—Centre County farmer, distinguished Jeffersonian
statesman, eight-term congressman, ex-secretary of state and
gubernatorial opponent of John A. Shulze. Andrew, son of
Roland and Jean Curtin, gained a portion of his academic
education at the school of the Reverend David Kirkpatrick
in Milton, home town of his friend James Pollock. After
further study under Bellefonte attorney and at Dickinson
College, young Curtin in 1839 was admitted to practice in
Centre County courts.

Andrew Curtin's political career began during the exciting
presidential campaign of 1840 when the Whigs were shouting
their campaign slogan of "Tippecanoe and Tyler Too." He
stumped for four successive Whig candidates in 1840, 1844,
1848, and 1852. In the two latter campaigns Curtin was
placed on the state Whig electoral ticket. A master of wit
and humor, possessed of unusual physical energy, and

---

[27] Actually the votes of the Native Americans determined
Cameron's victory. See Lee F. Crippen, *Simon Cameron: Ante-
Bellum Years* (Oxford, Ohio, 1942), 60.

[28] Forney to Morton McMichael, March 14, 1845, John W. Forney
Papers, LC.

exhibiting a genial personality, Andrew Curtin, after a decade, gained recognition as one of the leading Whig orators of the state.[29] He was the leading favorite for the gubernatorial nomination in the Whig convention of 1854, but gave way to his friend James Pollock.[30] Curtin managed an energetic campaign for Pollock and upon the latter's election was designated secretary of state in the incoming governor's cabinet. A nominal Whig plurality in the new legislature of 1855 offered an excellent opportunity for Curtin's election to the United States Senate if he were successful in securing Know-Nothing backing.

The appearance of 91 legislators in the Whig-American nominating caucus of 1855 (including nine Democrats) prevented the original Know-Nothings from exercising control of their own caucus. Cameron, who stood no chance of election as a Democratic candidate, had cleverly built a personal following by granting financial assistance to legis-lative candidates, by expressing his devotion to protection, and by signing a statement of American "principles." After the fifth ballot with Cameron leading Curtin by nine votes, twenty-nine Curtin men led by Francis Jordan of Bedford walked out of the caucus declaring that Cameron had pur-chased his votes.[31] A broadside published by the seceders branded Simon Cameron "one of the most intriguing if not the most corrupt politician in the state."[32] The rump nomin-

[29] For a sketch of Curtin see William C. Armour, *Lives of the Governors of Pennsylvania* (Norwich, Connecticut, 1874) ; William B. Parker, "Andrew Gregg Curtin," *Dictionary of American Biography,* IV, 606-07.
[30] Alexander K. McClure, "Life and Services of Andrew G. Curtin," an address delivered before the House of Representatives, Harrisburg, January 20, 1895.
[31] Philadelphia *Public Ledger,* Feb. 10, 1855.
[32] "American Petition," Feb. 12, 1855, Society Miscellaneous Collection, HSP.

ated Cameron but had not the strength to elect him. After a series of futile ballots it was seen that no candidate could secure the senatorship and the legislature postponed the election until fall.

Apparently there was little reason for the bitter personal enmity which developed between Curtin and Cameron during this contest. Curtin withdrew his candidacy and took no active part in directing charges against Cameron. Curtin supporters later took no active part in directing charges against Cameron. Cameron supporters later spread the tale that Curtin had violated a pledge to support Cameron in return for the latter's backing to make Curtin secretary of state under Pollock[33]—an obvious lie to any student who analyzes the campaign. Curtin's close confidant, Alexander K. McClure, attributed the enmity to a "personal reproach" cast upon Curtin by Cameron during the course of a party in which the latter had allowed his tongue to be loosened through over indulgence in liquid refreshments.[34] In Bellefonte, Curtin's hometown, the story was circulated that Cameron had referred to the questionable paternity of an illegitimate child. In any case the incident opened a breach that was never healed, and on the few occasions when it was necessary for the pair to face each other publicly only the coolest civilities were exchanged.

The Know-Nothing upheaval of 1854 in Pennsylvania was accompanied by another giving birth to a new major party, the Republican. Even during the course of the tedious congressional debates over the Kansas-Nebraska Bill which proposed to nullify the old principles of an established dividing line between the free and the slave, various mass

---

[33] James Bristow to John Covode, Nov. 28, 1859, Papers of John Covode, HSWP.
[34] McClure, *Notes*, I, 387.

meetings of anti-Nebraska men pledged their continued resistance to the impending legislation, designed, as they saw it, to impart new life blood to an archaic, barbarous institution. It was this one common denominator, their Wilmot Proviso sentiment, which coalesced former Whigs, Democrats, and minor groups into the new Republican Party.

Although anti-Nebraska men organized locally in Wilmot's territory and elsewhere in the fall of 1854, and four-fifths of Pennsylvania's newly elected congressmen opposed the Kansas-Nebraska Act,[35] the Republicans had effected no state organization within the Commonwealth. In August of the following year, representatives from ten counties issued a call from Reading for a state convention to meet at Pittsburgh, the geographic center of the anti-Nebraska men.[36] The radical complexion of the September Pittsburgh Convention, which in a moment of hysteria nominated a martyred abolitionist for canal commissioner, alienated the movement's conservative supporters. A last-minute attempt to fuse the Republicans, Whigs, and Americans into a "Union" ticket did not prevent the Democracy from electing a plurality candidate and gaining a working majority in the legislature. The new party did not achieve any important success immediately. Simon Cameron joined the Republicans in 1856 and soon was contending with David Wilmot for state leadership.

In spite of opposition groups, the Commonwealth's Democracy scored periodic successes. In 1851, William Bigler defeated the Whig governor William F. Johnston in

---

[35] Mueller, *Whig Party in Pennsylvania,* 220, 215.
[36] C. Maxwell Myers, "Rise of the Republican Party in Pennsylvania, 1854-1860," (MS, Pittsburgh, 1940) 62. The meeting is not to be confused with the free-soil controlled convention of the Americans at Reading in July.

his try for re-election. Tariff issues and the Nebraska controversy hurt the state Democracy but these losses were offset by the lawless excesses of abolitionists and radical free-soilers, as illustrated in the Lancaster County Christina riot where a slave owner was killed while demanding the return of his runaway slaves.

William Bigler, one of the state's leading Democratic leaders, had entered the political arena with publication of a Jackson sheet in Clearfield during the 1830's. A fortune amassed in the lumber business enabled him to devote his time to active politics. He served with distinction in the state senate, twice ocupying the office of speaker. As governor, he fought omnibus legislation, especially that which permitted wholesale chartering of banks. His capture of a seat in the United States Senate in 1856 compensated him for his defeat by the Whig-American combination when he attempted to succeed himself in the gubernatorial office. Bigler defended the policies of President Buchanan, whose characteristics of "dullness, ponderosity, and dogged industry" were similar to his own. He retained his political interests long after he retired from the Senate in 1861.[37]

The year 1856 would decide which of the several weaker opposition parties would emerge to do battle on a national scale with a scarred Democracy somewhat shorn, but still able to maintain its ranks unbroken. In Pennsylvania, a decadent Whiggism with its organization now practically defunct, had suffered itself to be inoculated with the prejudicial principles of "Americanism," a mixture providing no basis for permanency. Whiggism's exodus is to be found in the train of its successor. Judged by recent elections the Americans appeared strong but already antislavery issues

[37] Roy F. Nichols, *The Disruption of American Democracy* (New York, 1948), 55,

were in the process of cleaving their ranks. ". . . the
elements [slavery and antislavery] cannot dwell together,"
predicted the persevering Salmon P. Chase.[38]

The Americans had succeeded in effecting a national
organization but when their National Council injected the
slavery question (actually a *de facto* recognition of the
Nebraska Settlement) into their resolutions, former Governor
William F. Johnston of Pennsylvania led a group of 15
seceders from the hall. The same thing occurred at the
American National Convention of 1855 when New England
and Western states delegates withdrew; and again at the
Reading Convention a dissatisfied coterie of Philadelphians
walked out. Although the vague national plank of 1856
smacked only of a popular sovereignty flavor, the Johnston
junto, executing a repeat performance, joined with other
Northerners in a secession from the national convention,
and indicated its willingness to make a deal with the Republicans. The American State Council condemned the Johnston
faction and accepted Millard Fillmore. The demoralized
Whig remnants of the Commonwealth were expected to
support Fillmore, the Know-Nothing presidential candidate,
following his endorsement by a national meeting of Whigs at
Baltimore in the early fall of 1856, but many interior Whigs
rebelled and assisted in forming Union tickets with John C.
Frémont, the "People's" candidate included on their slate.[39]

The Keystone State was destined to play an important
role in the councils of the new sectional Republican Party
dating from its national organization in Pittsburgh, February
22, 1856. At that time a declaration of purposes, excoriating

---

[38] Chase to A.M.G. [sic], "Diary and Correspondence of Chase,"
American Historical Association, *Annual Report,* 1902, Volume II
(Washington, 1903), 272.

[39] Mueller, *Whig Party in Pennsylvania,* 217-27.

the Pierce Administration for its weaknesses and faithlessness, demanded the repeal of all laws which allowed slavery in "Territories once consecrated to Freedom" and proclaimed resistance by "every constitutional means the existence of slavery in any of the Territories. . . ."[40]

When the national nominating Republican Convention met at Philadelphia in June, Pennsylvania's delegates occupied 81 seats. The radical evangelistic fervor capturing the gathering is evidenced by the platform, presented by David Wilmot, reprobating the crime against Kansas and demanding liquidation in the territories of those twin relics of barbarism, "polygamy and slavery."[41] If taken seriously it could mean future criminal prosecution of members of the Pierce Administration from top to bottom. Pennsylvania's choice (more properly that of Thaddeus Stevens) for the Presidency, Justice John McLean of Ohio, was rejected and Frémont was chosen the party standard bearer.[42] Only the opposition of Francis P. Blair prevented Cameron from capturing the vice-presidential nomination.[43] The varied character of the gathering is illustrated in the presence of Thaddeus Stevens and Joseph Ritner, old Anti-Masonic leaders; Passmore Williamson, an abolitionist of the deepest hue; Henry C. Carey, economist and sociologist; James Black, prohibitionist; and E. D. Gazzam, Know-Nothing.

The Keystone Democracy's favorite son, James Buchanan, at last came into his own at the national convention held in Cincinnati. The Kansas fiasco decided the unavailability of

---

[40] *Official Proceedings of the Republican Convention, Pittsburgh* (Washington, 1856), 23-24.

[41] Stanwood, *History of the Presidency*, 272.

[42] At the state convention, June 17, the Pennsylvanians decided on McLean. On the first ballot at Philadelphia, the Stevens men gave McLean 23 votes.

[43] Myers, "Rise of the Republican Party," 102.

both Douglas and Pierce. Expediency demanded a man who could carry the two leading critical states of the North, Indiana and Pennsylvania; and Buchanan, who had been inadvertently "shelved" away from it all in London for the past several years, "was the right man for the times."[44] Senator William Bigler, Congressman J. Glancy Jones, and John W. Forney of the facile pen, all labored in the "Old Buck's" behalf to help bring about his nomination. The Democracy's platform called for continued endorsement of the Kansas-Nebraska principles (without agitation) which to date had brought them only one reward, flaming Kansas.

During the campaign of 1856, the Republicans lacked two major weapons which in the succeeding decades were to bring them victory, the tariff issue and an ample campaign chest. The tariff was forgotten in the crusade to eradicate the evil of slave-ridden territories, and the Democracy retained possession of the leading bankers. On the other hand, huge sums were spent by the Democrats to carry the October state elections and Buchanan.[45] By adding to the foregoing factors, Chairman Forney's numerous fraudulent registrations through "mass naturalization," and the fears of the conservative men, one has the best answers to the election returns.

It was a complete if narrow victory for the Democracy. Its candidates for state offices won over Union tickets by margins ranging from 2700 to 3700 votes. The Democracy succeeded in returning what looked like a working majority

---

[44] See Philip Shriver Klein, *President James Buchanan* (University Park, 1962). Lack of space makes it impossible to present a proper resumé of James Buchanan's career. It should be noted however that Buchanan was entering political eclipse in 1860 and exercised little influence on the period covered by this study.

[45] Job G. Patterson to Cameron, Sept. 18, 1856, Cameron Papers, Dauphin County Collection, Harrisburg.

in the General Assembly and three-fifths of the state's newly elected congressmen were Democrats. When the complete figures were finally tallied they showed the Buchanan electors chosen by a majority of little more than 800 votes. The results indicated not so much continued supremacy of the Democracy in the state as it did the surprising gains attained by an infant party only two years of age. The new sectional Republican Party had taken one more step in its seemingly inexorable march toward victory and it looked forward with confidence to the next four years.

In January, 1857, the time arrived for the Commonwealth to send another member to the United States Senate. A small majority on joint ballot of the two legislative houses apparently gave the Democrats the opportunity to entrench themselves in a strong spot for another six years. James Buchanan, anxious to reward his efficient campaign manager, and finding him unacceptable either as editor of the party organ or for a Cabinet post, practically dictated John W. Forney's nomination for senator in the Democratic caucus, thereby antagonizing many members who preferred Henry D. Foster.

The Republican nomination lay between David Wilmot and Simon Cameron. During the campaign of 1856 Cameron had been invited to participate in Republican conferences at the top level[46] and both Thaddeus Stevens and Wilmot had accepted him.[47] Even Andrew G. Curtin became "reconciled" to his candidacy.[48] After his defeat in 1855 Cameron had quietly gone his way, welding together a political machine built upon personal loyalty rather than party affili-

---

[46] E. D. Morgan to Cameron, Aug. 14, 1856, Cameron MSS, DCC.

[47] Stevens to E. D. Gazzam, Dec. 4, 1856, Edward McPherson Papers, Library of Congress ; Wilmot to Cameron, n.d., 1857, Simon Cameron Papers, Library of Congress.

[48] Samuel Purviance to Cameron, Dec. 3, 1856, *ibid.*

ation. His correspondence during the period indicated that he was making satisfactory progress, but few political observers would have predicted his election with Democratic support after he had turned his back on the party. But when Simon Cameron announced his desire for a minority party nomination, he did so with only one objective in mind—his successful election to the Senate.

Cameron possessed several advantages: Buchanan was known as his bitter enemy; there was general hatred for Forney among Republicans, Americans, and old Whigs because of his unfair campaign methods and the free use of his volatile pen; Cameron could pose as the leading champion of the tariff in the leading tariff state; his political machine functioned on a basis of rewards and punishments; and finally, he could afford to pay staggering sums for a few opposition votes. After three Democratic defectors[49] secretly pledged their vote to Cameron in the presence of coalition emissaries, the Republican-American caucus nominated him. In one of Pennsylvania's most dramatic senatorial contests, Simon Cameron emerged the victor over Forney. His election signified more than a victory over Buchanan and the State Democracy—he had secured recognition as the top Republican in Pennsylvania and could now operate on the national level with other members of his party. Moreover, he could conceivably become the Moses the party was seeking to lead it to victory in 1860.

But before the year would run its course, the Democracy would have an opportunity to secure a measure of compensation for its loss of the senatorship. It was time to select

---

[49] The end of W. B. Lebo, one of the three Democratic renegades, who dropped dead on the streets of Tamaqua twenty years later, made headlines. See Bellefonte *Democratic Watchman*, March 23, 1877.

a successor to Governor Pollock, who would retire in 1858. The party choice was William F. Packer, one-time journeyman printer under Cameron, former editor, canal and railroad builder, auditor general under Porter, and former Speaker of the House. Although Packer had labored to secure Buchanan's presidential nomination, he was considered Forney's candidate rather than the President's. At the time of his nomination Packer wrote secretly to Buchanan reprimanding him for his Kansas policy.[50]

The Republicans, believing they stood little chance of winning, decided the time was opportune to reorient their relationship with their former allies, the Americans, and to offer a political sacrifice if necessary, to clarify the issues. Posing as the great fish which had lately swallowed its Jonah, the Republicans, believing that the Americans had no choice except to follow, set up Union tickets in a condescending manner with the Americans relegated to the least important offices.

Their candidate for governor, David Wilmot, had gained widespread notoriety by virtue of his free-soil proviso. Had he accomplished nothing else in the realm of American political life, except to offer his amendment to bar the further spread of slavery, posterity would have remembered him. This citizen from northern Pennsylvania, with a reputation for slovenliness of dress, intemperance in eating and drinking, in addition to laziness, entered the House in 1845, and gained much attention and condemnation in his own state because of his vote to repeal the protective tariff of 1842. Wilmot was willing to resign his judgeship (temporarily it was understood), accept defeat, and perhaps gain recognition in the process, as the state's leading Republican. His primary

---

[50] Armor, *Lives of the Governors,* 443-44.

duty was "to fallow the ground for future harvest. . . ."[51] The party's promotion of Wilmot, who was considered little better than an abolitionist, proved that its managers were willing to gamble on the fast-increasing antislavery sentiment to more than compensate it for the loss of conservatives concentrated in the Philadelphia area. Before adjourning, the state convention passed antislavery resolutions and, taking a thrust at the Supreme Court of United States, asserted the plenary power of Congress over territories.

In spite of Wilmot's heroic efforts little interest was manifested by a public now in the process of reverting to political normalcy after the presidential campaign of 1856. Neither could Wilmot persuade Packer to accompany him on a tour of debates. Such practices, contended Charles Buckalew, the Democratic state chairman, eventually would lead to the selection of candidates "fit only for the stump."[52] The dormant tariff question reappeared but not in the same guise as before. Leading Republicans, proud of their protectionist proclivities, were chided by the Democracy for having chosen Wilmot, the "Free Trader," for their candidate. Wilmot struggled to rehabilitate himself on the tariff question but the spectral apparition of his tariff vote of 1846 would not down.

Had the effects of the Panic of 1857 been discernible to the public earlier, the protectionists would likely have seized upon the tariff as an issue; but the Republicans had to content themselves mainly with a repetition of the antislavery lines of the preceding year. The Americans, contrary to expectations, refused to play second fiddle in a Republican campaign and established their own slate of candidates for

---

[51] A. K. McClure, Pittsburgh *Gazette,* July 10, 1904, quoted in Charles B. Going, *David Wilmot* (New York, 1924), 497.

[52] Erie *Observer,* Aug. 8, 1857. Simon Cameron dipped into his own pocket to help finance Wilmot. See Wilmot to Cameron, Sept. 1, 1857, Cameron MSS, LC.

state offices. Not having completely divorced themselves from their former coalition, they destroyed their advantageous balance of power, and were witnessing the return of their proslavery wing to the Democratic fold.

Packer's excellent organization assisted in carrying him to an easy victory in a poll which netted 50,000 fewer votes than the preceding year. Although Wilmot's 146,000 votes fell 42,000 short of Packer's, they had almost equaled Frémont's. The poor vote polled by the American candidate, Hazlehurst, served only to reveal the party's weakness.[53] The Democrats had scored a clear-cut victory, but one of short duration. In another year the situation had changed completely; Packer was destined to become the last successful Democratic gubernatorial candidate until 1882.

The new administration began, unhappily, amidst the demoralizing effect of a nation-wide panic. During the late campaign the Democracy had boastingly attributed the prosperity of the last decade to their policies. The low tariff of 1857, possessing few protective features, was a Democratic measure; and the Republicans were quick to blame the nation's economic ills on a change in the tariff policy. Coming to the rescue of his party, President Buchanan explained: "It is apparent that our existing misfortunes have proceeded solely from our extravagant and vicious system of paper currency and book credits, exciting the people to wild speculation and gambling in stocks."[54] Governor Packer, sanctioning Buchanan's contentions, asked for uniform laws controlling the operations of banks and corporations.[55] On

---

[53] *The Pennsylvania Legislative Manual*, 1858, recorded: Packer, 188, 846 ; Wilmot, 146, 139 ; Hazlehurst, 28, 168.

[54] James D. Richardson (ed.), *A Compilation of the Messages and Papers of Presidents*, 1789-1897 (10 volumes, Washington, 1896-1899), VII, 2968.

[55] *Pennsylvania Archives, Fourth Series: Papers of the Governors*, VIII, 11-17.

the other hand, outgoing Governor James Pollock attributed the panic to the abandonment of the protective tariff.[56]

Protectionism had re-entered Pennsylvania's political arena to stay. The Democratic leader, Packer, had a premonition of the dangers which lay ahead if his party continued to deny the efficacy of protectionism. In his annual messages of 1859 and of 1860, the governor commented on the need for an increase in tariff rates. In 1859 he based his argument on the need for added revenue but in 1860 he called for protection for the mining and manufacturing interests.[57] The Jones-Schwartz case is a striking example of the growing insurgency fostered by Democratic protectionists within the ranks of the party. In Berks County a group of Democratic malcontents refused to accept Buchanan's sponsored congressional candidate, J. Glancy Jones, and nominated a protectionist anti-Lecompton candidate.[58] Buchanan attributed the defeat of his man to the protectionist leanings of Schwartz.[59]

Hardly had Buchanan's party swept into a commanding position in the Commonwealth than it began to weaken. There was a cloudy air of mysticism surrounding the heads of Republicans, Know-Nothings, and even erstwhile Anti-Masons and Whigs. The emergence of Thaddeus Stevens augured significant doings. An opposition was at work building an organization into which all souls, desirous of driving the Democracy from power, could enter. The atmosphere cleared when a motley gathering comprising such leaders as Ritner, Stevens, Galusha Grow, Alexander McClure and Morton McMichael, the Philadelphia editor, organized the

---

[56] *Ibid.*, VII, 943.
[57] *Ibid.*, VIII, 89-117 ; 173-97.
[58] *Cong. Globe*, 36 Cong., 1 Sess., 1951.
[59] John B. Moore (ed.), *Works of James Buchanan* (12 volumes, New York, 1908-1911), X, 229-30. Cited hereafter as *Works*.

People's Party. A new title for the united opposition would allow the discomfited Americans to rejoin without loss of face, and also it was hoped that a few promising Democrats like John Hickman and John M. Read, who had broken with Buchanan, would actively assist the new party.

The Democratic defeat of 1858 constituted more than a periodic reverse—it signified a political revolution. Never had the party of Jefferson suffered such a sudden reversal of confidence by the state's voters. John M. Read and William E. Frazer, the People's candidates for supreme judge and canal commissioner, won by majorities of 25,000 over their opponents.[60] The Democracy retained only a majority of one in the state senate, it elected only 32 members to the House, and succeeded in capturing but three of Pennsylvania's congressional seats. The results, it appeared to the *New York Times,* signified the state's "condemnation of Buchanan's Kansas policy . . . [and] a demand for protection of its industries, which Democratic candidates had ever and again promised, but never granted."[61] "We have met the enemy and we are theirs," commented the chagrined President. "This I have anticipated for three months and was not taken by surprise except as to the extent of our defeat."[62]

Factional disturbances continued to weaken the state Democracy. The state Democratic Convention of March 16, 1859, failed to endorse Governor Packer's policies, expressed "full confidence" in President Buchanan, asserted that the doctrine of popular sovereignty had met "continued [public] approbation," asked Congress for "discriminating protection" of the state's iron, coal, and industrial interests, and

[60] *Tribune Almanac,* 1859, 52-53.
[61] Lee L. Crippen, *Simon Cameron: Ante-bellum Years,* 189.
[62] Buchanan to H. Lane, Oct. 15, 1858, Moore, *Works,* X, 229,

named the party's candidates for state office.[63] But the well-known schism in the ranks of the Keystone Democracy was further publicized when a group of 99 bolters convened at Altoona under the leadership of John W. Forney and John Hickman, both of whom had defected from the Buchanan ranks. These "Forney-cators" endorsed Packer's policies, repudiated the platform of March 16, denounced the "weak, incompetent and corrupt" policies of Buchanan, and eulogized Stephen A. Douglas, the "heroic statesman."[64] Although plans to nominate a state anti-Lecompton ticket failed, the insurgents had scandalized the state Democracy and weakened the President's position.

The year 1859 revealed the strength of the new political machine of Simon Cameron. In the state House his candidate, W. C. Lawrence, defeated Curtin's man, Alexander K. McClure, for the speakership, and one of his creatures, David Taggart, presided at the state convention held in Harrisburg on June 8. Two supporters, John Covode and General C. P. Markle, were already pushing to have Cameron endorsed for the presidential nomination in 1860.[65] Andrew G. Curtin prudently decided to absent himself from the convention.[66] In the Senate, Simon Cameron had been calling for a protective tariff to aid revenues, industry, the farmer, and the mechanic; and the protectionists were looking to him for leadership.[67]

In the meantime the President was suffering further embarrassments. Besides acting as apologist for the

---

[63] Bedford *Gazette,* April 1, 1859.

[64] Erie *Observer,* April 23, 1859; Bedford *Gazette,* May 13, 1859.

[65] D. W. Shryock to Cameron, June (?), 1859, Cameron MSS, DCC.

[66] Curtin to E. Slifer, June 4, 1859, Slifer-Dill Papers (microfilm) PHMC.

[67] Bellefonte *Central Press,* Jan. 7, 1859.

Lecompton Constitution and the Tariff of 1857, the harried, tiring Buchanan found himself the storm center of charges and countercharges relating to elections in Pennsylvania. It started when Federal employees, campaigning against one "Honest John Covode" in Westmoreland County, stirred up a hornet's nest which developed into the Covode-Buchanan feud. Congressional action, arising out of Buchanan's charges of skulduggery in the Commonwealth's election, backfired into an investigation of the administration. Forney, the star witness, testifies that the Post Office Department had offered him $80,000 in contracts to support Buchanan's Kansas policy.[68] Protesting against the unconstitutional procedures of the investigating committee which he compared to England's infamous Court of the Star Chamber, the President could only cry out: "I defy all investigation. . . . Nothing but the basest perjury can sully my good name."[69]

But the fact remained that the President's position, through defections, schisms, dissatisfaction with his domestic policies, and charges of conduct unbecoming to a responsible public servant, had greatly weakened the position of Buchanan and his party in Pennsylvania. Political omens pointing to another Democratic defeat in 1859 were confirmed when the People's Party convincingly captured the fall elections. Both Democratic candidates for state office were defeated by large majorities and only one of the state senatorial seats fell to a Democrat. In the new state House, the defeated party was outnumbered two to one, and on joint ballot the Democracy would be able to muster only 46 votes to 87 for the opposition.[70] It is little wonder that the People's

---

[68] John A. Dodds, "Honest John Covode," *Western Pennsylvania Historical Magazine*, XVI (August, 1933).

[69] Moore, *Works*, X, 405.

[70] Davis, *Pennsylvania Politics*, 40.

Party looked eagerly forward to 1860 when it would be in position to capture the gubernatorial office and assist in repudiating the despised policies of James Buchanan.

II

The Republican Triumph of 1860

THE OPENING OF the new year, 1860, augured well for the success of the People's Party in Pennsylvania; the new Republicanism, so felt its followers, was about to come into its own. There had been a steady decline of the Democracy since the high tide of 1857 when it captured the gubernatorial office and swept the legislative elections. Dissatisfaction with the President's Kansas policy, the depression, the tariff issue, the Republican-American fusion—all were contributing factors in bringing about a landslide for the new party in the state and congressional elections of 1858. The following year saw a continuation of the same trend. The state People's-Republican Party, composing all elements opposed to the alleged offensive policies of the Democratic administration,[1] and maintaining that Congress dare not abdicate any portion of its authority (the right to restrict the growth of slavery) over the people of a territory,[2] was now on the verge of effecting a complete political triumph.

The prospects of the state Democracy, in spite of its late reverses, were by no means hopeless. Signs of rebellion against the Buchanan leadership in the state convention of 1858 had been effectively suppressed[3] and in 1859 the con-

[1] McClure, *Old Time Notes,* I, 342.
[2] *Official Proceedings of the Republican Convention at Pittsburgh, 1856.*
[3] Erie *Observer,* March 13, 1858.

vention expressed full confidence in the Chief Executive, although approval of the doctrine of popular sovereignty somewhat nullified such a resolution.[4] Buchanan's leadership, it was hoped, would yet secure adequate tariff protection for the interests of Pennsylvania. Republican contempt for the Supreme Court's decision in the Dred Scott case laid the party open to charges of destructive designs upon constitutional government.

In Pennsylvania each political year was inaugurated with the organization of the state legislature followed by the governor's annual message.[5] At such times the governor usually occupied the spotlight, but in January, 1860, the Democratic incumbent William F. Packer, a professed disciple of Douglas and private critic of Buchanan's Kansas policy, provoked little interest. Attention in political circles concentrated upon the coming nominations for the speakerships in the People's Party caucus. The outcome of the struggle for these key posts was expected to reveal the relative strength of the Cameron and Curtin factions in the legislature.

The anticipated factional fight for legislative office nominations did not develop within the People's Party. By unanimous votes William M. Francis of Venango and W. C. A. Lawrence of Dauphin were nominated speakers, respectively, of the state Senate and House.[6] Lawrence, a Cameron man, had upset A. K. McClure in an exciting contest for the speakership the preceding year, but Francis had not made himself conspicuous as a partisan of either group. The selection as Senate clerk of Russell Errett of the Pittsburgh *Gazette,* a strong Cameron organ, was looked upon as proof

[4] Bedford *Gazette,* April 1, 1859.
[5] Armor, *Lives of the Governors of Pennsylvania,* 445-46.
[6] Philadelphia *Press,* Jan. 4, 1860.

of Cameron's power of dispensing rewards to his worthy followers.

The chief factional struggle in the legislature developed in the contest for state treasurer between Eli Slifer of Northumberland and Henry D. Moore, second only to J. P. Sanderson as the leading Cameron lieutenant in the Philadelphia area. One aspect of the contest was between that of pure Republicanism as allegedly represented by the Slifer group and that of the eastern People's Party with a strong nucleus of Know-Nothingism centered in Philadelphia.[7] But Slifer's victory over Moore gave no hint of the anti-Cameron strength then latent in the Philadelphia area. Francis, Lawrence, and Slifer were easily elected over their Democratic opponents in the legislative elections.[8]

During the interlude prior to the meeting of the exciting party state conventions, the Republican majority of the new General Assembly demonstrated strength by steamrolling passage of a partisan joint resolution relative to the unseemly conduct of the national House of Representatives in its inability to organize, and castigating followers of the Buchanan Administration for uttering disunionist remarks in Congress. Another partisan resolution directed the grave charge of hypocrisy against the President for insincere recommendations on tariff revision.

With a functioning state organization and a willingness of the People's and Republican wings to act in harmony there apparently was little reason why the People's State Convention called for February 22, 1860, should not easily complete its main task of naming a suitable gubernatorial candidate, a slate of presidential electors, and a favorite choice for the

---

[7] Philadelphia *Public Ledger*, Jan. 17, 1860.

[8] *Journal of the Senate of Pennsylvania, 1860*, 6, 76 ; *Journal of the House of Representatives, 1860*, 6, 7.

Presidency; but actually the complete proceedings of the convention were determined and modified by the forces of Andrew G. Curtin and Simon Cameron. The latter, a presidential aspirant, was determined that the convention should not at the outset nominate his enemy for the governorship and then speedily disband without any guarantee of support for him at the national nominating convention. To secure these objectives, Cameron determined to endanger Curtin's nomination, thereby securing compensation for himself in the form of a compromise.

Among those mentioned for the gubernatorial chair were A. H. Reeder, Levi Kline, John M. Read, Joseph Casey, Eli Slifer, Thomas Howe, David Taggart, and John Covode; the last two named, next to Curtin, commanded the greatest strength. Personally, Cameron preferred Taggart of Northumberland, but Covode could summon more strength. It was part of Cameron's strategy to encourage a multiplicity of candidates, each with a small coterie of followers, thereby drawing off votes from Curtin. In addition Cameron was successful in weaning away a small group of delegates that were friendly to the aspirations of both Curtin and Cameron, and on the eve of the convention had maneuvered himself into a position where he could checkmate Curtin or perhaps even defeat him with a last-minute concentration on Covode.

The name of John Covode was well known in western Pennsylvania business circles. This grandson of a shanghaied redemptioner rose from humble surroundings to a position of wealth and eminence in his home county of Westmoreland. Beginning with the lowly office of justice of the peace, a service which earned him the useful sobriquet of "Honest John," Covode served two terms in the state legislature and in 1856, now a Republican neophyte, secured his second election to Congress.[9] There he participated in the notorious Grow-Keitt melee[10] and was soon to give his name to a nefarious congressional committee conducted for the purpose, so it seemed to Buchanan, of sullying the good name of the President.[11] Covode remained an important factor in Republican political circles until his death.

The Curtin grooming for the gubernatorial candidacy began in early 1859 after he expressed his determination to secure the prize if it were in his power.[12] The leading factors which determined his availability as a candidate were a conservative Republican attitude, past friendly relations with the Know-Nothings, interest in tariff protection as an ironmaster, experience as an administrator in his capacity as a former secretary of the Commonwealth, the geographical location of his home, unusual forensic abilities, and a genial personality. These qualities combined to make Curtin the ideal candidate to carry the crucial Keystone State of Pennsylvania, the one whose early election returns were regarded throughout the nation as the voice of political prophecy.

Management of the Curtin strategy fell chiefly upon William B. Mann of Philadelphia and Alexander K. McClure of Chambersburg, although ex-governor Pollock, state treasurer Eli Slifer, and the vociferous Thomas Marshall of Pittsburgh furnished aid and comfort. In Philadelphia, Cameron's inveterate's enemy, District Attorney William Mann, worked ceaselessly in lining up a favorable delegation from that city for Curtin and even managed the defeat of Cameron's lieutenant, J. P. Sanderson, as a delegate

[9] *Dictionary of American Biography,* IV, 470.
[10] James D. McCabe, *Behind the Scenes in Washington* (n.p., 1873).
[11] Moore, *Works,* X, 399-405.
[12] Curtin to Slifer, Feb. 26, 1859, Dill-Slifer MSS, PHMC,

to the state convention.[13] The Curtin men, anxious to eliminate Covode as a candidate, were working on a plan to urge him by questionable methods, it was said, to continue his congressional career. Curtin, perhaps overconfident of his strength, served notice on the Cameron camp of his intention to press the gubernatorial nomination as the first order of business at the convention.[14]

On February 21, delegates to the People's Party State Convention began arriving in the capital city of Harrisburg. That first night was spent by the delegates in getting acquainted, in "caucasing" at a late hour and making a preliminary survey of the relative strength of the various candidates. Following organizational preliminaries the next day, former governor James Pollock was elected permanent chairman. Pollock, the most available umpire acceptable to both factions, in the opening speech of the gathering established the conservative tone of the People's-Republican union in proclaiming lack of sympathy for fanaticism "whether in the form of Northern abolitionism or Southern slavery propagandism."[15]

The Cameron forces determined upon an early showdown of strength upon two key Cameron propositions; an endorsement of Simon Cameron for President, and selection of pledged national convention delegates by the state convention itself. The latter method, it was argued, was necessary in order to insure a united state front for Cameron at Chicago, a prime requisite for any presidential aspirant. When Morrow B. Lowry of Erie moved Cameron's endorsement as the convention's presidential choice, Thomas Marshall followed with one of the most violent and bitterest

[13] J. P. Sanderson to Cameron, Dec. 17, 1859, Cameron MSS, DCC.
[14] H. D. Moore to Cameron, Feb. 20, 1860, *ibid*.
[15] Philadelphia *Public Ledger*, Feb. 22, 23, 1860.

denunciations ever publicly given a candidate.[16] Public excitement mounted so rapidly that a mob forced its way into the House for the evening session to listen to rebuttals by J. N. Purviance and Glenni Scofield, followed by a powerful anti-Cameron blast from W. B. Mann who reiterated his district's antagonism to Cameron. Passage of Lowry's resolution by a vote of 89-39[17] constituted a minor victory for the Cameron forces. Presentation of the crucial motion to send convention selected delegates voting as a unit for Cameron provoked opposition counterproposals and a final test of strength. A. K. McClure's substitute resolution would allow each congressional district to select four delegates in its own fashion unpledged to the recommended presidential choice of the state convention, Simon Cameron.

At the end of a late night adjournment, the Cameron forces had determined to play their trump card—a threat of strength sufficient to block Curtin's impending gubernatorial nomination. According to McClure's version, two Cameron emissaries agreed to return ten lately stolen Curtin delegates in exchange for freedom of the congressional convention delegates if they so wished. This compromise, although it assured Curtin's nomination, did not guarantee a solid delegation for Cameron. Upon presentation of the compromise motion, McClure, with his eye centered upon the benefits of public fanfare, addressed the convention in a conciliatory speech, called for party harmony, and followed with a surprise amendment asking for acceptance of those delegates

---

[16] *Ibid.,* Feb. 23 ; Bedford *Gazette,* March 2, 1860.

[17] Although McClure recorded the vote at 80 to 44, the leading papers of the press listed the vote as above. McClure was evidently, as he often did in his *Notes,* relying upon his memory. Since the total vote of the convention totaled 133, the results indicated that several delegates refrained from voting. See McClure, *Old Time Notes,* I, 393–98.

already elected in the congressional districts. The compromise amendment together with McClure's and several others passed by a lopsided vote of 128 to 4.[18] The meagerness of the Cameron compensation is all the more evident when one notes that eleven congressional districts accepted convention pledged delegates; twelve others preferring to refer the decision to the local political units.[19]

With the Cameron problem behind it, the convention proceeded to the business of selecting a gubernatorial candidate. The Curtin-Cameron compromise left little doubt as to the final outcome, but both Covode and Taggart persisted in remaining in the running as candidates. On the first ballot, Curtin, Covode, Howe, and Taggart, received 56, 22, 18, and 16 votes, respectively. At the end of the second ballot, Curtin, still lacking one vote of the necessary 67, received 8 more and the nomination when a group of delegates announced a change in their votes.[20] Some of Covode's disappointed followers accused Cameron of perfidy,[21] but Cameron observed privately to a friend that he had done his best for Covode under the circumstances.[22] Before adjourning, the convention heard from its newly chosen gubernatorial candidate who stated (humorously it would seem) his intention to carry the unanimity of the convention to Chicago; then from orator William B. Mann declaiming the wedding of the Americans to the Republicans; and finally after accepting a slate of recommended presidential electors

---

[18] Philadelphia *Public Ledger,* Feb. 24, 1860.

[19] Davis, *Pennsylvania Politics,* 61-62.

[20] Philadelphia *Public Ledger,* Feb. 24, 1860 ; Altoona *Tribune,* March 1, 1860.

[21] J. G. McQuaide to Covode, March 1, 1860, Covode MSS, HSWP.

[22] Samuel B. Lauffer to Cameron, April 5, 1860, Cameron MSS, DCC.

and a series of resolutions, the convention concluded with a rousing three cheers and a tiger for Cameron and Curtin.[23]

The convention's resolutions reflected the peculiar interests of the state. They strongly criticized Buchanan's Administration for its disregard of the "just claims of the industrial interests of the country," for fostering sectionalism, for its corrupt administration, and finally for its "usurpation of states' rights," and those of the people. Borrowing a leaf from the party's national platform of 1856, the convention denounced the extension of slavery into free territory and added the African slave trade to the other twin relics of barbarism, polygamy and slavery. It was not the purpose of the party to seek destruction of slavery in the states by direct methods, because natural forces, moral, religious, and economic, would eventually bring about its end. The strong American complexion of the new party was reflected in the recognition of the evils wrought by the influx of foreign criminals into the country, but the strongest plank, the one considered somehow as lying alone within the private demesne of the Keystone State, demanded a systematic tariff providing for adequate protection of all classes of citizens.

The work of the convention was generally received with satisfaction by the People's press. Cameron organs like the Pittsburgh *Gazette* grudgingly accepted Curtin and then went on to extol the presidential aspirations of Pennsylvania's candidate in extravagant terms. Fortunately both Curtin and Cameron represented high protective tariff interests, and since such a tariff was considered absolutely essential to the Commonwealth's prosperity, acceptance of the pair was made easy. A few Republican organs, notably the Pittsburgh *Journal,* recalling the many accusations leveled at Cameron

---

[23] The Philadelphia *Public Ledger* of Feb. 23, 24, 1860, contains a complete text of the official proceedings and resolutions.

during the long course of his political career, deprecated use of the party to further his political ambitions.[24] Of course the volatile section of the Democratic press heaped abuse upon both men; Cameron as the living incarnation of corruption, and Curtin as the abolitionist nigger-loving enemy of those unfortunate enough to be born abroad.

Between the time of the adjournment of the People's State Convention of Pennsylvania in late February and the opening of the Republican National Convention scheduled for May 16, the nation was passing through the throes of one of the most tremendous political upheavals in its history. At Charleston, South Carolina, the disruptive forces of sectionalism had triumphed over the cohesive strength of party harmony, rending the proud party of the Democracy in twain with the ultimate outcome still in doubt. Another group, the Constitutional-Union Party, although dedicated to the gigantic task of stemming the tide of disunion, was by definition almost sectional because the border states were most mightily affected by threats of disunion. In a sectional contest carried on by a multiplicity of parties, and all omens at this time pointed to such a likelihood, the Republican Party, with its strength concentrated in the populous, heavy electoral states, stood the best chance to win. Although national Republican leaders openly expressed confidence in the outcome, it was commonly conceded that much depended upon the pivotal state of Pennsylvania.

During the second week of May, 1860, train after train bearing Pennsylvania's "irrepressibles" passed westward through a verdant landscape into a parched, thirsty country-side affected by the early May drouth; but truly there was no dearth of liquids inside the crowded, stinking, riding coaches. A boisterous mob variously estimated at 1200 to

[24] **Davis**, *Pennsylvania Politics,* 67,

2000 souls, including two bands, and 375-odd delegates and attached persons, was on its way to the giant Chicago Wigwam.[25] With sleeping space rented at one of the bursting hotels, and granted a stare at the sights of the prairie city, including the grotesque delegate from Oregon, Horace Greeley, the colorful pranksters, properly equipped with white hats and canes, were ready to settle down to serious convention work.

Although few political leaders among those gathered at Chicago conceded Cameron even an outside chance for the Presidency, his immediate followers took quite a different view of the situation. Building Cameron into a presidential possibility had been a laborious process and now his lieutenants were hopeful and eager for the spoils of victory.[26] As early as the spring of 1858 Cameron admirers were corresponding with the idea of creating a boom for him. In midsummer of the same year the New York *Herald* favorably commented at length upon his presidential aspirations. John P. Sanderson, formerly of the Philadelphia *Daily News,* and Russell Errett of the Pittsburgh *Gazette* accepted the journalistic burden of promoting his candidacy within the state. The Pittsburgh organ even published a fictitious list of Cameron counties in the state. In late September, 1859, the Cameron club of Chicago was organized under the leadership of Dr. Charles Leib[27] followed by organization of a Philadelphia Club headed by Isaac Hazlehurst, an outstanding Know-Nothing.[28] Having hurdled the state convention

---

[25] Passes for Pennsylvania's official party were furnished by the Pennsylvania Central and the Pittsburgh, Fort Wayne and Chicago Railroads. J. P. Sanderson to Cameron, April 17, 1860, Cameron MSS, DCC; G. W. Cass to Cameron, April 25, 1860, *ibid.*

[26] D. F. Williams to Cameron, Sept. 5, 1859, *ibid.*

[27] *Ibid.*

[28] Myers, "Rise of Republican Party," 257.

with partial success, the Cameron forces were early on the Chicago scene and soon discovered the unavailability of both William H. Seward of New York and of Salmon P. Chase of Ohio.

Two particularly distressing dilemmas facing the Cameron managers at Chicago were how to bring about and maintain a solid delegation vote as long as Cameron remained a candidate, and the question of support for Seward if Cameron dropped from the race. Thomas H. Dudley recorded the story of how John A. Andrew, only a day before the convention opened, persuaded both New Jersey and Pennsylvania to shelve their favorite sons, Dayton and Cameron, along with Andrew's favorite, Seward, in case a stronger candidate could be found—meaning Lincoln.[29] According to Charles P. Smith, Andrew headed another meeting at the Cameron camp on Thursday, followed by a night session in David Wilmot's room.[30] The net result revealed Lincoln's potential strength but no pledges followed, the Cameron men remaining adamant. On the other hand, Cameron's personal commitments to Seward[31] had no effect on the Curtin group who had been assured by their leader that Seward's nomination for the Presidency would result in certain defeat for their gubernatorial candidate in Pennsylvania. This decision, it was alleged by Horace Greeley, was made in the face of a cash offer from Seward's manager for Curtin's support.[32] Before adjournment about midnight, H. D. Moore and Russell Errett pleaded unsuccessfully for

[29] Thomas H. Dudley, "Inside Facts of Lincoln's Nomination," *Century*, XL (July, 1890), 477-78. Dudley, a New Jersey delegate, was an eyewitness of the events he described.
[30] Nevins, *Emergence of Lincoln*, II, 258.
[31] Seward to Weed, April 29, 1859, Thurlow Weed, *Memoir*, II, 256. The Pennsylvania movement against Seward was no secret. It appeared in the Philadelphia *Public Ledger* the next day, May 16.
[32] James S. Pike, *First Blows of the Civil War*, 520.

assurances of united support for Cameron on the morrow.[33] At this critical hour the Curtin faction would support neither Cameron nor Seward, and Thaddeus Stevens still insisted upon clinging to his ideal, Justice John McLean of Ohio.

Faced with the probability of humiliation for their candidate on the first ballot and a continued divided state delegation thereafter, the Cameron managers, Sanderson and J. Donald Cameron, made a quick decision to secure half a loaf if possible before morning. The eager Lincoln managers, Leonard Swett and David Davis, evidently not aware of the true state of affairs in the Pennsylvania delegation, quickly accepted what seemed to them to be a political manipulation of the first magnitude—a Cabinet position for Cameron in exchange for his faction's support on the second ballot.[34] Cameron could have had the Vice-Presidency but it was felt that such an arrangement would have smelled too strongly of a prearranged bargain.[35] Both Lincoln and Cameron were innocent of the transaction. Before dawn, Davis, exhibiting uncontrolled exuberance, proclaimed to a friend: "Damned if we haven't got them!"[36]

At an early hour on May 18—the day when the Republicans expected to choose their presidential nominee—a weary Pennsylvania delegation again gathered for the final decision —if any. At this time, wrote Henry D. Moore to Cameron, "oil was thrown on troubled waters," and the decision made which led to Cameron's heavy Pennsylvania vote on the first ballot.[37] McClure has the delegation's decision to back Cameron and Lincoln take place before the Cameron-

---

[33] H. D. Moore to Cameron, May 20, 1860; Russell Errett to Cameron, May 29, 1860, Cameron MSS, DCC.
[34] "Mr. Swett's Reminiscences," Weed, *Memoir,* II, 292.
[35] Samuel R. Purviance to Cameron, May 23, Cameron MSS, DCC.
[36] Nevins, *Emergence of Lincoln,* II, 257.
[37] Moore to Cameron, May 20, 1860, Cameron MSS, DCC.

Lincoln bargain, that is sometime before daylight of May 18,[38] but Moore wrote that "indeed up to the very hour of the meeting it looked as if we should get but little more than one half of the votes of your delegation. . . ."[39]

The gigantic Wigwam, packed to the roof, presented an awesome spectacle as the Pennsylvania delegation took its assigned seats flanked by the guardian Illinois delegation and far removed from any danger of last-minute propositions from the confident New York supporters of William H. Seward. With preliminaries soon out of the way, nominations began with that of Seward and Lincoln, the latter name eliciting even more deafening applause than the first. At the close of a mild public approbation for Dayton of New Jersey, Andrew H. Reeder presented the name of Simon Cameron. Several other nominations and seconds followed and the impatient audience screamed for immediate balloting. The first ballot yielded little beyond what was expected as Seward led Lincoln $173\frac{1}{2}$ to 102. Cameron's third-place vote of 50 actually created a stir in the convention and a buzz was heard making its rounds: "the opposition to Cameron was mightily small after all."[40] Of the 108 Pennsylvania delegates possessing one half vote each, 13 had refused to support Cameron. This was not unexpected as both William B. Mann and Thaddeus Stevens had served notice of their intentions. On the second ballot Reeder formally withdrew Cameron's name before Pennsylvania's vote of 48 for Lincoln could be announced. The second ballot had ended with Lincoln's vote of 181 trailing Seward by only $3\frac{1}{2}$. On the third ballot Pennsylvania contributed 52 votes to

[38] *Old Time Notes*, I, 406-07.
[39] Moore to Cameron, May 20, 1860, Cameron MSS, DCC. The statement made by some historians that the Pennsylvania delegation was in caucus all night is evidently in error.
[40] *Ibid.*

the Lincoln avalanche initiated by Massachusetts, and the wild suspense soon ended when Salmon P. Chase lost four of his Ohio votes.[41] ". . . from the crowd in the streets came a pandemonium of cheers, a wave of sound that mingled with the happy uproar inside the building."[42]

Other duties to be completed by the convention were the selection of a running mate for Lincoln and adoption of a party plank. The first was disposed of at the evening session after Lincoln's nomination when the Pennsylvania delegation brought on stage a huge banner inscribed "Pennsylvania Good for 20,000 majority for the People's Candidate—Abe Lincoln." On the first ballot, Pennsylvania distributed its vote among Andrew Reeder, John Hickman, Hannibal Hamlin, and a few others. Reeder withdrew before the delegation cast its entire 54 votes for Hannibal Hamlin, the winner.[43]

A clause in the party platform expressing opposition to the spread of slavery in the territories was taken for granted, but additional expressions of national policy appealing to particular interests or classes were needed to insure victory. These were forthcoming in the form of internal improvements, railroads, homesteads, and civil guarantees for the alien. To the Pennsylvanians the insertion of a protective tariff plank was an absolute essential. At the convention they discovered to their consternation that the West possessed little interest in protective principles and was in no mood to humor the arrogant Easterners.[44] However, the discomfited Pennsylvanians, concealing their chagrin at the ambiguously

[41] Stanwood, *History of the Presidency*, 295.

[42] Nevins, *Emergence of Lincoln*, II, 260.

[43] For the complete official version of the Chicago convention see *Proceedings of the First Three Republican Conventions of 1856, 1860, 1864*. (Minneapolis, n.d.)

[44] Thomas Pitkin, *Tariff and Early Republican Party*, 190.

worded compromise clause which advocated, on the basis of sound policy, such adjustments of the tariff as would encourage the development of the industrial interests of the whole country, went into spasms of joy, rising and swinging their hats and canes when the tariff clause was reported.[45]

Pennsylvania's performance at the convention had been sorry indeed. The dissension between the Curtin and Cameron factions was common knowledge. At no time did her political machinery function smoothly. "On nearly every ballot Pennsylvania was not in readiness when her name was called and her retirement for consultation became a joke."[46] Both Cameron and Russell Errett agreed that lack of unity had defeated Cameron at the convention.[47] While admitting that Pennsylvania's position has been "pitiable in the extreme," A. K. McClure, Curtin's leading lieutenant, consoled Cameron with the fact that they have been saved from positive disgrace through something like an approach to unanimity.[48]

The state Democracy, while in the process of rejoicing noisily over the dissension within the People's Party, certainly was not in any enviable position itself. Time after time Buchanan's loyal state organization was threatened with rebellions directed against the President's unpopular Kansas policy and his failure to secure a satisfactory protective tariff, the absence of which, now in retrospect, could safely be labeled as a prime cause of the economic depression dating from 1857. Buchanan's slim majority of 1856 in his own state took on the picture of an indictment rather than an endorsement, and the situation by 1860 was worse. Feuds

[45] Murat Halstead, *Caucuses of 1860* (Columbus, 1860), 135.
[46] *Ibid.,* 143.
[47] Errett to Cameron, May 29, 1860, Cameron MSS, DCC.
[48] McClure to Cameron, June 6, 1860, Cameron MSS, LC.

between the administration and Douglas men in the cities of Philadelphia and Pittsburgh were symptomatic of the evil days to come. But in the early spring of 1860 few could have foreseen the cataclysmal split which beginning at the national level was to permeate the state's hierarchical system to the very grassroots of the Keystone's Democracy where thousands would be at a loss to tell whom they followed.

The leading tasks performed by the state Democratic convention scheduled to meet at Reading in late February were similar to those completed at the People's convention a week earlier, except that it gave no endorsement to any presidential candidate and its members selected all delegates to the Charleston National Convention. Failure to attempt the creation of a unified instructed delegation was not an expression of the harmonious temperament prevailing at the convention, but rather was indicative of the near equal strength of the opposing Douglas and Buchanan-Breckinridge factions.

Of excellent Democratic gubernatorial timber there certainly was no dearth. The year 1860 had opened with little interest in potential candidates shown by the press,[49] but the Democratic leaders labored unselfishly to bolster their future presidential ticket with their strongest man. Among those prominently mentioned for the high office were Henry D. Foster of Westmoreland, William H. Witte of Philadelphia, Jacob Fry of Montgomery, John L. Dawson of Fayette, and George Sanderson of Lancaster. Because Foster was unwilling to become a candidate, Witte, who had carefully prepared his organization, was the leading contender. Fry was a former state officer of proven administrative ability. Dawson had valiantly defended the unpopular Lecompton

---

[49] Erie *Observer,* Jan. 7, 1860.

constitution before the 1858 state convention[50] and had earned the backing he was getting from President Buchanan and Jeremiah Black of Somerset County. Sanderson's pretensions could have been taken very lightly had he not secured the blessing of the powerful United States Senator William Bigler.[51]

The political complexion had altered considerably by the time of the opening of the convention of February 29. Witte, who in December was confident of the nomination,[52] had lost ground steadily. Prominent Democratic leaders expressed doubt of his ability to carry the state, he bungled his efforts with the Democratic legislators at Harrisburg, and, perhaps worst of all, his enemies circulated a whispering campaign relating to his alleged dishonest business transactions.[53] In the county of Westmoreland pressure was brought to bear upon Foster to promise acceptance of a tendered nomination.[54] When the delegates poured into Reading, February 28, on the eve of the Democratic State Convention, Witte was still in the lead only because of a rumored withdrawal of Dawson in his favor.[55]

Organization wrangling and the question of national convention delegates occupied the early hours of the Reading convention. Next, attention turned to the main task of nominating a gubernatorial candidate. Of the eleven names presented, those of Dawson, Foster, and A. S. Wilson were withdrawn. Although 68 votes were needed for a choice, Witte's full strength mustered on the second ballot yielded

---

[50] *Ibid.,* March 13, 1858.
[51] Sanderson to Bigler, Dec. 16, 1859, Bigler MSS, HSP.
[52] Witte to Bigler, Dec. 16, 1859, *Ibid.*
[53] J. M. Kibben to Bigler, Jan. 4, 1860 ; D. W. Moore to Bigler, Jan. 29, 1860 ; Jacob Turney to Bigler, Feb. 11, 1860, *Ibid.*
[54] D. W. Moore to Bigler, Jan. 29, 1860, Bigler MSS, HSP.
[55] Philadelphia *Public Ledger,* Feb. 29, 1860 ; James A. Gibson to Black, Feb. 18, 1860, Black MSS, LC.

only 56 votes. Fry with 35 was second and the remaining votes were rather evenly distributed among four other aspirants including Foster. At this juncture with a deadlock looming, nominations were reopened and the popular Foster was again placed in nomination. A stampede to him following the second ballot secured his nomination by a unanimous vote. An invitation to address the convention was graciously accepted by all the candidates except Witte who made no attempt at concealing his mortification.[56]

Lengthy, verbose, and obscure describes the resolutions passed by the convention. Agitation of the slavery question was branded as destructive of the bonds of Union; the question of slaveholding within the territories was declared to be only within the province of the judicial branch of government, and the doctrine of "irrepressible conflict" was declared abhorrent. Some clauses lent themselves to seemingly contradictory interpretations: The government consists of a union of sovereign states acting for the sovereign people who are bound together as one people by the general government. Another apparent contradiction was an endorsement of the principles of the party as set forth by the Cincinnati platform of 1856 (in which "progressive free trade throughout the world" was advocated[57]), and a request for an adequate protective tariff on iron, coal, wool, and other staples.[58] That, as proclaimed by the leading Democratic journals, there was universal satisfaction with the platform there could be little doubt, conceded the People's Party, because one could draw from it according to his individual needs.

Democratic interest soon transferred its attention

---

[56] For proceedings see Philadelphia *Public Ledger*, March 1, 2, 1860; Bedford *Gazette*, March 9, 1860.

[57] Stanwood, *History of the Presidency*, 268.

[58] Philadelphia *Public Ledger*, March 2, 1860,

from the state to the national scene centering upon the proceedings soon to take place at Charleston, South Carolina, chosen seat of the 1860 Democratic National Convention, where, it was realized, the issues so lightly glossed over at the state convention must now be squarely faced. In the deep South, where control of the party machinery had passed into the hands of the radical states' rights men, many of them of the Yancey-Rhett stripe, a new sectional party was in the rapid process of generation. That an amended, more radical "Alabama platform" was to be forced upon the coming convention there could be no doubt. This platform, if adopted as national policy, would have made it impossible to bar slavery from territory anywhere even at the express wish of its legislature. Slavery must be positively maintained under Federal protection.[59] To the Southern fire-eater the Douglas doctrine of popular sovereignty was, in its essence, even more insidious than that contained within the seeds of Black Republicanism. But what if the Douglas men, who in most cases really represented free states, should capture the convention!

The Charleston Democratic National Convention resulted in one of the most notable political fiascos on record. The Southern delegates walked dramatically out of the convention when they saw their platform defeated.[60] The Pennsylvania delegates, led by William Bigler, a Buchanan man, had first gotten out of hand by voting for Benjamin F. Butler's unchanged resolution (the old Cincinnati platform), and then followed with a rejection of the Douglas minority

[59] Dwight L. Dumond, *The Secession Movement* (New York, 1931), 33-34.

[60] Unless otherwise noted the material on the Charleston Convention is taken from the *Official Proceedings* authorized by National Democratic Executive Committee, Washington, 1860.

report, 15 to 12.[61] The Pennsylvanians remained seated with the Douglas rump, voting during most of 57 ballots for James Guthrie of Kentucky, thereby contributing substantially to the failure of Douglas to secure the 203 votes needed for a nomination. Criticism of the anti-Douglas vote, contended Bigler, was unjust because "we had never pretended to be for Douglas. . . ."[62] On May 3, the remnants decided to adjourn and meet again in Baltimore.

At home proponents of the several Democratic factions judged according to their individual prejudices, the work of the actions of their delegates at Charleston. Mass meetings and the press combined to express indignation at the results.[63] In the Douglas stronghold of western Pennsylvania, his supporters easily convinced themselves that their champion had been cheated of the nomination because he had received a vote exceeding two-thirds of the (rump) convention. Douglas organs, glossing over the facts, severely criticized Senator Bigler for his alleged secessionist activities. Few noted one simple fact—the Pennsylvania delegation had gone to Charleston uninstructed.

When the Democratic convention reassembled at Baltimore in mid-June, many of the Yanceyites reappeared, to the embarrassment of the Douglas men. The majority of the Pennsylvania delegation, still out of harmony with the Douglasites, and unable to sanction Breckinridge, continued their support for Guthrie, a Kentuckian of marked tariff principles. But the Douglas-minded convention, ignoring the tariff question, adopted its old Charleston platform

---

[61] The Democratic National Executive Committee in its "address" of July 18, 1860 claimed that Pennsylvania had voted for it. See Dumond, *Secession Movement,* 50.

[62] Bigler, "Letter on the Charleston Convention," May 26, 1860, Erie *Observer,* June 16, 1860.

[63] Davis, *Pennsylvania Politics,* 91-92.

unchanged and went on to nominate (by another rump) Douglas easily on the second ballot, 181½ to 13, over the combined opposition.[64]

The Southern seceders who had already met in various strength at three different places marshaled 231 delegates at Baltimore on June 23, and unanimously chose Vice-President John C. Breckinridge of Kentucky as their candidate. Although each of the 12 members of Pennsylvania's delegation presented credentials as a "regularly elected delegate,"[65] the names of only five appeared on the official Charleston list.[66] Two-thirds of the Pennsylvanians opposed the motion to nominate Breckinridge by acclamation.[67] The Southern report rejected at Charleston was adopted as the platform without opposition. From the White House, President Buchanan, although according recognition to neither of the Democratic Baltimore conventions in view of that fact that they could not claim to represent all the people, preferred to accept Breckinridge because "he sanctions and sustains the perfect equality of all the states within their common Territories, and the opinion of the Supreme Court . . . ."[68]

In the meantime the political year of the locust, 1860, had witnessed the appearance of a new national party allegedly innocent of all sectional and factional prejudices, but nevertheless particularly appealing to the border states. A residue of the decayed Whig and Know-Nothing parties, successfully completing a political metamorphosis, had emerged as the

---

[64] Stanwood, *History of the Presidency*, 286. A note of humor is to be seen in the decision of the Convention to count the disfranchised seceders, now numbered among the spectators, in order to acquire a quorum. This explains a second ballot.

[65] Dumond, *Secession Movement*, 90.

[66] Erie *Observer*, March 9, 1860.

[67] *Proceedings of the National Democratic Convention* (at Baltimore).

[68] Moore, *Works*, X, 458-59.

Constitutional Union Party for one purpose only—to preserve the bonds of union. Late in 1859 the movement had
mushroomed in various parts of the nation but owed more
to the venerable John J. Crittenden of Kentucky than to any
other source.[69]

The formal organization of the party in Pennsylvania,
dating from February 4, was necessitated ostensibly for the
purpose of preserving the Union, suppressing sectionalism,
and protecting a state's constitutional rights. At a Philadelphia meeting three weeks later the movement reported
organization of "Constitutional Union Associations" in
surrounding counties and at various interior points.[70] In
April the movement was reinforced with a party organ, the
independent Philadelphia *Evening Journal.*[71] The Lancaster
State Constitutional Union Convention of April 25 completed the usual program of such assemblies but failed to
endorse any presidential hopefuls.[72]

The Baltimore National Constitutional Convention of
May 9 found only 24 states represented. The gathering
transported national issues from the realm of reality to that
of ideas and attached itself to the guiding star of patriotism.
Its platform, which recognized only the principles of the
Constitution, the Union, and law enforcement,[73] certainly
had a national outlook but retained a considerable Southern
flavor. Essentially it stood for protection of minorities and
the states rather than for national supremacy. Most of its
leading adherents were either political nonentities or viewed
their political careers in retrospect. Its selection of John

---

[69] Allen E. Ragan in *Dictionary of American History,* II, 44.
[70] Philadelphia *Press,* Feb. 29, 1860.
[71] Elwyn B. Robinson, "The Public Press of Philadelphia During
the Civil War" (Ph.D. MS, Western Reserve University, 1936), 168.
[72] Davis, *Pennsylvania Politics,* 99.
[73] Stanwood, *History of the Presidency,* 289.

Bell and Edward Everett as standard bearers presented the somewhat incongruous picture of a procession of over-age political veterans led by the academic bib and tucker.

At the beginning of the presidential campaign of 1860 the Pennsylvania Democracy shared with the party members of its sister states the dilemma created by the party's schism —recognition of a bona fide candidate. Members of the electoral slate accepted at the Reading State Convention were pledged to support the nominee of the party, but identification of the individual in question was not easily ascertained. Logic, precedent, and technicalities went by the board as the proponents of Douglas and Breckinridge advanced the cause of their particular champion in accordance with the hopes, prejudices, and passions of the devotees. The Buchanan-Bigler coterie had little choice in the matter— the President's recent Lecompton feud with Douglas together with his natural Southern proclivities, placing him by the side of Breckinridge. The Haldeman-Wright-Montgomery faction threw its weight on the side of Douglas. Although liberal press support was held by both factions in all sections of the state, the western Pennsylvania Democratic organs usually supported Douglas. Prominent state leaders, grasping fully the gravity of the situation, took immediate steps to fill the breach.

Fortunately the torn Democracy found in the gubernatorial question a common ground on which to meet. Even the Republican opposition conceded the excellence of Henry Donnell Foster, the Democratic choice for governor. This remote cousin of both Stephen C. Foster and John C. Breckinridge received a fine education at Allegheny College, studied law in his uncle's office in Greensburg, and was admitted to the Westmoreland bar in 1829 before reaching his twenty-first birthday. In following his chosen profession he could find no satisfaction in the business of condemning criminals and consequently was generally found on the side of the defense. Only one other man in western Pennsylvania, Edgar Cowan, it was said, could match wits with Foster at the bar. In Congress the excellence of one of his speeches drew from John Quincy Adams his highest praise with the added observation that he saw in Foster the "coming man."[74] His genial qualities and personal magnetism matched even those of Andrew G. Curtin, who possessed them to an unusual degree.

First steps to heal the Democratic schism took place when the Democratic State Central Committee met in closed session in Philadelphia on July 2. Although strong, the Douglas faction could not persuade a majority of the Committee to accept their candidate. The Administration men agreed to a compromise in the form of a fusion of the Douglas and Breckinridge forces upon the Reading electoral ticket. According to this peculiar arrangement a voter would cast his vote for a Democratic presidential elector who in turn might vote for either Douglas or Breckinridge, depending upon the ability of the stronger to achieve the Presidency with the aid of Pennsylvania's electoral vote. The elector was unpledged if neither Democratic candidate could be elected.[75] To the Administration men a compromise was practically a victory and Buchanan was willing to bless any honest course calculated to defeat the Republicans.[76] But the anti-Administration journalist John W. Forney called for a purge of the Breckinridge men from the fusion ticket.[77]

---

[74] George D. Albert, *History of County of Westmoreland* (Philadelphia, 1882), 327; John N. Boucher, *History of Westmoreland County* (2 vols., New York, 1906), I, 351-52.

[75] Philadelphia *Press*, July 3, 1860.

[76] Philadelphia *Public Ledger*, July 12, 1860.

[77] Philadelphia *Press*, July 3, 1860.

The Douglas forces began an immediate fight to establish a separate electoral ticket in the state for their candidate. Not inappropriately, on Independence Day, in Independence Square, the Philadelphia Douglasites with much fanfare declared their independence of the Breckinridge faction.[78] Their spokesman, Richard J. Haldeman of Harrisburg, was Pennsylvania's representative on the Democratic National Committee. Within the next ten days Haldeman, taking action on his own responsibility[79] demanded by July 24 letters from each of the Reading appointed electors stating their position on Douglas. All those signifying their allegiance to Breckinridge or failing to reply were to be replaced at a Douglas state convention called for July 25. Haldeman's self-appointed duty, as he styled it, was soon clothed with the cloak of authority when the Douglas National Executive Committee issued an address July 17, calling for rejection of joint electoral tickets in all states and the substitution of pro-Douglas electors.[80]

The Haldeman convention of July 25, in Harrisburg, was remarkably well attended considering its extralegal features. Prominent Democratic leaders like Hendrick B. Wright and Richard Vaux added respectability to the gathering, but as the Erie *Observer* rather aptly observed, J. W. Forney was the head, and Haldeman the tail, of the convention and its "program of mischief."[81] It dispatched an ultimatum to the State Central Committee soon to meet at Cresson directing it to see that all Reading electors pledge themselves to support the regularly nominated candidates (meaning Douglas and Johnson), of the Democratic Party. If the

---

[78] *Ibid.*, July 6, 1860.
[79] Haldeman to Wright, July 13, 1860, Wright MSS, WHGS.
[80] Philadelphia *Public Ledger,* July 18, 1860.
[81] Erie *Observer,* Aug. 4, 1860,

Cresson meeting failed to produce the desired results, continued the Douglas directive, the Little Giant's supporters would call another convention and form their own electoral ticket.[82] Hendrick B. Wright was empowered to appoint a Douglas State Executive Committee, which he proceeded to do without waiting for the outcome of the Cresson meeting.[83]

At Cresson on August 9, the Douglas men could ill afford any compromise without loss of face, but at the end of prolonged wrangling their best efforts produced only an anomalous separate "amended fusion." The names of both Douglas and Breckinridge were now to head the national ticket as "candidates-at-large." If the one receiving the greater number of popular votes in the Commonwealth was the same that could be elected President with Pennsylvania's electoral vote, he was to receive it; but if it were possible to elect the minority candidate he was to receive it; and in case no candidate calling himself a Democrat could be elected the majority man received the state's entire electoral vote.[84] Administration leaders regarded the stormy session at Cresson successful because a facade of fusion had been maintained and the Douglas group reputedly "sewed up."[85] Many Douglas men were willing to accept amended fusion for sake of the common cause, but the radicals, backed by Forney's powerful Philadelphia *Press,* rejected it. The Douglas State Executive Committee, prematurely appointed by Hendrick B. Wright, immediately convened in secret session, arranged for a Douglas state electoral ticket, and

[82] Philadelphia *Public Ledger,* July 27, 1860.
[83] Hendrick B. Wright "memorandum," July 31, 1860, Wright MSS, WHGS.
[84] Altoona *Tribune,* Aug. 16, 1860.
[85] Thomas MacDowell to Bigler, Aug. 10, 1860, Bigler MSS, HSP,

made a tardy announcement of the slate only one month before the state elections.[86]

The People's Party, like that of the Democracy, likewise suffered from internal dissensions. Cameron's faction, charging "treason," persuaded the powerful Morgan-Weed-Seward combination of New York not to contribute financially to Curtin's campaign. The Cameron group, claimed the Curtin men, would be happy to see Foster defeat Curtin, if it did not contribute to a Republican defeat in the legislative, congressional, and presidential elections. Cameron's offer of financial aid to Foster's campaign in the form of a $1,000 gift[87] can hardly be viewed in any other light. On the other hand, the chairman of the People's State Central Committee, A. K. McClure, Curtin's closest confidant, made sincere efforts to effect a reconciliation. He recalled the forbearance of the Cameron's followers at Chicago, urged Cameron to attend the first meeting of the committe, and accepted Cameron's idea of making tariff protection, the "battle cry" of the campaign.[88] In reply, Cameron complained bitterly of attacks against him by Henry C. Carey and William B. Mann.[89]

In the meantime Cameron's two leading lieutenants, Russell Errett of Pittsburgh and John P. Sanderson of Philadelphia, devised a plan with the knowledge if not the connivance of Cameron to unhorse McClure by seizing control of the People's State Central Committee at the Cresson meeting. Because the majority of delegates "leaned toward Curtin," this fight was directed against McClure and

---

[86] Philadelphia *Public Ledger,* Aug. 16, Sept. 12, 1860.

[87] Albert, *History of County of Westmoreland,* 327.

[88] Pittsburgh *Post,* March 6, 1861 ; quoted in Davis, *Politics,* 171.

[89] Carey was a leading political economist. Mann, who was credited by Cameron himself with having blocked his nomination at Chicago, was especially furious at this point because Cameron succeeded in keeping him off the State Central Committee,

Mann rather than Curtin. Sanderson afterward justified the plan to humiliate McClure on the premise that victory in Pennsylvania was not possible without outside financial assistance from the Republican National Committee headed by E. D. Morgan of New York, a friend of Cameron.

McClure, having received no assurance from Cameron of his intention to attend the convention or to effect a compromise, planned and successfully executed a brilliant coup which completely foiled his opponents' plan to transfer directorship of the campaign to a hostile executive committee with a treasurer. On the eve of the convention, in the little town of Cresson, all the assembled delegates were entertained at a get-together frolic in an old hospital building. With a generous supply of spirits on tap the merry tipplers saw no reason to desert their card tables and cups before daybreak. All the Curtin men had secretly pledged themselves not to imbibe too freely of the wine or fail to answer roll call at the opening of the convention. The following morning, at a record-breaking session—at least for brevity— Curtin had his plan of campaign promptly approved and a resolution was passed to adjourn *sine die,* to meet again only on call of the chairman.[90] One Cameron participant, J. K. Moorhead of Pittsburgh, characterized the session as "hard" and excused acquiescence of the Cameron faction in the interest of harmony.[91]

McClure's victory, although spectacular, and undoubtedly a great source of personal satisfaction to him, boomeranged to his disadvantage. His methods were distasteful even to Thomas Marshall, so well remembered for his Cameronian

---

[90] McClure, *Old Time Notes,* I, 409-10. Apparently McClure is the only source for this story of his success, but related evidence corroborates it.

[91] Moorhead to Cameron, July 14, 1860, Cameron MSS, DCC.

philippic delivered at the state convention in February; and
the general mystery surrounding events at Cresson permitted
the Cameron faction to spread rumors of a fantastic plan to
elevate McClure to the governorship after Curtin resigned
to enter the Senate.[92] McClure now openly proclaimed the
People's State Central Committee defunct, and vowed never
to reassemble it. Personal attacks on him, asserted McClure,
together with the committee's inability to raise campaign
funds, had destroyed its usefulness; and the needed financial
contributions could be raised through his individual efforts.[93]
McClure could hardly be expected to state publicly his true
reason for not calling another committee meeting, but his
professed ability to raise the needed campaign funds
individually, in lieu of the efforts of a corps of trained
workers evoked knowing smiles even from his most intimate
friends.

J. P. Sanderson, determined to see McClure fry in his
own fat, laid plans for a new committee ostensibly for the
purpose of eliminating the party's financial plight, but actually with the intention of milking all available local sources,
thereby compelling McClure to operate in an economic
desert. After Curtin and Cameron concluded an unsatisfactory parley in Philadelphia, July 26,[94] Sanderson decided
to go ahead with his plans. McClure demanded an explana-
tion from Cameron, denounced the proposed action as a
reflection upon himself, and hinted that he might present
his case before the National Committee. Cameron's reply
to McClure's veiled threat was a masterpiece of political
sagacity: Some gentlemen had asked him to join a Repub-

---

[92] *Ibid.*
[93] J. P. Sanderson to Cameron, July 20, 1860, *ibid.*
[94] "Notation" by Cameron on Curtin to Cameron, July 22, 1860,
Cameron MSS, LC. Probably this is the only time the two enemies
ever met by appointment.

lican club with the understanding that its work would not interfere with McClure's committee. And now followed the unkindest cut of all: Was it true, asked Cameron, that McClure had given up hope of receiving funds, and did not intend to call another meeting of the State Central Committee?[95]

Lincoln, hearing of the dissension—it was not a secret—in the People's Party ranks of the Keystone State sent his man David Davis to make an on-the-spot investigation. McClure probably never learned of the Cameron conclave attended by Davis at the Girard House in Philadelphia where J. P. Sanderson was chosen the new secretary of the People's Party Auxiliary Committee of Philadelphia.[96] John Philip Sanderson, member of the Lebanon County bar, former state legislator and editor of the *Philadelphia Daily News,* was no stranger to the art of campaign management. As chairman of the American State Central Committee in 1856 he had carried on secret negotiations with John W. Forney, the Democratic leader, and betrayed a fusion plan of the Americans with the Republicans.[97] Sanderson's past political record seemed to qualify him admirably for his important post as first lieutenant of the political opportunist Simon Cameron.

This political "anti-pope" of McClure subdivided his Philadelphia committee into three groups, each bearing responsibility over a portion of the state, wrote reports directly to Lincoln, and never missed an opportunity to belittle or degrade either McClure or Curtin. In fact, a perusal of his letters to Lincoln and Cameron makes one

[95] Cameron to McClure, Aug. 1, 1860, *ibid*. Curtin had already given his consent to a Republican Club.

[96] William D. Kelley to Lincoln, Aug. 7, 1860, Lincoln MSS, LC.

[97] *Appletons' Cyclopedia of American Biography,* V, 386; Robinson, "Public Press of Philadelphia," 124.

wonder whether the chief enemy to be feared may not lie within the ranks of the People's Party. About the same time that Sanderson began operations, Davis and Leonard Swett, the Lincoln spokesmen, congratulated A. K. McClure on the excellence of his state organization.[98] The politically astute Lincoln, wishing to avail himself of all possible aid, did business with the legitimate state chairman, McClure, while at the same time, covertly, it seems, giving his blessing to the Sanderson anti-McClure committee.

The People's Party campaign in Pennsylvania was punctuated with such terms as protectionism, free homesteads, freedom, free labor, dignity of labor, disunion, the German vote, the Lecompton fraud, internal improvements, and Irish-Catholicism. The state organization emphasized issues which had local appeal, particularly the tariff. The Commonwealth's position as an industrial state, particularly its pre-eminence in iron, made such an issue imperative. The People's Party cleverly bound the tariff, slavery, and the free homesteads to the personal wants of most citizens—the economic well-being of the laboring man and his dignity as an individual. A protective tariff, by keeping cheap competitive foreign goods out of the country, would provide jobs to American laborers. Slavery not only weakened free labor economically because of its competitive nature but also degraded the dignity of honest labor. Often labeled by its enemies as the party of disunion, the People's Party countered by citing the secessionist activities of the Democratic Yanceyites. The state Democracy's attempt to pose as the party of protection was ridiculed because there seemed no chance of adequate protection under the national administration of a free trade

---

[98] McClure, *Old Time Notes,* I, 415.

party. The People's-Republican Party, including as it did an abolitionist wing, took pains to emphasize its conservative nature, omitting discussions of emancipation or Negro suffrage.

The burden of the Democratic attack was to show the logical outcome of a Republican sectional victory. The party's antislavery aims, claimed the Democracy, would lead to a disregard of states' rights and a breakup of the Union; and the camouflaged aims of abolitionism and Negro equality ("niggerism") would stand revealed with its triumph. The tariff could be regarded as a local issue rather than national, but a revenue tariff sufficiently protective in nature would eventually come under Democratic leadership. One point which the Democrats appeared to have scored with marked success in the Philadelphia area among businessmen was the probable disastrous effect of disunion on the business interests of Pennsylvania. Curtin's past Know-Nothing proclivities, coupled with the fact that his Irish father was a Catholic, furnished ammunition for his denunciation as a traitor to his ancestral heritage and faith.[99] The Bell men supported Foster, although, according to McClure, they were willing to switch to Curtin for a price—an amount too exhorbitant for his resources.[100]

The People's Party launched its state campaign on June 7, with an "Address" from the State Central Committee emphasizing Pennsylvania's pivotal position in the contest; victory for Curtin in Pennsylvania's early elections would presage a like one for Lincoln and would carry with it a powerful psychological value. Although the state was thoroughly organized, probably the greatest aid was secured through local clubs, the "Wide-Awakes." Members, clothed

---

[99] Boston *Pilot* quoted in Bellefonte *Central Press*, Sept. 27, 1860.
[100] McClure, *Old Time Notes*, I, 421-22.

in picturesque garb and bearing torches and banners inscribed with slogans—some patriotic, some political—sang, danced, and paraded through the streets on all kinds of festive occasions, arousing much enthusiasm by their antics. Oratory of the first order was delivered by a corps of nationally known speakers from outside the state who volunteered their services to save the Keystone Commonwealth. Only speakers acquainted with the tariff problem were acceptable. The tariff in Pennsylvania, Lincoln was informed, was of foremost importance in the conservative East; in the West it was on a par with the issue of "slave aggression" and in the North it was tolerated.[101]

Among the prominent out-of-state speakers were the Blairs, Montgomery and Frank; John Sherman and Justin S. Morrill, the darlings of the protectionists; Lucius Eugene Chittenden of Vermont fame; and Carl Schurz, brother to the German-Americans. At Philadelphia the "Wide-Awakes" spectacular torchlight procession indoctrinated Frank Blair with its enthusiasm and he responded with a mighty oration on the subject he loved best—slavery.[102] Concerning his tour, Chittenden amusingly related:

Where we travelled, what places we visited, I never inquired. The image of that fortnight upon my memory represents a continuous procession of committees of eminent citizens, mass meetings, torchlight procession, Wide-Awakes in uniform, shouting, singing political songs, and hurrahing for the ticket. In the afternoons Col. Blair and myself usually addressed the same mass-meeting. As soon as one had concluded he was hurried away to a distant town or city, to be in time for the evening meeting. The other made his speech and was rushed off in the opposite

[101] McClure to Lincoln, June 16, 1860 ; July 2, 1860, Lincoln MSS, LC.
[102] William E. Smith, *Francis Preston Blair Family in Politics* (2 vols., New York, 1933) I, 499,

direction. Some nights we were hundreds of miles apart, at noon the next day together. We were only permitted to see Republican newspapers which declared that our converts were numerous, our missionary work a success.[103]

Curtin, in his role as gubernatorial candidate of the People's Party was expected to carry a heavy share of the burden of state campaigning. The modest tariff plank of the Republican Party, added to his powerful forensic talents, made it possible for him to launch effective appeals to both the business and laboring men of the coal and iron regions. In mid-July he was making speeches within convenient distances of his home in Bellefonte, the geographic center of the state; a month later found him engaged in a tour of the northeastern counties, and throughout the period he made hasty trips to Philadelphia to confer with his manager, A. K. McClure. In September his itinerary resembled a great half circle from Easton through Erie to Pittsburgh. At Erie, Cameron assisted Curtin with an attack on his old enemy James Buchanan for his opposition to free homesteads—an example of the President's willingness to sacrifice the general welfare of the nation in an act of "slavish subservience" to a section of the country.[104] Curtin's tariff campaign received able support from the strong protectionist organ, the Philadelphia *North American.*[105]

There was much discussion, expectation, and wide public interest manifested over a widely circulated report that Curtin had challenged Foster to a series of public appearances somewhat on the order of the widely publicized Lincoln-Douglas debates. Bowing to public clamor, the

---

[103] L.[ucius] E. Chittenden, *Recollections of President Lincoln and His Administration* (New York, 1891), 10-11.
[104] Altoona *Tribune,* July 26, 1860; Bloomsburg *Columbia Democrat,* Aug. 11, 1860; Harrisburg *Telegraph,* Sept. 20, 1860,
[105] Robinson, "Public Press of Philadelphia," 82.

contestants' two campaign managers, McClure and Welsh, met twice presumably for the purpose of arranging details, drank and smoked their way through several hours of gentlemanly fellowship, and ended after one moment of deliberation in complete agreement—not to have the debates. As a guarantee of no loss of face to either side, each manager agreed to make public demands which he knew his opponent could not meet; and thus the proponents of each enjoyed the opportunity of accusing the other of declining the invitation. Curtin needed more time to canvass rural areas and Foster did not relish the idea of defending his dualistic godfather, Douglas and Breckinridge. Alexander McClure who related this charming story, assured his readers that to Curtin, the idea of meeting Foster was but a "passing thought" uttered in the heat of a campaign speech,[106] but in an earlier letter to Henry C. Carey he stated his intention to ask Foster "to meet me before the people and then I will be sustained."[107]

President Buchanan, the titular head of the Democratic Party in Pennsylvania, took no active part in the campaign. Between Douglas and Breckinridge, neither of whom he accepted as bona fide candidates, he chose the latter and considered every citizen free to make his own choice.[108] He gave Foster his full support because he considered his victory essential to Lincoln's defeat; but he doubted Foster's wisdom in endorsing the position of Douglas on the territories. Although there were many prominent Democrats such as Bigler, Dawson, Wright, and J. Glancey Jones, leadership in the ranks of the Democracy was not as pronounced as in the

---

[106] *Old Time Notes,* I, 428.
[107] Curtin to Carey, March 8, 1860, Carey Papers in Gardiner Collection, HSP.
[108] Moore, *Works,* X, 457-58,

People's Party, but each provincial leader accepted his share of the burden to bring victory to Foster.

The Democracy refused to accept the tariff question as an issue in the campaign and advanced Foster along with Curtin as the champion of protection and business. Their journals brushed aside the dust of sixteen years from the *Congressional Globe* and reprinted choice sections relating to Foster's past position on the tariff.[109] During the campaign he was proclaimed as a proponent of the Morrill Tariff Bill.[110] In 1856, it was recalled, Foster had fought for the relief of business through repeal of the tonnage tax. Foster's speech of September 17, in Independence Square, branded Republican principles as tending to sow dissension among the states and to destroy the Union. "Let me tell you," Foster shouted to the crowd, "that there is lying behind and underneath that purpose something deeper and far more destructive—a principle that endangers the existence of the Union itself." In reply to McClure's characterization of him as a freetrader, Foster cited his vote for protection in 1846 at the same time Hannibal Hamlin was voting against it.[111]

One of the most confusing aspects of the total contest in Pennsylvania was the Douglas campaign. At a meeting of the Democratic State Committee on August 9, the Douglas men turned down all efforts at compromise[112] and amended fusion definitely appeared at an end when the straight Douglas ticket appeared in September. Democratic organs repeatedly accused John Forney of deliberately sabotaging Democratic success by endorsing a separate Douglas ticket. Two decades later Forney, pleading guilty to these accusations, claimed that he had done his utmost to elect Lincoln

[109] Bedford *Gazette*, March 30, 1860.
[110] Bellefonte *Democratic-Watchman*, June 14, 1860.
[111] Erie *Observer*, Sept. 29, 1860.
[112] McClure to Lincoln, Aug. 11, 1860, Lincoln MSS, LC,

by supporting a straight Douglas ticket.[113] After the Pennsylvania state elections the Democratic State Committee and Douglas Executive Committee agreed to fusion unreservedly on the basis of the Reading ticket. Nevertheless a Douglas ticket apparently with the candidate's approval circulated through the mail and Forney obligingly contributed to the confusion with a Douglas ticket in his *Press*.[114] In Pennsylvania there is no telling how many Douglas men went to the polls, because the fusion vote undoubtedly included thousands of Douglas men. Douglas, during his few stops in Pennsylvania in September, lost no opportunity to speak as an exponent of modified protection.

The Bell and Breckinridge groups did not seem to create much stir during the contest. Both the Curtin and Foster men, hoping to secure the Bell vote for their candidate, waited anxiously for any news of a state ticket. On August 22, less than a quorum of the Bell Committee met and decided not to run a gubernatorial candidate. This shrunken Bell Committee was antagonistic to Curtin because businessmen feared a Republican victory would lead to a dissolution of the Union.[115] When the Philadelphia Constitutional-Union Committee endorsed Foster shortly before election, McClure publicly accused it of a sell-out to the Democrats. The State Constitutional Union Executive Committee at Harrisburg on September 27 decided once again not to run a gubernatorial candidate and selected a Bell state electoral ticket which appeared in the public press. Nothing was said about

[113] Forney, *Anecdotes of Public Men*, II, 421.

[114] Davis, *Pennsylvania Politics*, 133-34 ; Philadelphia *Press*, Oct. 19, 1860.

[115] McClure to Lincoln, Aug. 27, 1860, Lincoln MSS, LC. Russell Errett attributed the Bell anti-Curtin hostility to Curtin's commitments to Lincoln. Errett to J. Medill, July 21, 1860, Lincoln MSS, LC.

supporting Foster. Nevertheless, whether officially or not, the strong Bell group in the Philadelphia area gave its support to Foster.[116]

Lincoln certainly did not lack for information concerning the progress of the campaign in Pennsylvania: A. K. McClure, J. P. Sanderson, Cameron, and a host of self-appointed experts sent by mail much information together with comments to Lincoln in Springfield, who appeared peculiarly reluctant to make any public appearances. McClure's desperate quest for funds must have kept him quite busy, but he delivered five addresses in the Philadelphia area, and imported Carl Schurz at a handsome price specifically for the purpose of rehabilitating Curtin in the German areas. McClure informed Lincoln of Forney's fifth-column activities against Douglas, reported "cheery intelligence" from all parts of the state by mid-July, and later was certain his organization would save the state with a majority up to 30,000 for Curtin.[117] Sanderson grudgingly admitted, by mid-September, Curtin's ability to carry the state perhaps by 15,000, if in the meantime he didn't commit an act of folly; and accused the Curtin men of entering negotiations for the sale of a portion of the Lincoln electoral vote to Bell.[118] By August 1, Cameron could assure Lincoln of a much larger majority than Curtin's; and taking a sly poke at McClure's financial plight, protested the state's need for outside help. Both in private correspondence and publicly, leaders of the People's Party expressed confidence in the results of both October state elections and the presidential in November.

October 9, 1860, saw fulfillment of the most optimistic

---

[116] Philadelphia *Public Ledger,* Sept. 28, Oct. 8, 10, 1860.
[117] McClure to Lincoln, July 2, July 18, Aug. 11, Aug. 27, 1860, Lincoln MSS, LC.
[118] Sanderson to Lincoln, Aug. 27, Sept. 8, Sept. 18, *ibid.*

hopes of the People's Party in Pennsylvania. If, as was generally believed, Cameron hoped for Curtin's defeat by a narrow margin, he successfully concealed his chagrin in his telegram to Lincoln, "Pennsylvania comes greeting with 25,000 for Curtin."[119] In his retreat at Bellefonte, Curtin awaited anxiously for the news. First returns from his own normally strong Democratic Centre County gave him a small lead. A large pro-Curtin crowd gathered in front of the town's telegraph office shouting triumphantly as the returns filtered in. Before midnight, assurances of a Curtin victory from McClure led to a grand rush for Curtin's residence. ". . . he was hurried off to the Wigwam amid the long and loud acclamations of his friends and neighbors. On reaching the Wigwam the Col. was caught up by the people and borne on their heads . . . ."[120] Enthusiasm for Curtin's victory spread throughout the Republican North and the victorious party made the most of its 32,000-majority governor.[121] Legislative election results followed the Curtin trend. The 1861 General Assembly seated only 33 Democrats to 100 for the People's Party, a net gain of 13 members over the majority held in 1860.[122] Of the 12 state senators chosen in 1860, only 2 were Democrats. Foster's victory over Curtin in Philadelphia by 1,900 votes[123] was credited to the Bell elements. Curtin attributed his great victory in large measure to the "want felt for a protective tariff."[124]

"The October elections decided the presidential contest.

---

[119] Cameron to Lincoln, Oct. 10, 1860, Lincoln MSS, LC.
[120] Bellefonte *Central Press,* Oct. 11, 1860.
[121] The first "official" figures were Curtin, 262,349 ; Foster 230, 275, but the *Tribune Almanac* for 1861 listed 262, 403 for Curtin, 230, 329 for Foster.
[122] *Tribune Almanac* for 1861. At the beginning of the session the figures stood 35-98.
[123] Philadelphia *Ledger,* Oct. 13, 1860.
[124] Harrisburg *Telegraph,* Nov. 10, 1860.

Pennsylvania was the Keystone. 'As goes Pennsylvania, so goes the Union!' "[125] Chittenden's quoted observation, although altogether humdrum, could hardly be improved upon. With feeling so prevalent that it was all over, the presidential race lost interest and the November elections provided only an anticlimax. McClure did not relax his campaign efforts, although to Lincoln he confided: "The contest is altogether over in Pennsylvania—utterly abandoned by the Democrats . . . do not be surprised at 100,000 majority."[126] Simon Cameron, always with an eye on the potential fountain of patronage, sent $800 to aid in the weak counties of Illinois and had more (probably out of his own pocket) to send if necessary. McClure had not discovered such easy access to funds in his own state. Hearing of distress in the New England area, McClure, possessing neither silver nor gold, dispatched such as he had, Pennsylvania's 32,000-majority governor-elect, Andrew G. Curtin, to do yeoman's service.

In early November, the Democratic State Central Committee issued its last pre-election appeal. A Democratic vote, stated the Committee, "is a vote for the Constitution, the Union, and for the rights and property and safety of our southern brethren, and swells the great conservative body, which now stands as the only barrier to sectionalism and fanaticism."[127] Viewed in retrospect, the Democratic Erie *Observer's* evaluation of a vote for Lincoln sounded much like the voice of prophecy: ". . . Union or disunion is the question to be decided in November. The war of the North upon the South must produce its legitimate result and can

---

[125] Chittenden, *Recollections,* 17. James G. Blaine likewise emphasized Pennsylvania's importance, *Twenty Years,* I, 206-07.

[126] McClure to Lincoln, Oct. 15, 1860, Lincoln MSS, LC.

[127] "Address," Erie *Observer,* Nov. 3, 1860.

have but one end. There will come estrangement, then heated, then open and violent altercations, and then dissolution of the Federal Compact."[128] "The election of Lincoln," continued the *Observer* the following week, will mean "servile war, bloodshed and revolution, and no arm will be able to stay it."

Whether from one, a combination, or all of many reasons given: the pessimistic tone of the Democratic press, the continued machinations of John W. Forney, confusion and division in the Democratic camp, acceleration of People's Party growth through the election of Curtin, increasing popularity of a protective tariff, dissatisfaction with the policies of Pennsylvania's son seated in the White House, growth of the spirit of freedom, fear of a business slump, increase in stature of Lincoln, or even a desire to climb on the bandwagon, the Lincoln victory was considerably greater than Curtin's. Although 16,000 fewer people voted in November, Lincoln topped Curtin by 6,000 votes; and his majority over the combined tickets was 60,000, almost twice Curtin's. Lincoln received over 57 per cent of the total vote while Curtin's score was 53 per cent. The total popular vote gave Lincoln 268,030; the Fusion ticket 178,871, the Douglas straight ticket 16,765, and the Bell 12,776.[129] Although Philadelphia cast less than 20 per cent of the total vote she contributed over 60 per cent of the Douglas and Bell strength.[130] On the night of the election Cameron telegraphed enthusiastically to Lincoln, "Pennsylvania seventy thousand for you, New York safe, glory enough."[131]

To explain what the electorate had done in Pennsylvania

---

[128] Oct. 20, 1860.
[129] *Tribune Almanac* for 1861.
[130] *Ibid.*
[131] Cameron to Lincoln, Nov. 6, 1860, Lincoln MSS, LC.

is more difficult than to explain why it was done. Surely they were not voting for dissolution of the Union when they asked for containment of slavery. The vow of the deep South to secede the day a Black Republican should occupy the exalted office of the Presidency was to Pennsylvanians only a sample of the Southern fire-eater's bluster; and even if the threatened secession should occur, the deed was not of their own making. Within national Republican ranks they had heard of Seward's "higher law," of the "irrepressible conflict," and of the stern Puritanical principles of Salmon P. Chase; but few of their leaders were men of this stripe. Pennsylvania's contribution to the victory of sectionalism was unaccompanied with any desire to force dissolution of the Union or to coerce the South from the way of its domestic institutions. The antislavery movement as the moral force of righteousness against that of evil was, within the Commonwealth, still in its infancy and was yet to capture the imagination of her people. But the multiple reincarnation of the soul of John Brown was soon to find its way within the persons of thousands of devotees; and his body, containing the seeds of militant Republicanism, was beginning its inexorable march.

III

The Crisis

THE ELECTION OF Lincoln provided only one of the factors
leading to a final disruption of the Union. Earlier wedges
of separation multiplied manyfold during the 1850's and
rather strangely became concentrated within the question of
the territorial status of slavery. The Compromise of 1850
provided only a lull, and the contest over Kansas whetted
by a "Southern interpretation" of the Constitution in the
celebrated Dred Scott decision added fuel to the sectional
conflict. These differences became increasingly evident within
the halls of Congress where, with unrestrained tempers,
members occasionally engaged in personal combat to the
great disgrace of that body and the nation alike. The assault
upon the venerable John Hickman of Pennsylvania, a
respected House member, evoked much press comment.[1]
Simon Cameron, although on friendly terms with Jefferson
Davis, entered into a compact with Senators Wade and
Chandler to put an end to the "chronic insolence" of
Southern senators and if need be to carry the quarrel into
the coffin.[2] The execution of John Brown only a few days
before the opening of the new Congress contributed further
to the sectional tenseness.

The nearly matched parties in the newly assembled House
of Representatives, December 5, 1859, at once engaged in

[1] Feb. 25, 1860.
[2] "Memorandum," Cameron MSS, LC.

97

a prolonged contest to capture the speakership. Galusha A. Grow of Pennsylvania was a leading Republican contender for the honor. Upon Grow's withdrawal the party concentrated on John Sherman of Ohio, who was even less palatable to the Southerners than Grow. Weeks of balloting brought no election, and a group of determined Pennsylvanians including Thaddeus Stevens, Grow, Covode, E. Joy Morris, and Edward McPherson announced their intention to stay with Sherman indefinitely.[3] Abundant criticism from the press for prostituting public welfare to political bickerings had little effect upon the members. The Democratic press assailed the Republicans for their attempts to humiliate the South; while the Republican organs countered with tirades against the disunionist activities of their opponents. At the end of a three-week recess the Republicans successfully broke the deadlock by substituting William Pennington of New Jersey for Sherman.

Events of the succeeding months added to the prevailing pessimism. In Congress, Pennsylvania's representatives, Republican and Democratic alike, were disappointed in seeing a protective tariff go by the board, and in witnessing the death of Galusha Grow's Homestead Bill. It fell to the lot of Buchanan's already discredited administration to bear the brunt of attack for these failures. The summer months witnessed the work of another product of sectionalism, the disruption of the Democratic Party. Four major parties with four reputable candidates, all pledging fidelity to the Union but generally representing sectional interests, contested for the prize which was to decide the fate of the Union. The fall months brought Republican victories in many state and national elections, another triumph for sectionalism—a natural foe of nationalism, unity, and peace. Now only time

[3] Davis, *Pennsylvania Politics*, 45,

could confirm or deny the dire results predicted by the enemies of "Black Republicanism." According to the view of the victors and most independents, the decision had been made through our democratic process, the franchise, and it remained to be seen whether the will of the majority was to prevail.

The answer to this momentous question was not long in coming. South Carolina took immediate steps to call a "secession" convention and there was little doubt as to the outcome. Other Southern states were likely to follow her example. Southern moderates from the border states called for a solution through interstate conventions. From all points of the Union came all kinds of proposals ranging from suggestions of "four unions" to "two Presidents."[4] The harried President, Buchanan, anxious to avert a fratricidal conflict, brought upon himself storms of denunciation from both interested parties for his condemnation of secession and his advocacy of "peaceful constitutional remedies."[5] The President was voicing the opinion of his fellow Pennsylvanian, Attorney General Black, who could not see in coercion a constitutional remedy for the crisis.

Economic effects of the disruption were immediate within the Commonwealth. Exaggerated reports of Southern activities were well calculated to confirm the Northern businessman's worst fears. The chain of events which followed had all the earmarks of an economic depression. Reaction started with suspension of specie payments by Philadelphia banks, accompanied by a fall in prices and stocks, the cancellation of orders, the closing of manufacturing plants, and the resulting unemployment. The Democratic Bedford *Gazette,*

---

[4] James G. Randall, *Lincoln the President: Springfield to Gettysburg* (New York, 1946), I, 208-19.

[5] *Ibid.,* 220-21.

hailing the business paralysis as the first fruits of Lincoln's election, called on the President-elect to recede from his position or witness the end of a glorious republic, "another Rome reft of Empire and torn by bloody feuds of rival and jealous factions."[6] In Pittsburgh where the banks were forced to follow Philadelphia's example, the strongly Republican Pittsburgh *Gazette* pooh-poohed the gravity of the panic and criticized fellow sectional editors for assisting in the cause of disunion by creating hard times through the sheer power of evil suggestion.[7]

For over a month the victorious incoming state administration had remained publicly silent on the questions of public policy; and well might it do so in the absence of any go-ahead signal from Lincoln. But the public was sure to expect some comment from Curtin, McClure, and Morton McMichael, the featured speakers at a Philadelphia victory dinner held early in December, 1860. The addresses by these leaders could easily have served as commentaries upon the powerful pressure brought to bear by Philadelphia businessmen, who could see only bankruptcy as a concomitant of secession, if Curtin and his associates failed to agree in advance to a conciliatory attitude toward the South. Side-stepping the all-important question of the day—civil war, except indirectly, the carefully censored speeches "declared unqualifiedly that every constitutional right of the South must be sacredly maintained . . . ." Only one speaker, Wayne MacVeagh, wrote McClure, uttered the truth when he admonished the North to meet the "causeless rebellion" of the South and "accept civil war if necessary."[8]

---

[6] Nov. 30, 1860.

[7] Nov. 26, in Davis, *Pennsylvania Politics*, 140-41.

[8] McClure, *Old Time Notes*, I, 468-70. MacVeagh later succeeded to chairmanship of the State Central Committee, married Simon Cameron's daughter, and became Attorney General of the United States.

A Philadelphia mass meeting likewise expressed a conciliatory tone. Thousands of citizens assembled in Independence
Square on December 13, and listened to an open forum conducted by leaders representing all degrees of political opinion
it seemed, except abolitionism. George W. Woodward, Isaac
Hazlehurst, and the city's mayor were the leading speakers.
The resolutions placed emphasis upon the rights of states, of
owners of runaway slaves, and of territorial slave holders.
Of striking Christian incongruity, apparently, was the one
which branded arraignment of existing slavery in the states
as "inconsistent with the spirit of brotherhood." A parting
resolution invited an interstate convention for purposes of
consultation and possible remedial action based upon the
grievances of the South (nothing was said about Northern
grievances) and launched an appeal to the southernmost tier
of states to forbear from seceding.[12]

Two succeeding events which the unthinking public
related to one another caused much excitement in the
western part of the state. A few days after South Carolina's
secession from the Union on December 20, 1860, the public
learned of the War Secretary's order to ship south from
Pittsburgh heavy guns intended for two newly constructed
Federal forts in Louisiana and Texas.[13] This alleged
treacherous act by the Virginian, John B. Floyd, aroused
much excitement in Pittsburgh where there was general talk
of mob action to prevent removal of the ordnance. Protests
flooded Washington, citizens held mass meetings, and the
unfortunate James Buchanan stood accused throughout the
North of harboring traitors within his official family. The

[12] Philadelphia *Public Ledger,* Dec. 14, 1860.
[13] Philip G. Auchampaugh, *James Buchanan and His Cabinet on the Eve of Secession* (Privately Printed, 1926), 91.

voice of Simon Cameron, Buchanan's nemesis, could be heard speaking through the editorials of the Pittsburgh *Gazette* charging the President with collusion with South Carolina and with deliberately weakening the armed forces of the nation in order to reduce Lincoln's incoming government to impotence.[14] In Pittsburgh the furor gradually declined, the citizenry fortunately did not attempt to take matters into their own hands, and President Buchanan had the order revoked.

In December the governor-elect busied himself with the task of preparing an inaugural containing policies, he hoped, in agreement with those to be announced later by Lincoln. Although Curtin could not speak for the policies of the incoming Lincoln Administration, he realized that both the Commonwealth and nation expected the powerful Republican state of Pennsylvania to assume some position of leadership in the national crisis. According to A. K. McClure, Curtin organized a private spy ring which operated throughout the South and garnered information of great value as to the earnestness and disposition of the secessionist elements.[15] In mid-December, Curtin, promising faithful support to the President-elect, requested a conference with Lincoln for the purpose of harmonizing as far as possible his aims and statement of public policy with those of the incoming national administration.[16] Apparently Lincoln did not react favorably to Curtin's proposal. In his first address as governor-elect at Philadelphia on December 11, Curtin gave the election an economic interpretation: "a triumph of principles" which included as goals, liberalization of government, progress, development of wealth, and, most important

[14] The *Gazette* in Davis, *Pennsylvania Politics,* 151.
[15] McClure, *Old Time Notes,* I, 446.
[16] Curtin to Lincoln, Dec. 14, John G. Nicolay Papers, LC.

of all, "protection to the languishing interests of the people of Pennsylvania."[17] On the eve of the inaugural, two future state cabinet members together with A. K. McClure assisted Curtin in final preparation of his state paper.[18]

On New Year's Day, 1861, the General Assembly met in Harrisburg to organize preparatory to receiving the governor's message and to commence work on legislation. Moderate men still believing that further secession might be averted wished to see the body pass without further ado resolutions and legislation indicating their willingness to reconcile differences with the South. Events were soon to prove that the People's-Republican controlled legislature was in no mood for concessions, although the newly elected speaker of the Senate, Robert M. Palmer, suggested a study of the statutes relating to the rendition of fugitives held to labor services in other states with the idea in mind of promptly removing any just causes of complaint.[19] Palmer was referring to sections of the penal code of Pennsylvania which were contrary to the spirit and letter of the Federal Fugitive Slave Law. The speaker declared Pennsylvania's determination to resist every effort to destroy the Union but did not list the methods to be employed or to what extent the state was prepared to take the initiative.

Curtin's inaugural left no doubt of the position taken on the question of secession by the incoming administration. Curtin accepted Webster's concept of the Union as a compact of people. Concerning secession he said: "No part of the people, no state, nor combination of states can voluntarily secede from the Union, nor absolve themselves from their obligations to it. To permit a state to withdraw at

[17] Philadelphia *Press,* Dec. 3, 1860.
[18] McClure, *Old Time Notes,* I, 446-48.
[19] *Legislative Record of Pennsylvania,* 1861, 3.

pleasure from the Union, without the consent of the rest, is to confess that our government is a failure." Evidently Curtin envisaged the use of coercion if necessary to maintain the Union. "It is the first duty of the National authorities to stay the progress of anarchy and enforce the laws, and Pennsylvania . . . will give them an honest, faithful, and active support."[20] This view contradicted that of President Buchanan, who contended that a state could not legally be coerced because the Constitution had not delegated such power to the national government.[21] Curtin based his view primarily on the right of self-preservation and the acknowledged supremacy of the Union over the years.

The influence of the Curtin-Cameron feud was evident from the very beginning of the new administration in the makeup of Curtin's tiny "cabinet." The new governor's official family comprised one member who gave him six years of faithful service, and another, a Cameron man, who within a period of five months did much to discredit Curtin's regime. In the course of his campaign Curtin had surrounded himself with many able men capable and eager to fill leading appointive offices in the Commonwealth. Unfortunately the gubernatorial candidate was prone to allow, much to his later embarrassment, several aspirants to believe that he was the one particularly favored for a position.

Only two weeks before the time of his inauguration, a small group of friends assisted Curtin in selecting his secretary of the Commonwealth, Eli Slifer of Union County, a quiet unassuming successful businessman now completing his third term as state treasurer. During the past years Curtin

---

[20] *Pennsylvania Archives, Fourth Series, Papers of the Governors,* VIII (Harrisburg, 1902), 336-37.

[21] James D. Richardson, Compiler, *Messages . . . of the Presidents,* (10 vols. Washington, 1909), V, 635-36.

had frequent correspondence of a financial nature with Slifer and considered him a personal friend. At the same time Slifer had maintained friendly relations with Cameron. On December 29, 1860, Curtin tendered Slifer the office of secretary of the Commonwealth because of his fine qualifications, the high esteem in which he was held by the people, and their fine personal relations.[22] Immediately upon the announcement of Slifer's appointment, a coterie of Cameron men assembled in secret conference for the purpose of forcing Curtin to substitute Francis Jordan of Bedford for Slifer.[23] Jordan, according to McClure,[24] was originally Curtin's choice and his failure to receive the post impelled the disappointed candidate to desert to the Cameron camp. Curtin expressed both his surprise upon finding opposition from the Cameron group and regret for not knowing the facts sooner,[25] but would not publicly humiliate his friend Slifer by changing the appointment. Slifer's former office of state treasurer was assumed by Henry D. Moore of Philadelphia, Cameron's candidate for the office.

Cameron, still asserting his leadership of the People's Party in Pennsylvania, resolved to force one of his men upon the new state administration. Such an appointment would, to an uninformed public, indicate renewed harmony between the factions. Immediately upon Curtin's election, Samuel A. Purviance of Butler expressed his wish to have Cameron advance him for the post of Attorney General.[26] Purviance, having failed Cameron at the Chicago convention, now

[22] Curtin to Slifer, Dec. 29, 1860, Dill-Slifer Papers, Dickinson College Library.
[23] A. H. Reeder to Cameron, Jan. 2, 1861, Cameron MSS, LC.
[24] *Old Time Notes,* I, 436. But McClure's letter to Stevens, Nov. 7, 1860, (McPherson MSS), stated Curtin had "positively promised" Jordan the post of attorney general.
[25] G. L. Uliet to Cameron, Jan. 16, 1861, Cameron Papers, DCC.
[26] Purviance to Cameron, Oct. 11, 1860, *ibid,*

desired tangible manifestation of Cameron's continued confidence. Darwin A. Finney, Curtin's choice for the position, had one more year to serve in the state senate, and in order to effect a compromise, Titian J. Coffey suggested a temporary appointment of one year for Purviance. This would have the double effect of establishing state-wide prestige for the doubtful legal talents of Purviance and at the same time propitiate the Cameron faction. McClure claimed that Purviance accepted the office in full knowledge of his temporary appointment, but Purviance evidently expected to stay. Within three weeks of his incumbency, Purviance reported that McClure was contemplating his removal because of his close relations with Cameron.[27]

While Curtin was making preparations for taking office, journalists were suggesting remedial measures and prominent statesmen were voicing their appraisal of the crisis. Within the state, John W. Forney, having seen successful conclusion of his campaign to sabotage the presidential aspirations of Stephen A. Douglas, now called for an impartial evaluation of the incoming Lincoln Administration.[28] In a lengthy editorial, journalist Forney practically exhausted all the possibilities of his versatile pen in castigating antislavery itinerants from New England, on whom he heaped the entire responsibility for the crisis. Was it possible the state would have to shed blood for that apostle of abolitionism, John Brown, a saint "without piety or sanity"? Rather, advised Forney, it is for Pennsylvania to "calmly forbear, and look to arms only as a last resort."[29]

Two important leaders of the Democracy from Pennsylvania, both legalists of the first order, apparently placed no

---

[27] Purviance to Cameron, Feb. 7, 1861, *ibid.*
[28] Robinson, "Public Press of Philadelphia," 51.
[29] Philadelphia *Press,* Jan. 8, 1861.

blame upon the secessionists. George W. Woodward of the state supreme court actually seemed to be condoning secession when he wrote: "Bayonets can't keep a state in the Union. I believe that I rejoice to believe it."[30] For a long time, wrote Jeremiah Black, he had known that the Southern states would not agree to live under the same government if the party of abuse, the Republicans, came into power. The victors were intoxicated with their new power. Somewhat conscience-striken, however, Buchanan's new Secretary of State confided to Charles Buckalew that he would feel more comfortable if the skirts of the Buchanan Administration were clear, and he believed that the revolution might have been "throttled" at Charleston. "Lincoln," concluded Black, "is very small potatoes [whose] reputation grew out of making comical faces and telling smutty anecdotes."[31]

From the nation's capital, informed citizens began to hear of such terms as "the Committee of Thirteen," "the Critten-den Proposals," and the "Committee of Thirty-three" and to associate them with propositions to save the Union. The first named consisted of a group of distinguished senators comprising such names as Seward, Davis, Toombs, Douglas, Grimes, and Crittenden. Surely these statesmen could effect a solution if the will to compromise actually existed. The thirteen began its work coincidentally with South Carolina's act of secession and reported its failure on the last day of the year. The secessionist group desired failure as a means of ensuring defection of the border slave states while the radical Republicans would not sacrifice principles or make commit-ments. The venerable Senator Crittenden of Kentucky, perhaps possessed of a vision of the shades of Henry Clay, proposed to the thirteen his plan for extending the historic

---

[30] Woodward to Black, Dec. 10, 1861, Black MSS, LC.
[31] Black to Buckalew, Jan. 28, 1861, *ibid.*

Missouri Compromise line of 36°30, westward, with positive protection ensured for slavery south of that line, together with other safeguards; but the committee could not agree on his plan. Early in January, Crittenden succeeded in bringing his proposals to the floor of the Senate. The Committee of Thirty-Three, composed of one House member from each state, reported a series of minority proposals, some of which were passed as resolutions by the House.

Pennsylvania's United States senators, the Democratic ex-governor, William Bigler, and Simon Cameron, first Republican senator from the state, participated in the Crittenden debates. On January 14, 1861, Bigler moved to have the Crittenden proposals submitted to a popular vote of the people of the nation, and two days later he succeeded in getting all other business in the Senate postponed in order to consider them. Before the day was over all proponents of compromise were grieved to see a substitute motion passed which would kill all compromise including Crittenden's. Six Southern senators, seated on the floor, refused to vote on the substitute motion which passed, 25 to 23. Simon Cameron evidently changed his mind in the process and his independence among Republican Senators was unique. After voting for the substitute proposal along with all the Republican senators, he moved to have it reconsidered and the Senate passed his motion.[32] This meant that the Crittenden proposals were back on the calendar. Three days later, on January 21, Bigler delivered a long speech to an almost empty Senate chamber on behalf of modified Crittenden proposals. Bigler might well have been delivering a eulogy over a corpse; it was evident that the period of compromise had ended,

[32] John W. Burgess, *The Civil War and the Constitution* (New York, 1901), I, 111-12. Cox in his *Eight Years in Congress,* 28, recorded that Cameron voted against his own resolution.

because Georgia had just completed secession and Louisiana was about to follow suit.

The state's representatives in the Senate had shown a conciliatory attitude during the Senate proceedings. Bigler blamed the "unnecessary hostility" of people to slavery who had no connection with it as the fundamental cause of the crisis. But he could not recognize secession as a legitimate remedy for Southern ills and would resist it with all his power by peaceful means.[33] Cameron immediately followed his senior colleague on the floor of the Senate and expressed his hearty agreement with the "sentiments" expressed by Bigler. This statement was misunderstood by the public and sometimes misquoted and misinterpreted by the Democratic press as a full endorsement of everything Bigler had said. Cameron, as he himself later explained, did not agree with Bigler's interpretation of the crisis, but he did agree with his spirit of conciliation and patriotic efforts to maintain peace.[34] Cameron was willing to restore the old compromise line provided it applied only to territory already acquired. Perhaps Cameron's many letters from his constituents pleading for a peaceful solution led him to declare coercion a bad remedy and unquestionably the last; and he didn't know whether he would ever resort to it.

One more belated attempt to patch up sectional differences took place when a group of delegates representing only twenty-one states convened in Washington, February 4, upon invitation from Virginia's legislature. Curtin made Pennsylvania's participation in the conference entirely a partisan affair. Every one of his seven appointees, which included such names as Pollock, William Meredith, and David Wilmot, were Republicans. The legislative Democrats,

[33] Crippen, *Simon Cameron,* 229.
[34] Harrisburg *Telegraph,* Feb. 7, 1861.

whose votes had made participation possible, claimed they had been duped into voting for it upon the assurance several Democratic commissioners would be named. Certainly, the selection of Wilmot from the ranks of radicals who opposed participation appeared downright offensive to the Democracy. Pennsylvania's delegates were hamstrung with instructions not to support any amendment to the Constitution. Even the Republican-minded Philadelphia *Public Ledger* could not excuse Curtin's action.[35]

Whether or not the people of Pennsylvania would have approved a compromise will never be known, because no plan was ever submitted to popular vote. Cameron received many letters from various parts of the state approving his conciliatory attitude; and certainly it is erroneous to suppose that only the Philadelphia area supported him. The radical editor Russell Errett warned his good friend Cameron of the opposition to compromise prevailing in Pittsburgh, but admitted favorable sentiments in the Harrisburg area.[36] At the same time Cameron possessed a letter from a group of prominent Pittsburgh men approving of his stand. Samuel Collver, lately returned from a tour of western Virginia and southwestern Pennsylvania, reported "great applause" for Cameron in the area.[37] Actually the politically astute Cameron had written to various supporters throughout the state and had asked them to sound out public opinion in their area.[38] It is quite reasonable to assume that he thought he was speaking for his constituents during the crisis.

The Republican legislature took no steps which could be considered conciliatory. The Commonwealth's personal-

---

[35] Feb. 2, 1861, in Davis, *Pennsylvania Politics,* 166.
[36] Errett to Cameron, Jan. 23, Cameron MSS, LC.
[37] Collver to Cameron, Feb. 11, 1861, *ibid.*
[38] Cameron MSS, DCC.

liberty laws, which forbade state magistrates to accept jurisdiction in cases involving runaway slaves, imposed heavy
fines on anyone who might disturb the peace while in the
process of claiming a runaway, and outlawed the transfer
(sale) of captured fugitives. A motion in the General
Assembly for a study of "obnoxious laws" was defeated, and
bills to revise the penal code died in the committee stage.[39]
Only a resolution which acknowledged the common brotherhood of Pennsylvanians and "southern gentlemen" was
accepted. These Southern brethren were encouraged to continue in full enjoyment of their domestic institutions; but
the full strength of fraternal Pennsylvania, if it were
necessary, was pledged to prevent their close kinsmen from
creating a new fatherland.[40] The Democratic minority could
only express disapproval.

The first opportunity of the year for the state Democracy
to take an open blast at the Republicans came on January
30, 1861, when its state executive committee assembled. The
committee's "Address," released for public consumption
through Democratic organs, accused the Republican Party of
failing to meet "in a proper spirit of concession and compromise the overtures made for the adjustments of our National
difficulties." Then followed a very serious indictment of the
Republicans: "We are in the midst of a revolution,"
charged the committee, "brought about by the teachings of
an anti-constitutional party . . . ."[41]

The tone expressed by the state convention was more
moderate. Its platform dealing almost entirely with national
affairs was of great length. Taken as a whole the resolutions

[39] Davis, *Pennsylvania Politics,* 161-62.
[40] Pennsylvania *Journal of the House,* 1861, 140. The vote in the
House was 67-23.
[41] Bedford *Gazette,* Feb. 8, 1861.

were a prime example of legerdemain. The states were characterized as "sovereign and independent over every subject not surrendered to the control of the Federal government." The Federal government in its turn possessed supreme authority and the power to preserve itself, but should not use "armed aggression" upon seceding states so long as Northern states retained laws unjust to the South. The Crittenden proposals were acceptable as a "satisfactory basis" for adjustment of difficulties. Coercion was not to be used until the "rights of the South were secured." The platform did not list the Southern "rights" nor did it state who should judge the time when the rights had been secured.

The resignation of Southern members from Congress during the declining days of the Buchanan Administration made it possible for the Republicans to pass tariff legislation pleasing to the Pennsylvanians. Almost a year had gone by since E. Joy Morris of Philadelphia had made extravagant predictions concerning the newly introduced Morrill tariff. Cameron sought its passage because he considered it beneficial both to himself and his constituents. The state Democracy at that time had an added reason for advocating it—the coming elections. The Morrill tariff sailed easily through the House but struck a snag in the Senate, where it remained closeted. Within two days after the opening of the new session in December, 1860, Cameron was pressing for renewed action. Bigler exhibited an equal amount of zeal for the bill and even voted to postpone consideration of Crittenden's proposals in order to take up the tariff; and "when Douglas begged for the defeat of the Morrill Bill to pacify the South, it was Bigler who rose to refute him."[42] In the House, Pennsylvania Democrats assisted in its passage. "The passage of the Morrill Tariff was a blow to

---

[42] Stampp, *And the War Came*, 162.

border-state Unionists, but it brought joy to Pennsylvanians,
both compromising Democrats and 'stiff-backed' Republicans. Buchanan must have redeemed himself a little in his
home state when, like a loyal son, he signed the new revenue
law."[43] When Simon Cameron resigned from the Senate on
March 11, 1861, he signified his deep regret at the loss of
cherished personal relations but consoled himself with the
knowledge that after fifteen years of labor on behalf of tariff
laws he had witnessed the desired change at the close of his
senatorial service.[44]

The reason for Simon Cameron's departure from the
Senate was his tardy entrance into Lincoln's Cabinet as
Secretary of War. None of Lincoln's major appointments
created nearly as much comment or controversy and certainly none caused him as much grief. The amount of contemporary and secondary material on the subject is astound-
ing and its collection would result in a respectable-sized
volume.[45] As already related, Cameron's lieutenants at the
Chicago nominating convention secured a promise of a
Cabinet post from Lincoln's managers in return for Pennsylvania's support for Lincoln. At a secret meeting held
early in the campaign at Saratoga, New York, Lincoln's men
reiterated the pledge to Cameron in person.[46] Lincoln had
not been informed of the bargain at the time of his election,[47]
and did not include Cameron on the tentative list

---

[43] *Ibid.,* 163-64.
[44] *Papers of the Governors,* 1858-1871, 352.
[45] Two special studies are: Harry E. Pratt, "Simon Cameron's
Fight for a Place in Lincoln's Cabinet," Abraham Lincoln Association *Bulletin,* No. 49 (1937); and Elwin L. Page, *Cameron for
Lincoln's Cabinet* (Boston, 1954). The former work lacks notes from
the Robert Todd Lincoln Collection and the second draws from
neither of the two main Cameron collections.
[46] Pratt, Lincoln *Bulletin,* No. 49.
[47] McClure, *Old Time Notes,* I, 408.

he compiled the day after his election, nor did he list him among the possibilities.[48] In view of two premises which Lincoln came to accept during these torturous months; i.e., that the powerful state of Pennsylvania must be represented in his Cabinet, and that Cameron as the senior Republican senator and the most powerful political figure in the state must give his consent to the appointment, the outcome was quite logical. There is a good chance he would have secured the post whether a bargain had been struck or not.

There is little evidence to show that Cameron was advancing himself for a cabinet post; outside forces contributed largely to his candidacy. The tremendous pressure brought to bear upon Lincoln from Pennsylvania was based not upon Cameron's qualifications nor even his popularity; it rested largely upon the hopes of Cameron's supporters for personal advancement. This fact, the usually politically astute Lincoln did not seem to grasp. J. P. Sanderson desired a lucrative post in Washington; David Wilmot was angling for Cameron's support for the senatorship; Pollock had his eye on the directorship of the Mint; J. B. Thomas wanted the collectorship of the Port of Philadelphia; John Covode hoped Cameron could give him the gubernatorial nomination in 1863 which he had missed in 1860; J. K. Moorhead was a perennial suppliant of crumbs from the tables of Covode and Cameron; Edgar Cowan was paying his recent debt for the senatorship, and Russell Errett was likewise squaring accounts. With few exceptions Cameron's strongest supporters hungered to feed at the public trough. Strong out-of-state

---

[48] Portion of Gideon Welles MSS printed in Rufus Rockwell Wilson, *Intimate Memories of Lincoln* (Elmira, 1945), 352. Cassius M. Clay was not on the list but he later claimed that Lincoln had promised to make him Secretary of War—the post Cameron received. See A. T. Rice, *Reminiscences of Abraham Lincoln*, 298,

forces working for Cameron were the powerful Weed-Seward machine of New York[49] and David Davis, possessor of "strange power" over the President.[50]

On December 30, 1860, upon invitation, Cameron arrived at Springfield for conversations with Lincoln. From his hotel quarters Cameron dispatched a letter to Lincoln citing Leonard Swett's notes as explanatory of his coming and asking whether he should call. Early that same evening Lincoln had a two-hour conversation with Edward Bates of Missouri, J. P. Sanderson, and Cameron, in Cameron's rooms. According to Bates' account no mention was made of Cameron as a Cabinet possibility during the long interview.[51] On the following day Lincoln informed Cameron of his nomination to either the Treasury or War post and requested an early reply.[52] Cameron evidently felt elated over the offer, because upon his return to the East he tactlessly and publicly displayed Lincoln's offer wherever he went.[53]

Cameron's surprise appointment appearing in the press as early as January 1, 1861, evoked a storm of protest. Alexander K. McClure, lately rebuked by Cameron for his

---

[49] Weed, *Autobiography*, 607-08. Practically all the contemporary authorities, Welles, Nicolay and Hay, McClure, and Trumbull, agreed that Seward was urging Cameron's appointment. A notable exception was Henry Adams, who wrote: "Lincoln offered Cameron the Treasury without Seward's knowledge. Seward would have preferred any other man." See W. C. Ford, ed., *Letters of Henry Adams* (1858-1891), 78.

[50] "There is Davis, with that way of making a man do a thing whether he wants to or not, who has forced me [Lincoln] to appoint Archy William judge . . . and John Jones . . . in the State Department." See White, *Life of Lyman Trumbull*, 143.

[51] H. K. Beale, (ed.), "The Diary of Edward Bates, 1855-1866," *American Historical Association Report*, IV, 1930. Gideon Welles claimed that Cameron sought an interview with Lincoln, failed, and then invited Swett to Lochiel. See *Diary*, II, 390.

[52] Lincoln to Cameron, Dec. 31, 1860, Cameron MSS, LC.

[53] E. B. Washburne to Lincoln, Jan. 10, 1861, Lincoln MSS.

attempt to bargain for a seat in United States Senate, set out posthaste for Springfield. McClure in his interview with Lincoln objected to Cameron principally on the basis of his moral unfitness for high office and characterized the seemingly large support for Cameron as Cameron's own movement. Lincoln, on his part, looked upon McClure's opposition as part of a personal feud and requested tangible evidence of Cameron's unfitness. When McClure suggested either Thaddeus Stevens or David Wilmot for Cameron's place, Lincoln replied that Cameron would not consent to any appointment from Pennsylvania except himself. On the following day McClure informed the President-elect that although Curtin was "cautious" on the subject, both he and his new secretary of the Commonwealth were "content" to see no appointments made from Pennsylvania, and suggested William L. Dayton of New Jersey as a substitute.[54]

In recounting his visit to Lincoln, McClure wrote that strong pressure had compelled Lincoln to reconsider, and concluded: "I think at all events Lincoln will not act *hastily* again. I hope that the arch scoundrel of the state is thrown, and if I am entitled to any credit for it, I am willing to retire. I shall have done my state essential service."[55] Curtin, it seems, did not actually protest Cameron's appointment but he promised McClure and William B. Mann he would do so if it were necessary to keep Cameron out of Lincoln's Cabinet.[56] His pledge found its way into Lincoln's hands.

Lincoln's next moves seemed to preclude any Cabinet possibility for Cameron. Lincoln, not aware that Cameron had publicly displayed great satisfaction with the Cabinet offer, abruptly withdrew his promise, citing McClure's visit

---

[54] McClure to Lincoln, Jan. 3, 1861, *ibid.*
[55] A. K. M[cClure], to Stevens, Jan. 10, [1861], McPherson MSS, LC.
[56] Curtin to McClure, Jan. 1, 1861, Lincoln MSS.

as one reason in addition to a "more potent matter" outside Pennsylvania.[57] Later he sent an apologetic note and substituted a milder letter in lieu of the "rude" missive of January 3, which Cameron was privileged to exhibit. This antedated letter reiterated Lincoln's faith in Cameron and requested his public rejection of the offer as a boon to the writer. "With much pain," wrote Lincoln, "I now say to you, that you will relieve me from great embarrassment by allowing me to recall the offer."[58] His accompanying note promised no Cabinet appointments from Pennsylvania without consultation.

At first Cameron apparently intended to accept Lincoln's plea. He signified his acquiescence to Leonard Swett and urged Thaddeus Stevens in his place.[59] But other factors appeared which gave Cameron hardly any alternative to the course which he finally determined to pursue: A. K. McClure had boastfully predicted the end of Cameron's political career; Lincoln's request for a declination had been widely publicized; and Cameron could not afford such a blow to his prestige as a powerful dispenser of patronage. Certainly nothing was better calculated to bring out all the superb qualities of Cameron as a political warrior than a challenge, especially from the source most sensitive to him— his clientele. At the same time informants close to Lincoln advised Cameron to remain firm and not to relax until the end.[60] Realizing that a public declination of a Cabinet post

---

[57] Lincoln to Cameron, Jan. 3, 1861, Basler, Lincoln's *Works,* IV, 169-70.

[58] Lincoln to Cameron, Jan. 3 (actually Jan. 13), 1861, Cameron MSS, LC.

[59] Swett to Lincoln, Jan. 8, 1861 ; Stevens to Washburne, Jan. 19, 1861, Lincoln MSS.

[60] Elias Wampole to Cameron, Jan. 10, 1861, Cameron MSS, DCC ; David Davis to Cameron, Feb. 8, 1861, Cameron MSS, LC.

would appear farcical, Cameron determined to remain silent and force Lincoln to make the next move.

Other factors came into play which assisted Lincoln in solving his dilemma. Proof of Cameron's unfitness had not been presented.[61] Powerful railroad and iron interests, accepting Cameron as the champion of tariff protection, moved to heal the faction schism and to rally to his support. James Milliken, a Philadelphia ironmaster, assisted in bringing about a capitulation of the Curtin faction. At Harrisburg, Milliken assured Curtin and McClure that Cameron's appointments would be filled by men, "honest, capable and faithful," and that the aid of "friends"—meaning the Curtin faction—would be solicited when appointments were made. Milliken found Curtin conciliatory with no ax to grind; but McClure remained "jealous." Upon Lincoln's arrival in Philadelphia on February 21, arrangements were concluded to have him meet a deputation the next day. On February 22, James Milliken assured Lincoln that Curtin desired Cameron's appointment to the Treasury post and read a letter from McClure to the same effect. Eli Slifer and Samuel Purviance endorsed Milliken's statements. Morton McMichael, on behalf of himself and Henry C. Carey, likewise supported Cameron's candidacy. Although Lincoln had failed to commit himself, Milliken considered the interview satisfactory.[62]

Thus only a fortnight before the date set for Lincoln's inauguration the public accepted Cameron's entrance into the presidential family as a certainty. "Probably in the history of Political contest," announced the *New York*

---

[61] On December 31, Lincoln possessed a copy of charges. See "Memorandum" in Basler, Lincoln's *Works*, IV, 165.

[62] Milliken to Cameron, Feb. 19, 22; Purviance to Cameron, Feb. 23, Cameron MSS, LC.

Times, "no fight more bitter than that waged by the friends and enemies of Mr. Cameron is recorded. . . . today it is a settled point that Pennsylvania is to be represented in the cabinet by Mr. Cameron."[63] After Lincoln's arrival in Washington, conferences between the two centered around the question of the office Cameron was to occupy. Both Salmon P. Chase and Cameron wished to head the Treasury Department, but Chase had the stronger claim. Cameron, upon Lincoln's request, agreed to accept the War post and was nominated for the position on March 5, but did not take the oath of office until March 11. In the face of seeming defeat, this amazing politico had again emerged triumphant. If, as a prominent Lincoln scholar noted, the new Cabinet was composed of gentlemen comprising a wide diversity of political views, from the leading populous states and selected under the consistent principle of opportunism,[64] Cameron was hardly the least unworthy of the lot.

Cameron's entrance into Lincoln's Cabinet created the second vacancy in the Senate of United States which the Pennsylvania legislature was called upon to fill within a period of three months. The first election in early January, 1861, would choose a successor to outgoing Senator William A. Bigler. The Democratic Party now constituting a minority in the General Assembly could not hope to elect a senator, and Bigler did not consider himself a candidate for re-election. Consequently there rose from the ranks of the People's Party a multiplicity of senatorial aspirants seeking the aid of either the Cameron or Curtin faction, but most of them turning to Cameron, whose strength was considered the more powerful. Alexander K. McClure, backed by the influential William B. Mann of Philadelphia, circulated news

---

[63] Crippen, *Simon Cameron,* 242.
[64] Randall, *Lincoln: Springfield to Gettysburg,* I, 270.

of his own candidacy, tried to make a deal with Cameron, who spurned his offer,[65] and promptly dropped from the lists when Curtin let it be known that he could not support him. Thaddeus Stevens, rather naïvely, it would seem, consulted candidate McClure on his own chances and learned that they were not "formidable."[66] J. K. Moorhead of Pittsburgh hoped for the support of John Covode, who in turn was feeling out Cameron. To all aspirants except one Cameron gave the same answer—he would not interfere; but McClure's candidacy he would fight.[67]

David Wilmot, one of the early founders of the Republican Party in Pennsylvania, a national figure and experienced legislator, sought senatorial reward for his party services. Immediately after the state elections of 1860, rumors circulated of his unavailability because of the need for maintaining a conciliatory attitude toward the South. Wilmot, hearing of these rumors, appealed to Cameron, whose "active cooperation," he was certain, could elect him. Acting on instructions from Cameron, B. Rush Petrikin concluded a bargain in which Cameron would support Wilmot for the senatorship and Wilmot would push Cameron for the Cabinet. On the important question of the patronage, Wilmot would not "go as far" as the latter desired.[68] Cameron, vexed over the patronage and believing Wilmot owed him support anyway in view of his repeated promises, refused to ratify the bargain and cunningly based his reply upon a point of honor. He could not make himself a party "in the elevation of a colleague," answered Cameron, but if Wilmot failed to go to the Senate, he would "cheerfully

[65] Cameron to B. Rush Petriken, Dec. 11, 1860, Cameron MSS, LC.
[66] McClure to Stevens, Nov. 7, 1860, McPherson MSS, LC.
[67] Cameron to B. Rush Petrikin, Dec. 11, 1860, Cameron MSS, LC.
[68] B. Rush Petrikin to Cameron, Dec. 10, 1860, *ibid.*

consent" to have him go into the Cabinet.[69] Cameron's seemingly honorable and sacrificial reply led Wilmot to believe that he would exercise a benevolent hands off policy with regard to the senatorial race.

Andrew G. Curtin, on the other hand, gave Wilmot all the support he could muster. "We can rely on him," wrote the governor to his Secretary of the Commonwealth, Eli Slifer, and "if he can be elected by any fair means he should be. . . . You will all regret it when too late."[70] Curtin had already informed McClure of his determination to back Wilmot and his next step was to find out whether, as rumor had it, that Wilmot and Cameron had concluded an alliance. Again on the eve of the party caucus election Curtin reminded Slifer that "Wilmot is our man and put him in if you can."[71] Curtin's failure to hold McClure in line boomeranged to Cameron's advantage.

Covertly Cameron pursued a policy which gave him Edgar Cowan, the man he desired for the senatorship while at the same time he maintained his pose as an innocent bystander. In early November, an adherent of Edgar Cowan set forth to Cameron the future advantages to be gained in backing western Pennsylvania's favorite son—the popular, striking dynamic leader of Westmoreland's bar. In return for Cameron's aid in 1861, wrote D. W. Shryock of Greensburg, the western counties would support Cameron when he sought re-election to the Senate in 1863.[72] Shortly afterward Joseph Casey discovered that Cowan, who allegedly possessed "great force of character," was now "looming up"

[69] Cameron to B. Rush Petrikin, Dec. 11, 1860, *ibid.*
[70] Curtin to Slifer, Dec. 31, 1860, Dill-Slifer MSS.
[71] Curtin to Slifer, Jan. (n.d.), *ibid.*
[72] D. W. Shryock to Cameron, Nov. 1, 1860, Cameron MSS, DCC.

in the senatorial contest.[73] By middle November, J. P. Sanderson was satisfied with his candidacy and advised his chief to come to a friendly understanding with him.[74] Arrangements were carried out to have leading gentlemen of the People's Party meet with Cowan in his suite in Philadelphia. Before mid-December Cowan paid Cameron a visit at which time an understanding was reached between the two.[75]

The Cameron-Sanderson-Cowan plan worked perfectly, without leaks. Cameron stood mute while Sanderson advanced Cowan as his own candidate. In early January the press regarded the senatorial race as a contest between Cowan and Wilmot with the former possessing the edge. When Cameron returned to Harrisburg on January 5, he was besieged by Wilmot's supporters but remained inflexible in his determination to remain "neutral." Cameron, Wilmot assured his followers, could not be against him because the two had reached a "full understanding" on that point. "It looks favorable to my success. Indeed I believe I can make the election," confided the deluded Wilmot to the Machiavellian who was masterminding his defeat.[76] A. H. Reeder was fearful that Cowan could not be elected without Cameron's active intervention. "Your friends," implored Reeder, "don't know how to act or what to do till they hear what they *know* comes from you."[77] Following a secret conference of select Cameron men prior to the caucus, eager newsmen were untruthfully informed that Wilmot was slated

---

[73] Casey to David Davis, Nov. (n.d.) 1860, Lincoln MSS, LC.

[74] Sanderson to Cameron, Nov. 15, 1860, Cameron MSS, DCC.

[75] Cowan to Cameron, Dec. 15, 1960, *ibid*.

[76] Wilmot to Cameron, Jan. 5, 1861, *ibid*.

[77] Reeder to Cameron, Jan. 2, 1861. This is a pitiable commentary on the awe with which Cameron was held by members of his faction. These legislators were not at all representatives of the people of their Commonwealth—only Cameronian puppets unwilling to dance in their own way when privileged to do so,

for the full term of six years while Cowan would conclude Cameron's term after he entered the Cabinet.[78]

The electoral process began on January 3 in the legislature, where an unusually ridiculous number of nominations, totaling 48, were moved.[79] The two leading Democratic nominees were Bigler and Foster, the Democracy's recently defeated candidate for governor. In the People's Party caucus Cowan defeated Wilmot, 58 votes to 38, on the sixth ballot. A group of Cameron men, believing that he secretly desired Wilmot's election, voted against Cowan;[50] while some McClure men, refusing to follow Curtin's admonition, supported Cowan. On the following day when the two houses of the legislature met in joint session Cowan was elected by a straight party vote of 98 to 35 over Foster the Democratic nominee.[81] "You have a man in the senate," Sanderson confided to Cameron, "who will be right and is anxious to work with you . . . he is highly pleased with your behavior and will cordially and fully cooperate with you."[82] Judging from Cameron's interpretation of "cooperation" during the Wilmot-Petrikin negotiations this meant complete control for him of the state's federal patronage.

Edgar Cowan, the newly elected junior senator "from the Keystone state," appeared as one whom the Gods would seek to destroy. His Herculean frame, towering almost six feet four inches, was matched with classical features. His photograph in the Simon Gratz Autograph Collection portrays a clean-shaven, dark-haired, lean-boned individual with Alexandrian nose and firm jaws. Exceptionally well-

[78] Philadelphia *Public Ledger*, Jan. 8, 1861. The following day the *Ledger*'s Harrisburg correspondent apologized for the error, but insisted that "something" had happened afterwards.
[79] *Journal of the Senate*, 1861, 43-44.
[80] Sanderson to Cameron, Jan. 8, 1861, Cameron MSS, LC.
[81] *Journal of the Senate*, 1861, 57-58.
[82] Sanderson to Cameron, Jan. 8, 1861, Cameron MSS, LC.

steeped in Shakespearian witticisms and classical lore, his intellect harmonized perfectly with his physical bearing. Like Cameron he sprang from humble surroundings. His mother's earnings as a toll-gate attendant near West Newton enabled her to aid the boy, who lived with his grandfather. Upon graduation from Franklin College in 1839 at the head of his class, Cowan read law with Henry D. Foster in Greensburg. Three years later he was admitted to the Westmoreland County bar where he finally gained top recognition. It was said that he was connected with half of all the cases found on the Westmoreland docket from 1850 to 1860.

Cowan first entered politics as a Whig but switched to the new Republican Party in time to stump enthusiastically for Frémont in 1856. In 1860 he campaigned actively for the People's Party following an itinerary planned by McClure. His small group of followers had requested such a course in order to bring him into the limelight as a possible successor to Senator Bigler. At the very beginning of his tour he so offended the conservative and American elements that McClure transferred him into Wilmot's territory where his radicalism fell upon more willing ears.[83] If, as was alleged, Cowan was elected in Wilmot's place because of the latter's radicalism, the process seemed somewhat a case of substituting the kettle for the pot. Actually radicalism had no bearing on the outcome of the election which represented merely a personal triumph for Simon Cameron. But once installed safely for a long six-year term, Cowan went his own way, gradually becoming more tolerant in his attitude toward the South. Hindsight revealed Cowan's election to the United States Senate to be a major blow to radical Republicanism.[84]

---

[83] McClure, *Old Time Notes*, I, 443-44.
[84] On Edgar Cowan see *Dictionary of American Biography*, IV, 470-71 ; George D. Albert, *History of Westmoreland* ; John N. Boucher, *History of Westmoreland County*.

Wilmot had already swallowed a double dose of humble pie and was in no mood to digest another when the senatorial dish was again dangled before his avid eyes following Cameron's entrance into Lincoln's Cabinet. In a moment of anger following his defeat in January he had vowed not to accept the short term. With Cameron now a member of the presidential family and a recent senatorial victory behind him, there appeared to be no further reason to exclude Wilmot even on the basis of his radicalism. Rumor had it that Lincoln was hoping to see the free-soiler succeed Cameron. Wilmot was now assured of victory or he would never have allowed his name to be presented as a candidate. In the caucus of the People's Party he garnered 76 votes to 21 for all others. The Democratic caucus nomination meant little in this case and Witte who probably could have captured it withdrew. Thereupon William H. Welsh, chairman of the Democratic State Central Committee, accepted the honor. On March 14, 1861, Wilmot was elected easily over his opponent 95 to 34.[85]

The day that Lincoln received the delegation on Cameron's behalf in Philadelphia, and made a side trip to Harrisburg, was also his last before reaching Washington. His friends had seen or heard little within the last two weeks to encourage them. His enemies, scoffing at his laborious journey from Springfield, characterized it as a trail of buffoonery, handshaking, girl-kissing, whisker-raising, Highland-dancing, and cowardice. At Pittsburgh he had mentioned the tariff and at Harrisburg he had responded to Curtin's protestations of the Commonwealth's loyalty, but he exerted his greatest effort in Independence Hall at Philadelphia. Temporarily exhibiting the emotional stress under which he labored, the incoming President expressed his hope

[85] Philadelphia *Public Ledger,* Jan. 10, March 13, 14, 15, 1861.

that the principles established by the fathers of the Constitution might be instrumental in saving the nation. Nor was he asking for the shedding of blood; he envisioned the use of constraint only if force were first employed against the authority of the Federal government.[86] A fortnight later, the incoming Chief Executive threw aside the cautious reserve of four months and promised, upon the basis of his newly taken oath, enforcement of Federal authority within the boundaries of the nation. At the same time he maintained a conciliatory tone throughout his address and promised no interference with the South's peculiar institution, slavery.

The response of Pennsylvania's press to the President's message generally varied according to the political complexion of the organ. Condemnation from the state's three leading Democratic journals, the Philadelphia *Pennsylvanian,* the Harrisburg *Patriot,* and the Pittsburgh *Post* was to be expected. The *Pennsylvanian,* in comparing the two new sectional administrations, South and North, looked upon the first as asking only for peace while the latter was threatening coercion; the first the persecuted, the second the persecutor. It called upon Lincoln to evacuate Fort Sumter, and warned that any endeavor to strengthen its garrison would "sound the tocsin of a bloody civil war and the knell of the Union."[87] The Pittsburgh *Post* characterized Lincoln's message a "sad disappointment" containing nothing to lessen the public's apprehension, or to inspire confidence in the President.[88] The Philadelphia *Ledger,* well on its way to becoming a Republican organ, signified mild approval and

---

[86] Basler, Lincoln's *Works,* IV, 240-41.

[87] Robinson, "Public Press," 74. On April 2, 1861, this voice of the Democracy suspended publication and the party possessed no strong organ in the Philadelphia area until the spring of 1863 when the Philadelphia *Age* was launched.

[88] Pittsburgh *Post,* March 6, 1861, quoted in Davis, *Politics,* 171.

commented on the moderation exhibited in the inaugural. The Pittsburgh *Gazette* now with its mouthpiece Simon Cameron assisting in the execution of national policies, could do no less than to signify its hearty approbation.

During the first days of April events pointed to a final showdown on the question of Fort Sumter. Lincoln, anxious that some of the strong "loyal" states take cognizance of the existence of a civil strife, thereby strengthening his probable future action, requested Curtin to make an immediate public declaration.[89] The governor, on the advice of his friends, postponed his promised special message to the legislature and on the morning of April 9, the vexed President telegraphed: "I see you did nothing yesterday. I think if your action is to have any value you ought to come out without delay."[90] Curtin immediately addressed the General Assembly, calling its attention to the "existing deplorable and dangerous crisis of affairs." He pointed out the many deficiencies and inefficiencies existing in the state militia system and suggested remedies. He requested procurement of arms, the discarding of obsolete weapons, the establishment of a military bureau, and modification of the militia laws of the state so as to inject "vitality and energy" into its military organization.[91]

Earlier attempts in the year to reorganize the militia had fallen upon deaf ears in the legislature because of the negative effect it might have upon the critical border state of Maryland. This time action was prompt. A bill providing

---

[89] On April 6, Lincoln ordered that Governor Pickens of South Carolina be notified of the coming of the relief expedition. Lincoln had just crossed the Rubicon and hostile action seemed inevitable.

[90] Curtin to Rufus Wilson, Washington *Post,* Jan. 6, 1889.

[91] *Papers of the Governors,* 1858-1871, 363-66. At this time there were 500 militia companies comprising 20,000 men, unequipped, untrained except in rudimentary drill, and possessing only 42,000 effective small arms.

for reorganization of the state militia, accompanied with an appropriation of a half million dollars was passed over Democratic minority opposition. A properly staffed military department was to work under the direction of the governor.[92] Before passage of the bill had been completed, Curtin received official news of the attack on Fort Sumter. Curtin and McClure rushed to Washington, conferred with Lincoln on April 15, and in anticipation of the President's proclamation Curtin wired to his Secretary of the Commonwealth: "Accept all military organizations offered. Our services will be required immediately."[93]

The surrender of Fort Sumter on April 14 to the Confederates was followed the next day by one of the most momentous proclamations in the nation's history. Acting under an archaic act of 1795, Lincoln asked for the assembling of a gigantic national *posse comitatus* of 75,000 men to suppress powerful unlawful combinations within certain designated states. Part of the proclamation's immediate aftermath in the upper South was to let loose a new chain of secession led by Virginia and to result in further consolidation of the Confederacy. At the onset there was no lack of enthusiasm for the cause in the North. ". . . the air throbbed with mass meetings, rallies, cheers, resolutions, governors' proclamations, special legislative sessions, and parades with Revolutionary fife and drum. Rifle clubs and home guards were formed, arsenals seized, money subscribed, 'traitors' arrested, cannon mounted, flags raised, pro-Confederate establishments attacked, companies formed, and the Almighty importuned to wipe the enemy from the face of the earth."[94]

---

[92] Davis, *Pennsylvania Politics*, 173.
[93] Egle, ed., *Life of Curtin*, 212-213; Curtin and McClure to Lincoln, April 15 [1861], Nicolay MSS.
[94] Randall, *Lincoln: Springfield to Gettysburg*, I, 354,

Pennsylvania's response to the President's call was easily sufficient to have filled half the nation's quota. Leading the vanguard on April 16 came the Reading Ringgold Light Artillery followed by the Logan Guards of Lewistown and the Washington Artillery of Schuylkill County.[95] These first volunteers were quartered in the sheds of the agricultural fairground on the outskirts of Harrisburg. In a few days the rendezvous grew into Camp Curtin, best known of the state camps. William Bender Wilson, lately returned from his spying activities in the South, attached a relay magnet and key to a window sill in Curtin's office, thereby opening the first military telegraph office in America. For days the governor remained at his office until after midnight and returned at break of day.[96] On April 18, Pennsylvania's first contingent of 540 men reached Washington and received the official thanks of the House of Representatives. In Philadelphia where, only the day preceding Lincoln's call, Southern sympathizers were reported to be organizing into the Knights of the Golden Circle,[97] the response was enthusiastic. "Force alone," advised Morton McMichael's former conciliatory organ, the *North American*, "can now settle this great trouble . . . ."[98]

The energetic governor took steps to recall the newly departed legislature, summoned a competent staff of aides to Harrisburg, and initiated measures to provide for the transportation and welfare of thousands of men assembling from all parts of the state. In addition, thousands more pouring in from outside the state required care. Pennsylvania's original

---

[95] The Ringgold Artillery was the first military unit in the nation to reach Washington. See affidavits and endorsement by the Secretary of War, Cameron MSS, LC.
[96] William Bender Wilson in Egle, *Curtin*, 344-47.
[97] H. B. Robinson to Wright, April 14, 1861, Wright MSS, WHGS.
[98] Robinson, "Public Press" 85-86.

quota of April 15 was set at 16 regiments totaling 12,500 men, but on the following day the President reduced the number to 14 regiments.[99] Almost immediate filling of the state's quota necessitated numerous telegrams to various organizers of companies throughout the Commonwealth and spread much confusion and anger among the rejected volunteers.

In the meantime General Robert Patterson, area commandant, became panicky at rumors of a Confederate approach upon the capital and, on April 26, requested Curtin for an immediate additional requisition of 25 regiments of infantry and one of cavalry.[100] Without waiting for confirmation from the War Department Curtin hastily issued a proclamation calling for 25,000 troops to serve for either three years or the duration of the war. Again the response was enthusiastic and soon thousands were on their way to Harrisburg. But Patterson now flatly refused to accept the troops and the governor found himself in an embarrassing situation, the escape from which was likely to require unusual ingenuity. It seems quite likely that the inept Patterson, now in the Federal service, realized that he had no authority to issue an additional call for troops and decided to allow Curtin to assume the responsibility for his act.

On April 30, the same day Patterson wired Curtin of his rejection,[101] the governor protested Patterson's action to the Secretary of War and reminded him of the preparation made, of the assembling of many companies, and of the expense already involved.[102] Doubtless Cameron enjoyed Curtin's

---

[99] Cameron to Curtin, April 15, 16, 1861, Egle, *Curtin*, 219.
[100] Patterson to Curtin, April 26, 1861, *ibid.*, 256-57. McClure stated that Patterson made his request in person but Patterson's Philadelphia letter is printed verbatim in the source cited.
[101] Patterson to Curtin, April 30, 1861, *ibid.*, 262.
[102] Curtin to Cameron, April 30, 1861, *ibid.*, 222-23.

discomfiture immensely and was minded to allow the governor to fry in his own fat. Cameron had followed Lincoln's orders, and critics of the Secretary, while censuring him for rejecting Curtin's levy, have neglected to point out that acceptance of the additional 20,000 men would have compelled the Secretary to take an equal ratio from the other states and the Federal government could then have expected a mob of 225,000 militiamen, who about the time they could be properly equipped would be at liberty to walk home. As it was, Pennsylvania's original quota of 16 regiments was restored.

Fortunately for the overzealous governor, the Pennsylvania General Assembly rescued him from his dilemma. Curtin's reason for calling a special session of the legislature, as stated in his proclamation of April 20, was to seek legislation which would enable the governor to make the military powers of the state more available and efficient;[103] but when it convened the governor was impelled to ask for a great deal more. In his message of April 30, Curtin pointed out the unparalleled exigencies of the situation, stated that he had anticipated the need for more troops than Lincoln had requested and had accordingly accepted up to 23 regiments. Curtin cited Patterson's request as proof of his own foresight. Protection of the Commonwealth's southern border was offered as the chief reason for establishment of a force "exclusive of those called into the service of United States." On May 2, Curtin communicated to the legislature news of Federal rejection of his extra quota troops and laid the matter before the body with his recommendation for a state corps of 15 regiments.[104]

In this manner was born the famous Pennsylvania Reserve

---

[103] *Papers of the Governors,* 1858-1871, 370-71.
[104] *Ibid.,* 371-79.

Corps of some 16,000 men which completed its organization in May with George A. McCall in command. Two days prior to the Federal fiasco at Bull Run, the War Department announced its acceptance of the Reserves[105] and the major portion was rushed to Washington. Ardent partisans of the governor pointed out how his prudence and foresight probably prevented the Confederates from capturing the capital after the disintegration of General McDowell's army at Bull Run. Fortuitous circumstances had rescued the governor and in the end the national government completely reimbursed the state for the expense incurred by the Reserve Corps.

Concurrently Curtin was engaging in a verbal duel with the Secretary of War over state quotas and methods of enlistments. In answer to Curtin's inquiries Cameron replied that Pennsylvania's quota of militiamen could not be increased, but under the new Federal system of accepting three-year volunteers several additional regiments could be accepted. If supplies were not available from Federal depots the governor was authorized to supply the troops and present the bill.[106] On May 6, the governor sent a sharply worded dispatch to Cameron saying it would be well for him (Curtin) to understand how authority was divided so it would be possible to "move with certainty" and not risk having the people's ardor cooled.[107] The War Department, replied Cameron, recognized no divided authority, its jurisdiction being dominant over General Patterson who had acted

---

[105] L[orenzo] Thomas to Curtin, July 19, 1861, Egle, *Curtin,* 270. McClure in his *Notes,* I, 477, gives the reader the impression that the Pennsylvanian Reserves were not accepted until after Bull Run. Cameron, said McClure, did not envision the number of men that would be required. According to Cameron he wished to raise 500,000 but Lincoln and Seward did not agree with him. See *New York Times,* June 3, 1878.
[106] *Papers of the Governors,* 1858-1871, 382-83.
[107] Curtin to Cameron, May 6, 1861, Egle, *Curtin,* 266.

without authority or consent. Curtin next complained of Cameron's irregular procedures in sometimes arming private individuals in the state with authority to raise regiments. The governor determined to have several Cameron-authorized regiments, still in the embryo stage, consolidated under his own direction. With the assistance of William Meredith, his new efficient attorney general, and A. K. McClure, Curtin forced, as an alternative to a direct appeal to Lincoln, acquiescence upon Cameron in the matter.[108]

In Washington the besieged Secretary of War, equipped only with mediocre talents in the field of administration, was attempting to carry out duties which no mortal at that time could have performed properly during the early chaotic days of the Lincoln Administration. Frederick Seward discovered the harassed Secretary surrounded by a group of suppliants extolling the merits of their wares.[109] Albert Riddle found him without any of the ordinary equipment peculiar to offices, not even a secretary. The flustered Secretary of War would "find a piece of scrap paper, borrow your pencil, make a note, put the paper in one pocket of his trousers and your pencil in the other."[110] Others found office seekers using much of his valuable time. Certainly, Cameron, one of the master spoilsmen of his age, would not pass by the golden opportunity to create a clientele which would dwarf all previous efforts within his state. And already powerful men around the nation were giving him unsolicited advice on the conduct of his department and urging immediate vigorous prosecution of the war.[111] If Cameron had to be absent from his

---

[108] McClure, *Notes,* I, 387-90.
[109] Frederick Seward, *Reminiscences,* 163.
[110] Albert G. Riddle, *Recollections of War Times* (New York, 1895), 180.
[111] *Official Records,* Series III, I, 160.

office for a few days he was likely to ask Salmon P. Chase to assume responsibility. The coming of Thomas Scott into the War Office contributed much to clearing up its chaotic condition.

Cameron suffered much criticism for his manipulation of the patronage and the favoritism shown to Pennsylvanians. Complained the *New York Times*: "It is his dangerous partiality which has converted one-half the population of Pennsylvania into contractors."[112] Cameron men connected with the Harrisburg *Telegraph,* the Pittsburgh *Gazette,* the Philadelphia *Press,* and the Philadelphia Evening *Bulletin* received rewards. Five of the new paymasters, Brua Cameron, David Taggart, Russell Errett, Francis Jordan, and Andrew Sallade were closely associated with Cameron. J. P. Sanderson chose to remain at his side as chief clerk in the War Department. C. A. Walborn, Cameron's postmaster in Philadelphia, was able to take care of many lesser favorites. And it seemed as if Cameron had even succeeded in purloining some of Seward's prerogatives when he prevailed upon Lincoln to assign foreign missions to Jacob S. Haldeman and E. Joy Morris. Out of an early list of 127 military commissions, Pennsylvania received 20; Ohio was next with 12. The Keystone State received 18 of the 120 assistant quartermasterships, while New York received 16.[113] Cameron also had to take care of the President's favorites. The first notification Cameron received from Lincoln as Secretary of War was a request for an appointment for his good friend Elmer Ephraim Ellsworth.[114]

---

[112] West, *Gideon Welles,* 124.

[113] Cameron's Records of the War Department, Cameron MSS, LC; Robinson, "Public Press," 104-05, 153-54.

[114] Lincoln to Cameron, March 5, 1861, Cameron MSS, LC. This was a dashing leader of the Zouaves who got himself killed by tearing down a Confederate flag in Alexandria.

Curtin's administration suffered a new embarrassment following the resignation of his attorney general, Samuel A. Purviance. As already noted, the appointment of this prominent Cameron supporter was not intended to be permanent. Purviance believed that Curtin was willing to allow him to retain office but was afraid the governor would succumb to the evil influences (McClure) surrounding him.[115] Convinced that he was slated for removal at the end of the year, Purviance determined to bring discredit upon the Curtin administration in the form of an abrupt resignation purposely worded in such a way as to deceive the public and conceal his true motives. In late May, without warning, Purviance submitted his resignation for reasons "which appealed" to his "self-respect." Purviance could hardly have selected a more propitious moment to accomplish his purpose. On the same day the resignation appeared in the Philadelphia *Inquirer*, that journal devoted its editorial to a discussion of the merits of the Curtin administration which, stated the organ, "has for days been condemned for the very inferior equipment which was being provided the Pennsylvania soldiers in shoes, clothing, [and] blankets . . . ." It mentioned the resignation from the Curtin cabinet of Purviance a "citizen of unimpeachable integrity."[116] The implication was clear to any intelligent reader; Purviance the purist had resigned in protest to the governor's reign of shoddy and corruption. This patter was repeated in many leading journals of the state.

Severe indictments from the Democratic press was to be expected, but when bona fide Republican journals like the Pittsburgh *Gazette* chose to assail the governor, the charges, in the eyes of the public, took on more serious aspects.

---

[115] Purviance to Cameron, Feb. 7, 1861, Cameron MSS, DCC.
[116] Philadelphia *Inquirer*, May 25, 1861.

Senator Darwin Finney, under the circumstances, declined to succeed Purviance, and keeping in mind the imperative need for bolstering the fast-slipping Curtin administration, recommended William M. Meredith, a respected former United States Cabinet officer, for the post.

The Curtin administration succeeded in emerging from its first political recession with a measure of public confidence restored, but the resignation of Purviance coupled with charges of fraud in high places left scars that could not be erased. Meredith, whose health was poor, certainly did not relish the idea of pulling Curtin's chestnuts out of the fire; but as a public-spirited citizen, interested in maintaining the pre-eminent position of his native state in the war effort, he could hardly refuse. The Commonwealth had floated a $3 million loan and its full subscription was in doubt. Meredith accepted the post reluctantly and in conjunction with the governor took energetic measures directed toward securing a prompt return of public confidence in the state administration.[117] Curtin ordered an inquiry into the arms supply contracts and certain suspended bills.[118] The governor's commission found lack of competence exhibited by purchasing agents, absence of proper supervision, sharp business practices, some petty criminality, and faulty purchasing methods, but exonerated the governor of any participation in fraud. The report's criticism of Curtin referred to agents appointed by him for personal or partisan reasons.[119] With the aid of some prominent Philadelphia bankers, the Commonwealth's $3 million loan was fully subscribed at

---

[117] McClure, *Old Time Notes*, I, 513-20. McClure, who left a detailed account of the affair, emphasized the role which he played in solving the exigency; but did not seem to realize that he bore a large measure of blame for creating the crisis.

[118] Philadelphia *Inquirer*, May 31, 1861.

[119] Davis, *Pennsylvania Politics*, 188.

par.[120] Although Pennsylvania's debt increased to $43 million, the credit of the state remained unimpaired.

During the spring of 1861, the General Assembly of Pennsylvania was concerned mostly with the national problem of secession and the impending civil war; but there remained an old domestic problem, the tonnage tax on the Pennsylvania Central Railroad, which required solution. During the latter days of the Pollock administration, the legislature agreed to the sale of the main line of the Commonwealth's public works, consisting of canal and connecting rail lines between Philadelphia and Pittsburgh, to the Pennsylvania Central Railroad. The purchaser was asked to pay a bonus of $1,500,000; in exchange the legislature lifted the tonnage tax and specifically exempted all real and tangible assets of the railroad from taxation. In 1858 the supreme court of the state declared the tax exemption unconstitutional thereby restoring the tonnage tax which had been repealed in the same clause. When the state auditor general presented claims for collection of the back tax the company delayed payment through complicated litigation and sought relief, on the basis of breach of good faith, from the legislature.

In its earlier stages the controversy could not have been considered partisan although the Democratic governor, Packer, expressed no sympathy for the railroad company. The contest appeared as one between the common taxpayer and the business interests of the state. The leaders of the powerful People's Party in alliance with the railroad interests were pledged to repeal of the tax but, fearing defeat at the polls, proposed to postpone action until after the fall election of 1860. Thomas Scott, new vice-president of the Pennsylvania Railroad, fearful of further delay, pushed for immedi-

---

[120] Altoona *Tribune,* June 20, 1861.

ate repeal of the tonnage tax in April, 1860, but two prominent Curtin men, McClure and Finney, blocked it. Scott,
when privately advised that no action was contemplated for
immediate collection of the huge bill of over $700,000 then
due the state, reoriented his repeal campaign upon the next
session of the legislature. Realizing Cameron's personal influence over the state legislators, Scott implored the senator to
write a general letter urging repeal which he intended to cir-
culate among the members.[121] Doubtless, Cameron required
little urging in view of his huge financial stake in the Northern Central Railroad. Rather inappropriately, it seemed, the
ablest leadership against repeal of the tax was contributed
by a prominent Republican leader from Allegheny County,
John R. Penney, who was sensitive to the wishes of his
constituents.

The fight ended in a victory for the railroad interests. By
the use of very questionable methods, Scott secured passage
of the repeal bill and Curtin signed it on April 28, 1861. This
"frightful monument of blunders," McClure's appellation
for the tonnage tax, was finally erased.[122] The nature of the
repeal act is a commentary on the cunning and foresight of
its proponents. The statute, taking on the form of a contract
between the railroad company and the Commonwealth,
provided for annual payments of $460,000 to the latter over
a period of thirty years. The United States Supreme Court
had long proclaimed the sacred nature of contracts and there
was little likelihood that any future hostile legislature
could undo the work of Thomas E. Scott, entrepreneur-
extraordinary.

---

[121] Scott to Cameron, Jan. 30, 1861, Cameron MSS, DCC.
[122] *Legislative Record of Pennsylvania*, 1861, 667. McClure used
the tonnage tax as the subject for a whole chapter of his *Notes*, I,
478-89; and approximately one hundred pages of the *Legislative
Record* for 1861 is devoted to the same subject.

By early summer of 1861, the People's Party under the leadership of Andrew G. Curtin had left no doubt of its major policies. Starting with a conciliatory attitude toward the South following Lincoln's election, this was maintained until a late date, by Simon Cameron in the Senate. Curtin's first address as governor had in great measure anticipated Lincoln's inaugural, but appeared stronger in tone. The Republican controlled General Assembly had followed its chief executive with a resolution requesting the Federal government to maintain its authority and had pledged Pennsylvania's might to support such measures. Thus two months preceding the attack on Fort Sumter and Lincoln's call for the militia, the Commonwealth's executive and legislative branches were ready to accept remedial action for the crisis in the form of coercion. The goal was simple and unadorned; and at that time contemplated only sustenance of the Union. Advocacy of the protective tariff and the support given to repeal of the tonnage tax was indicative of the future influence big business was to exercise with the People's Party.

The Democracy, maintaining a conciliatory attitude until the last, had placed a large share of the blame for the unfortunate chain of events upon the triumph of the sectional Republican Party which refused to "recognize the rights" of all the states. During the secession crisis, Democracy's proponents had offered an abundance of confused logic and the party faithful knew not where they were going. But the Confederate capture of Fort Sumter did much to clarify the issues. Now thousands of patriotic Democrats could see no partisan motives in the use of armed might to preserve the glorious Union. The fratricidal conflict must now be accepted by the party as a *fait accompli*. Its leaders now representing a minority group sought to regain their lost position through the negative process of criticism of the majority party. This attack, beginning with a censure of the Republican conduct of the war, was soon to assume many ramifications. In 1861 the State Democracy possessed neither the power nor the ability to prescribe positive policies for the nation.

IV

Curtin Rides the Tide

CURTIN'S ENTRANCE INTO the gubernatorial chair in January, 1861, marked the beginning of a three-year term of office. Not until October, 1863, would the electorate of the state be called upon to judge the stewardship of their chief executive. But during the interim the voters would have the opportunity in municipal, county, district, state, and congressional elections to signify their approval of the policies followed by the People's Party. In the fall of 1861 all the 100 seats of the state House and one-third of the 33 in the Senate would be filled. Many recent converts from the ranks of the Democrats, Whigs, or Americans, could not be counted upon to remain faithful to the new Republican party. On the other hand, the Democracy's great leader, James Buchanan, had retired to his country estate near Lancaster and was engaged in the task of preparing an apology for his much maligned administration. Democratic district leaders were left to carry on the struggle according to their own devices.

Issues appeared fewer after Bull Run. The public realized that the civil conflict was certain to be prolonged beyond their original expectation but expected General George B. McClellan, using the Pennsylvania reserves as a nucleus, to crush the Confederates before the end of the year. The governor's administration had undoubtedly suffered from the effects of the Purviance episode and from revelations of graft and corruption in connection with war contracts. The

141

leaders of the People's Party, in view of a spirit of dissatisfaction and uneasiness pervading the Commonwealth, were
much concerned over the probable loss of the lower house
of the General Assembly. Neither could it be concealed that
the People's Party had taken the lead in bringing about
repeal of the tonnage tax. Current rumors of prostitution of
public interest in the legislative halls of the state in exchange
for bribes from the railroad interests were widely believed
and consequently the ire of thousands of taxpayers was
aroused.

A. K. McClure, acting Chairman of the People's State
Central Committee chose "harmony" for his party's theme
in 1861. In a spirit of conciliation he asked Simon Cameron
to attend the June meeting of the Central Committee and
congratulated the Secretary of War on a recent address.[1]
McClure proposed to neutralize the strength of the Democracy in doubtful districts by running Democrats who
approved of a vigorous prosecution of the war on a Union
ticket.[2] This strategy of bipartisanship in the name of patriotism and preservation of the Union succeeded in several
legislative districts. Members of the Democratic party were
now separated into two factions, War Democrats and Peace
Democrats—both asking for preservation of the Union. The
former group, because it agreed with the People's Party that
only successful conclusion of the war could reunite the
Union, often became confused with Republicans under the
title of "Unionist" and consequently many prominent War
Democrats finally found their way into the Republican camp.
On the other hand the Peace Democrats, who believed that a
negotiated peace with the Confederacy could bring about
reunification, were soon dubbed by their enemies with the

---

[1] McClure to Cameron, June 1, 1861, Cameron MSS, LC.
[2] McClure, *Old Time Notes,* I, 502-03.

ANDREW GREGG CURTIN: Governor of Pennsylvania, 1861-1867; Minister to Russia, 1869-1872; Congressman, 1881-1887. *Courtesy of Pennsylvania Historical and Museum Commission.*

opprobrious title of Copperheads. Attempts at harmony brought a confusing array of local tickets—People's Republican, Democratic, Union, No Party, Democratic-Union, Republican-Union, and even Constitutional-Union. Contention among Republican and Democratic candidates for places on the "Union" tickets killed the movement in several districts.

To analyze the legislative election returns held on October 8, 1861, is simple. The average tax-paying voter, full of righteous indignation at the favoritism shown the Pennsylvania Railroad corporation by the "corrupt" legislature, had taken his vengeance in the most effective manner possible—simply by defeating for re-election those who had voted for the obnoxious measure. With the exception of the city of Philadelphia which favored repeal, only one House member who had voted for lifting the tax was returned and that particular member had represented the wishes of his constituents. The only two state senators returned, Republican John Penney and Democrat Hiester Clymer, were the two who had led the fight in the state senate against repeal. The Republicans had greatly outnumbered the Democrats in voting for repeal and had suffered accordingly. For the House the voters had selected 32 Republicans including People's Party candidates, 51 Democrats, 13 Union Republicans, and 4 Union Democrats.[3] The new Senate, including old members, would seat 22 Republicans, 10 Democrats and 1 Union Republican. Out of the 11 new members elected to the Senate only 2 were bona fide Republicans; and it seems quite evident that had every senatorial seat been at stake in

[3] *Tribune Almanac,* 1862. Davis, *Pennsylvania Politics,* 207, listed only 42 Democrats elected to House. He also listed 13 Union-Democrats and 22 Union-Republicans. Contested seats explain the discrepancy.

1861, the Democrats would have captured that body. Although the future augured well for the Democratic party the legislative elections had proved little except that legislators had best beware of an aroused electorate.

Charges arising from the 1861 elections brought to a head the question of the soldiers' vote. An act of 1839 gave the franchise to militiamen or volunteers called into active service either under state or national authority. In 1861, military elections, according to the provisions of the act, were held and supervised by commanding officers. Under these conditions it is not surprising that charges of fraudulent voting were soon made. Among the devices apparently used were coercion of the soldiers by officers and the manufacture of fictitious votes from nonexistent military units. Charges of fraud in military voting arising from the 1861 fall elections led to the contesting of five seats in the House of Representatives. In all cases, the legislators, fearful of their political future, admitted the validity of the soldiers' vote.[4] The following spring a Democratic state supreme court ruled the soldier voting statute of 1839 unconstitutional.[5] The majority opinion was written by puisne justice George W. Woodward, the next gubernatorial candidate of the Democratic party. The Republican press, ignoring the provision of the state constitution which clearly required a voter to live in the same district in which he cast his vote, assailed the court for depriving the nation's defenders of their franchise.

The confusion arising from the fall elections of 1861 was reflected in the organization of the General Assembly of January, 1862. Union-Republicans and regular Republicans, aware of their precarious position in the House, determined

---

[4] For a fuller discussion of this subject see Davis, *Pennsylvania Politics*, 209-11.
[5] Philadelphia *Evening Bulletin*, May 22, 1862.

to use the same tactics that they had used with moderate success in the fall elections. For speaker they supported former Surveyor General John Rowe, a Democratic-Unionist. This strategy detracted from the strength of the line Democrats who nominated William Hopkins for the office. The coalition of the Republicans with the Union Democrats, who possessed the balance of power was easily sufficient to elect Rowe over Hopkins, 53 to 45.[6] Rowe's election had the added effect of producing dissension within the Democratic ranks. Orthodox Democrats looked askance upon their political brethren, who, in preference to their bona fide caucus candidate, had supported the candidate of the Black Republicans.[7] In the Senate the Republicans experienced no difficulty in electing Louis Hall speaker. Republicans made a bid for opposition support by approving Democratic appointments to important committees. The re-election of Simon Cameron's man, Henry D. Moore, to the state treasureship over William V. McGrath[8] one week following the Secretary of War's departure from Lincoln's Cabinet, spoke well for the strength of the Cameron machine at a time when Cameron had sunk to the nadir of his public prestige.

Immediately upon completing its organization the legislature received the governor's annual message. Curtin reviewed favorably the Commonwealth's participation in the war effort and the legislation connected with it. He pointed with pride to the Pennsylvania Reserve Corps which had rushed to fill the gap created by the Bull Run defeat. The governor, in commenting on the Commonwealth's strategic and economic position, promoted Pennsylvania to the

---

[6] Altoona *Tribune,* Jan. 9, 1862.
[7] G. P. Steele to Wright, Jan. 9, 1862, Wright MSS, WHGS.
[8] *Journal of the House,* 1862, 78.

position of a sovereign state which could not "afford to have a foreign power" bounding her on any side. He noted his triumph over the War Department (Cameron) in terminating the practice of permitting individual raising of volunteers. He was proud to report Pennsylvania's total enlistments to date at approximately 110,000 men. Of domestic interest were the results of investigations arising out of charges of fraudulent contracts, the state treasury balance of one and one-half million dollars, and the complaints of banks penalized for suspending specie payments during the national crisis.[9] The governor had made no mention of war aims aside from the restoration of the Union. Although Radicals were displeased, the message calmed the fears of the Democratic press which was already expressing concern over rumors that the Negro problem would determine new national policies.

The early months of the 1862 legislative session were devoted mainly to the problem of judging contested seats, to the investigation of alleged fraud in connection with repeal of the tonnage tax, and to an attempt at the restoration of the tonnage tax. The political aspirations of the Democratic chieftain from Bedford County, John Cessna, led to a union of two of these problems into one unit. Cessna had won the unique honor of election to the speakership of the state House of Representatives while still in his thirtieth year. In 1860 he had attended the Charleston Convention and managed Witte's unsuccessful gubernatorial candidacy.[10] Cessna, a leading hopeful for the coming Democratic nomination for 1863, could not afford a legislative defeat in 1861. Although bested by his Republican

---

[9] *Papers of the Governors,* 1858-1871, 413-35.
[10] McNair and Robson, *Biographical Encyclopedia of Pennsylvania,* 518 ; Bedford *Gazette,* Mar. 9, 1860.

opponent, George W. Householder, in the combined legislative district of Bedford and Somerset which returned two
members, Cessna contested his right to a seat on a technical-
ity based upon a constitutional guarantee of 1790 which
gave one seat to Bedford, the county which he had carried.
Cessna, the War Democrat, had received strong Republican
support in his home county, and comprehending the
disastrous effect on the Republican Party of the Hopkins
investigation then in progress, approached A. K. McClure
on the subject of a bargain profitable to both parties.
McClure agreed to assist Cessna; in return Cessna obligated
himself to see that the pending investigation of alleged frauds
connected with the Tonnage Repeal Act were terminated
before the Union-Republicans had suffered irreparable harm.
Cessna won his seat through a friendly committee predom-
inantly Democratic and therefore the covert Republican aid
was not required; but Cessna for reasons agreeable to both
his sense of honor and personal profit, proceeded to carry out
his part of the bargain.[11]

Simultaneously with efforts to restore the tonnage tax,
the Democratic state representative from Washington
County, William Hopkins, introduced his resolution for
creation of an investigating committee to inquire into "all
the facts" connected with the passage of the Commutation
of Tonnage Act of 1861. Hopkins found many citizens who
believed that improper influence had been used in bringing
about repeal of the Pennsylvania Railroad tax.[12] Hopkins
was undoubtedly sincere in his efforts to bring the guilty to

[11] McClure, *Old Time Notes*, I, 526-28. The Committee was
selected by lot. If McClure continued to act as Householder's counsel
in this case, he must have been guilty of a grave violation of legal
ethics. See Davis, *Pennsylvania Politics*, 216. Bedford County was
separated in April, 1862. See *Journal of the House* 1862, 621.
[12] *Journal of the House,* 1862, 67.

justice, but at the same time he was well aware of the immense personal capital he was likely to derive from a successful exposé of corrupt Republicanism in league with equally corrupt Pennsylvania Railroad business interests.

Hopkins' opponents used two successful devices to fight his investigation: Speaker Rowe was persuaded to appoint "conservative" men approved by railroad magnate Thomas Scott to "assist" Hopkins; and through Cessna's influence the committee was forced to submit its final report and accept liquidation before legislative adjournment. The powerful railroad interests had been forced to pay well for its favorable legislation and undoubtedly J. Edgar Thomson, its president, and Thomas Scott, both of whom conveniently escaped the ambarrassment of testifying before the investigating committee, would have derived much satisfaction in seeing their legislative blackmailers punished, but such a procedure would have led to their own exposure. Cessna was consummating more than an agreement when he put an end to Hopkins' inquiry; he was at the same time spiking a potential boom for the committee chairman which conceivably could have carried Hopkins into the governor's mansion.[13] Stripped of partisan implications the committee's report showed that legislative blackmail had been used freely upon the railroad interests by members of the General Assembly.

Efforts to restore the tonnage tax likewise came to naught. Although such a bill would have constituted violation of a contract, the legislators, mindful of the lessons derived from the recent fall elections, were afraid to oppose such a measure openly. On February 13, 1862, the Judiciary Committee of the House reported a bill calling for repeal of the

---

[13] McClure *Old Time Notes*, I, 532. The Hopkins' inquiry is related frankly and fully by McClure.

statute providing for commutation of the tonnage tax on the Pennsylvania Railroad.[14] A month later the bill passed by a vote of 70 to 28[15] and was sent to the state Senate where it was assigned to a hostile committee. The bill was reported so that its opponents could load the proposal with unpalatable amendments. One such amendment laid a tax on all tonnage transportation through or within the Commonwealth including all "products of mines, forests, and farms." The amended tax bill now appeared not as the special enemy of the Pennsylvania Railroad interests but as a general foe, inimical to all transportation facilities within the Commonwealth. The House rejected the Senate amendment, 71 to 25[16] and took no steps to effect a compromise with the Senate. This time the confused voters could not pinpoint responsibilty for the failure.

By 1862 a rapidly growing force was making its influence felt on both state and national levels. This was abolitionism, the *bête noir* of the South and her supporters. With the coming of the civil conflict, exponents of the cause were discovering the possibility of rapidly expanding horizons. Moral issues could now be associated with and supplemented by the goals of victory and unionism. A group, the Radicals, had criticized Lincoln from the beginning of his administration for what they considered his mild policy toward the South. National frustration growing out of military defeats and failure of the Lincoln Administration to achieve an early victory over the Confederacy led to increased pressure by this group upon the President. In the autumn of 1861 Thaddeus Stevens spoke well for the extremists when he called for the wasting of the South if necessary and its re-

---

[14] Philadelphia *Evening Bulletin*, Feb. 13, 1862.
[15] *Journal of the House*, 1862, 439.
[16] *Ibid.*, 814.

peopling by freedmen."[17] After the President removed General Frémont, following the freeing of the slaves of Confederate supporters in the Missouri district, radicals and abolitionists united in their criticism of Lincoln. When in late October, 1861, the Pennsylvania Anti-Slavery Society met at Westchester, Lincoln's treatment of Frémont was denounced.[18] Although many other factors were involved in Frémont's dismissal, these the abolitionists chose to ignore. Cameron's Pittsburgh *Gazette,* "speaking for the people" on Frémont's behalf, noted how "sadly and coldly" Lincoln's modifications had been received.[19] Again when Cameron retired from the office of Secretary of War early in 1862, the abolitionists hailed his removal as a Lincoln sacrifice to the conservative camp.

The Curtin faction of the People's Party joined with Union Democrats in taking a conservative stand on the abolitionist question. The many letters directed to Hendrick B. Wright, a strong Union-Democrat, during the last half of 1861 indicated the wishes of his group to sidestep the slavery question while at the same time striving to restore the Union.[20] Inclusion of emancipation of the Negro among the administration's war aims was likely to assure the return of a group of War Democrats to the regular fold of the Democracy. A. K. McClure, in the course of his frequent visits to the President, seized upon every opportunity to admonish Lincoln on the political perils of emancipation.[21] Increasing opposition by the strong Republican press to the governor's conservative views was evidenced by its attacks on Senator

[17] Randall, *Civil War and Reconstruction,* 371.

[18] Randall, *Lincoln: Springfield to Gettysburg,* II, 25.

[19] Sept. 3, Nov. 7, 1861, quoted in Davis, *Pennsylvania Politics,* 236-37.

[20] Wright MSS. Many comments are cited in *ibid.,* 233.

[21] *Old Time Notes,* I, 558.

Edgar Cowan, an opponent of the Federal Confiscation Act freeing slaves. But the People's State Central Committee on May 1, 1862, carefully following the party line of the preceding year, called upon *all loyal citizens* of the state to assist in choosing delegates to the coming state convention. This opened the way to continued Democratic support of the war effort.

On July 17, 1862, only five days before Lincoln's Cabinet first learned of his determination to propose emancipation,[22] a gathering known variously as the People's, the Union, or the Republican and People's Convention met at Harrisburg to nominate candidates for state offices, to define the purposes and opinions of the party, and to "unite in sustaining the national administration."[23] The election of John C. Knox, a former Democratic state officer, as permanent president, and the liberties granted John W. Forney, indicated an all-out effort by the People's Party to garner support from every possible source. John Rowe, Charles Schriner, and George M. Lauman were among the prominent Union-Democrats in attendance. This state Union Party convention nominated without opposition William S. Ross for surveyor general and Thomas E. Cochran for auditor general, the former a Democrat of long standing. Seven formal resolutions adopted by the gathering included praise for members of the armed services and confidence in Lincoln, Curtin, and Wilmot. The state's senior senator, Edgar Cowan, was conveniently forgotten. The convention sought to emphasize its conservative nature by condemning groups which were "openly or covertly endeavoring to sever the country."[24]

---

[22] David Donald (ed.), *Inside Lincoln's Cabinet: Civil War Diaries of Salmon P. Chase* (New York, 1954), 99.
[23] Philadelphia *Evening Bulletin*, July 17, 1862.
[24] Harrisburg *Telegraph*, July 18, 1862; Philadelphia *Evening Bulletin*, July 17, 18, 1862.

The Democratic State Convention of July 4 found the Breckinridge-Douglas schism largely healed and members of the Democracy enthusiastic over their chances of success in capturing state, legislative, and congressional offices in the fall of 1862. Francis W. Hughes, president of the convention and chairman of the Democratic State Central Committee, was representative of the very conservative nature of the gathering. Allegedly Hughes had prepared resolutions of a treasonable nature the preceding year but thought best not to present them.[25] Resolutions of the convention criticized the administration's conduct of the war, questioned the righteousness of its war aims, and protested the high-handed measures which deprived citizens of their constitutional rights. The only declared object of the Democratic Party was "restoration of the Union as it was, and the preservation of the Constitution as it was." Northern abolitionist activities were placed on a par with Southern secession as a prime source of the nation's calamities. Negroes must not be admitted to "political or social equality" by a government established originally and "exclusively for the white man." The delegates thanked the soldiers for their efforts to restore the Union, "such a purpose alone [being] worthy of the awful sacrifice" already entailed. Isaac Slenker was nominated for auditor general, and James P. Barr, editor of the Pittsburgh *Post,* was named candidate for surveyor general. The Democrats along with the Unionists had asked for a continuation of the war effort, but as the party of the opposition, they were enjoying the privileges of destructive criticism.

Some current happenings of the time which undoubtedly influenced the Commonwealth's electorate of 1862 were the unsatisfactory progress of the war effort, the President's two

---

[25] Philadelphia *Press,* Oct. 3, 1862.

requisitions for a national levy of 600,000 troops, the enforcement of a state draft, the announcement of Lincoln's proposed Emancipation Proclamation, Curtin's call for additional militia, the two Confederate invasions, and the Altoona Conference of governors.

On July 1, 1862, in immediate response to a request from eighteen governors that more men be called to "speedily crush the rebellion," Lincoln, "fully concurring in the wisdom of the views expressed," requested the states to furnish 300,000 additional men.[26] Curtin's reply of July 4 assured the President that everything possible would be done to meet the demand of the government in the emergency. However, enlistment for only six months, said Curtin, would have brought better response.[27] Over 100,000 Pennsylvanians were already in the field and approximately another 30,000 *hors de combat.* The governor, following a precedent established in other states, wished to offer a state bounty but no funds were available. Curtin issued a proclamation asking for the bounties to be furnished by municipal, county, and private subscription; and the response from Philadelphia and a few counties was good. Through strenuous efforts, 38 regiments comprising 40,000 troops were raised in response to the President's July call.[28]

Lincoln gave the governors a double dose of their own medicine when he followed a month later with a request for an additional 300,000 troops to be raised by state draft if

---

[26] *Official Records,* Series III, volume II, 180-81, 187-88. In his annual message, January 7, 1863, Curtin erroneously stated that Lincoln had called for troops on July 7. See Egle (ed.), *Curtin,* 240.

[27] Curtin to Lincoln via telegraph, July 4, 1862, Lincoln MSS.

[28] Egle (ed.), *Curtin,* 240-41, 254. The state was actually credited with only 30,000 of her quota of 45,000. See *Official Records,* Series III, Vol. II, 188f.n. McClure in *Notes,* I, 540, erred in setting Pennsylvania's quota at approximately 18,000 men.

necessary under the act of July 17, 1862.[29] To fill the President's second quota through any system of volunteering looked impossible and the state administration resorted, as authorized, to a draft. A. K. McClure, the state director, realized the political implications of the task and resolved to make the unpleasant task as bipartisan as possible. The commissioner and surgeon of the draft of each county were required to be of opposite political faith. In Schuylkill County the Molly Maguires defied conscription and threatened bodily injury to their neighbors who accepted it. Federal troops were made available to enforce the draft but few could doubt the impropriety of using them. Deficiencies, with the connivance of state authorities and apparently that of Lincoln also, were accounted for in Schuylkill County and Philadelphia by crediting fictitous volunteering to make up the difference.[30] In troublesome Cass Township of Schuylkill, Catholic priests cooperated in quieting the turbulent Mollies. By October 27, 1862, resistance was over.[31] Throughout the state, however, there was much complaint of a draft which allowed the rich to escape by furnishing a substitute while the poor were enlisted. Curtin, fearful of the effects of the draft upon the coming election, directed postponement for the nine-months service men until after the electorate went to the polls. It was necessary, Curtin publicly stated, to postpone the draft because the governor's special militia requisitions had called many men away.[32] A total of 32,000 men, probably including the fictitious lists,

---

[29] Randall, *Lincoln: Springfield to Gettysburg,* II, 291.

[30] According to McClure, *Notes,* I, 546-48, Stanton was insisting upon the use of troops to enforce the draft, while Curtin was resisting it ; but on October 22 and 23, Curtin wired to Stanton requesting permission to use troops. See Russell, *Biography of McClure,* 279-80.

[31] Russell, *McClure,* 280.

[32] Philadelphia *Bulletin,* Sept. 24, 1862,

was raised in Pennsylvania under the conscription call; of these approximately 10,000 were bona fide draftees.[33]

The halo of mystery surrounding the famous governors' conference at Altoona on September 24, 1862, has made it difficult to evaluate this event. All sessions were held in secret[34] and newspaper correspondents had to rely upon hearsay, rumors, and leaks. As years passed the surviving governors liked to think of themselves as having participated in a unified effort to support the deified Lincoln. Actually the majority of the governors probably accepted the invitation to attend with the idea of forcing Lincoln to adopt radical policies and to bring about General McClellan's downfall. According to Curtin, the conference had its inception in a letter written by him to Governor Andrew of Massachusetts informing him "that in my opinion the time had come to give the war a definite aim and end, and that the Governors of the loyal states should take prompt united and decided action in the matter." After more correspondence between the two executives and the coming of the national military crisis of early September, the pair decided to see Lincoln before proceeding further. Lincoln discussed with them his tentative Emancipation Proclamation and asked the advisability of having the governors request its issuance. Had this happened Lincoln would have lost the obvious advantages of the initiative. Andrew and Curtin advised Lincoln to first issue a notice of his coming proclamation and then they would follow with a commendation.[35]

[23] *Official Records,* Series III, Vol. II, 291 f.n. ; Egle (ed.), *Curtin,* 254.

[24] Altoona *Tribune,* Sept. 24, 1862.

[35] Curtin to correspondent, Bellefonte, Jan. 5, 1889, Washington *Post,* Jan. 6, 1889. The account by Russell Young in Egle, *Curtin,* 305-30, is based on a manuscript by Austin Blair who was not present at the Altoona meeting. See Hesseltine, *Lincoln and the War Governors,* 249-62.

On September 14, 1862, Curtin, Governor Tod of Ohio, and F. H. Pierpoint, governor of the fictitious state of "loyal Virginia," sent out a call for the governors of all loyal states to meet at Altoona, September 24. On the appointed day fourteen governors or their proxies assembled at the mushrooming little city of Altoona. A sightseeing tour around the famous Horseshoe Bend consumed the morning hours and the first meeting was held in the early afternoon. Two later sessions carried the conversations past the hour of midnight.[36] The announcement of Lincoln's preliminary Emancipation Proclamation only two days before the Altoona Conference made it look as if the wily President had "cut the ground from under the Radicals"; but both Curtin and Andrew knew this would happen before they issued the call for the conference. Although the limitations of the Proclamation disappointed the radicals, there was little they could do and Curtin was assigned the task of drafting an "Address of the Loyal Governors" to the President. The document promised Lincoln full support "without hesitation," asked for a large force of reserves, thanked Lincoln for freeing the slaves, and admonished him to pursue the war with "utmost vigor."[37]

The members could not agree to include a strong indictment of McClellan in such a public document and decided to hold the final session of the conference at Washington in consultation with the President. Lincoln politely thanked the governors for their "Address" and intimated there was no cause for further parley. When Governor Kirkwood of Iowa blustered out the real reason for their visit—a demand for McClellan's dismissal—Lincoln reddened and administered a rebuke to Kirkwood for doubting his general's loyalty. Lincoln emerged from the affair with added prestige and the

[36] Philadelphia *Bulletin*, September 25, 1862.
[37] Egle, *Curtin*, 318-20.

radicals apparently had gained but little. Curtin may have connived at bringing mortification to some of his radical colleagues, but he was sincerely interested in forcing a more vigorous prosecution of the war. Although Lincoln had issued the proclamation only as a tool of war, conservatives were frightened with its implications and the steps which were likely to follow in logical sequence.[38]

Lee's invasion of September, 1862, and Jeb Stuart's later October raid into Pennsylvania created consternation throughout the Commonwealth. Before Lee was checked at Antietam by McClellan the apprehensive governor called out an additional 25,000 militiamen, who suffered mostly foot service in the Cumberland Valley.[39] Captain James Brisbin disdainfully related the governor's militia campaign in northern Maryland where he remained "safe" until Lee's army retired. Then after Curtin had marched his men home and thanked them for their "gallantry," the Confederates seized Chambersburg.[40] During the troublesome September days Lincoln received much urgent advice and exaggerated information from his impromptu field commander, Governor Andrew G. Curtin.[41]

It was therefore within an atmosphere of war weariness and disgust at the apparent failures of Lincoln's policies that the people of Pennsylvania went to the polls on October 14. Early reports from Philadelphia indicated a victory for the Unionists, but their premature rejoicing soon turned to gloom when the final returns filtered in. The two Democratic

---

[38] The evidence from Curtin, Washington *Post,* Jan. 6, 1889, indicated that Lincoln was thinking of the Altoona Conference as well as Antietam when he timed his preliminary emancipation proclamation.

[39] *Papers of the Governors,* 1858-1871, 455-56.

[40] Brisbin to Cameron, Oct. 25, 1862, Cameron MSS, LC.

[41] Curtin to Lincoln, Sept. 11, 12, 14, 16, 17, 1862, Lincoln MSS.

candidates for state office, Isaac Slenker and James P. Barr, achieved victory by a slim margin of less than 3,800 votes out of a total of approximately 430,000 cast.[42] In the lower house where every member was newly elected, the Democrats scored an easy victory, 55 to 45, but in the Senate where only 12 new members were chosen, the Unionists won 8 seats to 4 for the Democrats and retained their majority 21 to 12. The Democracy including three Union-Democrats, with a margin of one vote in joint session was now in position to elect a state treasurer and a United States senator if party lines held. The battle for congressmen proved to be a draw, each party succeeding in sending 12 members. Philadelphia returned only one Democrat, Samuel J. Randall, but elsewhere the Democracy more than held its own. Two prominent Republicans, Speaker Galusha Grow and Edward McPherson, were defeated for re-election. The latter blamed his failure on the recent Confederate invasions.[43]

Without some support from the War Democrats, the state administration efforts to cooperate fully with Lincoln were likely to be hamstrung. "The voting in 1862 was as much for or against Lincoln's administration as it was a judgment upon congressmen for their purely legislative records."[44] Pennsylvania was not alone in her protests against Lincoln policies. The majority cast for Lincoln in 1860 by New York, Ohio, Illinois, and Indiana went to Democratic candidates in 1862. Thaddeus Stevens, the iron-willed radical from Lancaster, returned to the House, using his dictatorial methods unsparingly for the purpose of keeping the reduced Republican majority in line. In the Keystone state, the last-

---

[42] *Tribune Almanac,* 1863. Buchanan privately expressed his confidence in a Democratic victory, John N. Eberman to Bigler, Aug. 13, 1862, Bigler MSS.

[43] Russell, *McClure,* 277.

[44] Randall, *Lincoln: Springfield to Gettysburg,* II, 237.

minute "Address" of the Union State Central Committee, pleading for the casting aside of party issues and support for the "unconditional friends of the Union," had fallen upon deaf ears.[45]

On January 1, 1863, Lincoln proclaimed the emancipation of all slaves within the Confederate lines. Characteristic of the Democratic response were the Erie *Observer*'s comments: ". . . we have opposed it as unconstitutional, impolitic and contrary to the rules of civilized warfare, and we do not now see any cause for changing our mind."[46] But Simon Cameron, now seeking recognition as the national administration's leading man in the state, compared Lincoln's dictum to the principles of the Christian religion which would "work silently, quietly, but surely upon the hearts of thousands and bring help and strength to our cause when we least expect and most need it."[47] Governor Curtin's avoidance of the emancipation question received favorable comment from the Democratic press. The governor's annual message of January, 1863, dwelt upon the improved state of the treasury, the sinking fund, the burden upon state banks, the unfortunate disfranchisement of service men, the raising of militia, and the problem of bounties.[48]

In the legislature the evenly balanced parties fought desperately for the slightest advantage. George V. Lawrence, a Cameron man, succeeded Hall as speaker of the Senate; while in the House, John Cessna, a War Democrat, was elected to the presiding chair. The Democracy's one vote majority on joint ballot enabled it to elect William V. McGrath state treasurer and to send a Democrat to the

---

[45] Philadelphia *Bulletin,* Oct. 3, 1862.
[46] Jan. 10, 1862.
[47] Cameron to S. P. Chase, Jan. 7, 1863, Chase MSS, HSP.
[48] Altoona *Tribune*, Jan. 13, 1863.

United States Senate to replace David Wilmot. Actually the Republicans of Pennsylvania no longer possessed representation in the Senate, because Edgar Cowan was consistently voting with the Democratic opposition.

During the early days of 1863, the state Democracy was riding high. If the trend of the last two years continued the party would wrest control of the state executive chair from the Republicans. Curtin's formal announcement on April 15 that he was not a candidate for re-election[49] appeared to remove the most formidable obstacle in that direction. Numerous expressions of discontent appeared in the organs of both parties. Service men deluged their relatives, local editors, state legislators, and congressmen with long lists of grievances. Death on the field of battle, concluded one group of frustrated convalescents, was preferable to their present treatment.[50] In the border counties of Franklin and Adams impoverished citizens complained of the destruction wrought by Confederate raids.

Leaders of the state Democracy gathered at Harrisburg for their state convention on June 17. Among the gubernatorial hopefuls were Henry D. Foster, the defeated candidate of 1860; John Cessna, the leading War Democrat; William Hopkins, nemesis of the railroad interests; George W. Cass, Pittsburgh railroad magnate; William H. Witte, leading contender of 1860; Hiester Clymer, favorite of the eastern Democracy; and George W. Woodward, conservative member of the state supreme court. The powerful state chairman, Francis W. Hughes, who agreed with William Bigler that the Democracy must take a strong stand "squarely against this disunion war," was backing Witte.[51] The Democratic stal-

---

[49] *Papers of the Governors,* 1858-1871, 500-01.
[50] Nineteen convalescents to John Covode, Jan. 29, 1863, Covode MSS, LC.
[51] Hughes to Bigler, Mar. 31, 1863, Bigler MSS, HSP.

warts were in no mood to support Cessna whose recent collusions in the legislature with the Republicans had left doubts of his orthodoxy. On the first ballot Witte led Clymer by 14 votes, but at the end of eight ballots with Clymer in the lead Hughes withdrew Witte's name in favor of Judge Woodward. Following a period of pandemonium Woodward defeated Clymer 75 votes to 53. Walter H. Lowrie was nominated the candidate for supreme judge by acclamation.[52]

The convention wished to issue a strong indictment of the Curtin and Lincoln policies while at the same time refraining from any statement which might be construed as treasonable. Discussion of probable resolutions went back to the Democratic caucus of March 26 whose memorials were considered too weak by William Wallace, Clymer, and Cyrus Pershing, because the question of the "rights of the states and conscription" had been omitted.[53] The resolutions stressed the recent violation of the time-honored personal rights—life, liberty, property, and trial by jury—and reminded the nation that there could be no free government without a free press. The state Democracy, disclaiming any sympathy for the "traitors in arms," would consent to no terms involving "dismemberment of the Union"; but claimed at the same time the right to consider publicly any measures which were likely to lead to a restoration of the Union. In addition the Democracy accused the Republican Party of deviating from its avowed purpose of waging war— the preservation of the Union. A vote of thanks was rendered the "lion-hearted Democracy" of Ohio for its "manly vindication" of the Constitution in the case of Clement L. Vallandigham.[54]

---

[52] Erie *Observer,* June 27, 1863.
[53] Wallace to Bigler, Nov. 26, 1863, Bigler MSS.
[54] Erie *Observer,* June 27, 1863.

George Washington Woodward, the Democratic choice for governor, was no stranger to the political world. In 1845, as the Democratic caucus candidate for United States senator, he had seen Simon Cameron rob him of his prize. This native of Wayne County received a fine academic training and in 1830, at twenty-one years of age, began an illustrious judicial career. He appeared as a prominent participant in the constitutional convention of 1837-1838. In 1841, Woodward was chosen president judge of the Fourth judicial district. His selection by the Democracy in 1845 to succeed Buchanan in the Senate indicated his respected position in the party. Seven years later his party elected him to the supreme bench of the state for a term of 15 years. Reputedly Woodward had stated: "If the Union is to be divided, I want the line of separation to run north of Pennsylvania."[55] Unionists, following Woodward's ruling against state conscription, branded him a traitor to the cause. That the physical and mental giant, George Washington Woodward, was certain to be a worthy opponent of any candidate the Unionists might present, both friend and foe agreed. His nomination was a deliberate move by the Democratic Party to avoid selection of a man likely to be accepted by the Unionists as a coalition candidate, and was proof of the party's confidence in its ability to capture the gubernatorial prize without the aid of the War Democrats.[56]

The question most frequently asked in state political circles during the first half of 1863 was: "Is Curtin a candi-

---

[55] George P. Lathrop, *History of the Union League of Philadelphia* (Philadelphia, 1884), 11.

[56] On Woodward see Philadelphia *Age,* Aug. 25, 1863 ; Appleton's *Cyclopedia,* VI, 607 ; McClure, *Notes,* I, 93-94. The impression that Cameron and Woodward were bitter personal enemies is erroneous. Woodward solicited aid from Cameron in 1863. See Cameron's notation on Wood to Rice, n.d., Cameron MSS, LC.

date for re-election?" From the public's viewpoint there seemed little excuse for the governor's vacillating policy; but the governor's very poor health, the opposition of the Cameron faction, the probability of a Union-Democratic coalition, the attitude of the Lincoln Administration, Curtin's popularity with the soldiers and the grassroots of his party, the highly touted strength of state's Democracy in 1863, and the changing fortunes of the military strife—all were factors which the governor must consider in arriving at a final decision.

Simon Cameron, embittered following his return from Russia by the boastfulness of Curtin's followers and his defeat for the senatorship, determined to prevent the governor's renomination by promoting the candidacy of John Covode, now a recognized leader of the radicals. Cameron requested Covode to ascertain Lincoln's attitude toward his candidacy and found that although the administration considered Covode as owing Curtin nothing, yet it didn't wish to be "setting the pins" against Curtin.[57] This answer gave the green light to Cameron, who was seeking to rehabilitate himself by following the Lincoln way and who therefore was careful not to offend the President.

In the meantime Curtin proceeded to throw a fly into the Covode ointment with his suggestion, circulated in private circles, that General William B. Franklin, a popular War Democrat, be presented as a Union-Democratic coalition candidate for governor. The governor, whose health was near the breaking point in the early months of 1863, was anxious to insure the election in his place of an ardent supporter of the war effort; but all potential gubernatorial candidates of the Democracy, in expectation of a Democratic victory, refused to consider any coalition with the Unionists.

---

[57] Covode to Cameron, Feb. 11, 1863, Cameron MSS, DCC.

It was clear that the gubernatorial contest of 1863 was to be fought on strict party lines with bona fide candidates representing each group and under these conditions it would be difficult for Curtin to refuse a proffered renomination.

Suddenly, as if by magic, Curtin's impending candidacy appeared liquidated. Although close friends doubted the governor's physical abilities to carry on another strenuous campaign, it was the tearful entreaties of Curtin's wife, Catherine, who feared for her husband's life, which led to his decision, in consultation with close advisers, to retire from the contest if the maneuver could be executed gracefully and without loss of face. Alexander K. McClure and John W. Forney enlisted the aid of Simon Cameron who, of course, readily agreed to assist in removing his foe from the political scene. In presenting the case to Lincoln, McClure, in addition to listing Curtin's poor health as a factor, argued Curtin's re-election a poor risk because many of Pennsylvania's soldiers would be unable to vote. The plan was to have Lincoln offer Curtin an important diplomatic post at the end of his gubernatorial term in early 1864.[58] Although at that time no first-class missions were vacant, Lincoln immediately wrote a note to Curtin, for public consumption, promising him, if possible, a future appointment upon termination of his gubernatorial services.[59]

Curtin's formal announcement on April 15 of his intention to retire created somewhat of a bombshell in political circles. The heavy duties of his office, explained Curtin, had seriously impaired his health; he had therefore decided to accept Lincoln's proffer to high office at the end of his present term. Reaction to the governor's announcement

[58] McClure, *Notes*, II, 41-48.
[59] Lincoln to Curtin, April 13, 1863, facsimile in McClure, *Lincoln and Men of War Times*, 244.

varied widely in Republican circles, The rank and file of the party refused to believe their ears and continued to elect convention delegates pledged to Curtin. The Cameron journals had little comment on the subject. The opposition Clinton *Democrat* sarcastically hailed the "wise, thoughtful and magnanimous" governor for his decision "not to curse the people of the state" with another administration.[60]

The governor's decision to retire produced a fresh crop of gubernatorial hopefuls including J. P. Penney, Henry D. Moore, Benjamin Harrison Brewster, Louis D. Hall and W. W. Ketcham, all of whom were friendly to Cameron. In the meantime that politico must have suffered considerable discomfiture when his lieutenants reported Curtin still the strongest with the Republican voters, and the wish of local organizations to send Curtin delegations to the coming convention. During the month of May rumors continued to mount that Curtin would accept a renomination from his party but the governor failed to spike such reports with any reiteration of his determination not to accept. When the state executive undertook a good-will tour of the northern area of the state, addressing Republican audiences up to seven times in one day, the *Republican* anti-Curtin press, demanding to know the real purpose of all the music, bonfires, fireworks, and fanfare, requested Curtin to remember his pledge and to put an end to all speculation.[61] Actually, the governor was bound to remain silent until he learned the outcome of the Democratic convention scheduled for June 17. A nomination for General Franklin would have provided the best insurance against Curtin's candidacy but the Democracy did not wish to avail itself of the opportunity.

Cameron's keen political perceptions now told him that

---

[60] Quoted in Bellefonte *Democratic-Watchman*, May 1, 1863.
[61] Pittsburgh *Gazette*, June 5, 1863.

Curtin would finally accept a renomination and he immediately took steps to block it. To his lieutenant, C. A. Walborn of Philadelphia, he wrote: ". . . Curtin is in his true character of cheating. You and others of the Delegates can check mate him . . . perhaps it will be best to go for Covode as the easiest means of disposing of him, I am for any honest man."[62] A week later, A. K. McClure, Curtin's closest confidant, confessed that he feared Curtin was "assenting involuntarily" to the use of his name for renomination.[63] In the meantime, Benjamin Harrison Brewster, easily the most servile of Cameron's creatures, received assurance from Lincoln that the President would not interfere and preferred to leave the Union men of Pennsylvania to their "own good judgment" in the selection of a candidate.[64] Convenient postponement of the Union state convention until August 5, allegedly because of Lee's invasion, strengthened public belief of the governor's interest in another term.

Theorizing regarding Curtin's course ended only three weeks prior to convention date. On July 13 the wavering tortured mind of Curtin sought an outlet and possible relief through a long conference with McClure at the latter's home in Chambersburg. The following morning McClure learned of the governor's decision not to refuse a nomination. On July 15, McClure's Chambersburg *Franklin Respository* announced Curtin's decision, asked for public support, and predicted a two-thirds vote for him at the convention. William B. Mann, Cameron's old Philadelphia nemesis, put machinery in motion to line up delegates in that area for Curtin.[65] The Pittsburgh *Gazette* and Harrisburg *Telegraph*,

---

[62] Cameron to Walborn, June 2, 1863, Autograph Collection, HSP.
[63] McClure to Eli Slifer, June 9, 1863, Slifer-Dill MSS, DCL.
[64] S. P. Chase to Brewster, June 9, 1863, Cameron MSS, DCC.
[65] Russell, *McClure*, 295-96.

the two strongest Cameron mouthpieces, severely criticized Curtin; the former actually exercising the role of a party opposition organ while the latter steadfastly refused to recognize the legitimacy of the governor's candidacy. Only a week before convention time, Attorney General William Meredith expressed his fear that the Lincoln Administration would actually intervene to defeat him if he attempted to run.[66]

The Union state convention met in Pittsburgh, the anti-Curtin capital of Pennsylvania, on August 5. Lee's retreat from Gettysburg and Grant's capture of Vicksburg had contributed much to restoring public confidence in the final success of the Union armies and the tone of the meeting was one of optimism. The results of an early pro-Curtin caucus and the election of his friend Henry D. Maxwell to the temporary chairmanship of the convention presaged a Curtin victory. The Pittsburgh group, perceiving Covode's chances nil, conspired with the Cameron men to eliminate Curtin as a candidate by promoting the withdrawal of both candidates, ostensibly in the name of party harmony, thereby paving the way for either Moore or Penney. But the motion to consider the withdrawal resolution before proceeding to a nomination was easily voted down 84 to 45. After Curtin's name had been placed in nomination "amid applause and hisses," the anti-Curtin coalition played its last trump— the presentation of a letter from Covode withdrawing himself from nomination in the interests of harmony so a united party could agree on "some new man." Ironically, the finale was enacted by Alexander Cummings, whose disreputable management of war contracts under

---

[66] Meredith to Slifer, Slifer-Dill MSS. Seward, Chase, and Stanton, the three strongest members of Lincoln's cabinet were considered hostile to Curtin, especially Stanton. See McClure to Slifer, June 9, 1863, *ibid.*

Secretary of War Cameron was a national scandal. Curtin, observed Cummings, did not possess the confidence of his party.[67]

But nothing could stop the swing to Curtin. "It was evident," observed Wayne MacVeagh, "that the Republicans must either nominate Curtin or practically surrender the battle."[68] Curtin's 90 votes on the first ballot gave him the nomination. Penney received 14 votes, mostly from the Pittsburgh area, and Moore, the eastern Cameron man, garnered 18.[69] Little interest was manifested in other state offices, and at the evening session Daniel Agnew of Beaver was chosen by acclamation the candidate for supreme judge. The convention's resolutions endorsed the Lincoln Administration, lauded Curtin for his past support of the Federal government and his solicitude for the soldier's welfare, thanked the gallant defenders of the Commonwealth, and requested a constitutional amendment permitting an absentee vote for soldiers. As an afterthought the convention endorsed the bold stand of Lincoln's Administration in summarily arresting persons guilty of "traitorous practices," but a move to endorse Secretary of War Stanton was greeted with jeers and hisses.

It was now up to the Cameron faction to make the best of what was to them an ill situation. Party harmony demanded support for the Union candidate and not even the most

---

[67] Erie *Observer,* Aug. 15, 1863. Cummings, one of Cameron's "plundering patriots," had lately been appointed to the job of revising tax assessments throughout the state. He emerged from the war a breveted brigadier general and President Johnson appointed him governor of Colorado Territory.

[68] Wayne MacVeagh, "Curtin Re-elected Governor," Egle, *Curtin,* 162.

[69] These figures are given by MacVeagh, the Harrisburg *Patriot and Union,* the Philadelphia *North American,* and the Bellefonte *Central Press.* But the Pittsburgh *Gazette* and Philadelphia *Bulletin* gave Curtin 95, Moore 17, and Penney 16.

rabid anti-Curtin Republican sheet preferred Woodward to Curtin.[70] A Philadelphia *Press* editorial on the day following Curtin's victory found that at the convention, arguments and calculations of the politicians possessed no favor with the people.[71] The disgruntled John Covode consulted with his fellow radical Salmon P. Chase "as to the proper course to be taken in Pennsylvania" in view of Curtin's potential as a presidential candidate. No speculations on Curtin's future, advised Chase "could excuse the loyal men from supporting him now."[72]

The gubernatorial campaign of 1863 did not lack for issues—most of which originated with the beginning of the civil strife. In addition to the failure of the national administration to bring the war to a successful conclusion, questions arose as to the full meaning of Lincoln's Emancipation Proclamation, the suppression of the cherished liberties of free speech, freedom of the press, and exercise of the right to a speedy trial by jury. This suppression of civil liberties grew out of the alleged treasonable activities of groups called Copperheads, Butternuts, and Knights of the Golden Circle. The term Copperhead was used early in the war to designate opponents of Lincoln's war effort, the Peace Democrats.[73] The Butternut badge was emblematic of the humble origins of its members and a cross section of the badge was indicative of the union of the hearts of the North and the South.

The Union press carried highly colored accounts of Copperhead activity, some of it undoubtedly fictional.[74] Resistance to the draft in the areas of Philadelphia and Pittsburgh and the counties of Berks, Cambria, and Schuyl-

[70] Aug. 25, 1863 quoted in Davis, *Pennsylvania Politics*, 300.
[71] Philadelphia *Press*, Aug. 6, 1863.
[72] Donald (ed.), *Inside Lincoln's Cabinet*, 179.
[73] Wood Gray, *The Hidden Civil War*, 140-41.
[74] Pittsburgh *Gazette*, Oct. 2, 1863 ; Sept. 21, 1863.

kill were looked upon as Copperhead inspired. Fear of the Copperheads is seen in the "Address" of the loyal governors attending the Altoona-Washington Conference in which the state executives pledged "vigorous exercise" of all "lawful and proper powers contending against treason . . . and public enemies . . . ."[75] When prominent old-line Democratic leaders were named Copperheads by the Unionist press, many War Democrats joined the Unionist ranks as bona fide members to escape the stigmatization accorded their more conservative brethren. The rebels and Copperheads, charged the Pittsburgh *Gazette,* are one; their "fortunes rise and fall together. If one triumphs so will the other."[76]

The allegedly seditious activity of the Copperhead press led to suppression of their organs and to the imprisonment of their editors. The new Philadelphia *Age,* the Philadelphia *Evening Journal,* the Lancaster *Intelligencer,* and the Erie *Observer* were considered leading Copperhead journals by the Unionists. The Kittanning *Mentor,* the Bellefonte *Democratic Watchman,* the Easton *Sentinel,* the Westchester *Jeffersonian,* and the Meadville *Democrat* are good examples of the rabid local press. The case of Albert D. Boileau, editor of the Philadelphia *Evening Journal,* attracted state-wide attention. Shortly after Lincoln proclaimed emancipation, Boileau quoted the attack of Jefferson Davis on Lincoln, expressed his approval, and compared Lincoln's Administration unfavorably with that of Davis. A week later he was hustled off to Fort McHenry, where after a chastisement of several days' duration, he was released.[77] Mob attacks on Democratic presses were reported from Sunbury, Meadville,

---

[75] *Official Records,* Series III, Vol. II, 583.
[76] Oct. 12, 1863.
[77] Erie *Observer,* Feb. 7, 1863 ; Robinson, "Public Press," 171.

Easton, Carlisle, Kittanning, Westchester, and Huntingdon.
The controversial nature of these attacks is illustrated in the
case of the Huntingdon *Monitor*. A Democratic organ placed
the blame on an abolitionist-Unionist mob; but the Altoona
Tribune's reporter who interviewed all those placed under
arrest, found it included a party of indignant soldiers, the
majority of whom were Democrats.[78]

Curtin's reaction to the indignities and summary treatment dealt the Commonwealth's citizens by military authorities operating in a sphere where remedies could be sought in
civil courts must have given the radicals a severe jolt. In a
special message to the General Assembly the governor
deprecated interposition by the federal government in the
liberty of Pennsylvania's citizens whose only redress was the
judiciary; such interference was "dangerous." The state
administration, reported the vexed governor, was not privy
to any arrests of such nature; and fortunately there were
only a few wretches plotting betrayal and so comforting the
rebels. Curtin questioned Lincoln's constitutional right to
suspend the writ of *habeas corpus* and requested the legislature to pass resolutions urging Congress to pass a law
"defining and punishing offenses of the class referred
to . . . ."[79] By this action early in 1863 the governor relieved
himself of any blame for abridgment of the right of free
speech. Undoubtedly Curtin's appeal for preservation of a
cherished right in the face of radical disapproval stood him
in good stead during his campaign for re-election.

The burden of the Democratic strategy in the coming
campaign, it seemed to many sincere Democrats, should be
directed toward removing the stigma of disloyalty and
treason imposed upon it by the Unionists; but its leaders

[78] Altoona *Tribune,* June 9, 1863.
[79] *Papers of the Governors,* 1858-1871, 492-94.

chose rather to raise the bugbear of abolitionism as a specter of frightfulness in order to terrify the state's electorate into voting against Curtin. The "Address" of the Democratic State Central Committee, in reviewing the background of the war, termed Lincoln's election a "triumph of abolitionism" over the Democratic conservatives of the North. Slavery, a "state problem" obviously could not be a cause of the war. Pennsylvania's interests could not be served by a "fanatical faction" which perverted and protracted the war for "ruinous and perhaps unattainable ends." The Republican abolitionist policy promised nothing better than a "Southern Poland ruled by Northern despotism." Abolitionism, *not* reunion, concluded the Democratic Committee, was the chief war aim of Lincoln's government and consequently reunion was unattainable on such principles.[80] The Democratic Pittsburgh *Post* wrote of the multitudes in the South that were prevented from coming back into the Union because of property confiscations and the emancipation of their slaves.[81] The influential Philadelphia *Age* looked upon the contest as a fight for a survival of Anglo-Saxon freedom.[82]

Judge Woodward, mindful that the judiciary and politics should be kept unmixed, made few speeches during the campaign. The chief oratorical burdens were shifted to J. Glancy Jones, William Porter, William Bigler, and Jeremiah Black. The last-named was assigned the task of making Woodward's position clear to the public. To Woodward it seemed that the only impression his enemies had made on the public mind prejudicial to his interests related to his "Unionism" or loyalty. Woodward instructed Black: "If I am a traitor, I pray you tell the people of Pennsylvania so,

---

[80] Philadelphia *Age*, Aug. 13, 1863.
[81] July 30, 1863, quoted in Davis, *Pennsylvania Politics*, 305.
[82] Aug. 18, 1863.

but tell them also *to* whom I would betray a people among whom I was born and have always lived with and with whom my all of earthly goods and honor is embarked . . . ." Woodward did believe that a force was seeking to overthrow the work of the Founding Fathers and to establish upon its ruins a "negro despotism."[83] Black's carefully prepared speech was delivered at Lancaster on September 17. After tracing the constitutional development of personal and state liberties, the eminent jurist emphasized that these alone were not sufficient if the Chief Executive were allowed to take upon himself powers (suspension of the writ of *habeas corpus*) belonging exclusively to the legislative department of government. If the Union is restored, cried Black, it must be accomplished solely on the basis of the Constitution and laws.[84] Whether consciously or not, Woodward revealed his true position when he congratulated Black on his fine address and then asked: "[But] why did you scout the sacred right of revolution?"[85]

James Buchanan in retirement satisfied himself with giving the Democratic candidate advice while his friend William Bigler took the stump. The evils of conscription, currently being used as a theme in the New York elections, must be avoided, warned Buchanan. Issues greater than conscription were dependent upon Woodward's election—issues which would decide the welfare or woe of the nation, cautioned the Sage of Wheatland.[86] At that time a ruling by the state supreme court on the constitutionality of the national conscription act was pending and Buchanan advised Woodward not to vote against its constitutionality. This particular dilem-

---

[83] Woodward to Black, Sept. 10, 1863, Black MSS, LC.
[84] Philadelphia *Age*, Sept. 24, 1863.
[85] Woodward to Black, Oct. 31, 1863, Black MSS, LC.
[86] Buchanan to Woodward, Sept. 5, 1863, Moore, *Works*, XI, 346-47.

ma was solved by postponing the court's decision until after election. Bigler in his speech at New Hope had little to say on the subject of Curtin or the state administration and criticized the Lincoln Administration for making little effort to effect a settlement of the civil strife and to accomplish reunion. "Is subjugation or extermination," asked Bigler, "to be the word?" Two weeks later in his letter to the "Erie men," Bigler asserted that the Republican radicals, "because of their impracticable motions about slavery, and the intensified hostility so long cherished between them and the leading men of the South [were] hopelessly incapable of adopting a policy calculated to restore the Union . . . ."[87]

The Democratic gubernatorial campaign of 1863 may therefore be looked upon primarily not so much as an assault upon Governor Curtin and his policies as it was upon the Lincoln Administration. The Democratic press, it is true, often spoke of Curtin, the "shoddy" candidate; the man who robbed the state's taxpayers when he assisted in repeal of the tonnage tax; the governor from whose cabinet Samuel Purviance had resigned in order to maintain his self-respect; and cracker of the mythical Pennsylvania Dutchman's double skull. Actually, the leaders of the state Democracy were asking the state's electorate to show their disapproval of radical Republicanism by defeating Curtin, the exponent of aggressive war policies but not of abolitionism or radicalism.

A powerful new factor in deciding election returns, the Union League, made its debut during the gubernatorial campaign of 1863. In Philadelphia the organization was inaugurated in the early spring of 1863 under the title of the National Union Club. At the largest mass meeting reputedly

---

[87] Bigler to the Erie men, Oct. 3, 1863, Erie *Observer,* Oct. 10, 1863.

held in that city since 1860, the chairman, Morton McMichael, pronounced the club "an instrument to assist the national government in crushing the wicked rebellion."[88] In addition to Benjamin Harrison Brewster, H. B. Wright, and Governor Curtin, the huge gathering was privileged to hear the loyal military governor of Tennessee, Andrew Johnson, and Senator Doolittle of Wisconsin. Local chapters sprang up like mushrooms in all the principal towns of the state. From its inception the Democracy looked upon the League with fear and distrust. The Erie *Observer* warned all good Democrats to have nothing to do with the League because with few exceptions all members in Erie were known Republicans.[89] Forney saw in the League a useful instrument for promoting patriotism, fellowship; proper performance of political duties, and enlightenment (propaganda) of the mind.[90] Starting out as a semisecret organization, the League threw aside its mummery and developed into a strong adjunct of the Republican Party. Frustrated Democrats could only protest that no special organization was needed to support the Union and that their party was likewise a bulwark of unionism.

Curtin's main speaking itinerary of the campaign began at West Chester, September 23, with scheduled engagements at Beaver, Washington, Indiana, Wilkes-Barre, Scranton, Towanda, Bellefonte, York, Reading, Pottsville, and ending at Philadelphia on the eve of the election. At the last-named city, Curtin delivered a short but powerful address charged with logic and based upon moral principles. It was not important, Curtin reminded his audience, that either he or

---

[88] Philadelphia *Bulletin,* March 12, 1863.
[89] April 4, 1863.
[90] Philadelphia *Press,* March 28, 1863, quoted in Davis, *Pennsylvania Politics,* 301.

Woodward should triumph; but it was imperative that right should triumph over evil and he sincerely believed in the righteousness of his cause. For his part he purposed stead-fastly to sustain the President. He acknowledged no under-standing of a "bogus loyalty" which professed fidelity to the government concurrently with its refusal to give it support.[91]

During his tour Curtin found no difficulty in justifying his title, The Soldiers' Friend. He had done everything within his power to administer to the wants of the soldier whether in the field or in the hospital; he had made personal appeals to the legislature when Pennsylvania's regiments were in arrears of pay and when families were suffering because no arrangements had been made for bounties.[92] The governor had secured permission to have the state quartermaster general purchase clothing for troops when necessary and he had secured pensions for widows and the fatherless children.[93] Complaints from the soldiers received individual replies from either the governor or his efficient secretary, Matthew Quay. Provisions were even made for bringing back the bodies of the dead.

The necessity for a Republican victory in the Keystone state prior to the decisive presidential election of 1864 was fully realized by the party's national managers. That Curtin was detested by many leading figures in the party was no secret, but this was not a popularity contest and political sages doubted whether a Republican President could be elected in 1864 if Curtin were defeated. Various devices were used to procure Curtin additional votes. The prominent War Democrat, General Benjamin F. Butler, spoke in the governor's behalf at Harrisburg on September 19. In Phila-

[91] Philadelphia *Bulletin*, Sept. 22, Oct. 12, 1863.
[92] *Papers of the Governors*, 1858-71, 490.
[93] *Laws of Pennsylvania*, 1861, 765 ; *ibid.*, 488.

delphia's Concert Hall, the radical Henry Winter Davis
stood amid bloodstained battle flags to deliver his "bloody
shirt" address,[94] representative of a new type of effective
oratory. MacVeagh made appeals to the servicemen for
support from their friends and relatives at home; and
William Meredith urged Secretary of War Stanton to send
home every man he could spare, be it soldier or civilian.
The final "Address" of the Union State Central Committee
recalled Woodward's avowal of the "right of secession" and
reminded the voter that he had only *one* question to decide
when he went to the polls: "It was whether he was for the
Union or against it."[95]

On October 14, Pennsylvania's electorate decided the
state elections. Although many thousands of servicemen
were absent from the state, the total gubernatorial vote of
524,000 exceeded by 30,000 that of 1860. Curtin's 270,000
votes gave him a majority of 16,000 over Woodward, half
his majority of 1860.[96] Daniel Agnew the Unionist candidate
for supreme judge defeated Lowrie by 12,000 votes. The
results of the legislative elections gave the Unionists a scant
majority in each house. In the new Senate 17 unionists
(including Republicans, People's, and National Unionists)
would face 16 Democrats. The next House would consist of
51 Unionists and 49 Democrats.[97] The Unionists had re-
elected Curtin by a respectable majority, placed a Republican
judge on the supreme court, and scored a scant working
majority in the General Assembly.

---

[94] Philadelphia *Age,* Sept. 22, 1863 ; Philadelphia *Bulletin,* Sept. 25,
1863.

[95] Pittsburgh *Gazette,* Oct. 10, 1863.

[96] Smull's *Legislative Handbook,* 1873, 193.

[97] The election results actually gave the Unionists a majority of
only one in the House. For a complete breakdown of the returns
see Davis, *Pennsylvania Politics,* 314-15.

Curtin achieved his victory through a combination of factors; and not the least of these was the new trend of military events dispelling war weariness. At the end of 1862, seemingly little progress had been completed in crushing the rebellion, but by October, 1863, the Confederacy had been cut in twain in the west and Lee's invasion of Pennsylvania, the Confederacy's greatest offensive operation, had been successfully repulsed. Few now doubted the ultimate outcome. Chairman MacVeagh's fine organizational work at all levels and in all spheres contributed much in getting out the Unionist vote. The "bread and butter" vote of the Federal and state clientele added to the ballots of furloughed servicemen, was considerable. But the personal factor was the greatest of all. Both parties agreed that only Curtin could have beaten Woodward. The people of Pennsylvania had expressed their confidence not in radicals, nor even in an exponent of Lincoln's policies, but rather in a governor who had pledged the entire resources of the state to crushing the rebellion.

V

Triumph of the Cameron Machine

WHEN SIMON CAMERON retired from the office of Secretary of War in the early days of 1862 to enter upon his "Siberian exile," few would have dared to predict that the famed politico was yet to enjoy his greatest triumphs. The story of the rebuilding of the state's greatest political machine following his disgrace and return from Russia is unparalleled in the Commonwealth's history. Cameron's ante-bellum machine which had depended upon personal loyalty rather than party regularity became the nucleus of the postwar organization, a pyramidal hierarchy with Cameron at its pinnacle. The example of the powerful patron of the War Office doling out lucrative rewards to the members of his numerous clientele was one not easily forgotten either by those who enjoyed its fruits nor by those denied them. When Cameron chose the Lincoln way to rehabilitate himself, his pathway was made easier by a horde of followers eager to partake of the loaves and fishes.

During the early months of the Lincoln Administration Simon Cameron was easily overwhelmed by the duties of an office, which, according to contemporary observers, would have consumed the energy of ten competent Secretaries. The problems encountered in the War Office would have tested the wisdom of a Solomon or the efficiency of a Hamilton, but of either talent Cameron possessed but little. Although endowed with a goodly measure of common sense, the

Secretary's better judgment invariably flew out the window when an opportunity to please a friend presented itself. His inadequacies for high office he frequently confessed to his closest friends; but nevertheless, Cameron resented William H. Seward's early attempts to act as a minister of all talents in Lincoln's Cabinet and came to rely upon Salmon P. Chase for help. A strong friendship developed between the two Secretaries which continued unabated through the years.

Lincoln's greatest immediate dilemma, the question of Fort Sumter, was discussed before Cameron entered upon his Cabinet duties, and it wasn't until after the meeting of March 15 that the new Secretary of War, relying mainly upon the expert advice of General Winfield Scott, agreed with the majority of the Cabinet that it would be unwise to attempt relief of the fort.[1] But after March 29 following another Cabinet discussion on the subject, Cameron became a proponent of relief.[2] On April 4 Cameron gave Major Anderson at Fort Sumter information on the projected relief expedition, expressed confidence in the commander, and authorized him to capitulate if and when he deemed it necessary.[3] A fortnight later the fort was in Confederate hands and Major Anderson reported to the Secretary of War that after 34 hours of attack with "quarters entirely burnt . . . the magazines surrounded by flames . . . and no provisions remaining but pork," he had surrendered.[4] Before receiving Anderson's official report Lincoln issued his call for volunteers.

Overnight Cameron's office was converted into a center of chaos. Fresh hordes of office seekers besieged the Secretary,

---

[1] *Official Records,* Series I, Vol. I, 196-98.
[2] "Reminiscences" of George Harrington quoted in Wylie Samuel Crawford, *Genesis of the Civil War* (New York, 1887), 367-68.
[3] *Ibid.,* 382.
[4] *Official Records,* Series I, Vol. I, 12.

SIMON CAMERON: United States Senator, 1845-1849, 1857-1861, 1867-1877; Secretary of War, 1861-1862; Minister to Russia, 1862-1863. *Courtesy of Pennsylvania Historical and Museum Commission.*

and floods of telegrams concerning troop movements, general inquiries, and unsolicited advice poured in from the loyal states. Six border states rejected the idea of furnishing troops to coerce their Southern brethren, the governor of Missouri answering Cameron that his requisition was "illegal, unconstitutional, revolutionary, inhuman, [and] diabolical."[5] Shortly the War Secretary was busily engaged in supervising the railroad and telegraph lines, directing the movement of troops, and recommending high military appointments. He took time to investigate the alleged traitorous activities of former Secretary of War John B. Floyd, accused of arming the South during the declining days of the Buchanan Administration,[6] and through General Ripley issued a misleading report on the subject.

Soon complaints of Cameron's conduct of the War Office appeared. Critics thought that he could have better used his time in seeking arms from Europe instead of allowing Confederate emissaries, Northern speculators, and state agents to monopolize the field. Instead of advocating a regular standing army, Cameron spoke for the civilian voluntee system because "no government is so strong as that whose foundation rest immovably in the hearts of the people."[7] Before the debacle at Bull Run it seemed to J. B. Fry that Cameron sensed the coming disaster because "his countenance showed apprehension of evil."[8] After Bull Run, the War Secretary reiterated his faith in ultimate victory; but the struggle to come would be "long and fearful enough to sink small men and raise great ones."[9]

The activities of three Federal military leaders—Benjamin

[5] Moore, *Rebellion Record*, I, 27-30.
[6] *Official Records*, Series III, Vol. I, 321-22.
[7] Moore, *Rebellion Record*, II, 231.
[8] "McDowell's Advance to Bull Run," *Battles and Leaders*, I, 183.
[9] Cameron to S. P. Chase, July 21, 1861, Chase MSS, HSP.

F. Butler, John C. Frémont, and W. T. Sherman—commanded special attention from Cameron. Butler in command at Fortress Monroe had refused early in the conflict to give up fugitive slaves, classifying them as essentially contraband of war.[10] Following the passage of a "confiscation" act, Cameron advised Butler of his right to retain the slaves of disloyal masters but warned him against harboring or encouraging runaways of loyal masters.[11] At this point the Secretary was in complete agreement with Lincoln on the need of a cautious approach to the problem of runaways. The later case of Frémont, commander in Missouri, also involved the question of slavery. In late August, 1861, the impetuous commander, without consulting Lincoln, had emancipated the slaves of disloyal masters. Cameron congratulated Frémont on his initiative and prepared to have his office issue a formal endorsement; but to his mortification, Lincoln asked Frémont to modify his order in conformity with existing law. In early October, Cameron, on an "inspection" trip through the West, carried the order for Frémont's dismissal; but after consultation with the humiliated general he brought the President's dismissal order back to Washington undelivered.[12] Cameron visited Sherman at Louisville on his return route and was astonished to learn that 200,000 troops would be required for offensive operations in that theater of war. Sherman was furious to find his confidential report featured as an "insane request" by the nation's leading dailies. Cameron failed to offer any explanations to the "crazy" general.[13]

---

[10] Benjamin F. Butler, *Butler's Book* (Boston, 1892), 257-59.
[11] Cameron to Butler, Aug. 8, 1861, McPherson, *History of the Rebellion*, 245.
[12] Cameron to Lincoln, Oct. 12, 14, 1861, Lincoln MSS.
[13] William T. Sherman, *Personal Memoirs* (New York, 1891), I, 231-34, 242.

The greatest criticism directed against Cameron during his tenure of office grew out of his selection of irresponsible or corrupt agents empowered to grant lucrative war contracts. The most notorious of these agents was Alexander Cummings, formerly a Cameron lieutenant in Pennsylvania who at that time was editor of the New York *World*. Condemned government carbines which had been sold by the government for $2 each were bought back by Cummings at $15. Later the same carbines were sold by the government for $3.50 and then re-purchased at $12.50 by Simon Stevens, a law associate of Thaddeus Stevens, and resold to the government for $22.50.[14] A lighter side of the incriminating evidence showed purchases by Cummings of an enormous supply of linen trousers, 25 cases of Scotch and ale, and 280 pints of ale and porter. A total of $140,000 expended by Cameron's crony remained unaccounted for. At Huntingdon, Pennsylvania, contractors were allowed an average of $117 for the purchase of 1,000 cavalry horses. It is estimated that the government lost $50,000 on a deal which netted only 350 good horses.[15] For political reasons Cameron authorized the purchase of 600 mules in Kentucky at $125 each.[16] Similar tales from the record of questionable transactions could be recited *ad nauseam*.

Several months after Cameron relinquished charge of the War Department, the House of Representatives passed a resolution censuring the former Secretary for "investing Alexander Cummings with the control of large sums of public money, and authority to purchase military sup-

---

[14] *Congressional Globe,* 37 Cong., 2 Sess., 308.

[15] Meneely, *The War Department,* 1861, 264-65. The Altoona *Tribune,* Oct. 2, 1861, reported however that the agents' rejection of horses ran to 90 per cent and in no case was more than 25 per cent of a lot accepted.

[16] *Official Records,* Series I, Vol. IV, 277-78.

plies . . ." without sufficient guarantees."[17] On May 26,
Lincoln magnanimously accepted a share of the blame
heaped upon his fallen Secretary: "It is due to Mr. Cameron
to say that although he fully approved the proceedings, they
were not moved nor suggested by himself, and that not only
the President, but all the other heads of departments were at
least equally responsible with him for whatever error, wrong,
or fault was committed . . . ."[18] But no amount of the
President's whitewash, charged Administration enemies,
could remove the stigma from "Corruption Cameron." The
President, it is to be noted, was defending his own extralegal
methods which to his way of thinking were necessary to the
salvation of the Union; but the House censure did not relate
to the President's emergency actions. The House was actually
censuring Cameron for the manner in which he exercised his
authority. Moreover Lincoln's apologetical message did not
deny that Cameron was at fault; it merely placed the
responsibility upon many shoulders instead of one.

In early May, 1862, at a Harrisburg banquet, Cameron
defended his actions. He had found his Department "desti-
tute of the means of defense; without guns, and with little
prospect of purchasing the *material* of war." There was
hardly a man in the Department he could trust. The Adjutant
General and the Quartermaster General had disappeared
and the Commissary General was near death. Cameron
recalled that Edwin D. Morgan, governor of New York,
together with three other men, shared Cummings' responsibility.[19] Regarding some of the congressmen who voted to
censure him, Cameron said: "[They] were ever besieging my
doors, and often patiently waiting for hours to catch a part

---

[17] *Cong. Globe,* 37 Cong., 2 Sess., 1888.

[18] Basler, *Works,* V, 243.

[19] Harrisburg *Telegraph,* May 5, 1862.

of the drippings from the War Department."[20] In reviewing his past conduct the former Secretary saw no act of his which he would not repeat under the same circumstances.

Some of the facts concerning Cameron's retirement from the War Office need clarification, although A. K. McClure, Seward, Thurlow Weed, Gideon Welles, Nicolay, Hay, Montgomery Blair, Forney, S. P. Chase, and Senators Browning, Fessenden, Wade, and Henry Wilson contributed their views. This much is clear: Cameron had expressed his desire to be relieved of his duties[21] (if it could be accomplished without loss of face) and Lincoln was looking for the opportunity to rid himself of Cameron if it could be done in the manner which the Secretary desired.[22] The opportunity presented itself when Cassius M. Clay, minister to Russia, signified his desire to come home. On January 11, 1862, Lincoln notified Cameron of his intention to nominate him, in accordance with Cameron's expressed desire for a change, to the post of minister to Russia.[23] In a letter of acknowledgment antedated the same day Cameron reviewed his services in the War Department, acknowledged some mistakes, avowed he had done his best, and "gratefully" accepted the "new distinction"[24] Lincoln had bestowed upon him. Almost a year later Cameron wrote confidentially to his friend S. P. Chase: ". . . the president said he needed a 'scapegoat' and

---

[20] Cameron to Chase, May 2, 1862, Chase MSS, HSP.

[21] B. F. Wade to H. Wilson, June 18, 1870; Chase to Cameron, July 4, 1870; M. Blair to McClure (copy), Sept. 29, 1870; J. M. Cameron Papers, Crippen Notes.

[22] Browning, *Diary,* I, 595. Lincoln told Browning that ". . . he wanted some place to put Cameron to get him out of the War Department . . . ."

[23] Lincoln's short brusque note of January 11 is in the Library of Congress, but the milder antedated letter used for public consumption was in the J. M. Cameron Papers at Harrisburg.

[24] Cameron to Lincoln (copy), Jan. 11, 1862, Cameron MSS, LC.

I needed no second whisper to induce me to give place to another."[25]

No one factor was decisive in bringing about Cameron's retirement. His inefficient conduct of the War Department coupled with charges of corruption led to a weakening of public confidence. Two powerful pressure groups, one representing the banking interests of New York[26] and the other the border states, clamored for his removal, the latter group suffering great mortification from Cameron's report of December 1, 1861, in which he had recommended the arming of slaves. One clause of this report read: "If it shall be found that the men who have been held by the rebels as slaves are capable of bearing arms and performing efficient military services it is right, and may become the duty of the government to arm and equip them . . . ."[27] Lincoln could not allow his Secretary to act as policy maker and ordered Postmaster General Montgomery Blair to recall the report but the unaltered version appeared in many newspapers.

Edwin McMaster Stanton, Cameron's successor, was a Pennsylvanian only by adoption. This son of a Steubenville, Ohio, physician went to work early in life to support his widowed mother. He earned his way through three years of college, turned to the study of law, and was admitted to the Ohio bar in 1836. His Pennsylvania residence began in 1847 when he moved to Pittsburgh, but for five years preceding his entrance into the War Office he lived in Washington. His proven extraordinary legal talents had led him, with the aid

---

[25] Cameron to Chase, Dec. 24, 1862, Chase MSS, HSP.

[26] J. W. Butterworth to Fessenden, July 3, 1861 quoted in Carman and Luthin, *Lincoln and the Patronage,* 129 ; A. K. McClure quoted by Lancaster *Intelligencer,* July 26, 1865. McClure insisted that pressure from the banking interests was the vital factor.

[27] Original manuscript in Cameron MSS, LC. The altered report is printed in full in *Official Records,* Series III, Vol. I, 704-08.

of Jeremiah Black, into Buchanan's Cabinet for a short period of service. Supposedly Stanton detested "Black Republicans," and his comment on the "imbecility of the Lincoln Administration" was well publicized. He had assisted Cameron in the preparation of the Secretary of War's annual report—the "last straw" in the chain of events leading to Cameron's forced retirement. Lincoln had replaced Cameron with an obnoxious radical who gave the President as many headaches as his predecessor; but fortunately Stanton possessed no clientele to whom he owed political debts. The new Secretary's administration was marked by energetic measures and as much honesty as Stanton's prejudicial nature would allow.

Cameron's troubles did not end when he left the Cabinet in preparation for his new duties in Russia. In the executive session of the Senate on January 17, 1862, his confirmation to the new post was savagely assailed by Senator Trumbull, who labeled the mission a "whitewash to enable him to recover his seat in the Senate."[28] Wilson, Fessenden, and Sumner defended Cameron, the last-named senator expressing grief over Lincoln's modification of the rejected report.[29] His plans for sailing were changed because of lack of steamer accommodations and his arrest by Pierce Butler for "alleged false imprisonment" the preceding summer.[30] Then on April 30 came the censure by the national House of Representatives. Added to this disgraceful stigma were the bitter taunts of the jublilant Democratic press hailing the departure of the "Old Winnebago Chief" into the Siberian wastes. *Leslie's Weekly* featured the "Exiles of Siberia" and *Harper's Weekly* lampooned Cameron in a cartoon portraying him with a

---

[28] White, *Life of Trumbull,* 187.
[29] Charles Sumner, *Memoir,* IV, 63.
[30] Moore, *Rebellion Record,* IV, 89.

carpet bag en route to Russia. The public stock of Simon Cameron was never lower than in May, 1862.

There were some redeeming features, however, for the degraded Secretary. Neither A. G. Curtin nor A. K. McClure publicly gloated over Cameron's fall. The governor invited Cameron to attend a social function at his home and McClure expressed hope that he would be able to drop into his office for "an hour's chat" before departure.[31] The Cameron newspapers continued their support while at the same time withholding criticism of Lincoln. His numerous friendly correspondents pretended to believe that their chieftain still retained the President's confidence. His friends even encouraged him to arrange for David Wilmot to go to Russia while he slipped into the free-soiler's seat in the Senate; and Cameron actually circulated feelers with the proposal in mind.[32] As a fitting finale before his sailing, Cameron's friends staged a mammoth farewell dinner in his honor at Harrisburg on May 2. Mayor Kepner introduced 150 Cameronian devotees to their honored guest, "a Pennsylvanian who has never forgotten his native state . . . ." At the conclusion of a lengthy response Cameron admonished his fellow Pennsylvanians to support Lincoln's "wise and patriotic measures."[33]

Cameron's absence from the United States was of exactly six months' duration, half of which was spent going or coming. He had no intention of remaining in Russia when he left[34] and the day following his reception by the Czar, the

---

[31] Curtin to Cameron, April 10, 1862 ; McClure to Cameron, April 24, 1862, Cameron MSS, LC.

[32] Cameron to W. Harris, Feb. 6, 1862, Simon Gratz Autograph Collection, HSP ; Cameron to Chase Feb. 11, 1862, Chase MSS, HSP.

[33] Harrisburg *Telegraph*, May 3, 1862 ; "Banquet to the Honorable Simon Cameron," Cameron MSS, LC.

[34] Cameron to Harris, May 3, 1862, Gratz Collection, HSP.

minister wrote two important letters: the first to Lincoln thanking him for accepting his share of the House censure—"a good act bravely done";[35] the second to Secretary Seward requesting an immediate furlough. After some delay Seward granted the request on September 6.[36] Cameron received it in Marseilles on his way home. During his stay in Russia the minister sent only nine dispatches to the State Department, although he found ample time to carry on a voluminous correspondence with friends in the United States and to advise the President on distribution of the patronage.

Soon after his arrival home at Lochiel, Cameron was pleasantly surprised to learn that he was no longer considered a political outcast by important party men. His old supporters expressed complete faith in his ability to stage a comeback. He received correspondence from B. H. Brewster, Forney, Chase, and James G. Blaine, all extending their best wishes. The old Cameron lieutenants J. K. Moorhead, George V. Lawrence, Francis Jordan, Samuel Purviance, and J. P. Sanderson encouraged Cameron to remain in the United States where he could be of great service especially if he were to re-enter the Senate. Salmon P. Chase, taking note of Lincoln's impending Emancipation Proclamation, observed to Cameron that Lincoln and Seward had now arrived at the same position "we occupied a year ago."[37] Because the former Secretary of War in late 1861 had asked for the arming of slaves, the public was now looking upon his as a prophet without honor in his own country. "You will be surprised to learn," wrote Forney, "that you return home stronger than you have ever been in your life."[38]

---

[35] Cameron to Lincoln, June 26, 1862, Lincoln MSS.
[36] *Foreign Relations of United States,* 1861-1862, Part II, 454.
[37] Chase to Cameron, Nov. 16, 1862, Cameron MSS, DCC.
[38] Forney to Cameron, Nov. 2, 15, 1862, *ibid.*

The urging of Cameron's followers to have him re-enter the Senate was somewhat analogous to inciting a land animal to come out of the water. The Senate was Cameron's perfect medium—the one which he had mastered and in which he felt perfectly at home. During his despondent stay in Russia he had resolved to "reject in the future all ambitious schemes" which would "entangle" him with office. "For him his course was run."[39] The two main obstacles in his path to the Senate were the majority of one vote which the Democrats would possess in the joint legislative session of January, 1863, and the obvious wish of David Wilmot to succeed himself. But his followers could see little difficulty ahead for a strategist who had triumphed over the caucus nominee of his own party in 1845 and who had secured three Democratic votes in 1857 when he won election to the Senate as the minority party's nominee—a feat usually considered impossible. Truly the Wilmot case was a delicate one; Cameron had given Wilmot his word not to oppose the incumbent if he desired a renomination by his party, a wish Wilmot had already expressed.[40]

With the senatorial election less than two months away Cameron arrived at a quick decision to try for it as a surprise candidate, and to solicit administration aid. Nothing would contribute more to his complete rehabilitation than a return to the Senate in 1863. From Chase he had already elicited a promise to steer Wilmot into a judgeship or to assist in procuring him a mission abroad, but Wilmot remained adamant in his resolution to remain a candidate[41] although he did not see how he could procure his own election. Cameron

[39] Cameron to B. H. Brewster, n.d., Savidge, *Life of Brewster,* 97, 99.
[40] Cameron to Chase, Aug. 18, 1862, Chase MSS, HSP; Forney to Cameron, June 11, 1862, Cameron MSS, LC.
[41] Forney to Cameron, Dec. 9, 1862, *ibid.*

requested Stanton to procure a commission for the son of a Democratic legislator who had promised his vote.[42] Next he visited Lincoln[43] and presented the first lady with an exquisite watch he had purchased abroad.

Cameron's ability to defeat Wilmot for the Union Party caucus nomination depended upon proof of his power to garner enough Democratic votes to insure his election over the Democratic majority candidate. Theoretically a switch of one legislative vote from the Democratic to the Union ranks would insure Cameron's election; but the cunning politico was too well informed on behind-the-scenes manipulations to stake his chance of success on a single vote. Cameron's confidants suggested the names of several Democrats who could be induced to vote for him.[44] But one man on whom Cameron apparently relied to deliver a Democratic vote was Dr. T. Jefferson Boyer of Clearfield. Cameron requested J. L. Rightmeyer of the Northern Central Railroad (Cameron's road), to have Colonel John C. Myers of Philadelphia influence Boyer to vote for him. Myers was glad "to go to work for Simon—God Bless Him," and promised to see Boyer at Reading. On January 7, 1863, one week before the senatorial election, Cameron confided to Salmon P. Chase: "Mr. Wilmot is still a candidate under the delusion that he can succeed . . . . I could have been elected—and possibly might be yet, if he were out of the way—but while he is there, my democratic friends, naturally timid in these times, are afraid to risk themselves in the face of what they

---

[42] Cameron to Stanton, Nov. 24, 1862, Stanton MSS, LC.
[43] Lincoln to Cameron, Dec. 14, 1862 (telegraph), Cameron MSS, DCC.
[44] W. Wiley to Cameron, Dec. 7, 1862; E. O. Jackson to Cameron, Dec. 20, 1862; C. S. Minor to Cameron, Jan. 3, 1862; J. C. Meyers to Dear Larry [Rightmeyer], Nov. 24, 1862, Cameron MSS, DCC.

are told is a division in our ranks."[45] Early in January, Cameron had not made it clear to some of his trusted lieutenants whether or not he was a candidate.[46]

The Democrats were determined not to allow Cameron to rob them of the fruits of victory as he had done in the last year, 1857, that they were in position to elect a United States senator. Friend and foe alike agreed that Cameron would exercise no difficulty in commanding the necessary Democratic votes to elect him if the election could be kept free from coercion or fear of reprisals. For weeks Democratic spokesmen publicly declared that any Democrat who voted for Cameron would never leave the legislative hall alive. Arrangements were made to admit a large gang of murderous Philadelphia Democrats led by "experienced leaders in ruffianism" to insure the carrying out of the threat.[47] The Curtin administration adroitly refused to yield to Cameron's importune pleas for military supervision of the election because it could not be made a party "to such an atrocious violation of the fundamental principles of civil government."[48] Cameron's sole consolation was a House resolution requiring the sergeant-at-arms to hire additional help for the maintenance of order.[49]

Democratic prospects of victory in the contest increased the number of senatorial hopefuls. Henry D. Foster, Francis W. Hughes, James Campbell, Charles Buckalew, J. Glancey Jones and William Bigler headed the list of prospects. Jones was trying for the support of the Buchanan-Bigler faction, but this group no longer controlled the state organization and

[45] Cameron to Chase, Jan. 7, 1863, Chase MSS, HSP.
[46] S. A. Purviance to Cameron, Jan. 3, 1863, Cameron MSS, DCC.
[47] Philadelphia *Bulletin,* Jan. 12, 1863.
[48] McClure, *Notes,* 11, 36.
[49] *Legislative Record,* 1863, 24.

Bigler himself made no attempt to win the prize.[50] In the Democratic caucus, Buckalew and Campbell proved the strongest, the former receiving the nomination on the sixth ballot, 40 votes to his opponent's 19. Hughes retained most of his supporters to the end.[51]

The Union caucus encountered much more difficulty in arriving at a decision. A secret special committee, charged with the task of determining the relative chances for election of Wilmot and Cameron, learned that the former had no hope of eliciting any Democratic votes, but Cameron assured the committee of his ability to command the Democratic support needed to guarantee his election. On the eve of the Union caucus, Forney's *Press* falsely reported that Cameron was quietly enjoying himself at home possessed of no ambition to return to the Senate and of his hope to see Wilmot renominated.[52]

The Democratic-controlled House, ignoring M. B. Lowry's senatorial resolution to postpone the election in order to avoid the "danger of violence," prepared to convene in joint session with the Senate on January 13 for the purpose of electing a senator. The Republican members, who had gone into the caucus at eight o'clock on the morning of the election, arrived late for the joint session and intimated that Wilmot was their caucus nominee.

In his *Notes*, A. K. McClure has left his readers a graphic account of this dramatic electoral scene; and an imaginative muckraker of a later age wrote: "the aisles and galleries

---

[50] Jones to Bigler, Nov. 8, 1863, Bigler MSS, HSP; Bigler to Buchanan Nov. 29, 1862, quoted in Davis, *Pennsylvania Politics*, 271, f.n.

[51] Cameron to Chase, Jan. 7, 1863, Chase MSS, LC; Pittsburgh *Gazette*, Jan. 14, 1863.

[52] Philadelphia *Public Ledger*, Jan. 13, 1863; Erie *Observer*, Jan. 17, 1863.

were thronged with a band of determined Democrats . . . each with a revolver in his right coat pocket and his hand on his revolver ready for business."[53] Not until the clerk called the name of the first Republican elector did the audience know for certain that Cameron was the Union candidate. More significantly it meant that the Union nominee was expecting Democratic support. One Democratic member created some excitement when he announced his vote for Buckalew in the face of a large cash offer to vote for Cameron. All Republican senators voted for Cameron while all Democratic members voted for Buckalew. On the House list, Boyer who was number seven on the roster voted for Buckalew, but LaPorte, a Republican supporter of Wilmot, bolted and voted for William D. Kelley. This meant that Cameron would need two additional Democratic votes from the remaining list of House members but none were forthcoming, and Buckalew was elected, with 67 votes to Cameron's 65.[54]

Although the public agreed with the Pittsburgh *Gazette* that "an armed mob of bullies" had determined Buckalew's victory, Cameron placed the determining factors elsewhere. To Lincoln he wrote: "I would have been elected only for the treachery of Wilmot." To Chase he confided: ". . . my election was *certain* but Mr. LaPorte, the friend of Wilmot . . . voted for Judge Kelly [sic] and thereby alarmed the gentlemen of the democratic party whose names come after him."[55] But of his trusted lieutenant, Walborn of Philadelphia, he inquired: "Can you tell me why it was that our friend *Milward* [sic] was not in *the House* that day, as

---

[53] Blankenberg, "Forty Years in the Wilderness," *Arena,* XXXIII (January 1905), 8.

[54] *Legislative Record* 1863, 26-27; *Journal of the Senate* 1863, 50.

[55] Cameron to Lincoln, Jan. 13, 1863, Lincoln MSS; Cameron to Chase, Jan. 12, 1863, Chase MSS, HSP.

you said he would. From that came all the blunder."[56] On the day of the election this much is certain—Cameron was not expecting his winning vote to come from Boyer. According to A. K. McClure, Cameron had no chance of being elected, because four Republicans had pledged themselves to bolt the party nomination, if necessary, in order to insure his defeat.[57]

Before the election took place it was rumored that T. Jefferson Boyer, the Democratic representative from Clearfield, would vote for Cameron. The House Democratic majority, anxious to bring to light a story of bribery and political corruption upon their opponents, appointed a special committee to investigate charges of corruption in connection with the senatorial election. The committee held 43 sessions and examined 30 witnesses. Boyer, according to his own testimony, met Cameron and his agent William Brobst several times and finally accepted an offer of $20,000 to support Cameron. In the presence of Dr. Fuller, agent of the Republican caucus, he reaffirmed his pledge to vote for Cameron. However, testified Boyer, he had no intention of voting for Cameron, but was merely baiting him so no other Democratic member could be corrupted. Cameron's agents admitted the alleged contacts, contended that Boyer had first approached them, and denied the involvement of any money in the bargain. It was fully established that Cameron met Boyer on several occasions. ". . . unlawful means were employed," concluded the committee, "to secure the election of Simon Cameron to the Senate of the United States . . . ."[58]

---

[56] Cameron to Walborn, Jan. 20, 1863, Society Autograph Collection, HSP. William Millward was United States marshal for eastern district of Pennsylvania.

[57] *Notes,* II, 32.

[58] "Report" of the Committee on Frauds, Pamphlet Collection. No. 1963, PSL. The Myers-Rightmeyer correspondence of Nov. 24, 26, 1862, proves that Cameron took the initiative in contacting Boyer, Cameron MSS, DCC.

In the months ahead Simon Cameron experienced further setbacks and disappointments. Although outwardly indifferent to the outcome of the senatorial election, his defeat must have gone hard with him since he attributed it to members of his own party rather than to the Democracy. The Curtin faction along with his enemies in the minority party publicly rejoiced at Cameron's discomfiture and again announced that he had been destroyed. A few weeks later came official announcement of his resignation as minister to Russia. Lincoln, who was willing to allow Cassius M. Clay to return to his old post in Russia, requested Cameron to give him an answer on his wish to return to Russia—the decision being entirely Cameron's. In resigning, wrote Cameron, he was thinking not only of his family's health, but also of his desire to "associate with his countrymen," and to "assist the Government" to the best of his ability in overthrowing the rebellion.[59] But probably the bitterest pill Cameron had to swallow in 1863 was Andrew Curtin's gubernatorial candidacy. Cameron, realizing the probable disastrous effect of a Republican defeat in the state elections of 1863 upon the presidential election of 1864, reluctantly gave lip endorsement to Curtin.

Unquestionably one of Cameron's cleverest political accomplishments of his career was the manner in which he retrieved his position with the Lincoln Administration. One might have expected him to show bitterness toward Lincoln, but the latter's magnanimity in shouldering the blame for a portion of Cameron's poor conduct of the War Department moved the former Secretary to write from Russia: "At all events, I can assure you that I will never cease to be grateful."[60] But while he was supporting Lincoln openly, Cameron

[59] Cameron to Lincoln, Feb. 23, 1863, Lincoln MSS.
[60] Cameron to Lincoln, June 26, 1862, *ibid.*

was working secretly to bring his friend Benjamin F. Butler before the public eye, with the idea that the general could be made available in 1864 for the presidential nomination.[61] That Cameron was able to support Lincoln publicly and Butler privately, while at the same time keeping on the best of terms with Secretary Chase who had powerful patronage, speaks well for his political sagacity.[62] To better himself in the eyes of Lincoln, Cameron added Curtin to the list of potential candidates aspiring to take the President's place in the White House.[63]

By the end of 1863 Cameron was convinced that Lincoln could be re-elected and he determined to secure the prestige of initiating the movement for his renomination. His conclusions regarding Lincoln were based upon a private poll conducted throughout the state by his local lieutenants. When Cameron interviewed Lincoln on the subject, the President confided that he didn't like the idea of having both Chase and Benjamin F. Wade against him.[64] Then Cameron proceeded to relate how the Pennsylvania legislature had requested Jackson to run again after he had pledged himself to one term. Cameron's angling brought forth the desired request. "Could you get me a letter like that?" inquired Lincoln; and the shrewd Cameron replied: "Yes, I think I might." On January 5, 1864, all Union members of the Pennsylvania legislature subscribed to a request for Lincoln's

---

[61] Butler, *Private and Official Correspondence*, II, 590 ; Cameron to Butler, April 23, 1863 ; *ibid.*, III, 58.

[62] Carl Sandburg concurred with a newspaper article which stated that Cameron joined the Lincoln movement to "pay off old scores against Chase." *The War Years*, II, 644-45. The friendly correspondence between Cameron and Chase does not bear out this assertion.

[63] Cameron to Lincoln, Oct. 10, 1863, Lincoln MSS.

[64] "Simon Cameron at Home," *New York Times*, June 3, 1878. The article erroneously printed *Weed* instead of *Wade*. See New York *Tribune*, July 5, 1878.

renomination.[65] "I have kept my promise," wrote the exuberant politico to Lincoln. A week later the Union League of Philadelphia endorsed Lincoln's renomination and provided for a committee of 76 men to promote the same.[66] Forney's *Press* followed suit. "You are now fairly launched on your second voyage," Cameron assured Lincoln.[67]

In the meantime the Commonwealth was witnessing the inauguration of its war governor for a second term. On January 19, Harrisburg was treated with a colorful procession of cavalry, infantry, and artillery led by the state's leading soldier, Major General Winfield Hancock. An open barouche drawn by four white horses bore the governor and his legislative committee through the inclement weather to a platform in front of the capitol where the acting speaker of the Senate administered the oath of office.[68] Curtin's annual message devoted much space to the subject of the currency, greenbacks, and the new banking system. The governor requested proper care for the orphans and scored the legislative body for its pernicious practice of passing hundreds of bills during the last few days of its session. Of the civil conflict he said: "Whatever blood and treasure may still be necessary—whatever sacrifices may be necessary, there will remain the inexorable determination of our people to fight this thing out to the end—to preserve and perpetuate this union."[69]

The lower house had organized easily with the placing of H. C. Johnson, the Cameron candidate, in the speaker's

[65] "Pennsylvania Legislative Memorial for Lincoln's Renomination," Pittsburgh *Gazette,* January 18, 1864. One Union member, Senator Harry White, was in Confederate prison.

[66] Philadelphia *Bulletin,* Jan. 12, 1864.

[67] Nicolay and Hay, *Lincoln,* IX, 53.

[68] Pittsburgh *Gazette,* Jan. 21, 1864; Philadelphia *Age,* Jan. 20, 1864.

[69] Erie *Observer,* Jan. 16, 1864; Altoona *Tribune,* Jan. 13, 1864.

chair, but the Senate failed to follow suit. The deadlock in the state Senate was occasioned by the absence of Harry White of Indiana presently in Libby prison at Richmond. The Democratic opposition regarded White no longer a bona fide member of the Senate and charged that the senator's father had failed to forward White's resignation to the legislature. The Democracy offered a compromise on the basis of division of Senate offices with the Republicans taking the speakership, but the Unionists insisted upon all the offices on the basis of a victory at the polls. After two months of wrangling, Penney, the old speaker, relinquished his chair and was promptly re-elected by the deciding vote of Hiester Clymer, the Democratic candidate for the same office.[70]

Cameron's early move for Lincoln confounded A. K. McClure, Thaddeus Stevens, and Wayne MacVeagh, the latter two being supporters of Salmon P. Chase.[71] Cameron possessed a copy of the "Pomeroy Circular," a paper circulated for the purpose of promoting Chase for the Presidency, and he knew that Chase's powerful Treasury clientele was working in the Secretary's behalf in creating a reaction in Pennsylvania's legislature against the President's re-election. "But I can tell you," assured Cameron, ". . . the Devil and all his imps cannot take Pennsylvania from you."[72] In his *Notes*, McClure claimed that he was as sincerely in favor of Lincoln's renomination as Cameron; but on March 9, 1864, he wrote to Thaddeus Stevens: "I *fear* we cannot carry Lincoln . . . can we get Grant? Lincoln is very strong but could his personal strength compensate for the errors which will be charged to him? Finally—if Lincoln should be

---

[70] Philadelphia *Press*, Jan. 5, 1864; Erie *Observer*, Jan. 23, 1864.
[71] McClure, Notes, II, 133-34; MacVeagh to Chase, Jan. 23, 1864, Chase MSS, LC.
[72] Cameron to Lincoln, Feb. 13, 1864, Lincoln MSS.

deemed unavailable by intelligent and disinterested men, *could* his nomination be defeated?"[73]

After the meeting of the Union State Central Committee on April 6, which made plans for the state convention, Cameron reported another victory for the Lincoln forces. The Curtin-McClure faction failed to have a postponement of the Union National Convention recommended.[74] Through such action the anti-Lincoln wing would have more time to look for an "available" candidate. The Cameron forces continued their triumphant march at the Union State Convention of April 28. The convention endorsed Lincoln, instructed the four delegates at large (McClure was one) to "adhere to Abraham Lincoln first and last," and moved "against all attempts to postpone the day of nomination." No official mention was made of the Vice-Presidency but prevailing sentiment favored James Guthrie of Kentucky. In face of a petition signed by 80 members to have McClure made chairman of the State Central Committee, George V. Lawrence waited until the convention adjourned and then appointed Cameron.[75]

The Democratic State Convention proved to be a colorless affair. Former President Buchanan could perceive no issues on which his party could "fight a Presidential battle." Success for the Democracy in the coming election, believed the tiring Sage of Wheatland, could add only to further embarrassment for his party.[76] The state Democracy met at Philadelphia, March 24, under the direction of Charles J. Biddle,

[73] McClure to Stevens, March 9 [1864], McPherson MSS.

[74] Cameron to Lincoln, April 7, 1864, Lincoln MSS. A few days later Montgomery Blair wrote to Cameron that both Curtin and Forney wished to postpone the national convention.

[75] On Union State Convention see Pittsburgh *Gazette,* April 29, 1864 ; Bedford *Gazette,* May 6, 1864 ; Cameron to Lincoln, April 28, 1864, Lincoln MSS.

[76] Buchanan to Nahum Capen, Jan. 27, March 14, 1864, Moore (ed.), *Works,* XI, 355, 357-58.

scion of the city's proudest family. The convention found
only one type of issue involved in the coming contest—the
kind which would "effect the welfare and liberties of . . .
sister states . . . ." The Democracy requested the nomination of McClellan, the elimination of the corrupt Federal
administration, and the restoration of the national welfare.
Adjournment followed cheers for the Union and McClellan.[77]
Democratic state leadership was satisfied to follow in the
train of the national organization and to defer the question
of principles to the Chicago national convention. The Unionist Pittsburgh *Gazette* asked how the convention could
denounce Lincoln and conveniently forget to condemn the
"infernal rebellion."

Lincoln, hoping to bolster his ticket with a War Democrat
as a running mate, determined to approach General Benjamin F. Butler on the subject. Cameron, selected as liaison
agent, visited his friend at Fortress Monroe in late March,
enjoyed a pleasant talk with the General, and brought back
the surprising news that Butler was not interested in the
Vice-Presidency. Lincoln then selected another War Democrat, Andrew Johnson of Tennessee, to supplant Hannibal
Hamlin. Apparently Lincoln disclosed his plan to only two
men in Pennsylvania, Simon Cameron and A. K. McClure;
thus insuring the support of both Unionist factions at the
national convention.[78] Cameron evidently concealed from
Lincoln his own aspiration to be given second place on the
ticket, but his ambition was no secret to his top henchmen.[79]

---

[77] Erie *Observer*, April 2, 1864, Pittsburgh *Gazette*, March 28,
1864.

[78] Butler's *Book*, 632-33 ; Burr's interview with Cameron quoted in
McClure, *Men of War Times*, 442-42. Cameron to Lincoln, March
29, 1864, Lincoln MSS.

[79] John N. Purviance to Cameron, Feb. 12, 1864, Cameron MS,
DCC. Rather ironically, Lincoln's close friend, Ward H. Lamon,
went to the convention ostensibly as a "Cameron man."

At the Union National Convention at Baltimore the Lincoln strategists were triumphant. With one exception the entire Pennsylvania delegation, many of whom were beneficiaries of the Lincoln-Cameron patronage, went along with the idea of supporting Johnson for the Vice-Presidency. Thaddeus Stevens growled that he couldn't see the necessity of going into "damned rebel provinces" to procure Lincoln's running mate. Cameron cleverly concealed the plan to shelve Hamlin. First he threw the convention into pandemonium with a resolution to have both Lincoln and Hamlin nominated in one "package"—something he knew the convention would not accept. After enjoying the spectacle which he had created, Cameron withdrew his motion and substituted one to nominate Lincoln by acclamation. This was changed to a vote by states and Lincoln received every vote except Missouri's. Although Thaddeus Stevens, who now knew what was coming, warned the convention that no seceded state could be represented in the electoral college, Johnson of Tennessee was accepted as a candidate for the Vice-Presidency and received 200 votes to Hamlin's 145 on the first ballot. Then in accordance with the Lincoln-Cameron-McClure plan, Cameron, who was chairman of his delegation, remained on his feet to inform the convention that the Pennsylvania delegation had directed him to give the state's 52 votes to Johnson. By the time the scramble to jump on the Johnson bandwagon was over, Hamlin retained but 9 votes.[80] Cameron had performed his work so skillfully that Hamlin never realized what had actually happened and placed the blame for his defeat on Massachusetts although

---

[80] On Union National Convention see Johnson, *Proceedings;* Tweedy *Proceedings;* McClure, *Notes,* II, 137-141; Pittsburgh *Gazette,* June 10, 1864.

he "didn't know why." The deluded Hamlin actually thanked Cameron for his "generous support."[81]

The national convention of the Democracy at Chicago carried out the expressed wishes of the Keystone Democrats —it did select General George B. McClellan for its presidential standard bearer and it issued a strong statement of principles. The Pennsylvania delegation included such notables as C. L. Ward, George W. Cass, Francis Hughes, W. V. McGrath, Asa Packer, and William Bigler, the last-named acting as temporary chairman of the convention. The optimistic delegation worked in a medium of Keystone club supporters, brass bands, fine weather, jubilant crowds, and much "bad whiskey."[82] On the third day of the convention R. Bruce Petrikin moved for nominations and Pennsylvania cast its 26 votes for McClellan, who received the full convention vote except for $28\frac{1}{2}$ for Thomas Seymour. "No man except McClellan," commented James Buchanan, "could have been nominated at Chicago. The convention was neither more nor less than a ratification meeting of the decree of the people."[83] For Vice-President the state cast a favorite-son vote for George W. Cass. On second trial George Pendleton was unanimously nominated. The convention declared the war a failure as a means of restoring the Union, protested the disregard shown constitutional rights, condemned the interference of military authorities in elections, and asked for efforts toward a cessation of hostilities on the basis of preservation of the Union.[84]

[81] Hamlin to Cameron, June 18, 1864, Cameron MSS. J. G. Nicolay refused to believe that Lincoln had masterminded Johnson's substitution for Hamlin. See correspondence on subject in McClure, *Men of War Times*, 425.

[82] Pittsburgh *Gazette.* August 31, 1864.

[83] Buchanan to J. B. Henry, Sept. 24, 1864 ; Moore (ed.), *Works*, XI, 371-72.

[84] *Official Proceedings* of the Democratic National Convention (Chicago, 1864).

Simon Cameron, chairman of the Union State Central Committee in 1864 and now the recognized "Lincoln man" of the state was entrusted with complete charge of his party's campaign. More than the election of a President was involved; all congressmen's seats were at stake as well as the seats of all state representatives and one-third of the state senators. State senatorial results in 1864 were significant to one who was already laying plans to seize the senatorship in January, 1867. Cameron called a special meeting of his committee on July 2, selected an executive subcommittee, laid general plans for the campaign, designated Philadelphia the state headquarters, and then disappeared into the wilds of Cameron County on a week's fishing trip with Montgomery Blair.[85] The state chairman's nonchalant attitude outwardly remained unchanged after the state's electorate voted on July 2 to allow an absentee soldiers' vote.[86] Admittedly McClellan was popular with the armed servicemen, but the Unionists believed that the majority would support Lincoln.

Actually many leaders of the Union Party questioned Lincoln's ability to defeat McClellan. Cameron confessed his doubts to national chairman Henry J. Raymond, who agreed and then rather ill-advisedly passed his misgivings on to Lincoln.[87] Under proddings from Lincoln, the state chairman exhibited renewed energy, collected assessments from the clientele, and solicited donations from prominent businessmen. William J. Bullock, fashioner of wooden legs, offered the heaviest contribution and Jay Cooke's enterprise

---

[85] Pittsburgh *Gazette,* July 3, 1864 ; Smith, *Blair Family,* II, 272.
[86] The 14 counties showing the highest percentage against the soldiers' vote all went Democratic in November. See "Record of Clymer and Geary," Pamphlet Collection, No. 676, PSL.
[87] Raymond to Cameron, Aug. 19, 1864, Cameron MSS, LC ; Raymond to Lincoln, Aug. 22, 1864, Lincoln MSS.

contributed $1,000.[88] Luzerne County and quite likely other doubtful counties received special aid. Acknowledgments contained in the Cameron collections indicate that Cameron sent $100 to each county only a few weeks before the presidential election. In an irritable strain he wrote to Stanton: "We can carry Pennsylvania and if you will give us half the help Col. Curtin got last year from the Govt. *we will win* it."[89] The Union League was again called into the service and the state's political heirarchy functioned down to the grass roots with a responsible captain in charge of each county. On September 6, Cameron reported favorable on the situation.

The militant Philadelphia *Age* accepted the brunt of expounding the Democracy's case. It "repelled the charge of treason levelled at all critics of the [Lincoln] administration," and denounced Lincoln's suspension of the writ of *habeas corpus*. To the *Age,* the October contest was no ordinary one: "It is the initial struggle in Pennsylvania for human freedom throughout the world [against] the fruits of Mr. Lincoln's wicked policy." Reunion should be the only condition of peace.[90] An ardent Democratic sheet, the Lancaster *Intelligencer,* assisted with such severe attacks against Cameron that it looked as if he were the presidential candidate in place of Lincoln.[91]

Very late on the night of the October state elections in Pennsylvania Lincoln wired anxiously to Cameron: "How does it stand?" The answer to this question came slowly and painfully as the returns filtered in. As late as October 20, nine days after the balloting, the Republican Pittsburgh

---

[88] W. G. Moorhead to Cameron, July 22, 1864, Cameron MSS, LC; Cameron to Nicolay, Aug. 25, 1865, Nicolay MSS, LC.
[89] Cameron to Stanton, Sept. 20, 1864, Stanton MSS, LC.
[90] Philadelphia *Age,* Oct. 8, 1864.
[91] Aug. 4, 1864.

Gazette reported a state majority of only 626 for the Unionists with two congressional seats still in doubt. When the fog cleared it was revealed that the Unionists had gained three seats in the Senate and thirteen in the House, or a majority of 35 votes on joint ballot. The Unionist strength of the Commonwealth in the new Congress would double that of the Democracy, but a state majority of only 15,000 votes was too close for comfort, and Lincoln requested Cameron to have McClure work closely with him during the remaining few weeks of the presidential contest.

The confidence and enthusiasm shown by the Democracy during the campaign was well founded. Repeated calls for more troops, continued Confederate forays, failure to win the expected victory in 1863, suppression of civil rights and the growing influence of the radicals at Washington together with the narrowness of the October returns, led the Democrats to believe that there was a good chance to elect McClellan. In August, Confederate raids had led to the burning of Chambersburg and a call by Curtin for 30,000 militiamen to stop the rebel advance.[92] The total call for troops in 1864 totaled 91,740, twice that of 1863.[93]

Governor Curtin, under the August mandate of the people permitting the absentee soldiers to vote, appointed a commission, eight of whom were Democrats to supervise the field elections. According to Cameron the governor's bipartisan methods "destroyed the usefulness of those who were well disposed" and backed with party funds he selected over one hundred men "to visit every part of the army in the field" thereby securing for the Unionists a "full vote."[94] The

[92] Pittsburgh *Gazette,* Aug. 4, 1864. Although McClure's press of the Chambersburg *Franklin Repository* was destroyed, the organ missed only three issues. See *Repository,* Aug. 24, 1864.
[93] Egle, *Illustrated History of the Commonwealth,* 270.
[94] Cameron to Lincoln, Nov. 1, 1864, Lincoln MSS.

governor, Cameron warned Lincoln, had appointed a state supervisor "whose heart was not with the administration." At the same time, Curtin, who had gone to Cuba for rest, was receiving congratulation from the Democratic press for his fairness.[95]

Political omens during the closing weeks of the campaign pointed to a Lincoln victory in November. Forney's powerful Philadelphia *Press* contributed its bit by consistently identifying the Democratic cause with that of the Confederacy and emphasizing the rebels' wish to see McClellan elected. The protectionist *North American* of the same city found all friends of the rebellion, all spies, and all advocates of a degrading peace associated with the Democratic Party.[96] A few days before the election Cameron privately expressed confidence to his friend General B. F. Butler. On November 8, 1864, the electorate of Pennsylvania gave Lincoln a majority of 20,000 votes over McClellan. His majority of only 5,700 on the home vote but over 14,000 on the soldiers' vote justified the strenuous effort made by the Unionists to distribute soldiers' ballots and grant furloughs.[97] It looked as if the Lincoln-Cameron coalition would have no worries within the Keystone state for the next two years.[98]

When one considers the fact that Cameron held no public office during the years, 1863 through 1866, it is indeed remarkable that he was able to maintain a very respectable patronage and to repair a political machine which paid off dividends in 1867. He remained on the best of terms with Chase and evidently had influence with Stanton, as the many

---

[95] Erie *Observer,* Nov. 3, 1864.
[96] Robinson, *Public Press,* 96, 152.
[97] Philadelphia *Age,* Aug. 5, Nov. 8, 1864.
[98] Tribune *Almanac,* 1864. The official vote for Lincoln, 296, 389 ; for McClellan, 276, 308. See Stanwood *History of the Presidency,* 307. McClellan carried 35 of the Commonwealth's 65 counties.

letters from grateful recipients of army commissions and sinecures testified. His relations with Lincoln after his retirement from the Cabinet were much better than is generally supposed. He recommended Isaac Hazlehurst, an old Philadelphia Know-Nothing, for the supreme bench—an appointment he felt would be most creditable to the President.[99] While in Russia, Cameron submitted five names to Chase for Collectorships in Pennsylvania.[100] Many letters could be cited indicating Cameron's ability to secure patronage; in fact, he had done so well after retirement from the War Office that Curtin complained to Lincoln: "It has so happened that since the commencement of your administration not one important appointment has been made on my recommendation." To McClure's way of thought Lincoln "had not met anything like reasonable expectations."[101]

After Lincoln's re-election, Cameron's influence over him was recognized by leading Pennsylvanians. George W. Childs asked Cameron to oppose Sherman for Secretary of the Treasury. Wayne MacVeagh, chairman of the State Central Committee in 1863, requested Cameron for help because "Mr. Lincoln listens to nobody else from Pennsylvania as he does to you."[102] Cameron's election to chairmanship of the Union Central Committee was attributed by the Democratic opposition to the President's influence exerted against Curtin.[103] So greatly was Cameron's power felt and feared that local contesting Union candidates sometimes left the choice of the nominees to him. Those who hoped to be advanced in favor wrote fawning letters protesting their

[99] Cameron to Lincoln, April 30, 1862, Lincoln MSS.

[100] Cameron to Chase, July 20, 1862, Chase MSS, HSP.

[101] Curtin to Lincoln, July 6, 1862 ; McClure to Lincoln, Sept. 11, 1863, Lincoln MSS, LC.

[102] MacVeagh to Cameron, Jan. 2, 1865 ; Cameron MSS, LC.

[103] Lancaster *Intelligencer,* Oct. 27, 1864.

complete loyalty. One Cameron man apologized for appearing at a Unionist dinner with A. K. McClure. United States Marshal William Millward, hearing of a rumored split between his boss and Forney, assured Cameron that he was opposed "to anybody that opposes you."[104] It is necessary for one to read the letters written to Cameron during the years, 1864 and 1865, in order to grasp fully the awe in which he was held—this at a time when outwardly he was powerless to dispense patronage and with the full power of the Curtin administration against him.

Two events of 1865, the death of Lincoln and the results of the Union State Convention, it was hoped by Cameron's enemies, would checkmate his growing strength. But Cameron, quite aware of the significance of the powerful Federal patronage, supported the new President, Andrew Johnson, through 1865 and was able to keep his important men in office against the strong McClure faction which was only lukewarm in its support of Johnson. Not until the summer of 1866 when the President began wielding the ax wildly in order to gain support for his plan of reconstruction did Cameron break openly with him. Soon thereafter Johnson's appointments were held in abeyance by the radical-controlled Senate. This state of political confusion over the matter of Federal patronage lasted until the end of the Johnson regime. At the Union State Convention of August 17, 1865, Cameron failed to impress his slate of state officers upon the Keystone's Unionists, but a year later he succeeded in capturing the state convention.

Simon Cameron, the senatorial aspirant, realized fully that popular conventions could not elect or defeat him. Prior to the passage of the Seventeenth Amendment, the election

---

[104] Millward to Cameron, July 17, 1865, Cameron MSS, LC.

of a United States senator, in accordance with the purpose of our Constitutional fathers, was hardly a Democratic process. Removal of the upper chamber from popular control made it comparatively easy for senatorial hopefuls to canvass every legislative elector of the General Assembly. True, candidates for legislative office usually bound themselves to support specific men or were instructed by local conventions but frequently these pledges were ignored or forgotten. Consequently contests for the senatorship often resolved themselves into a gigantic game—a play for political stakes which history recorded as possessing no rules. Intimidation, bribes, expectation of reward, personal prejudices and loyalties, all played their part in the nominating caucus of the majority party; but success in such a caucus did not always insure election—a fact already demonstrated by Simon Cameron.

The master strategist had laid his groundwork well, beginning with the state senatorial elections of 1864. Able lieutenants in the local districts were requiring Union candidates for legislative offices to make their positions known in advance, and financial assistance was made available for pledged legislative aspirants. For example by 1864, the Huntingdon County Union committee was reported already under control and in 1865 the state senatorial candidate from Cameron County had pledged his vote for January, 1867, to Cameron.[105] Similar reports came in from other counties. By August, 1865, Cameron's candidacy was common knowledge.[106]

In Pennsylvania the senatorial contest of 1867 was one of unequaled fury. It was a battle not between candidates of two opposing parties, but between the two Cameron and Curtin factions struggling for control of the victorious

---

[105] F. B. Hackett to Cameron, Aug. 8, 1865, *ibid.*
[106] Welles, *Diary,* II, 349.

Union-Republican Party's state organization. Chances of Democratic success were nil without a coalition with one of the disappointed Republican aspirants. David R. Porter's private fears expressed to James Buchanan were confirmed when the legislative elections of 1866 brought no change in Radical Republican control of the General Assembly, although it did reduce the Unionist majority on joint ballot from 43 to 35 votes.[107]

It was taken for granted among those in position to know that both Cameron and Curtin would be senatorial candidates in 1867, and that no other aspirant had much chance of success. Curtin faced the double problem of not only fighting the Cameron faction, but also retaining the radicals within his own following. Curtin was accused successively by Thomas Williams, Edwin Stanton, and Simon Cameron of having Democratic leanings;[108] and the virulence of Democratic press attacks upon Cameron, contrasted with the rather mild criticisms directed against the Curtin administration, gave some credence to these charges. The governor, realizing this sentiment, attempted desperately during the course of the gubernatorial contest of 1866 to retrieve his position with the radicals. His militant Brooklyn speech advocated the use of coercion if necessary to force Southern acceptance of the proposed radical program.[109] A "monstrous proposition," it was, stated the governor, to submit a proposed constitutional amendment to the former Confederate states.[110] Apparently Curtin was making a last-minute bid for support from the Thaddeus Stevens faction.[111]

---

[107] Porter to Buchanan, July 21, 1866, Buchanan MSS, HSP; Tribune *Almanac*, 1866, 1867.

[108] Burton A. Konkle, *Life and Speeches of Thomas Williams*, II, 454, 479.

[109] Harrisburg *Patriot and Union*, Nov. 13, 1866.

[110] *Papers of the Governors*, 1858–71, 750-51.

[111] Harrisburg *Patriot and Union*, Jan. 3, 1867.

The recent election of John White Geary, a Cameron man, to the governorship added to Curtin's list of obstacles. The case of James W. Fuller, a leading corporate lobbyist and friend of Curtin, illustrated the power the new governor threw behind the Cameron camp. Fuller was given to understand that if "he wished to maintain his old relations with the state authorities," he would have to desert Curtin.[112] When Geary made Benjamin Harrison Brewster his attorney general, the appointment was interpreted to mean that the new governor was under Cameron's control. Brewster, although admitting that his appointment may have strengthened the Cameron forces, insisted the matter was purely the governor's own doing.[113]

Curtin's strongest weapon was his popularity with the Republican press and the masses. The neutral protectionist Pottsville *Miners' Journal,* listing three-fourths of Schuykill's Republican electorate for Curtin, was certain Cameron could not be the people's choice, although that organ had no personal objection to him.[114] The *Journal* vouched for the validity of Alexander K. McClure's *Franklin Repository* list of 46 organs for Curtin, 12 for Cameron, and 5 for Stevens.[115] In western Pennsylvania, the Beaver *Argus* agreed that Curtin was the most popular man in the state.[116]

John W. Forney's entrance into the senatorial lists in the summer of 1866 is difficult to explain except on a basis of Forney's well-known flair for the spectacular. By the middle of December Forney had withdrawn and was urging the senatorship upon Stevens. After praising Curtin's annual

---

[112] McClure, *Old Time Notes,* II, 204.
[113] L. Kauffman to Stevens, January 4, 1867, Stevens MSS, LC.
[114] Pottsville *Miners' Journal,* Jan. 5, 1867.
[115] *Ibid.,* Dec. 29, 1866.
[116] The Beaver *Argus* at this time was not under the control of Matthew Quay, a Curtin lieutenant.

message the erratic Forney branded Simon Cameron the last man to send to the Senate, one whose election was certain to bring disgrace if not defeat upon the party.[117]

Stevens had formally announced his preferment for the senatorship in July. Next to Curtin, he was most popular with the masses but his candidacy was punctuated with a variety of "ifs." If he had been younger, if he had built up a state machine, if he were not considered indispensable in his present position, and if only his candidacy could be taken seriously, he would have made a formidable antagonist. Even among members of the state legislature, Stevens' followers had difficulty in convincing their colleagues that the sardonic czar of the national House of Representatives was not taking his own candidacy as a grim joke.[118] In late December, 1866, only one organ, his hometown Lancaster *Express* still considered him a bona fide candidate.

Other Unionist aspirants besides Cameron, Curtin, and Stevens were J. K. Moorhead, Thomas Williams, and Galusha A. Grow. The political veteran James Buchanan, from his haven at Bedford Springs, thought that among the list of Republican candidates—*"such candidates,"* there was very little choice, but Cameron's chance was the best.[119] A Democratic survey of the Republican field revealed "Curtin, the meanest of all, Cameron the wiley [sic] trickster, Grow the vain and unscrupulous, and 'Old Thad' who thirty years ago threw his conscience to the devil . . . . So far as we can judge Simon points up."[120] Cameron's own observations two months preceding the legislative elections of 1866 is a

---

[117] Philedalphia *Press,* June 25, Dec. 19, 1866 ; Jan. 1, 3, 1867.

[118] John J. Cochran to Stevens, Oct. 22, 23, 1866 ; E. Griest to Stevens, Oct. 23, 1866, Stevens MSS, LC.

[119] Buchanan to Mrs. Johnston, July 30, 1866, Moore (ed.), *Works,* XI, 422.

[120] Meadville *Crawford Democrat,* Jan. 6, 1867.

commentary on the efficiency of his political machine: "I don't see how the combination can defeat me, and yet I shall not be easy till its over . . . . Curtin will be the greatest competitor and may be elected . . . and yet if the way does not greatly change I shall whip them."[121]

Candidates for the Democratic nomination drew little attention even from the Democratic press. It was taken for granted that the Democracy stood no chance of electing its nominee. Senator Edgar Cowan's leadership of the Johnson Republicans in 1866 earned him no place with the Democracy; in fact, many Democrats looked upon him with suspicion and distrust. Nevertheless many Democratic organs including the influential Harrisburg *Patriot and Union* regarded him a leading senatorial prospect to replace himself. But the logical man for the honor was William Wallace of Clearfield, characterized as the ablest of the Democratic organizers of his day.[122] He had first attracted attention in the state senatorial contest of 1862, emerging the victor in a normally strong Republican district. While still in his thirties he secured top party recognition in the state with his election as chairman of the Democratic State Central Committee in 1866. Wallace considered a nomination at that time damaging to his prestige and he determined to shift the doubtful honor to Cowan. In the face of a "decided disposition" by the caucus to nominate a regular Democrat, Wallace was forced to direct personal appeals to his friends in order to defeat his own nomination.[123] Whether Cowan realized it or not, his senatorial nomination by the Democratic caucus occurred only because Wallace steadfastly refused it.

The battle between the Union candidates began in the

---

[121] Cameron to Charles Dana, Aug. 12, 1866, Cameron MSS, LC.
[122] McClure, *Notes*, II, 389.
[123] Wallace to Bigler, Jan. 11, 1867, Bigler MSS, HSP.

caucus to select candidates for the speakership of the state House. Because the Stevens men erroneously believed Curtin to be the strongest, J. Donald Cameron was able to take the first trick for his father by exacting a pledge from a majority of the Stevens men to support John P. Glass, his candidate. In desperation, Matthew Quay, the Curtin candidate, offered to support a Stevens man for the speakership and Stevens' lieutenants who had just arrived late on the scene wired to their chief that his delegation was already out of control.[124] One can hardly conceive of a more ludicrous political situation than that existing at noontide, December 31, 1866. There were the Curtin men offering to support Waddell, the candidate of Stevens whose delegation had bolted to the Cameron camp. After J. Donald Cameron paid a visit to Waddell that same afternoon he was no longer an aspirant for the speakership—"he felt bound by [the previous] action,"[125] a pledge which he had not personally taken. This was only one of the many notorious Cameron conferences which rarely failed to convince a party disciple of his error. Stevens' confused last-minute instructions to defeat Quay[126] merely placed his blessing upon a Cameronian *fait accompli*. On January 1, 1867, J. P. Glass was elected speaker of the House by a party vote of 61 to 37 over the Democratic nominee, A. D. Markley. Quay, on the advice of Curtin, had withdrawn his candidacy. The idea prevailed that nothing could stop Cameron.

On the other hand, Cameron was radiating confidence among his friends. Christmas Day greetings to Benjamin F. Butler included the announcement: "I expect and intend to

[124] R. W. Shenk to Stevens, Dec. 29, 1866; E. Reilly to Stevens, Dec. 31, 1866, Shenk and Billingfelt to Stevens, Dec. 31, 1866, Stevens MSS, LC.
[125] E. Reilly to Stevens, Dec. 31, 1866, *ibid*.
[126] Stevens to Sypher and Shenk, n.d., *ibid*.

win."[127] At the end of the first week of the new year, Cameron wrote a clear synopsis of the situation to Salmon P. Chase:

I am, I think, going to win. Indeed, I do not see how I can be defeated—but my opponents have worked themselves into the position of enemies. Forney and Stevens and Grow all believed the fight would be so violent and so evenly divided between Curtin and me, that one of them would get the prize—and each believed himself the fortunate expectant, but my strength was developed so early that they found Curtin was beaten—and now they are combining against me. I feel certain they will be disappointed again. They are all to be here, in person, and for the next 4 days I will be the best abused man in 'these parts.' I like a fight, and if I don't whip them they will have more luck than they merit.[128]

Cameron's use of the word "early" can have only one interpretation—some members ostensibly in the anti-Cameron group had secretly pledged themselves to support Cameron.

The first move to organize a coalition for the purpose of defeating Cameron in the caucus was made by a Curtin group which conferred with Stevens on the subject; but Curtin denied he had any plans for a coalition.[129] Stevens followed with an open letter. In the past, wailed the Commoner, bribery had controlled the actions of the legislature; indeed it had become proverbial for the largest purse to win, but fortunately the present legislature was "above suspicion."[130] Stevens did not explain why he possessed implicit faith in the current legislature after reviewing its past history; moreover his lieutenants had warned him Cameron gold was in circulation. Cried L. Kauffman: "Oh shame where is thy blush when men can be bought as so many oxen and

---

[127] Butler, *Correspondence*, V, 717.

[128] Cameron to Chase, Jan. 7, 1867, Chase MSS, HSP.

[129] Philadelphia *Press*, Jan. 5, 1867; Harrisburg *Patriot*, Jan. 8, 1867.

[130] *Ibid.*, Jan. 9, 1867.

asses?"[131] Although Stevens announced his intention of staying away from Harrisburg, he appeared in the capital a few days later in the company of J. K. Moorhead, the Pittsburgh senatorial hopeful, and had a long conference the results of which were not disclosed.[132]

On January 11, 1867, the same day the Union caucus nomination was to be made, the anti-Cameron coalition forces made their last desperate attempt to arrive at an understanding. The prelude began with a group of "portly Philadelphians" in the basement bar of the Brady House intermingling their drinks with curses directed at Cameron. Old Thad Stevens, hobbling down from his garret in the Jones House, made his way to John Wien Forney's rooms at the State Capitol Hotel. Mid-afternoon found such worthies as Galusha Grow, Forney, Stevens, Hartranft, General Fisher, Major Todd, Senator Billingfelt, and T. J. Bigham, Moorhead's lieutenant—thirty-two in all, gathered in Forney's suite. From the Lochiel House, J. Donald Cameron must have smiled at the covey of "ducklings" gathered under the wings of the great "dead duck," Forney. Cameron, agreed the leaders, would win the caucus nomination, and consequently his defeat could be attained only by bolting the Union Party ticket and seeking enough Democratic votes to insure the election of a coalition candidate. He had come to the meeting, growled Stevens, to avoid a great calamity, but because—as he understood it—Cameron could procure any number of votes he needed, he chose to remain a candidate lest a worse man secure the vote of his friends. Curtin reminded Stevens that the people had chosen enough pledged members to elect the former but

---

[131] Kauffman to Stevens, Jan. 4, 1867, Stevens MSS, LC. In Woodburn's *Stevens,* page 599, this is quoted as "men *were* bought."
[132] Philadelphia *Press,* Jan. 8, 1867.

it was now too late to block Cameron. Failing to agree on any one candidate, the group disbanded with all hope of stopping Cameron gone.[133]

The Lancaster *Intelligencer* gave its Democratic readers an amusing, embellished "account" of the Union caucus nomination and its aftermath. At 7:30 P.M., the great sachem George Bergner, acting for the Winnebago chief, Simon Cameron, marched "forty odd men . . . all wearing Indian moccasins . . . in Indian file" to the state House of Representatives.[134] There behind barred doors, the closing act of a long, intense, political drama quickly came to a close. Rejection of a motion to delay the caucus was followed by a ballot which netted Cameron 46 votes, exactly twice the number cast for Curtin. Stevens and Grow polled seven and five votes, respectively.[135] In accordance with a prearranged plan, Quay moved to make Cameron's nomination unanimous. Great excitement immediately prevailed among the Curtin men. A Philadelphian screamed: "Bring me a bell. I say bring me a bell. There is an auction going on here and I intend to cry it." For the high bid of a chew of tobacco or a kick the auctioneer sold the districts of the members who had disregarded their instructions.[136]

Cameron's election over Cowan on January 15, 1867, contributed only a mild anticlimax to the previous Union caucus contest. The Democrats accepted the Republican renegade Edgar Cowan as their party candidate, and the

---

[133] Lancaster *Intelligencer*, Jan. 16, 1867; Huntingdon *Globe*, Jan. 16, 1867; Harrisburg *Patriot*, Jan. 18, 19, 1867. The coalition, according to McClure, could have defeated "the power of a subsidized caucus," had not the same influence "demoralized the Democratic members." Harrisburg *Patriot*, Jan. 19, 1867, quoting McClure's *Repository*.

[134] Jan. 17, 1867.

[135] Harrisburg *Patriot*, Jan. 12, 18, 1867; Huntingdon *Globe*, Jan. 16, 1867.

[136] Lancaster *Intelligencer*, Jan. 16, 1867.

Union Republicans supported Cameron with a straight party vote. The first ballot gave Cameron 81 votes to Cowan's 47. Cameron's friends immediately gathered around him in the Lochiel Hotel dining room and heard these words: "I thank God that in spite of the slanders . . . my fellow citizens have always stood by my side . . . . This last struggle of my political life has ended in victory." And then as if to anticipate the cries of corruption on the morrow, Cameron concluded: "The names of those voting for Cameron were as pure and honorable as that of the ones voting for his rivals."[137] From Governor Geary, Cameron's "true friend," felicitations read: *"Victory—Congratulations.* May Heaven's choicest blessing rest upon the evening of your well-spent life."[138]

Surprisingly little comment on Cameron's election, with the exception of McClure's *Franklin Repository,* was found in the Republican press. The Philadelphia *Public Ledger* omitted any mention of it while the neutral *Evening Telegraph* preferred Cameron to Cowan in spite of his unfitness. The strong protectionist Pottsville *Miners' Journal* openly accused Cameron of purchasing his nomination. "Why Simon Cameron was chosen," fumed the chagrined McClure, "I need not repeat. The story is familiar to all." Curtin should have been named on the first ballot but a "just nomination had been bartered for a price."[139] Naturally the two strong Democratic organs, the Lancaster *Intelligencer* and the Harrisburg *Patriot,* strongly approved McClure's accusation of bribery.[140] But Gideon Welles thought Cameron

---

[137] Huntingdon *Journal and American,* Jan. 23, 1867.

[138] Geary to Cameron, Jan. 11, 1867, Cameron MSS, LC.

[139] *Franklin Repository* quoted in Harrisburg *Patriot,* Jan. 19, 1867.

[140] Lancaster *Intelligencer,* Jan. 16, 1867; Harrisburg *Patriot,* Jan. 19, 1867.

greatly preferable to his competitors because "No worse man than Stevens could have been elected" and Curtin was "limber, deceptive and unreliable."[141]

Actually Cameron's perfectly functioning organization had triumphed over Andrew G. Curtin's well-known state popularity—a fact which Curtin's friends, the public, and a large part of the press did not seem to realize. The vote at the caucus, 2 to 1 in Cameron's favor, revealed there had been little need for the use of Cameron's gold. McClure's claim that 21 pledged Curtin men had voted for Cameron seems extravagant. Cameron's confidence expressed privately long before some of these men were "instructed" can be explained only on the basis of his ability to count his votes. However, McClure actually identified only "three monuments to perfidy" to Curtin; and one of these, F. S. Stambaugh, was a Stevens man. Philadelphia, which McClure largely ignored as a factor, is the more likely spot to look for the answer to Curtin's defeat. Under the leadership of William B. Mann, a special Cameron hater, it had been a Curtin stronghold; but 10 of the city's 15 representatives in the Republican caucus supported Cameron.[142] Senator M. B. Lowry of Crawford, at the time a professed independent, justified his vote for Cameron on the ground that Curtin was "not sound politically, but was a Johnson man."[143]

The boast of Curtin's followers that the "scepter of power was in their hands and could not be wrenched from them"[144] proved empty indeed. Curtin, greatly grieved and humiliated, retired in silence to his home in Bellefonte, Centre County.

---

[141] *Diary,* III, 16.

[142] Philadelphia *Evening Telegraph,* Jan. 11, 1867. H. W. Watts informed Stevens of rumored defection among the Philadelphians, Jan. 7, 1867, Stevens MSS, LC.

[143] Meadville *Crawford Democrat,* June 15, 1867.

[144] Blaine, *Twenty Years,* II, 242.

The triumphant Cameron entered upon a reign of such strength that when he chose to relinquish it a decade later, his scepter passed easily into the hands of his political heirs, J. Donald Cameron and Matthew Quay.

VI

The First Fruits of Victory

THE COLLAPSE OF the Confederacy in 1865 ushered in a regretable era of American history. The commonest name, Reconstruction, is a political misnomer, but the many dissimilar terms applied to it by a host of competent scholars make it clear that no single theme can satisfactorily interpret the war's aftermath. Especially was it an opportune age for the military hero and business enterpreneur alike, when political and social thinking would find itself dominated by nationalistic and business ideologies.

Heading the political arena was Lincoln's successor, Andrew Johnson, alternately hailed as the arch-traitor of all time or as the coming messiah of constitutional government. Among the leading political leaders were Benjamin Wade, Simon Cameron, Roscoe Conkling, Charles Sumner, Thaddeus Stevens, Benjamin F. Butler, and Zachariah Chandler. The Pennsylvanians, Cameron and Stevens, came to occupy special niches in the post-bellum era. Cameron was generally regarded as the ablest and most astute politico of his age; whereas Old Thad caught the public eye in his role as congressional leader of the anti-Johnson Radicals and czar of the national House of Representatives. These were the men who controlled the nation's political destinies during the age of "Reconstruction."

Military victory had settled the immediate questions of secession and slavery but many other problems remained.

Northern political leaders, especially, had to adjust them-selves to a changing economic pattern involving the new demands of the industrialists, farmers, and laborers. At the war's end, the United States contained a large group of newly born capitalists, many of whom had fattened at the public trough and who were eager to use their sudden wealth on a scale scarcely dreamed of in the ante-bellum age. More-over many cared little what means should be used to achieve their ends. America's great natural resources, scarcely tapped, lay at their feet—a potential bonanza.

The Southern agrarian aristocracy of ante-bellum days had been crushed but a new agrarian power was rising—the great mass of small farmers throughout the nation. Post-bellum conditions combined to create economic dissatisfaction among these folk. The higher prices during the war had encouraged long-time credits and expansion. The farmer of 1866 found a mortgage on the one hand and a poor crop on the other. In 1866 and 1867 the price both of grain and of land fell, and credit became scarce. The debt-burdened farmer found himself in a position from which there appeared few avenues of escape. Added to this he suffered grievances from the railroad lines which were spreading westward. Within a few years the oppressed farmer was to turn to the Granger movement, through which he hoped to find solutions for his problems.

The laboring classes likewise had their complaints. Since 1860, prices had risen proportionately higher than wages. In October, 1866, in terms of currency, wheat was $11.55 per barrel, cotton $40\frac{3}{4}$ cents per pound, beef $15.50 per barrel, butter 37 cents a pound, and tea $97\frac{1}{2}$ cents a pound. In terms of gold these items represented various increases of 31 to 147 per cent over the mean price for the years 1859-

1862.[1] The movement for higher wages faced an uphill fight in a nation where labor had not yet been able to organize effectively and where human rights appeared to have no place in the post-bellum business man's philosophy of property rights.

All of these groups, the industrialists, farmers, and laborers, had a keen interest, though for different reasons, in the protective tariff. It was the avowed purpose of the industrialists of the age to maintain protection for American industry by continuing their alliance with the triumphant Republican Party and by engaging in a program of education with the assistance of the press and party platforms for the benefit of the laborers and farmers. The high Civil War tariffs were made an integral part of the economic and political order. Industry had received an impetus during the prolonged conflict which assisted in strengthening the party pledged to maintaining protection.

This vast postwar industrial empire of the Commonwealth which was destined to play an increasingly important role in the political destinies of the state was a new civilization of oil, coal, and iron with the nucleus of the last-named located within Allegheny County. To list great names in Pennsylvania iron is to list the public leaders of the era. Henry W. Oliver, John Fritz, and Andrew Carnegie were the new smiths of Vulcan. Daniel Morrell of the Cambria works was a worthy colleague of the high protectionist William D. "Pig Iron" Kelley. Although all omens pointed to Pennsylvania as a future titan of industry, at the war's end most of the state's citizens still lived a rural life.

The post-bellum era, reputedly, was one of ostentatious display, riotous living, corruption, and evildoing, but the

---

[1] Ellis P. Oberholtzer, *United States Since the Civil War* (New York, 1937), I, 190-91.

mass of the people still took seriously their moral and spiritual life. The Bible in its entirety was the word of God, and was, in most cases, to be interpreted literally. There was a strong movement on foot to promote temperance through the organization of lodges. Political leaders, not at all averse to taking a drink within their own congenial circles, often found it expedient to support such movements; in fact the community's political boss was likely to be president of the local temperance chapter. The state legislature, in recognition of the public pressure, passed a bill "for more strict supervision of places and persons concerned in the traffic of intoxicating liquors." Bars were required to close by midnight and no liquor was sold to an habitual drunkard, nor, upon request of a wife, to a luckless spouse.[2] The theater often presented the temperance theme. Possibly as a lesson for those revelers whose heads were just beginning to clear, the Pittsburgh Opera House in 1867 presented for its New Year's matinee, *Ten Nights in a Bar Room*. The next day as a chaser, it played *The Drunkard,* a "theme of great moral value."[3]

The gentry of the day were likely to seek recreation in building up fine stables with which to vie with those of their neighbors. There was no better method of impressing the public with one's station in life than by taking a Sunday-afternoon ride equipped with the most gorgeous rig and attire. If the gentleman of quality wished to vacation at a spa within the state he was likely to be found at the fashionable Bedford Springs Hotel, where as many as 700 guests in a season were accommodated. A glance at the hotel register might reveal a list of Pennsylvania's bitterest political enemies congregated under one roof. Further snooping on

[2] *Appleton's Annual Cyclopaedia, 1867,* 619.
[3] *Ibid.,* 621

the ground would bring to light a more astonishing fact—sworn political enemies chatting together pleasantly or enjoying Scotch over a friendly game. Here was Pennsylvania's political Truce of God. This did not mean that political activity was taboo at the haven—on the contrary, "stooges" and political lieutenants checked in frequently to report on their local political vanes and to procure assistance in working out problems. One suspects that as much political strategy was planned in this beautiful sylvan retreat as was ever accomplished in the more notorious centers of Philadelphia and Harrisburg.

The end of the war brought new meaning to common political terms and added new ones. In 1865, victory had been realized for the militant Unionist administration of Abraham Lincoln and now the Democratic Party found itself disgraced because of its past halfhearted efforts toward achieving a complete military victory. The Democratic press had constantly minimized Union victories and directed the severest invectives against the Lincoln Administration. Immediately after the outpouring of blood at Gettysburg the Harrisburg *Patriot and Union,* a leading organ of the Democracy, advised: "Let us hold out to the Southern people the olive branch asking from them no other condition than a return to the old order of things."[4] During the war a Copperhead usually signified a Democrat who was opposed to the war effort; now the Republican press generally stigmatized all Democrats as Copperheads; and consequently many former War Democrats were now to be found in the ranks of the Radical-Republicans.

Although the party leaders still relied upon James Buchanan and William Bigler for advice, active direction of the party had passed to United States Senator Charles

---

[4] July 6, 1863.

Buckalew and to William Wallace. In 1867 the party reluctantly received the renegade Senator Edgar Cowan when the Republicans read him out of their party because of his support of President Johnson's reconstruction policies. The elevation of the martyred Lincoln into national sainthood had placed a valuable weapon in the hands of the Democracy's enemies. Loyal citizens were constantly reminded that it was the "disloyal Democracy" that had heaped odium upon the late beloved President. By 1866 the Democratic leaders were placed in the awkward position of contributing support to a President whom they had lately labeled a traitor to their party. With the much-abused Buchanan in retirement, the Democracy was forced by circumstances to accept Andrew Johnson as a national leader.

At the end of the war, the Republican Party was known officially as the National Union Party; but more frequently its members went under the name of Radicals. This majority wing of the Republicans, bent on a vindictive policy toward the beaten South, rejoiced in the name and members felt flattered when addressed as such. For example, in Pennsylvania the radical wing of the Republicans included a progressive bloc endorsing Negro rights, increased subsidies for education, favorable labor legislation, and an expanded currency as opposed to a conservative wing which received aid and comfort from the new postwar corporations and railroad interests. The Republican Party which had originally come into being largely because of popular opposition to the spread of slavery in the Territories, had successfully appealed for support from both the industrialist and the laborer by calling for a strong protective tariff for American industry, and to the land-hungry Westerner with the passage of a homestead act. In 1864, the Republican-Unionists had triumphed largely because of the war issues. Now with conclusion of the conflict, a different approach was required to maintain party strength and unity. President Johnson's defection from the post war radical program of the party confronted it with an additional problem. Might not the renegade Executive draw with him the conservatives, who represented a considerable proportion of the Unionists?

Upon the assassination of Lincoln in April, 1865, all segments of Pennsylvania's Union Party led by Curtin, McClure, and Cameron joined with the press headed by Forney in pledging their support to the new President. Johnson's answer to a Cameron-led delegation must have satisfied the most fervent Radical of the lot. "Treason is a crime," the President pronounced in the sternest of tones, "and there are men who ought to suffer the penalty of their treason."[5] Again the Chief Executive was assured of hearty support from a state which had steadfastly sustained the national government in its efforts to crush the rebellion.[6] The irrepressible Forney went through his not unusual routine of journalistic gymnastics, requesting Johnson to approve prospective articles for his *Press* and *Chronicle,* changing an editorial proclaiming the demise of state governments through rebellion, and concluded with the reassuring statement that "you are to see that I am square upon your platform and shall continue to stand there until the bitter end."[7] McClure's *Franklin Repository* hoped the new administration would not depart from the accepted Lincoln policy because "in it was the nation's hope."[8]

The state Democracy on its part could not agree on the question of support for President Johnson. The Lancaster

---

[5] Blaine, *Twenty Years of Congress,* II, 12-13.
[6] Curtin to Johnson, April 25, 1865, Johnson MSS, LC.
[7] Forney to Johnson, April 20, May 1, 1865, *ibid.*
[8] Lancaster *Intelligencer,* April 26, 1865.

Intelligencer, announcing cooperation for the new President in every effort he might make toward promoting lasting peace and restoration of the Union, hoped Johnson would give "wide berth to radical fanatics."[9] But the distinguished Democratic leader William Bigler advised: "Not only for our party but for the country's sake no uncertain ground should be assumed at the [Democratic] state convention. It should be assumed that we are to oppose Mr. Johnson's administration simply because he was elected by the Republican Party."[10] Buchanan doubted whether Johnson could secure the confidence of the Democracy as long as he remained under the influence of the Blairs and Forney. "If President A. Johnson should fall into their hands," he wrote, "I shall not say what I apprehend though I agree with him on his plan of reconstruction."[11]

A visit by Charles Mason to Johnson in June, 1865, led him to believe that the President was strongly inclined to return to the Democratic fold. Johnson's pronounced views on the subject of states' rights led Mason to urge Jeremiah Black's influence upon the President. Thus within two months of Lincoln's death the Democracy had fair hopes of weaning Johnson from the Radical camp. One event had served to mar Mason's visit to the President—on his way out he met Cameron coming in. Mason concluded: "I do not augur well of such birds of ill omen but I trust he will do no . . . harm."[12]

When the Union state convention met on August 17, 1865, to select its slate of state offices, its temporary chairman,

[9] May 10, 1865.
[10] Bigler to I. D. Stites [?], May 14, 1865, Bigler MSS, HSP.
[11] Buchanan to Dr. Blake, July 25, 1865, Moore (ed.), *Works,* XI,, 395.
[12] Mason to Black, June 14, 1865, Black MSS, LC.

John Covode, flattered the President in glowing terms.[13] The convention responded with a resolution commending Johnson for his past record and expressing hope for his future conduct because Lincoln could best be honored by giving support to his successor. The President's unbending patriotism in the past, thought the convention, was a sure guarantee that in the future the authority of the government would be upheld and the rights and liberties of all citizens be secured. The last clause of another resolution, condemning the South for failing to accept the President's generosity, held that the laws governing seceded states belonged within the sphere of the lawmaking branch of government—a direct thrust at Johnson. Despite this discordant note from the Keystone state, the President's waning strength was sufficient to secure him an endorsement from the Union State Central Committee in November.

Thaddeus Stevens, Alexander K. McClure, and William D. Kelley were the first important state Republican leaders to break with the President. Stevens stepped into the lead with a double blast at the President. He had failed to find a single Northern leader who approved of Johnson's reconstruction policy—a course which would lead to the destruction of the party itself.[14] In response to an invitation from the President in late October of 1865, A. K. McClure and Governor Curtin spent an unpleasant hour with Johnson arguing over the President's reconstruction policy. Johnson, according to McClure's account, "exhibited impatience and petulance at every opposing suggestion" and expressed amazement at doubts his plan would fail of congressional recognition. Curtin's lieutenant recorded his parting of the ways with these words: "It would be foolish to disguise the

---

[13] Beaver *Argus,* August 23, 1865.
[14] Stevens to Johnson, July 6, 1865, Johnson MSS, LC.

fact that the president, both by word and deed, disclaims the position of a partisan Executive . . .; that he is not insensible to the flattering approval of his administration by the Democratic party [and that he] will adhere to the political fortunes of the Southern States without regard to political consequences."[15]

Cameron, with everything to lose and nothing to gain in the important matter of patronage, was biding his time. His job would be to woo the new President and go along with him as far as he dared. His correspondence with Johnson exhibited remarkable restraint and was not as demanding as some he had written to Lincoln. After the fall elections are carried, Cameron promised the President, "we will sustain your policy be it what it may."[16] Three weeks later his Harrisburg mouthpiece the *Telegraph* viciously attacked McClure for his break with Johnson.[17] The need for patronage was too great, reasoned Cameron, to squabble over an issue still in doubt.

Lincoln was not yet in his grave before the Union factions of Pennsylvania began angling for Johnson's patronage. Rumors spread like wildfire of contemplated changes thus leading to another chain reaction of inquiries by anxious aspirants and worried officeholders. Congressman J. K. Moorhead of Pittsburgh moved to protect his Allegheny fief[18] and in Philadelphia John Wien Forney made plans to dispense Johnson's patronage[19] in a city where the choicest plums were held by Cameron men. Governor Curtin joined

---

[15] McClure, *Recollections of Half a Century,* 88 ; Lancaster *Intelligencer,* November 15, 1865, quoting Chambersburg *Franklin Repository*.

[16] Cameron to Johnson, Sept. 20, 1865, Johnson MSS, LC.

[17] Harrisburg *Telegraph,* Nov. 10, 1865.

[18] James Park to Moorhead, April 18 [?], 1865, Johnson MSS, LC.

[19] Forney to Johnson, April 20, July 17, 1865, *ibid*.

in the Philadelphia patronage battle, insisting upon removal of C. A. Walborn, a leading Cameron lieutenant, from the postmastership. Curtin explained to Johnson that he was not asking for direct distribution of patronage in Pennsylvania, but was earnestly requesting that no one hostile to him be appointed.[20] To Curtin this meant of course all Cameron men. But Cameron was able to keep both Bergner at Harrisburg and Walborn at Philadelphia in office during 1865 in spite of strong state administration pressures, and it was not until September, 1866, that Cameron consoled Walborn upon the loss of his sinecure with the promise of a better one. McClure admitted Cameron's closeness to the President and his ability to dispense Federal patronage, but attributed Cameron's triumph to the political chaos of the period. The net result enabled Cameron to seize control of the Union state convention the following year. At the end of 1865, neither Cameron nor Curtin had broken with Johnson, both preferring to await the test of the President's strength in the newly assembled Thirty-ninth Congress.

The crucial year 1866 witnessed only one important political figure of the Unionist-Republican group from Pennsylvania still aligned on the side of the embattled President. Edgar Cowan chose to remain loyal to President Johnson and his policies. His senatorial election in 1861, it will be recalled, was possible only with Cameron's aid. Under the circumstances, it was believed Cowan would prove amenable to Cameron's leadership, but he preferred to choose his own course. Cowan by-passed the ordinary period of Senate apprenticeship, preferring to participate in the debates from the first. His peculiar voice, which ranged into two octaves when speaking, together with his great bulk, caused no little comment and attention. Blaine rated his

[20] Curtin to Johnson, June 22, 1865, *ibid.*

EDGAR COWAN: United States Senator, 1861-1867. *Courtesy of Historical Society of Pennsylvania.*

ability high,[21] Welles admitted his legislative ability along with his ignorance of political machinery,[22] while Thomas Hendricks characterized him as a dashing debater capable of maintaining himself against great odds.[23] His opposition to radical bills during the war impelled Benjamin Wade to dub him the watchdog of slavery. He opposed the Confiscation Act, the Legal Tender Act, and the National Banking Act, all on constitutional grounds. He touched even the heart of the self-righteous Charles Sumner with his unique humanitarian resolution to send quinine into the Confederacy. Cowan's answer to "Parson" William G. Brownlow's attack on President Johnson illustrates the deadliness of his rebuttals:

This is the first time in the history of the Senate, unquestionably, that such a dropping as this has fallen from so foul a bird into this chamber, and it is the first time . . . where members of this body would sit patiently by and not vindicate themselves from the charge of being accessories to such vituperation.[24]

Under Lincoln, Cowan had given evidence of how he would stand on the question of readmitting the seceded states when he inquired of the Vice-President, upon counting the electoral returns, whether there were any more returns to be counted [Louisiana and Tennessee], and if so "why they are not submitted to this body in joint convention, which alone is capable of determining whether they should be counted or not."[25] On the vote to form the select Committee on Reconstruction, December 12, 1865, Cowan indicated that he would follow Johnson rather than the mass of his party. Only two other Republicans joined with the small

---

[21] Blaine, *Twenty Years of Congress,* I, 321.
[22] Gideon Welles, *Diary of Gideon Welles,* II, 637.
[23] Boucher, "Edgar Cowan," *Americana,* XXVI, 249.
[24] *Cong. Globe,* 39 Cong., 1 Sess., 3957.
[25] Stanwood, *History of the Presidency,* I, 311.

Democratic band to oppose this measure. From this time onward Cowan supported the President. True, Johnson at times had difficulty in keeping him in line, but publicly Cowan never deviated from his thesis of defending the principles of constitutional government.

Legislative bodies, party conventions, and the press jointly carried out the Cowan purge. On March 3, 1866, the state legislature of Pennsylvania by a strict party vote carried a resolution requesting Cowan's resignation. Following suit five days later the Union state convention resolved that Cowan had "disappointed the hopes and forfeited the confidence" of those electing him and therefore that body was most earnestly requesting his resignation.[26] The Union press for the most part condemned Cowan for refusing to follow the party although the Philadelphia *Evening Telegraph*, taking exception to the rule, commended the senator for his honest and conscientious fight.[27]

Johnson and his little group of followers realized that the outcome of the fall congressional elections of 1866 would determine victory or defeat. To Cowan was given the task of leading the presidential forces in his own state. In retrospect the task looked like an impossible one. To the Johnson Republicans it did not appear so.

Johnson's first test of strength in Pennsylvania came at the Union state convention of March 7, 1866. Alexander K. McClure had been corresponding with Stevens as to the proper method of blocking any endorsement for the President, and in the absence of any approbation from Curtin, coupled with Cameron's lukewarm attitude toward Johnson, it must be assumed that McClure led the Radical forces in the convention. According to McClure, Cameron planned to

---

[26] Philadelphia *Press,* March 8, 1866.
[27] January 25, 1866.

have the convention endorse the Johnson Administration but the plan failed when the anti-Cameron forces threatened to split the convention and nominate an anti-Cameron candidate for governor. What followed was an ambiguous statement from the convention thanking the President for his past services and ending with an appeal for him to depend upon the loyal support of the masses who would uphold "all measures by which treason shall be stigmatized."[28]

As was to be expected, the resolution was interpreted by the friends and enemies of the President each in his own fashion. Although, as McClure pointed out, the resolution did not constitute an endorsement of the President's policies, to the casual reader it appeared to do so. When Cameron's Harrisburg *Telegraph* interpreted the resolution favorably for the administration, McClure's *Franklin Repository* and Forney's powerful *Press,* which was now taking the lead in its attacks upon the President, hastened to correct the misapprehension.

Governor Curtin who had been vacationing in Cuba for his health returned to deliver his annual message of 1866. In it he noted his former policy of not discussing national affairs, but promised that the principle expressed in the message of the President at the commencement of the session of Congress would receive his cordial support.[29] Following a visit to Johnson by Curtin shortly after adjournment of the Union State Convention, the air was rife with rumors of the governor's entry into the Johnson camp. While Forney's *Press* contended there was no danger of the governor's default, Curtin's home paper, the Bellefonte *Democratic Watchman,* declared that he had privately announced his sympathy for the President and had blamed

---

[28] Beaver *Argus,* March 14, 1866.
[29] *Papers of the Governors,* 1858-1871, 709-32.

Stevens and Summer for keeping the country in a state of excitement.[30] Later the *Watchman* accused Curtin of angling for a mission to Italy. If true, this accusation meant Curtin was hoping to use the position as the means for a graceful exit in case of his defeat for the senatorship the following January. At the opening of the Geary gubernatorial campaign at York in August, 1866, Curtin set all minds at rest regarding his position when he attacked Johnson and the proposed Philadelphia Convention.

The Pennsylvania Republican supporters of Johnson were now presented with a distressing dilemma. If sufficient candidates of the regular Union Party could not be secured favorable to the President's program it would be necessary to vote for the Democratic opposition in order to give him that support—a pill too bitter for most Republicans to swallow. The Johnson Republicans, observed the Bedford *Climber*, hardly able to support a Radical candidate for governor, would welcome a gubernatorial candidate of their own.[31] Perhaps the only satisfactory release from the dilemma was the organization of a state Johnson-Republican party with a full slate of candidates. Such were the hopes of Johnson's followers but unfortunately for them the movement never developed beyond the convention stage.

The Johnson movement was formally inaugurated in Philadelphia, May 19, at the Academy of Music. The enthusiastic delegates, after proper entertainment by the Liberty Cornet Band which "discoursed some very fine music," settled down to work. Very properly the newly formed national Union Johnson Club announced as its purpose the support of President Johnson and his Cabinet. One resolution of the twelve accepted stated that, according

[30] June 29, 1866.
[31] July 7, 1866.

to the Constitution, "the right to prescribe qualifications of electors is left to the states," and at present seven were entitled to be represented.[32] Addresses by the Republican Senators Cowan, Doolittle, and Norton were denounced by Forney's *Press,* which hailed the meeting as "an auspicious commencement of the attempt to break up the Union Party and to help the Copperheads into power."[33]

The highwater mark of the Johnson movement was achieved during the August days of the famous Philadelphia Union Convention. Montgomery Blair, wrote William E. Smith, originated the idea because he hoped to build up a new conservative party with himself at the head.[34] Henry J. Raymond, national chairman of the Union-Republican Party, did not wish to support a movement which had for its object the formation of a new national party, but the Blair-Doolittle group convinced Johnson of its necessity. On June 23, three days before the call appeared in the press, the final work was completed in the President's study with the assistance of Cowan and six others.[35] A later request by the committee urged every state and territory to send delegates to help devise a "plan of political action calculated to restore unity, fraternity, harmony, and enduring peace."[36] The erection of a huge wigwam reputed to seat 15,000 persons proved no pains were spared to make the gathering a spectacular one. The night before the convention opened Cowan was inspecting the mammoth pile to the accompaniment of saws and hammers.

---

[32] Philadelphia *Age,* May 21, 1866.

[33] Philadelphia *Press,* May 21, 1866.

[34] Smith, *Blair Family,* II, 366-67 ; Claude G. Bowers gave Johnson credit for originating the Convention, *Tragic Era,* 121.

[35] Welles, *Diary,* II, 538 ; Browning, *Diary,* II, 81.

[36] Smith, *Blair Family,* II, 367.

Prominent Republican leaders of Pennsylvania were conspicuous by their absence at the convention. Cowan was the only man of prominence present with the exception of former Governor William F. Johnston who had been ostracized by the Union-Republicans because of his leadership at the anti-Lincoln-Frémont convention of 1864. The Democracy sent a strong delegation including Porter, Bigler, and Packer, three ex-governors. These were reinforced by George Woodward, Jeremiah Black, and Cyrus Pershing. Vallandigham, the prominent Copperhead from neighboring Ohio, embarrassed the gathering and was excluded upon the protest of Hiester Clymer, Democratic candidate for governor. Other characters like the irrepressible Reverdy Johnson and the dashing General Custer added color to the motley gathering.

Cowan presented the resolutions adopted by the convention. The doctrines they contained were "simply those of the President's Reconstruction policy, the doctrine that the 'states' in our Federal system are indestructible and immaculate, and . . . always possessed of the rights of local self-government and of representation in the national Government."[37] The logic of the resolutions, commented John Burgess, led to such extremes that Johnson's cause was damaged rather than helped in the North. The only work of the convention that could be construed as bearing on the important congressional elections was a call from the Johnson National Committee for mass meetings in the counties to ratify the action of the convention. Unfortunately no action was taken to provide for Johnson state organizations throughout the several states with separate Johnson tickets. The convention adjourned on August 16, with cheers

---

[37] John W. Burgess, *Reconstruction and the Constitution*, 99.

for Cowan, the Union, the Constitution, and Johnson."[38]

The Radical organs led by Forney enjoyed a journalistic field day, vying with one another in heaping opprobrium upon the heterogeneous Johnson gathering. A sample of titles includes such gems as "Bread and Butter," "Copper-Johnson," and "Arm-in-arm." Some compared the convention to the collection of beasts in Noah's ark—"clean beasts, and of beasts not clean." Proceedings of the convention were embodied in editor Forney's classic headline: "They came, they met, they got wet." The *Press* pondered over the absence of James Buchanan, the Sage of Wheatland: "Was there none poor enough to do him reverence?"

In order to render void the influence of the Johnson convention, a call, allegedly from Southern "loyalists," went out for a Union North-South convention in the city of brotherly love. Governor Curtin suggested (humerously, perhaps), on the basis of Southern unionist support, that Stevens and his radical colleagues would assist in its promotion.[39] In addition to a pair of delegates from each congressional district, Curtin, Cameron, John W. Geary, and Forney were appointed delegates-at-large. There would be no place for the Cowan coterie at this loyalist convention; thanks to Stevens, they had been properly read out of the party.

When the delegates assembled in Philadelphia, September 3, there was a marked contrast to the reception tendered the Johnson men at their convention. The principal city functionaires only lately returned from their "vacations" were now back in the city smiling and bowing like the good hosts they were. The Radicalized Union League entertained

---

[38] On Johnson Convention see Philadelphia *Press*, Aug. 14-17, 1866; Harrisburg *Patriot and Union*, Aug. 17, 1866; Philadelphia *Evening Telegraph*, Aug. 14-16, 1866.

[39] Curtin to Stevens, August 23, 1866, Thaddeus Stevens MSS, LC.

royally the not-yet-baptized scalawags and carpetbaggers. Significantly, the lion did not see fit to lie down with the lamb in this quest for national brotherhood. After a mass meeting in Independence Square, the two groups met in separate conventions allegedly in order to allow the Southern delegates to act freely and to make their declarations appear more significant. Actually, Stevens, who was acting as generalissimo of the affair, separated the two groups because of his alarm over some arm-in-arm manifestations. "It does not become radicals like us," he wrote, "to particularly object—but it was certainly unfortunate at this time. The old prejudices, now revived, will lose us some votes. Why it was done I cannot see except as a foolish bravado."[40] No doubt Old Thad suffered further embarrassment when he heard how gubernatorial candidate Geary, Governor Curtin, and Simon Cameron, along with the fuzzy General Burnside, had been discovered as spectators at the Southern convention and escorted to the platform amid a perfect furor of enthusiasm.[41] During the five days the Southern convention was in session it zestfully waved the Bloody Shirt but in the end failed to endorse Negro suffrage. The Northern delegates, constituting in reality only a huge reception committee, gathered at the Union League Hall where Governor Curtin presided in his glory for the last time.

The battle of conventions continued in Pittsburgh and lesser cities of the Commonwealth to the end of the campaign, but all failed to produce a Johnson slate of state offices. In April it had been announced that a Johnson nominating convention would meet in Pittsburgh sometime in July, and a month later General Dick Coulter was rumored

---

[40] Stevens to William D. Kelley, Sept. 6, 1866, *ibid.*
[41] Philadelphia *Press*, Sept. 5, 1866.

to be the Johnson gubernatorial candidate. However, the movement never developed beyond the formation of a state central committee with J. R. Flannigan as chairman.[42] When the electorate of Pennsylvania went to the polls in October, 1866, it had no way of showing its preference for Andrew Johnson's policies except by voting for Democratic congressional candidates; and possibly a vote for Hiester Clymer, the Democracy's candidate for governor.

One of the few weapons that Johnson possessed in his fight with the radical-controlled Congress was that of Federal patronage. When, beginning in the spring of 1866, the President began using the ax profusely to gain supporters, a contest developed between Johnson's Republican supporters and his Democratic friends for "Bread and Butter," thereby creating one of the greatest impediments toward realization of the Johnson goal—unity of the two factions. When Democrats were granted patronage the President's small Republican following complained because they had not been properly rewarded for their loyalty; but on the other hand Democrats felt they should receive the major portion of the spoils because they constituted Johnson's chief pillar of congressional support. A majority of the many districts and postmaster appointments in Pennsylvania were channeled through Secretary Hugh McCulloch and Senator Cowan.[43] When Thaddeus Stevens attempted to secure a paltry $100 postmastership for a friend he was furious to discover an order from the President directing Cowan's approval for all appointments.[44]

With the summer's progress angry, frustrated Democrats, increasingly disturbed over Johnson's distribution of the

[42] Titusville *Morning Herald,* Sept. 27, 1866.
[43] Appointment lists, Johnson MSS, LC.
[44] Copy of "Speech" delivered at Bedford, Sept. 4, 1866, Stevens MSS, LC.

patronage, wrote letters of protest to William Bigler and Jeremiah Black praying for increased Democratic appointments.[45] William Wallace, chairman of the Democratic State Central Committee visited the President twice concerning the matter and gave an encouraging report to Bigler.[46] Before the election was over a number of Johnson's Republican clients saw the handwriting on the wall and resigned to save themselves from the forthcoming Radical guillotine. R. B. Carnahan, the President's man in Allegheny County, repudiated him with an announcement of his support for the Union-Republicans, while the former Governor Pollock, although a Lincoln appointee, resigned his position as Director of the Mint to avoid a charge of guilt by association.

The Administration's opposition used a variety of methods to checkmate it. The Radical controlled Senate used freely its constitutional weapon against Johnson's patronage. As opposition to the President mounted, the Senate rejected or failed to act on many Johnson appointments. A few members of the old Cameron clientele kept their jobs by passing themselves off as War Democrats. Colonel William B. Thomas, anticipating the provisions of the Tenure of Office Act upon his removal as Collector of the Port of Philadelphia, "resolved to test the question whether the President of United States can make such an appointment when no vacancy has 'happened' without the advice and consent of the Senate." He also questioned the power of the Chief Executive to renominate a person once rejected.[47]

President Andrew Johnson, realizing the unlikely possibility of victory through the media of mass meetings, conventions, and patronage resolved to carry his fight to the people.

[45] Bigler MSS, HSP; Black MSS, LC.
[46] Wallace to Bigler, Aug. 28, 1866, Bigler MSS, HSP.
[47] Philadelphia *Press*, Aug. 13, 1866.

When the President began his unfortunate swing around the circle at Philadelphia, August 28, the city fathers, with the exception of a small group of business men, were again on vacation, but he received a rousing welcome from the multitude over a two-mile march. General Meade, under orders from Stanton, received the President with military honors and escorted him through the city.[48] Peace, conciliation, one people, and one Union were the keynotes of Johnson's two addresses delivered in the city. From Philadelphia the Chief Executive passed on to New York and then westward as far as Chicago and St. Louis.

Mid-September found Johnson back in Pennsylvania on the concluding lap of a tragic tour. At Pittsburgh the mob's uproar was so great that Johnson was unable to speak; the populace would hear only Grant. The Democratic State Central Committee arranged to have David Porter meet the Chief Executive at Johnstown for the purpose of escorting him eastward to Harrisburg, but the tragedy of a collapsing platform, bringing death and injury to dozens, marred the Porter reception. In Altoona the party assembled at the Logan House, site of the famous War Governors' Conference of 1862. Of the group composed of Cowan, Welles, Custer, Johnson, Farragut, and Grant, the last two named received, as usual, the major portion of the popular huzzas. Fortunately the crowd behaved itself and made no attempt to heckle the Chief Executive who appeared in the guise of a tribune of the people bearing to Altoona a flag of thirty-six stars.[49] Although it was a different story at the next stop, Tyrone, where the President reddened to the cry of three cheers for Congress, the rousing welcome accorded the party at Harrisburg granted partial compensation for the recent dis-

---

[48] George G. Meade, *Life and Letters,* II, 288.
[49] Altoona *Tribune,* Sept. 22, 1866.

courtesies suffered. Porter, waxing eloquent over the Harrisburg reception, described it as "magnificent beyond anything that was ever witnessed" there.[50]

To cynical Thaddeus Stevens the swing took on the character of a traveling circus built around the antics of two clowns with a side show starring a tumbler, his monkey, and an organ. The tumbler was Montgomery Blair and the monkey was Senator Doolittle, who "looked so much like one." In his Lancaster speech, Stevens commented on Johnson, the elder "clown":

But coming round, they told you, or one of them did, that he had been everything but one. He had been a tailor. I think he did not say drunken tailor; no he had been a tailor (laughter); he had been a constable (laughter); he had been a city Alderman (renewed laughter); he had been in the legislature. God help that legislature! (Great merriment). He had been in Congress, and now he was President. He had been everything but one—he had never been a hangman, and he asked leave to hang Thad Stevens.[51]

Through 1865, it will be recalled, state Democratic leaders considered it dangerous to endorse Johnson's policies because he was theoretically still a Republican. By February, 1866, when it was clear that the Union Party and the Chief Executive were not of one fold, the Democratic State Central Committee released a post-mortem political announcement to the effect that the Democracy's electorate had already endorsed Johnson's policy. From the floor of the Democratic state convention of March, 1866, the President was proclaimed the modern Moses, a man raised by God to lead his people. It was further "revealed" via private sources that Johnson was a Democrat through all his public offices.[52]

---

[50] Porter to Buchanan, Sept. 16, 1866, Buchanan MSS, HSP.
[51] Titusville *Morning Herald,* Oct. 3, 1866.
[52] Lancaster *Intelligencer,* March 7, 1866.

Considering the amount of platform oratory devoted to an exposition of the President's unexcelled qualities and the character of his messianic mission, the resolution endorsing Johnson was lame indeed. The Democracy's convention found the President "entitled to respect and confidence."[53]

Hiester Clymer, the Democratic choice for gubernatorial honors, found himself in an embarrassing position. Not being able to foretell whether the Johnson forces would effect a coalition with the Democracy in the coming campaign, he straddled the situation with the announcement that he stood broadly upon the platform of Andrew Johnson. The Philadelphia *Evening Telegraph* countered with the printing of a devastating statement alleged to have been made by Clymer in 1863: "I know Sir, that Andrew Johnson has gone as far as the farthest and is ready to go still farther and uproot every principle upon which this great and good government of ours is founded."[54]

Behind the scenes, state Democratic leaders were working fast in order to determine the relationship between the two groups during the coming campaign. Fresh from a visit to Johnson, Buckalew brought back the news that the President expressed no hostility past or present toward Clymer.[55] The Democratic state chairman, William Wallace, highly suspicious of the Blairs and A. W. Randall, was determined to prevent a Johnson-Republican wedge in the Democratic organization. Although the Johnson movement must be encouraged in so far as it will affect the radicals, wrote Wallace, it must not in any way effect the present status of the party.[56] James Buchanan, voicing the same sentiments

---

[53] Harrisburg *Patriot and Union,* March 7, 1866.
[54] March 10, 1866.
[55] Wallace to Bigler, March 28, 1866, Bigler MSS, HSP.
[56] Wallace to Bigler, *ibid.*

upon approach of the Philadelphia convention, warned that
formation of a new party with new names and principles
would only make the Democratic cause helpless.[57] The party
fathers had spoken and no new party composed of Johnson-
Republicans and Democrats was formed. If the Johnson-
Republican group nominated a candidate pledged to Democratic principles, well and good; if not, the people could show
their devotion to the same principles by voting for Democratic candidates.

To show, however, evidence of solidarity existing between
the groups, Johnson-Clymer clubs were formed in local
communities. When such a club was organized, the local
radical press, usually hailing it as a Copper-Johnson club,
took pride in pointing out its usual elements—a few Democrats plus the Johnson Bread and Butter men. On the other
hand some local Democratic leaders protested against the
growing influence exerted by the Johnson men within their
rank; for example in Mercer County where a pseudo-
Democrat had himself chosen as a Democratic state
committeeman.[58]

There appears to be only a few instances where coalition
candidates were so designated. Samuel J. Reynolds, Stevens'
opponent for Congress, was listed in the Lancaster *Intelligencer* as the Democratic-Conservative candidate. In Bedford County, B. F. Meyer ran for the legislature on a Democratic and National-Union ticket. In Pittsburgh the county
Democracy accepted a slate nominated by the Allegheny
County National-Unionists. In Philadelphia the Johnson
men were not able to put any candidates in the field against
the radicals, William D. Kelley, Charles O'Neill, and

---

[57] Moore, *Works,* XI, 423.
[58] R. M. DeFrance to Bigler, July 21, Aug. 6, 1866, Bigler MSS,
HSP.

Leonard Myers. The apathy shown the Johnson movement in Philadelphia was attributed by Forney to the President's own speeches.[59]

The Johnson-Democratic forces were seriously handicapped by lack of funds.[60] In districts where the vote was close, victory usually went to the party possessing the largest campaign chest. Although Joseph R. Flannigan, Johnson's state chairman, performed the unpleasant duty of assessing Federal officeholders within the Commonwealth, such methods did not always bring about the desired results. Numerous accounts appeared in the press reciting the story of patriotic citizens resigning in protest against such measures, or sticking to their guns until removed. During the campaign Wallace asked William Bigler to impress upon the President the vital need for funds and additional patronage in the Philadelphia area. In addition Wallace dispatched a fund-raising committee to New York for the express purpose of contributing to the defeat of General Henry Cake, a successful coal operator who could afford to contribute to his own campaign coffers in the Tenth Congressional District. Wallace's cry of bankruptcy availed him little and the committee returned empty-handed.[61]

Two districts, the Twentieth and Twenty-first, commanded the most interest in the congressional race. In the former, General A. B. McCalmont, the Democratic candidate, was a special target of the Radicals because of his "sweet communion with unrepentant rebels" at the Copper-Johnson Philadelphia convention.[62] In the Twenty-first, which included Cowan's home county, Westmoreland, a victory for the

---

[59] Forney to Fessenden, Sept. 1, 1866, Forney MSS, LC.
[60] Wallace to the "President and Secretary," Sept. 15, 1866, Bigler MSS, HSP.
[61] Wallace to Bigler, Oct. 3, 1866, *ibid*.
[62] Titusville *Morning Herald*, Sept. 24, 1866.

radical John Covode would be interpreted as a personal triumph over Johnson's state lieutenant rather than over the Democratic congressional candidate Hugh H. Weir. Cowan, informed of a Radical chest of $13,000 for Covode, implored the President to appoint two suppliants to lucrative army posts in exchange for a campaign contribution of $4,000 from the successful petitioners. Although the President complied with Cowan's request, it likely had little influence on the outcome of the contest because wealthy John Covode could and did pay for the necessary votes, as a perusal of his personal papers reveals. Even Thomas Scott of the powerful Pennsylvania Railroad interests entered the lists to procure Covode's election.[63]

Near the end of the campaign, Democracy's leaders within the Commonwealth privately expressed confidence in victory. William F. Johnston saw hope of gaining five members in Congress with a good chance of breaking even in the state legislature.[64] William Bigler expected a gain of from two to five seats in Congress although he conceded that the Radicals had a good chance to win the gubernatorial contest.[65] Both state chairman Wallace and the President's man, Montgomery Blair, thought the prospects were good within the Keystone state.[66]

The Republicans progressively gained more confidence as the time approached for the elections. They began by claiming a 20,000 majority and fourteen congressmen but upped it to 25,000 and fifteen congressmen following the Philadelphia Johnson convention. After the President completed his sorry "Swing around the Circle" the radicals extrava-

[63] Painter to Covode, Oct. 4, 1866, Covode MSS, HSWP.
[64] Johnston to [?], Sept. 20, 1866, Bigler MSS, HSP.
[65] Bigler to Johnson, Oct. 1, 1866, Johnson MSS, LC.
[66] Wallace to Bigler, Oct. 5, 1866, Bigler MSS, HSP; Milton, *Age of Hate*, 375.

gantly claimed twenty seats in Congress including all from Philadelphia.

The results of the congressional elections of October 9 did not sustain the extravagant claims of the Radicals, but their predictions were closer to the truth than that of their opponents. In 1864, Pennsylvania had elected fifteen Republicans and nine Democrats to Congress. The elections of 1866 gave the Republicans eighteen seats and the Democrats six, representing a gain of three seats for the former in the new Congress. Victory for Henry Cake and John Covode aroused special rejoicing in the ranks of the Radical Republicans.

The Republicans polled 303,790 votes to 292,351 for the Democrats, a majority of 11,000.[67] John White Geary, the Republican gubernatorial aspirant, was elected by a majority of 17,000 over the Democratic candidate Clymer. The Democratic congressional candidates received about 2,250 more votes than Clymer, but the Geary vote topped the Union-Republican congressional candidates by 3,500 votes. The Radical candidates for Congress had received only 50.9 per cent of the total districts votes, so in spite of what appeared to be a Republican landslide a change of less than 2 per cent could have brought a Republican defeat. Johnson's policy, so it would seem from an analysis of the vote, was actually more popular in the state than was the Democratic candidate for governor. Democracy's leader in Philadelphia, Samuel J. Randall, remained firmly entrenched in his district although his party lost the other four by narrow margins. James G. Blaine and others attributed the surprising Democratic gains in Philadelphia to corruption at the polls.[68] The

---

[67] *Tribune Almanac,* 1867, 62.
[68] Blaine, *Twenty Years,* II, 405 ; McQuaide to Covode, Oct. 20, 1866, Covode MSS, HSWP,

state Republican majority of 21,000 in 1865 had been cut in half.

Although actually the Democratic defeat was not as bad as it appeared both William Bigler and Senator Cowan were deeply dejected. Johnson's only consolation was the existence of a beaten minority of 290,000 people willing to stand by him on constitutional rights. Cowan, who continued to advise Johnson until the end of his term, could find little solace in becoming a candidate for re-election to the United State Senate with a hostile majority against him in the state legislature. The President, genuinely grateful for Cowan's services, nominated him minister to Austria but the Senate did not deign to act on the appointment. Cowan retired to his home at Greensburg where he went about repairing his private affairs. He had wasted six or seven years of his life, he wrote, and quarreled with his party "to boot."[69]

The new Radical, Simon Cameron, with the senatorial prize again within his grasp, and the martyred Lincoln silent, belied his secret position as a Johnson agent at the 1864 Union nominating convention and now "revealed the fact" that he had warned the Baltimore convention against Johnson. At that time, so Cameron told his audience of veterans, he did not believe such a low white of the South was fit to become President, and if he were a lawyer in Congress, he'd be the first to impeach Johnson.[70]

The mandate of the people was clear, or so it seemed to the victorious Radical-Unionists. Congress must start anew to reconstruct the rebellious states. Shortly before the verdict at the polls, Vindex had asked: "Brothers have ye bled in vain . . . are all our sacrifices for naught?"[71] The people

---

[69] Cowan to S. R. Phillips, Nov. 28, 1867, Gratz Autograph Collection, HSP.
[70] "Address" of Simon Cameron, Nov. 7, 1866, Johnson MSS, LC.
[71] Titusville *Morning Herald,* Sept. 17, 1866.

had answered "*No*." The bloody shirt had won its first great victory in Pennsylvania but not its last.

VII

The Emergence of John White Geary

UPON TERMINATION OF the fratricidal conflict, Andrew G. Curtin was the most popular man in the state and could have had any elective office befitting his position. The Democratic press had commended him for his fairness and his fight to maintain civil liberties. The Harrisburg *Patriot* suggested Curtin for Stanton's place when it was rumored he would resign. But in many respects 1865 was an unhappy year for him. Following his disappointing interview with Lincoln's successor, Curtin suffered a recurrence of old symptoms accompanied with a partial loss of the use of his limbs. A major portion of the summer was spent in rest and treatment at Bedford Springs and in the fall he underwent surgery in New York. In the meantime he suffered the loss of his youngest child. After another period of illness at his home in Bellefonte he sailed for Cuba. There, in the warmth of the tropical sunshine, he showed much improvement and meditated on his past strenuous war duties.[1] It was therefore left to A. K. McClure, Curtin's lieutenant, to protect the faction's interests; this he performed willingly and efficiently.

The Union state convention met on August 17, 1865. At first the Cameron and Curtin factions agreed upon John A.

---

[1] Curtin to Slifer, May 31, June 9, Aug. 9, Dec. 21, 28, 1865, Slifer-Dill MSS; Chambersburg *Franklin Repository*, Aug. 9, 1865; Curtin to Meredith, Nov. 13, 1865, Meredith MSS; Beaver *Argus*, Nov. 29, 1865.

Hiestand for auditor general. But when Cameron attempted to "hog" the convention by having H. C. Johnson selected permanent chairman and perhaps himself made chairman of the state central committee, the forces of Curtin, Stevens, Major Todd, and John Cessna agreed secretly to allow Johnson to be elected chairman and then to humiliate Cameron. The plan was entirely successful. General John F. Hartranft, the coalition's surprise candidate, defeated Hiestand, 63 to 39, and Colonel Jacob Campbell of Johnstown was named for surveyor general. John Cessna received the chairmanship of the Union State Central Committee.[2] A Stevens-inspired resolution passed by the convention called for continued subjugation of the "Rebellious States" with the laws governing them provided by the "law-making power of the nation, to which it legitimately belongs."[3] The Republicans of Pennsylvania had taken an early lead in advancing a vindictive militant policy toward the prostrate South, and had "arraigned" the Democratic leaders before the people's bar for their "obstruction of efforts" to maintain the "life of the Republic."[4]

The Democracy, realizing along with the Unionists the electorate's preference for military heroes, likewise nominated army veterans for state office. Colonel W. W. H. Davis of Bucks was named for auditor general over Isaac Slenker; and Colonel John P. Linton of Cambria triumphed over James P. Barr, the Pittsburgh journalist, for surveyor general. The convention agreed with Johnson that the South

---

[2] Chambersburg *Franklin Repository*, Aug. 23, 1865; McClure *Notes*, II, 186-90. According to McClure, Hartranft was not considered a candidate for state office. Actually, he had angled for Cameron's support in late June. See Wood to Cameron, June 29, 1865, Cameron MSS, DCC.

[3] *Tribune Almanac*, 1866, 44.

[4] Bradford *Reporter*, Aug. 24, 1865.

had really never been out of the Union, and recorded its opposition to Negro suffrage; but not until late in the campaign did the Democratic State Central Committee "distinctly" affirmed its support of Johnson's reconstruction policy. It reiterated its opposition to Negro suffrage and equality, and asked the electorate whether it was willing to hazard the superiority of the white race.[5] The "Black Issue," injected late in the campaign, emerged, in the opinion of the leading organ of the Democracy in Philadelphia, as the main issue of the campaign.[6]

The feud which broke out between Cameron and William D. Kelley of Philadelphia easily stole the show from a dull off-year state political contest. C. A. Walborn, Cameron's postmaster at Philadelphia, had been rebuffed in 1864 when he sought Kelley's aid in having the House censure of Cameron expunged; thereupon he used his utmost efforts to defeat Kelley's renomination to Congress. In the summer of 1865 Kelley retaliated by eliciting a promise from President Johnson to dismiss Walborn, and he actually succeeded in having Millward, another Cameron man, dismissed from his sinecure. In an address at the Girard House on August 10, Cameron made pointed reference to Kelley's activities: he could recall with pleasure the days when members of Congress from Philadelphia were too proud to go job hunting. Kelley replied with the most scathing public denunciation given to Cameron since the People's state convention of 1860. The first time he ever heard of Cameron, recalled Kelley, was in connection with crime, and it was clear that Cameron "had never been false to his criminal instincts." His children, concluded Kelley, would be able to vindicate his good name merely by pointing to the fact that

[5] Harrisburg *Patriot,* Sept. 28, 1865.
[6] Philadelphia *Age,* Sept. 19, 1865.

"Cameron and his friends were ever hostile" to him.[7]

On October 12, two days after the state elections, the Democratic *Patriot and Union* reluctantly confessed: "We have met the enemy and we are theirs." Hartranft and Campbell had easily triumphed over their Democratic opponents for state offices by a 22,000 majority. The number of Unionist representatives doubled that of the Democracy and the new state Senate of 1866 would seat 21 Unionists to the Democrats' 12.[8] All omens pointed to a victorious year ahead when the state's electorate would select a successor to Governor Curtin who could not succeed himself.

In 1865 the press and political leaders began speculating on probable Union gubernatorial candidates. Before the nominating convention met, the names of Winthrop W. Ketcham, Francis Jordan, John Cessna, John White Geary, and James K. Moorhead received mention but only three were to receive serious consideration. Ketcham's unusual achievement of getting himself elected to the state Senate from a normally strong Democratic district, had attracted state-wide attention. Once characterized by Cameron as one of Lincoln's most reliable friends,[9] Ketcham of Luzerne decided to build his own political following after Cameron failed to back him for the most lucrative plum in the state, the Collectorship of the Port of Philadelphia.[10] A. K. McClure turned from his first choice, General Winfield Hancock, to Francis Jordan when Curtin urged tardy recognition of a once faithful follower who had deserted his camp in

---

[7] *Ibid.,* Aug. 16, 1865. See also Chambersburg *Franklin Repository,* Aug. 16, 23, 1865.

[8] The official returns were Hartranft, 238,400; Davis, 215,740; Campbell 237,967; Linton, 215,981. House elections; Unionists 67, Democrats 33. *Tribune Almanac* 1866, 54-55.

[9] Cameron to Lincoln, June 20, 1864, Lincoln MSS.

[10] W. W. Ketcham to Cameron, Jan. 13, 1865, Cameron MSS, DCC.

disgust after the new governor in 1861 failed to carry out his promises.[11] But a specter from Jordan's county of Bedford, John Cessna, rose to haunt his prospects. Cessna, upon failing to secure the Democratic gubernatorial nomination in 1863, deserted to the Union camp, tried desperately to secure McClure's support, and withdrew from the race too late to help Jordan.

John White Geary was a native of Westmoreland County. Family financial difficulties and the death of his father compelled him to leave Jefferson College before graduation. After engaging in teaching and various other occupations, he finished college, studying both law and engineering. His experience outside his state enabled him to gain the assistant superintendency of the Allegheny Portage Railroad Company. Following the outbreak of the Mexican War, he organized a company of volunteers, led them to Pittsburgh, and was consequently elected lieutenant colonel of an infantry regiment. By April, 1847, Geary and his men were at Veracruz ready to participate in the march on Mexico City. Geary recorded his charge on Chapultepec: "Your humble servant was [wound]ed smartly in the groin with a grape shot when leading his regiment within 100 yards of the *Work* I was disabled for a few minutes, and cheered my boys on . . .—amidst a perfect storm of iron hail." As a compliment to the gallantry of Geary and regiment he was given command of the Citadel.[12]

Not long after his return to Pennsylvania, Geary secured from President Polk the postmastership of San Francisco. The trip to California via the Panama route with his family

[11] McClure to Slifer, June 10, 1865, Slifer-Dill MSS; Lawrence to Cameron, May 4, 1865, Cameron MSS, DCC.

[12] Geary to Edward Geary, Sept. 21, 1847. Letters of John White Geary, Oregon Historical Society, on loan to Pennsylvania Historical and Museum Commission. Cited hereafter as the Geary MSS.

JOHN WHITE GEARY: Territorial Governor of Kansas, 1856-1857; Brevet Major General of Union Armies, 1865; Governor of Pennsylvania, 1867-1873. *Courtesy of Pennsylvania Historical and Museum Commission.*

was an arduous one. During his stay on the Isthmus, Geary organized lodge societies, printed an American newspaper, "hunted" chickens to keep from starving, and held his own in a brawl with a dozen thieving native guardsmen. In San Francisco, the city of magnificent opportunities, he amassed and lost a fortune. He became the first citizen of the city— first alcade and later its mayor. He was credited with getting the Free State clause inserted in California's constitution.[13] Geary obtained a leave of absence to return to Pennsylvania and remained there.

In July, 1856, Geary was appointed governor of turbulent Kansas. He worked actively to restrain the factions and brought a measure of order out of chaos. Obtaining no support from the proslavery Kansas legislature, hindered by the jurist Lecompte, overwhelmed by land squabbles, and failing to secure needed troops, Geary resigned, rather significantly, on the same day Buchanan came into office. Geary placed the brunt of his lack of support from the Democratic Administration upon Buchanan, whom he characterized as the "Old wretch who sits at the head of this nation." It was Buchanan's "settled determination," wrote Geary, to disgrace him if possible.[14]

Geary's entrance into the civil conflict of 1861 may be attributed mainly to his desire to sustain the Union. His war record was excellent. In the East he participated in the battles of Cedar Mountain, Chancellorsville, and Gettysburg. In the West, he won fame in the Chattanooga campaign, leading the famous charge up Lookout Mountain. His troops participated in Sherman's march to sea and were the first to enter Savannah. The citizens of Savannah commended him for his fair governorship of the city. After the death

---

[13] "Record of Clymer and Geary," Pamphlet No. 827, PSL.
[14] Geary to Edward Geary, Sept. 13, 1857, Geary MSS, PHMC,

of his son in battle, the war took on the character of a crusade to avenge his loss. When his troops burned the town of Ringgold, Georgia, Geary gloated: "It was a sweet revenge to sweep them like a hurricane to know I was avenging *Wauhatchie's bloody glen.*"[15]

General John White Geary's candidacy was first promoted by his powerful neighbor, Radical Congressman John Covode of Westmoreland. The two were in correspondence as early as April, 1865, when Geary was stationed at Raleigh, North Carolina. At that time Geary was thankful for the efforts Covode had exerted in his behalf and expressed his intention of seeing Covode soon in Washington.[16] Covode had some explaining to do when General C. P. Markle, whom Geary had approached, questioned the wisdom of supporting a "new man" from the ranks of the Democracy.

That Geary's antecedents were strongly Democratic there could be no doubt. Not long after he had resigned the governorship of "Bloody Kansas" in 1857, he had written: "I am a Democrat of the old school, have always been one, and hope always to be so." In 1860 Geary believed that the Union could be preserved only "upon a compromise . . . based upon non-intervention of the Congress and Popular Sovereignty in the Territories."[17] For public consumption it was "revealed" in March, 1866, that he had voted for Lincoln in 1864.[18] According to McClure, Geary, three months prior to the time of the Republican nominating convention of 1866, consented to having his name presented for

---

[15] Geary to Edward Geary, Feb. 24, 1864, *ibid.*
[16] J. W. Geary to Edward Geary, Sept. 13, 1857, *ibid.*
[17] Geary to Edward Geary, Nov. 10, 1860, *ibid.*
[18] Philadelphia *North American,* March 8, 1866. In November, 1864, Geary was in Georgia preparing his men for their march to the sea.

the Democratic gubernatorial nomination.[19] But long after Geary had accepted the Republican nomination, the Harrisburg *Patriot,* which had no partisan reason for favoring Geary, reported the letter in question as having been written on August 14, 1865, and that Geary had simply declared himself still a Democrat.[20] Geary, on his part, denied that he had ever considered accepting Democratic proffers.[21]

By mid-January General Geary felt that he was well on his way to the candidacy. His late talks with Covode he treasured as the "laws of the Medes and Persians which . . . altereth not," and now Covode must assist him in planning his *"Modus Operandi."* He urged Covode to have Generals Markle and Purviance work harder on his behalf.[22] Purviance's acceptance of Geary's candidacy was of unusual significance—it meant that Simon Cameron had determined to support Geary. At about the same time, Simon Cameron, speaking at a banquet, publicly announced his support of Geary.[23] In Philadelphia, Covode's friend, W. H. Painter was carrying the fight into Ketcham's stronghold through newspaper articles which would frighten the people out of choosing a civilian for governor.[24]

By February, Union Party factional lines were clear. Absence of strong protest from leading Union organs against acceptance of a "new man" indicated little support for Geary's leading opponents, W. W. Ketcham and J. K. Moorhead. Forney's *Press* and the Bradford *McKean Miner* finding in Geary's name "a synonym of strength," came out

---

[19] McClure, *Notes,* II, 193.

[20] Sept. 5, 1866.

[21] Philadelphia *Press,* Aug. 31, 1866.

[22] Geary to Covode, Jan. 18, Feb. 9, 1866, Covode MSS, HSWP.

[23] Bellefonte *Central Press,* Jan. 19, 1866 ; While governor of Kansas, Geary termed himself Cameron's friend.

[24] Painter to Covode, [Feb.] 8, 1866, Covode MSS, HSWP.

strongly for the Cameron candidate. The Curtin-McClure group, perceiving no hope for either Jordan or Cessna, was throwing its strength to Ketcham. From Lancaster came news that the county delegation, controlled by Thaddeus Stevens, was instructed for Geary. Thus with the support of Cameron, Forney, and Stevens, Geary had every reason to feel confident.

The press exhibited little interest in speculating over prospective Democratic candidates. Hiester Clymer, who had contested unsuccessfully against Woodward for the prize in 1863, was most frequently mentioned because of his recognized leadership of the Democratic forces in the state legislature. The two other men most frequently mentioned for the honor were George Cass of Pittsburg and Asa Packer of Mauch Chunk, both railroad magnates. William Wallace, chairman of the Democratic State Central Committee, was looked upon as the logical candidate for the Senate and was not mentioned for gubernatorial honors.

The Democracy held its state convention at Harrisburg on March 5. Long "opening" speeches by John Latta, S. K. Kerr, Hiester Clymer, General Cass, Richard Vaux, and others praised President Johnson's policies and asked for the nomination of a staunch supporter of constitutional rights. The convention's resolutions, reflecting the fight brewing in Congress, asked for restored Southern representation in Congress, the exclusive right of each state to determine voting qualifications, the denial of Negro suffrage, confidence in the President's policies, and an equalized bounty for soldiers and sailors.[25] The Democracy had accepted a *fait accompli,* the extinction of slavery; but it did not consider the Negro entitled to the franchise. The Republican Philadelphia *Press* thanked the Democracy for the candor of

---

[25] Harrisburg *Patriot,* March 6, 7, 1866.

its program and the *North American* thought it could detect a deviation from the usual Copperhead platforms.[26] Considering the multiplicity of candidates (nine names were presented), the convention encountered little difficulty in arriving at a choice. At the evening session, Hiester Clymer's 72 votes on the fourth ballot gave him the nomination. Cass, Vaux, and Packer received 34, 13, and 11 votes, respectively. Clymer, reported the disinterested Philadelphia *Telegraph,* owed his victory primarily to the indefatigable efforts of William Wallace.[27] To the *Telegraph,* the conservative platform was less conservative than its candidate and the Philadelphia *Press* doubted whether Clymer would be bound by his own platform.[28]

The Unionists convened at Harrisburg on March 7. Upon arrival at Harrisburg, the anti-Geary forces led by McClure, Marshall, and Mann, were shocked to find the situation already out of hand. Curtin's warning to McClure and Eli Slifer of a coming "packed" Cameron convention proved correct.[29] On the other hand, the Geary forces arrived confident of their strength. Cameron, with his usual thoroughness, had requested Samuel Purviance to make a survey of the delegates in late February. His report predicted a total of at least 74 votes for Geary or seven more than the required number.[30] The election of Covode as permanent chairman over Cessna presaged the outcome. But the fight was furious not only on the floor of the convention but also in the bars and hotels where Ketcham and Geary men engaged in personal combat. Geary was denounced loudly as a "white-

---

[26] March 7, 1866.
[27] March 7, 1866.
[28] Philadelphia *Telegraph,* March 6, 1866 ; Philadelphia *Press,* March 7, 1866.
[29] Curtin to Slifer, Dec. 28, 1865, Slifer-Dill MSS.
[30] Purviance to Covode, [Feb.] 24, 1866, Covode MSS, HSP.

washed Locofoco [and a] Reconstructed Democrat."[31] Within the convention walls Marshall and McClure thundered their protests to no avail against the selection of a new and untried man. Covode had successfully completed his task of assuring the delegates that Geary was "reliable on the great issue of the colored *man* and the tariff."[32]

A threatened party split at the convention was averted largely because it was likely to strengthen the Johnson movement. McClure rejected Matthew Quay's plan of "revolutionary action," and elicited from Geary the promise of "a straightforward Republican administration . . . free from the influence of faction." McClure had doubts of Geary's sincerity but promised to support him if nominated.[33] Geary's 81 votes nominated him on the first ballot and Ketcham received 30 votes, only two more than Purviance had conceded to him. J. K. Moorhead and Harry White received the remaining ballots. But Cameron could not persuade the convention to endorse Johnson's Administration. "Conservative Pennsylvania men were amazed at the Radical frenzy; [it was] almost a hand-picked Stevens rally."[34] Before the convention adjourned it was revealed that Geary, a newly baptized member of the Stevens brotherhood of Radicals, had heartily approved the Commoner's policies.

Various factors contributing to Geary's victory were the influence of Stevens, Covode, Cameron, Forney, and the Pennsylvania Railroad interests; the last-named, so it seemed to the Lancaster *Intelligencer,* contributing more than even "the money and the corrupt influence of Cameron."[35] The personnel of Geary's cabinet later reflected his indebtedness

[31] Lancaster *Intelligencer,* March 14, 1866.
[32] W. H. Painter to Covode, Feb. 8, 1866, Covode MSS, HSP.
[33] McClure, *Notes,* II, 196.
[34] George F. Milton, *The Age of Hate* (New York, 1930), 288.
[35] March 14, 1866.

to Cameron, and McClure agreed that Cameron named the Union Republican candidate for governor. Certainly, Geary satisfied the clamor of the press for a soldier candidate and in addition he could capitalize on the old abuses he had allegedly suffered from Buchanan.

The multiplicity of parliamentary problems arising from the introduction of seventeen resolutions on the floor of the convention, proved much too weighty for its inept chairman, John Covode, who lost entire control of the situation, much to the delight of the McClure coterie. The Democratic press likewise rejoiced at the spectacle created by the Radical "ignoramus" who had so skillfully "put them fellows through."[36] The lengthy platform dealing almost entirely with national affairs, called for protection of the "natural rights" of Negroes, the reorganization by Congress of the late insurrectionary states, and a protective tariff for "all branches of productive industry." The virtues of Stanton, Grant, Curtin, and Geary were commended; the latter for his high personal character, patriotism, valor, military skill, faithful attachment to the cause of human freedom and support of American protective principles.[37]

Geary was at once bombarded with a volley of questions which he was expected to answer publicly. A Pittsburgh group, disturbed over the backing given Geary by the Pennsylvania Railroad interests, wanted to know whether his election meant that *one* railroad corporation would be allowed a monopoly, and if he favored a general law to regulate railroad construction. As a friend of internal improvements, replied the candidate, he favored protection for railroad corporations should they continue to act their

---

[36] Bellefonte *Democratic Watchman,* March 16, 1866.

[37] Philadelphia *Press,* March 8, 15, 1866 ; Beaver *Argus,* March 14, 1866 ; Harrisburg *Patriot,* March 8, 1866.

part as public servants, under the law which they were bound to observe. A general regulatory law he favored, but it *must originate* with the legislature.[38] Geary had executed a remarkably graceful straddle on the railroad question. His views on Negro suffrage and Johnson's reconstruction policy, requested by the Philadelphia *Age*,[39] remained unanswered for four months. Geary was pledged to follow in the train of Simon Cameron, who as yet had not openly broken with Johnson, and Negro suffrage he sidetracked by eliminating it as a present issue.

The chief attacks directed by the Democracy against Geary were his doubtful Radical orthodoxy because of recent defection from Democratic ranks, his alleged Know-Nothing antecedents, and his support of Negro suffrage. His status as a Democratic "renegade" seemed to create little stir among the Republican voters. According to an unlikely story widely circulated by Democratic organs, General Geary, during the late war, had arrested a group of Catholic sisters possessing passes from General Scott.[40] These unfortunate sisters were first left unguarded among gangs of rough soldiers and then sent to Frederick. The Titusville *Morning Herald* branded the tale an infamous falsehood manufactured out of whole cloth and reminded the voters that the late Bishop Young of Erie had been a friend of Geary and a most ardent supporter. The charge that Geary wished to see Negro suffrage both within the Commonwealth and the reconstructed states probably had the most harmful effect.

Few state elections evoked such hearty cooperation among the Union factions or such an imposing display of oratorical

---

[38] Philadelphia *Telegraph*, April 10, 1866.
[39] March 31, 1866.
[40] Harrisburg *Patriot*, Sept. 21, 1866,

talent as the one to defeat Clymer and his helpmeet, the President. The Curtin camp contributed the governor himself along with A. K. McClure, Francis Jordan, Thomas Marshall, Wayne MacVeagh, William B. Mann, and John Cessna—all powerful orators. Cameron added his services aided by Louis B. Hall, John Scott, and General Geary. The independents of the hour, Galusha Grow, John W. Forney, and Stevens, completed the all-star team. The first great Republican rally of the campaign, held at York on August 9, called for an excursion train of twenty cars from Harrisburg. The many delegations were grouped together under their local banners, possessing one common slogan—"we vote as we fight."[41] The Reverend Mr. Slayman was just beginning the huge mass meeting with an address to the Throne of Grace when part of the stage collapsed and precipitated its occupants to the earth. After order was restored, the minister thanked God for his "signal favors to this people in the past."

Geary and Curtin were the principal speakers at the opening York rally, the latter setting the pattern for the campaign. The question of Negro suffrage, he insisted, could not be presented before the people of the Commonwealth, bcause constitutional limitations prevented another amendment before 1870. The governor, capitalizing on the recent civic disturbances in New Orleans, recommended an army large enough to compel "obedience" all over the land. The impending Johnson convention at Philadelphia he effectively brushed aside with the newly born "bloody shirt." Such a gathering of men whose hands are stained with the blood of innocent people, protested Curtin, should not meet within his own state of Pennsylvania. Geary, speaking in general terms, asked for universal justice and freedom. His bid for the Catholic vote was reflected in his wish to see an Irish minister

---

[41] *Ibid.,* Aug. 9, 1866.

in Washington and his sympathy for the oppressed peoples of Poland, Hungary, and Ireland. He ignored the two questions of the day—the Negro vote and reconstruction of the defeated South. In later appearances he aped Curtin's opening speech.

The Union State Central Committee planned a speaking itinerary covering the twenty leading towns of the state and ending at Mill Springs in Montgomery County on October 2. Seldom were Cameron and Curtin seen together, the pair appearing on the same platform only three times during the campaign. Mid-September witnessed the "big guns" of the party at Erie, all booming at the same time. Three stands at different points of the compass were erected for the accommodation of the state's leading figures. Cameron, suddenly promoting himself to the Radical vanguard, attributed the disturbances in the late rebellious states to the leniency of the North and advocated harsher measures. Geary, who had lately explained that the proposed civil rights amendment did not "necessarily" include Negro suffrage,[42] dwelt at length upon the constitutional aspects of civil rights and congressional representation, and labeled the three-fifths clause unfair because "all persons" in the South were not represented. Approximating Charles Summer's theory of "state suicide," Geary would grant the seceded states no rights because they had committed treason. The gubernatorial candidate's contention that the Democracy had abandoned its old truths appeared like an apology for his desertion from the party. The portion of his address devoted to an attack on President Johnson revealed him as a man of remarkable clairvoyant qualities: "I knew he was never true from the first time when he was nominated. I was in Tennessee. I knew him to be insincere and threw up

---

[42] Philadelphia *Press*, Aug. 31, 1866.

my hands in despair."[43] Geary, unlike Johnson, had determined not to "prove a traitor" to the Union.[44]

Near the end of the canvass the Unionist-Republicans
separated into groups. At Warren, Cameron predicted the
outbreak of a second rebellion if the Union Party failed to
carry the congressional elections.[45] John Forney seized the
opportunity to berate one of the state's top Democratic
leaders, William Bigler, while operating in his territory.
Cessna, presently outside the Cameron pale, canvassed the
strong McClure strongholds around Chambersburg and
Gettysburg. At Bedford, Thaddeus Stevens, using the major
portion of his time to direct a devastating diatribe against
Edgar Cowan, commented only briefly upon Geary's superb
qualities. "A purer patriot," solemnly affirmed the Commoner, "never breathed the air . . . He risked all to save
the country."[46] In company with the notorious Radical Benjamin F. Butler, Geary attended the opening of the Dauphin
County Soldiers Monument Fair, and then the pair appeared
in Pittsburgh at the Soldiers and Sailors Convention on
September 25 where Butler was the main show. The candidate's last speech of the campaign, delivered at Harrisburg,
denounced President Johnson in the bitterest terms. "No
tyrant in any age—not even that of Nero . . . ever
descended so low in his efforts to debauch or reached so
high in his efforts to destroy as Andrew Johnson."[47]

In 1866 the attitude of the Radical Union Party in Pennsylvania in no way differed from its chief Radical representative in Congress, Thaddeus Stevens. The Keystone

---

[43] *Ibid.,* Sept. 13, 1866.
[44] Harrisburg *Patriot,* Sept. 1, 1866.
[45] Philadelphia *Press,* Sept. 15, 1866.
[46] "The Pending Canvass," Stevens MSS, LC.
[47] Philadelphia *Press,* quoted in Lancaster *Intelligencer,* Oct. 17,
1866.

state's leaders were not asking for a rapid healing of the wounds engendered through civil strife nor an immediate restoration of the Union. A militant coercive program based upon the obsolete *lex talionis,* it was hoped, would govern the victorious North's relations with the beaten South. The Union-Republican Party had conducted an intensive campaign of two months; and the willingness of all factions to work together for party victory proved how seriously its leaders viewed the situation. In the eyes of the Unionist chieftains, a victory for Hiester Clymer, who had endorsed the President's policies, was a victory for the still non-recanting, rebellious South, and could conceivably lead to a loss of all the gains achieved through the sacrifice of Northern manhood and substance.

The Democracy's gubernatorial candidate was the beau ideal of post-bellum society. Brilliant, handsome, courtly, and possessed of a luxuriant handlebar mustache and goatee, Clymer, the perfect gentleman, radiated personality. Hiester Clymer was born in 1827, near Morgantown in Berks, the county of the solid Pennsylvania German. His Christian name reflected his connection with one of the county's foremost families, the Hiesters. Clymer completed his preliminary education at Easton and then studied law at Princeton, graduating in 1847. In law school Clymer had for his roommate the later notorious Secretary of War, W. W. Belknap. In the fading hours of the Grant Administration, it was to be Congressman Clymer's painful duty to move the impeachment of his old college chum for malfeasance in office.

On admission to the bar in 1849, Clymer practiced law in Berks for two years, then moved to Schuylkill where he obtained top recognition in his profession. In 1856 he returned to Berks, a Democratic stronghold. Clymer moved into the ranks of the Democracy when his party, the Whig, expired, and he attended his new party's conventions at both Charleston and Baltimore. The same year he was elected to the state Senate, where at the end of two terms of service he was undisputed leader of the little group of Democrats in the upper chamber. Before the end of the war, the Unionists named him among the leading Copperheads of the state. After his defeat in 1866, Clymer served four terms in Congress. At the time of his death in 1884, Clymer was vice-president of the Union Trust Company of Philadelphia, president of the Clymer Iron Company, and director of the Reading Insurance Company.[48]

It is surprising how little Clymer was attacked by the radical leaders, most of the assaults upon him coming from the Radical press and campaign literature. Thomas Marshall said that Clymer "was personally a very estimable man," but his course during the war rendered it impossible for any loyal man to vote for him. Geary was quoted as having nothing against Clymer, "but the soldiers knew his record." The Republicans organs, *Miners' Journal,* Philadelphia *Press,* Beaver *Argus,* and Altoona *Tribune,* all condemned the "record" rather than the man.[49] According to a radical broadside and the Bradford *Reporter,* Clymer had opposed arming of the state during the crisis of 1861, the collection of a direct Federal tax, a vote for the soldiers, bounties for volunteers, and pay increases for members of the armed services.[50] Reputedly he had perceived *no treason* in secession

[48] Benjamin Fryer, *Congressional History of Berks (Pa.) District, 1789-1939* (Reading, 1939), 193-202.
[49] Pottsville *Miners' Journal,* March 24, 1866; Beaver *Argus,* March 14, 1866; Altoona *Tribune,* March 10, 1866.
[50] "Record of Clymer and . . . Geary," Pamphlet No. 827, PSL; Bradford *Reporter,* April 26, 1866.

and had characterized Lincoln as a tyrant, usurper, buffoon, and assassin.[51]

An examination of the *Legislative Record* somewhat softens these accusations against Clymer. He fought the increase in pay for soldiers because the declining value of the greenback would make the increase meaningless. The proposed increase, he insisted, must be paid in gold. His answers to his accusers on March 30, 1865, did not have the ring of a Copperhead: "You shall not evade an answer by calling me disloyal . . . . Why do you continue to pay him [the foreign minister], who is basking . . . on the smiles of royalty, and refuse it to him, who . . . is battling in your defense?" Clymer could not understand why those parading as the soldiers' friend would make believe that everyone outside the pale of the political communion was his enemy.[52] Clymer gave two reasons for his nay on the soldiers' vote. The state legislature could not legalize by passage what the courts had declared unconstitutional; the proper remedy was a constitutional amendment. Secondly, "by a strict [Republican] party vote every measure proposed by the Democrats . . . to prevent fraud . . . had been stricken out."[53] His opposition therefore was based on constitutional grounds and the fear that the soldiers would be coerced into voting for the Union Party.

There is surprisingly little material appearing in the press relating to Clymer's campaign and his speeches. The leading organ of the Democracy in the state, the Harrisburg *Patriot and Union,* between August 22 and October 2, failed to print a single address by its candidate; but during the same period the organ was printing verbatim portions of speeches by

[51] Harrisburg *Telegraph* quoted by Beaver *Argus,* May 9, 1866.
[52] *Legislative Record, 1864,* 149.
[53] *Ibid.,* 509.

Curtin and Geary. Clymer began his campaign in August and by September 15 he reported having campaigned in all regions of the state.[54] At Titusville, Clymer described the legislative program of the Republican Congress as intended for the suffrage and benefit merely of the Negro. Near the end of his lone, long campaign, nearing physical exhaustion, Clymer climaxed his tour with a speech at Independence Hall. He considered himself the "white man's candidate"; but Geary had practically admitted that he would endorse the Negro ballot in 1870. Finally, Clymer publicly denied that he had ever been against the soldiers' vote. So spoke the Democratic–Johnson Republican candidate for governor.

Although outwardly the Clymer and Johnson factions made every appearance of working together harmoniously, the President's coterie could not swallow the candidacy of one who had publicly castigated Johnson during his tenure as military governor of Tennessee. After organization of the Johnson National Union State Executive Committee, active steps were taken to bring pressure to bear upon the Democratic state leaders to substitute another gubernatorial candidate—one likely to be much more palatable to the Johnson men. Late in August, after Clymer had already begun his campaign, two presidential emissaries of the Johnson Committee called upon him and made a most astonishing proposition to the Democratic candidate. President Johnson proposed to nominate him for the mission to Russia or Spain in return for a withdrawal of candidacy in favor of Asa Packer. Clymer quickly declined in "determined language"[55] that which he regarded as a studied insult from the presidential chair. The Johnson National Executive Committee had acted

---

[54] Clymer to J. T. Hoffman, Sept. 15, 1866, Miscellaneous Collection, HSP.

[55] Wallace to Bigler, Aug. 28, 1866, Bigler MSS, HSP,

rashly without consulting either the Democratic state chairman, William Wallace, or William Bigler. When the committee belatedly notified Wallace of its action, he promptly informed Bigler and wrote the committee that such action could not be entertained.[56]

To Clymer's great relief none of his Democratic friends were privy to the attempted subversion, although at first he reasonably suspected Bigler on the basis of the latter's conduct at the time of Clymer's nomination when Bigler had used all his persuasive powers to induce him to refuse the nomination.[57] In haste Clymer wrote to Bigler expressing his "regrets that he did Bigler the injustice to believe . . . [him] connected with the infamous scheme. God knows," continued Clymer, "I did not wish to believe it. It fairly paralyzed me . . . and had I not felt that I had a deep hold upon the affection and confidence of the party . . . I should have sank under it . . . . I shall go on with renewed effort."[58] Fortunately very few persons knew of Johnson's efforts to have Clymer supplanted, and the story never leaked out. Its revelation would have destroyed even the outward unity which existed between the Johnson Republicans and the Keystone Democracy. It must have been very difficult for Clymer to declaim publicly his support of the President's policies. Although no mention of Edgar Cowan's name is found in the correspondence relative to the proposed deal it is inconceivable that Cowan, the President's man in Pennsylvania, was in ignorance of the move.

Buchanan was then in secluded retirement and took no active part in the campaign. But "Old Public Functionary" could not resist the temptation to do a little private snooping

---

[56] *Ibid.*
[57] Bigler to Johnson, Oct. 18, 1866, Johnson MSS, LC.
[58] Clymer to Bigler, Sept. 6, 1866, Bigler MSS, HSP,

on his own when he learned that his old enemy who had vowed to "hit him under the fifth rib"[59] at the end of the Kansas fiasco, was now the Radical candidate for governor. Buchanan wrote to a friend in the State Department requesting information on Geary's official resignation as governor of Kansas and on the candidate's brother, Edward Geary, at that time Federal Superintendent of Indian affairs for Oregon and Washington.[60] Before the war Geary had written to his brother, "If you want anything further only let me know, for I'm as good a fiddler as ever drew a bow."[61] It seems unlikely, however, that "the Old Buck" succeeded in manufacturing any shells for Clymer's campaign artillery. The campaign was remarkably free from personal attacks, although Geary once rebuked Clymer for not refraining from personalities.

Democratic leaders were divided in their opinions as to the outcome. On the basis of an early study made by David Porter, whom the former President considered one of the "shrewdest calculators"[62] in the state, Buchanan predicted victory for Clymer. The state chairman, Wallace, regarded the situation "encouraging," and Bigler expected victory in the congressional elections but doubted that Clymer would "carry the day."[63] The probability of his election, reasoned Clymer, was punctuated with a big "if." If he could hold the McClellan vote of 1864 (and this he felt confident of doing)[64] and gain in addition the support of the Johnson men,

[59] Geary to Edward Geary, Sept. 13, 1857, Geary MSS, PHMC.
[60] W. G. Hunter to Buchanan, March 17, 19, 1866, Buchanan MSS, HSP.
[61] Geary to Edward Geary, Dec. 22, 1859, Geary MSS, PHMC.
[62] Buchanan to Mrs. Johnston, July 30, 1866, Moore (ed.), *Works,* XI, 442.
[63] Wallace to Bigler, Oct. 2, 1866, Bigler MSS, HSP; Bigler to Johnson, Oct. 1, 1866, Johnson MSS, LC.
[64] Clymer to Hoffman, Sept. 15, 1866, Miscellaneous Collection, HSP,

his election was insured; unless the President's friends "cheated" him.[65]

In 1864 Lincoln had carried the state by 20,000 votes over McClellan. The Union majority in the state elections of 1865 were approximately the same as the preceding year. Thus if only 4 per cent of the 300,000 Republicans likely to turn out for the election remained true to Johnson and voted for Clymer as directed, he was certain of election. It was not unreasonable to assume that the President could command at least 12,000 votes from the Unionist ranks.

On October 9, the voters of Pennsylvania gave Geary 307,270 votes to Clymer's 290,096, a majority exceeding 17,000. The total congressional vote for Democratic candidates exceeded Clymer's by 2,255 votes; but at the same time, Geary scored a majority of 3,564 over his Republican congressional running mates. This proved that a sizable bloc of voters favored Johnson's plan of reconstruction but had not voted for the Democratic gubernatorial candidate. Apparently (as Clymer had feared), the Johnson Republicans had failed him. Clymer carried every county that McClellan won in 1864, except Perry, which Geary took by a scant majority of 86.

The battle had really centered around the national issue of reconstruction. The fruits of victory, insisted the Union-Republicans, could be realized only by supporting the party which had made victory possible. To vote for the Democracy, reasoned the Radicals, was equivalent to a shameless repudiation of the heroic deed and an insult to the living veteran. The Democracy had asked for the speedy restoration of the Union—an acceptance of constitutional rights; but the immediate application of such worthy principles was too much to expect from a people shorn of thousands

---

[65] Clymer to Bigler, Sept. 20, 1866, Bigler MSS, HSP,   .

of its beloved sons n the bloody conflict. The policy of "Thorough" had triumphed. The Radicals, knowing well the danger of accepting Negro suffrage as an issue in 1866, had cleverly refused to recognize its existence.

The gubernatorial contest in Pennsylvania was looked upon nationally with special interest. She was still one of the October states which furnished an advanced barometer of public feeling. Wrote Blaine: "The vote for these candidates [Geary and Clymer] was looked upon as giving the aggregate popular expression touching the merits of the administration."[66] With veteran votes a decisive factor, the Democracy would have done well to have selected a prominent soldier rather than a civilian—and least of all a civilian of Clymer's stamp. William Bigler realized this fully when he wrote that the true strength of the Radicals was to be found "in the prejudices and passions still cherished in the hearts of the people."[67]

The day of January 15, 1867, was a somber one for the forces of Andrew Curtin. The great war governor, forced to relinquish the chair which he had filled so ably for six years, and defeated for the senatorship which he felt was rightfully his, must now retire to private life. In his place Curtin saw John White Geary, reputedly the creature of his archenemy, Simon Cameron. If this were so, the "great Winnebago Chief" was now the undisputed political boss of the state. That his loyal followers must either allow themselves to be converted to Cameronism or suffer permanent ostracism within the ranks of the party, Curtin fully realized. Moreover, Cameron, the cunning political veteran, was not likely to leave unguarded any openings through which the former governor might seek rehabilitation.

---

[66] *Twenty Years,* II, 239.
[67] Bigler to Johnson,, Oct. 18, 1866, Johnson MSS, LC.

On inauguration day, the crowd in Harrisburg viewed a magnificent specimen of manhood, over six feet five inches in stature, being sworn into the gubernatorial chair. Geary's long, black, flowing beard concealed the jaw of a determined individual, who according to his own evaluation was not designed by nature to become the puppet of another. The new state executive must have viewed the ten fire departments and seven divisions that participated in the mammoth parade somewhat in the same light of a victorious general reviewing his conquering host. Geary had not forgotten one iota of his hatred for the South. In a vein of criticism against the national government's leniency he said: "I cannot refrain from an expression of regret that the general Government has not taken any steps to inflict proper penalties . . . upon the leaders of those who rudely and ferociously invaded the ever sacred soil of our state."[68] The new governor had bluntly expressed his views and proved his physical courage to all. He was confident, proud, and headstrong. It remained to be seen whether his moral courage could weather the assaults of three years by rings of past masters of the most treacherous of all games—politics.

In 1867, A. K. McClure charged that Geary bartered his office as directed by Cameron,[69] and thirty-seven years later he reiterated that Geary's cabinet was made by Cameron.[70] True, the make-up of the tiny "cabinet" did reflect the influence of Cameron, but Francis Jordan, the secretary of the Commonwealth, was not his choice. Cameron promised to support Henry C. Johnson of Meadville and succeeded in extracting a pledge from Geary on March 19, 1866, that he

---

[68] Philadelphia *Evening Telegraph*, Jan. 18, 1867.
[69] Chambersburg *Franklin Repository*, quoted by *Erie Observer*, Jan. 24, 1867.
[70] McClure, *Notes*, II, 201.

would make Johnson secretary of the Commonwealth. Geary's violation of his pledge proved that strong pressure was being brought to bear upon him from other sources. Louis Hall of Hollidaysburg, from John Scott's district, was the prime mover behind Jordan's appointment. Louis Hall had been dubbed Geary's "principal wire worker" at the convention which nominated him.[71] The powerful Hall, Speaker of the Senate, was desirous of having his sister's husband, Francis Jordan, occupy the first post. Jordan, an ancient enemy of Cameron, had become embittered when Curtin failed him in 1861, but his appointment as Pennsylvania agent by the governor, at a salary of $3,000, partially healed the breach.

But Benjamin Harrison Brewster, Geary's new attorney general, did owe his position to Cameron. Brewster, a leading Philadelphia lawyer, had served Cameron for over a decade. He traced his ancestry to early colonial stock and liked to pretend his descent from the illustrious Pilgrim father William Brewster. For his second wife he had chosen a daughter of Robert J. Walker, successor to Geary's headaches in Kansas. Under President Arthur he was to achieve fame in his role of prosecutor of the notorious Star Route frauds. This is the gentleman whom Cameron characterized for Lincoln elucidation, "one of the most remarkable men that I have ever met."[72] Cameron, according to Brewster's biographer, would have supported his friend for the senatorship in January 1867, had he not decided to take it for himself.[73] Strangely, it was Brewster's hated, ostracized half

---

[71] Bellefonte *Democratic Watchman,* March 16, 1866.
[72] Cameron to Lincoln, Feb. 13, 1864, Lincoln MSS.
[73] Eugene C. Savidge, *Life of Benjamin H. Brewster* (Philadelphia, 1891), 99.

brother, who also aspired to a position in the Geary cabinet and pleaded for Cameron's assistance.[74]

Geary's leading supporters besieged him on behalf of their local clientele but there simply wasn't enough "bread and butter" to go around. Waiting in line were the followers of John Covode, Thaddeus Stevens, John Forney, and Simon Cameron. Apparently the Curtin faction received no consideration.[75] Some of the offices attainable through state patronage were numerous inspectorships of flour, lumber, salted provisions, domestic spirits, sole leather and harness, bark, petroleum, illuminating gas, and pickled fish. In addition there were auctioneers, slaters of weights, measurers, railroad policemen, county marshals, quarantine masters and superintendents—about twenty types of positions in all, and in some cases one was appointed for each county. The hundreds of local and county appointments were for the small fry. Although Cameron intended to take care of his best men through Federal patronage, Geary assigned him his own private niche in the Democratic fifteenth congressional district (York, Cumberland, Perry).

In Washington the harried President, engaged in combat with a hostile Senate, was losing the patronage battle. Until March, 1867, when Cameron would displace the Republican renegade Senator Edgar Cowan, the Radicals of Pennsylvania were forced temporarily to rely upon Radical senators from other states to represent their interests. They found an ardent advocate in the person of Benjamin L. Wade of Ohio—one of Johnson's bitterest enemies. General Irwin of Beaver and John Mattern of Huntingdon requested Wade to defeat Johnson's candidates for regional collectors and

---

[74] F. Carroll Brewster to Cameron, Nov. 26, 1866, Cameron MSS, LC.
[75] McClure, *Notes,* II, 200-01.

assessors of internal revenue.[76] Wade was successful, the Senate rejected the appointments; and as a result of these cases of stalemate being repeated many times, most collector-ships were left undecided.[77] The Senate even rejected the appointment of former Governor W. F. Johnston to the Collectorship of the Port of Philadelphia. When Cowan accused the Senate of rejecting Johnston's appointment on political grounds, Senator John Sherman replied: "It is not for him [Cowan] nor the President to say what reason actuated the Senate.[78] The Federal patronage was in such confusion in Philadelphia during April, 1867, that the positions of collector, naval officer, surveyor, and director of the mint were all open simultaneously. In spite of his break with the President, Cameron succeeded in having his man named postmaster of Philadelphia. On May 3, 1867, Henry Bingham, formerly of Hollidaysburg, announced that he had "assumed control" of United States Court House and Post Office Building. The Cameron housecleaning in Phila-delphia had begun.[79]

With a short era of peace on the state political horizon, three of the state's Radical leaders went on "vacation": McClure to Montana where he possessed mining interests; Cameron on an excursion to Kansas where a railroad fever was brewing; and John W. Forney to Europe seeking inspir-ation for a new series of articles to appear in his *Press.* Andrew G. Curtin was back at his home in Bellefonte and his successor, Geary, was busy grappling with the problems of his new office in Harrisburg. At the national capital, Nebraska had been admitted into the Union over the President's veto. Radical military reconstruction born of the

---

[76] Feb. 13, 1867, Papers of Benjamin L. Wade, LC.
[77] Altoona *Tribune,* April 3, 1867.
[78] *Cong. Globe,* 39 Cong., 2 Sess., 436.
[79] Henry H. Bingham to Charles Gilpin, Gilpin Papers, HSP.

legislative branch of government was begun and passage of
the Tenure of Office Act presaged the fast falling prestige
of the Chief Executive's office. The new Fortieth Congress
assembled eight months early for a hectic session; and with
public attention focused upon the more exciting national
scene in Washington, the year 1867 was a so-called "off year"
in the Commonwealth's political life. But this was the same
year when the state's Democracy would score a minor
victory and was encouraged to believe that the high tide of
Radicalism was receding within the Keystone state.

George Washington Woodward, Pennsylvania's premier
jurist on the state supreme bench was retiring from the
court after fifteen years of service and the state's electorate
was required to select a successor.[80] State Democratic Chairman William Wallace, the choice of William Bigler and the
most popular man of his party, could have been named to
succeed Woodward had he wished. "I am annoyed with
request to allow my name to be used for judge," wrote
Wallace to his partner, Bigler. "I am averse to this and I
think I should peremptorily forbid it."[81] Bigler then turned
to Warren Woodward, a relative of the retiring jurist and
received another negative reply. Three weeks before the
convention opened, Bigler had ascertained a prevailing sentiment for Judge George Sharswood of Philadelphia, but was
not sure that a majority of the delegates would vote for
him.[82]

The Democratic state convention met on June 11 for
the purpose of choosing its candidate for supreme judge and
to express officially the present sentiments of the party

---

[80] Woodward gave President Johnson the benefit of his legal
talents, and was successful in getting himself elected to Congress.
DeWitt, *Impeachment and Trial of President Johnson,* 366.

[81] Wallace to Bigler, Feb. 12, 1867, Bigler MSS, HSP.

[82] Bigler to Black, May 22, 1867, Black MSS, LC,

regarding the critical problems of reconstruction and Negro suffrage. George Sharswood had no difficulty in defeating Judge Maynard Ryan of Schuylkill, Woodward's choice. Wallace was re-elected chairman of the Democratic State Central Committee—a distinction he was to hold for two more years. The Keystone's Democracy, affirmed the convention, was opposed to amending the state constitution for the purpose of granting Negro suffrage; and it reaffirmed the right of each state to prescribe the qualifications of its electorate. A resolution directed at the Radical congress complained because some states were "denied the right" to be represented in Congress. The state Democracy was cognizant of the political implications involved in a Radical "reconstruction" of the South, but could do little beyond registering a protest. The convention's final resolution scored the strong Republican state legislature which had "distinguished . . . itself for the number of unwise and unconstitutional enactments" passed since January, 1867.[83]

The Democracy's candidate for supreme judge, George Sharswood, was a native Philadelphian. At fifteen years of age he entered the sophomore class of the University of Pennsylvania and graduated with first honors. Three years later he was admitted to the bar. In 1837 he began the first of his three terms in the state legislature. At thirty-five he became assistant judge of the District Court of Pennsylvania. During these years he continued his studies and acquired a good knowledge of Latin, French, and Spanish. While serving as president judge in Philadelphia he became interested in the law school of the University of Pennsylvania. There he became a professor of law and was credited

---

[83] Harrisburg *Patriot*, June 12, 1867.

with being the real founder of that university's law school.[84] John A. Johnson said of him: "On rule days many cases were disposed of with unsurpassed speed, and his charges to juries were models of excellence.[85]

The Union-Republicans held their state convention at Williamsport on June 26. John Scott of Huntingdon presided and the assembly received its usual share of verbosity from Thomas Marshall, assisted by T. J. Bigham. Cameron's faction was directed by his new son-in-law, Wayne Mac-Veagh, a recent recruit from the Curtin camp. The former governor's thinning forces were represented by William B. Mann, the powerful district attorney of Philadelphia, whom Cameron never succeeded in smashing. After nine ballots, Henry W. Williams, who was supported by MacVeagh, triumphed over M. Russell Thayer, Mann's choice, 65 to 40.[86] The results, observed the Democratic Erie *Observer,* was a triumph as usual for the "Old Winnebago Chief." Resolutions condemned President Johnson for his "reckless pardons" and his administration for its faithlessness. The convention asked for adequate protection for American industry, praised the new governor for his honesty and courage, and endorsed its candidate for supreme judge in glowing terms.

Henry Williams, the Union candidate, suffered much criticism from the opposition press. Lately graduated from Yale, Williams, the ambitious Connecticut Yankee, had

[84] Samuel Dickson, "George Sharswood–Teacher and Friend," *American Law Register,* LV (October 1907), 401-27.

[85] John A. Johnson, Joseph A. Kneass Scrapbook, HSP.

[86] McClure made the erroneous statement that the convention was not disturbed by factional strife; that Williams was nominated unanimously, and that Williams was at the time serving on the Supreme Court as an appointee. According to Smull's *Legislative Handbook* for 1873, Williams was appointed in 1868. Possibly McClure confused this convention with that of 1869 when Williams again received the nomination for supreme judge. See *Notes,* II, 212.

migrated to Allegheny County, Pennsylvania, where he secured election as judge. The youthful candidate, noted the Clearfield *Republican,* had no reputation outside Pittsburgh and "his mind was largely developed with reference to negro equality, women's rights, and spirit rappings."[87] To the Lancaster *Intelligencer,* a vote for Williams was a vote for continued disunion, Negro domination, prohibition, impoverishment of the South, military despotism, impeachment of the President, and a victory for Thaddeus Stevens' doctrine of miscegenation. The proponents of liquor were actually much concerned over Williams' attitude on the prohibition issue. John Cessna, a vice-president of the State Temperance Union, was reported at work on a bill, and the temperance views of the new governor were well publicized. After his inauguration Geary had entertained selected members of the legislature and his executive family—thirty thirsty guests in all—with a hearty draught of cold water.[88] Thousands of stein-loving Germans viewed with apprehension the antics of the Union-Republican temperance leaders.

The Union press attacked Judge Sharswood principally on his past record as a legislator and jurist. The moderate Philadelphia *Evening Telegraph* thought that Sharswood "owed it to himself as a jurist [and] to his reputation as an honest man to repudiate [the declaration against negro suffrage] this infamous plank in the Democratic Platform."[89] The Clearfield *Raftsman's Journal* recalled Sharswood's dissenting vote in a district court ruling which validated the constitutionality of the greenbacks.[90] The Philadelphia *Press* accused Sharswood of representing, not the democracy of

[87] Quoted in Clearfield *Raftsman's Journal,* July 17, 1867.
[88] Beaver *Argus,* April 17, 1867.
[89] June 13, 1867.
[90] July 17, 1867.

Jackson, but rather that of Calhoun whom he had toasted twenty years earlier.[91]

The public indicated little interest in the campaign, and newspapers featured news of national interest. None of the Radical leaders seemed to have done much stumping for Williams. McClure noted Curtin's lack of participation in the contest, but the Philadelphia *Press* recorded two addresses by him at the end of the campaign; one before the Union League at Philadelphia, and the other at Manayunk.[92] The Clearfield *Raftsman's Journal,* in an effort to arouse the Republicans from their apathy, warned that a "Copperhead" victory would be interpreted as an endorsement of the President's policies and would encourage him to persist in his resistance to Congress.[93] The Philadelphia *Press* felt it expedient to wave the bloody shirt—a device which had proved highly successful in the preceding year's campaign: "The public peril is again so great that we need not ask every American who loves his country to vote the Republican ticket. To the bad men who hate their country, who desired to see the rebellion succeed, [and] who mourned when our armies triumphed, it will be a pleasant and an easy thing to vote for Sharswood."[94]

The Democracy was highly enthusiastic over the results of the state elections held on October 8. Sharswood was elected supreme judge over Williams, 267,746 votes to 266,824—a scant majority of 922 votes.[95] The day following the election a Democratic band paraded past the office of the Philadelphia *Press,* reported its chagrined editor, playing the "appropriate rebel strains of Dixie." If one were to base the

---

[91] Oct. 4, 1867.
[92] Oct. 7, 1867.
[93] Sept. 21, 1867.
[94] Oct. 8, 1867.
[95] Appleton's *Annual Cyclopaedia, 1867,* 620.

Democratic gains solely upon Sharswood's victory, the triumph would seem mainly a personal one, but the results of the legislative election showed a Democratic trend. In the legislature of 1867, the Republicans counted a majority of 33, but in the new General Assembly this lead would be cut to thirteen, five in the Senate and eight in the House.

A summary of the views of contemporaries lists four reasons for the Democratic resurgence: (1) Antipathy within the Republican party to Cameron's leadership,[96] (2) Johnson's "demoralizing" of the Union-Republicans,[97] (3) Sharswood's personal popularity,[98] and (4) prejudice against granting the Negro a vote. There appears little evidence that the Republicans would consider a vote for Sharswood as a vote against Cameron. A campaign of public enlightenment would have been necessary to have accomplished it and both Curtin and McClure said nothing on the subject. Neither did the press report any such campaign from William B. Mann in Philadelphia. Johnson's "demoralizing" influence should have been less in 1867 than in 1866 when he failed and Cowan, who was no longer in the Senate, took no active part in the campaign.[99] In Philadelphia, Sharwood's victory did look like a personal one because Geary had carried the city by 5,338 votes. Outside Philadelphia only two counties, Franklin and Jefferson, changed to the Democratic column. Somerset moved into the Republican column.

The Democratic trend was not peculiar to Pennsylvania. Her neighbors, New York and New Jersey, also went Democratic, and in all the Northern states carried by the Repub-

[96] *Notes*, II, 212.

[97] Forney, *Anecdotes* of Public Men, 286.

[98] Charles R. Deacon, Manager, *Biographical Album of Prominent Pennsylvanians*, First Series, 121.

[99] Cowan to S. R. Phillips, Nov. 28, 1867, Simon Gratz Autograph Collection, HSP.

licans the minority party showed gains. The Democratic
victory was therefore a reaction common to several states.
The resistance to Negro suffrage was considered one of the
common factors. In addition there was a falling off of
business, the Greenback agitation was beginning and the
working man showed a disposition to express himself. The
union of the laborer with the Democrats was illustrated by
the December elections in Pittsburgh. There the Democrats
made no nominations for mayor and assisted the workingmen in electing their nominee James Blackmore to the city's
chief executive office.[100] Fred Haynes stated that Greenback-
ism captured the principal leaders of the wage earners in
1867.[101] In Pennsylvania, the feeling against contraction of
the currency was making itself felt mainly within the ranks
of the Democrats who were allied with the workingmen. In
addition to the reasons given by contemporaries for the
Democratic resurgence of 1867, one must also look upon the
results as an expression of dissatisfaction against existing
economic conditions.

What then would be the effects of the state elections upon
the Radicals? Would they consider the results a mandate
from the people to alter their program? The elections did
not mean a repudiation of the Radical program, asserted
Charles Summer, the senatorial leader: "Those elections [in
Ohio and Pennsylvania] only show more imperatively the
necessity for impeachment."[102] According to James F.
Rhodes, the elections had the effect of "consolidating the
members of Congress into support of the Reconstruction
Acts as . . . a party policy."[103] Congressional elections had

[100] Pittsburgh *Gazette,* Dec. 10, 1867.
[101] Fred E. Haynes, *Third Party Movements Since the Civil War*
(Iowa City, 1916), 93.
[102] Milton, *Age of Hate,* 471.
[103] Rhodes, *History of United States,* VI, 204.

not been held in 1867 so the Radical Party there remained intact; but if the trend were to continue in 1868, it might mean the scrapping of the whole Radical program of reconstruction and a death blow to Republican entrenchment in the occupied South. The Democracy in Pennsylvania now believed that the pinnacle of Radicalism was attained in 1866 and that continued reaction would carry them to victory in 1868. Would a Moses arise around which the faltering Union-Republicans could rally their banners? The next twelve months would answer that question.

VIII

The Cameronian Path of Empire

TWO PENNSYLVANIANS, Andrew G. Curtin and Galusha A. Grow, determined to try for the Vice-Presidency in 1868.[1] The former governor's prestige had waned since his defeat for senator of the preceding year, but there was still magic enough left in his old war title of "The Soldier's Friend" to stir popular imagination. Grow, author of the Homestead Act, had secured national recognition through his election to the speakership of the House in 1861. Although a fighter, Grow lacked ability to sense popular opinion, to appraise properly political situations, and to perceive practical implications. Without consulting either John White Geary or Cameron, Grow requested John Covode for support. In optimistic vein he wrote: "Unless something occurs that I don't know now, . . . it seems to me I will be a pretty sure thing in the national convention."[2]

A. K. McClure, recognizing the pro-Curtin complexion of the Union-Republican state convention meeting at Philadelphia on March 10, employed steamroller methods worthy of the Cameron machine to promote Curtin's candidacy. Immediately upon the convention's organization, H. B. Swope moved "that the representatives of the people of the

---

[1] Curtin to McPherson, Feb. 6, 1868, McPherson MSS, LC; Harrisburg *Telegraph,* Feb. 27, 1868. In his *Notes,* McClure's memory slipped when he named "early spring" as the time when Curtin's candidacy was first pushed by his friends.

[2] Grow to Covode, Oct. 17, 1867, Covode MSS, HSP.

state now assembled in this convention declare it to be the will of the Republican party of Pennsylvania that Ulysses S. Grant and Andrew G. Curtin be the candidates respectively for President and Vice-President of the United States." Russell Errett's motion to insert Benjamin Wade's name in the place of Curtin ended in bedlam. The convention then decided to act separately on the candidates, and Grant was named that body's choice for the Presidency by acclamation. Although Curtin received 109 votes to Wade's 22, McClure had failed to secure a unanimous endorsement for his candidate.[3] The deluded Grow received not a single vote.

At the evening session, McClure succeeded, by a vote of 85 to 47, in passing his notorious resolution designed to send a united Curtin delegation to Chicago regardless of the wishes and votes of the districts. District delegates would be accepted if pledged for Curtin; if not they would be rejected and others appointed in their places. This unusual procedure, reversing the custom of allowing congressional districts freedom in election of delegates to the national convention, was aimed especially at J. Donald Cameron, Simon's son, who had been elected in the Dauphin district. Another McClure resolution bound Pennsylvania's delegates to vote as a unit at the national convention, and the Curtin lieutenant had himself named head of the state delegation. J. Donald Cameron, refusing to accept his unhorsing, contested for his seat at the national convention and succeeded in gaining an honorary seat for his pains.[4] With little ado the state convention selected Generals John F. Hartranft and Jacob Campbell candidates, respectively, for auditor and surveyor general. Before adjourning the Radical-minded body praised

[3] McClure erred (*Notes,* II, 217) in writing that the Cameron faction threw its support to Grow. Benjamin Wade was evidently its choice.
[4] Blaine, *Twenty Years,* II, 390.

Congress for its determination to impeach Johnson and thanked Secretary Stanton for his firmness, courage, and patriotism.[5]

McClure's victory proved barren indeed. His dictatorial methods boomeranged when fifteen Republican state organs expressed their disapproval of the methods used to procure Curtin's endorsement,[6] although the great majority supported him. The Radicals, who cared little for Curtin, were so certain of Johnson's removal that they were reflecting on the make-up of Wade's cabinet. Two Pennsylvanians, Thomas Williams and Benjamin Harrison Brewster, were being boomed for positions in Wade's new cabinet. Curtin never succeeded in convincing the Radicals of his orthodoxy. The Philadelphia *Morning Post* doubted whether the Chicago convention would dare to nominate a "hesitating, doubting man" like Curtin and predicted that he could save himself only by "embracing Dinah."[7]

The Union Republican Party held its national nominating convention in Chicago at the end of the third week in May. Pennsylvania's delegation was led by Alexander McClure, John Scott, John Wien Forney, and General Harry White. The permanent chairman thanked the Almighty for Abraham Lincoln, invoked wisdom for the present convention, and further indicated that Grant might be the Deity's next choice. The alleged unwilling candidate, General Grant, was nominated without ado or opposition. Only Grant, agreed Curtin, could carry his state for the Republicans.[8] McClure gave Forney credit for securing the General's con-

[5] On the Republican state convention see Harrisburg *Telegraph*, March 12, 13, 1866; Hollidaysburg *Register*, March 18, 1868; McClure, *Notes*, II, 217-18.

[6] Harrisburg *Telegraph*, April 11, 1868.

[7] Quoted by Reading *Eagle*, March 18, 1868.

[8] Curtin to Washburne, Oct. 17, 1867, Elihu Washburne Papers, LC.

sent and commented on Grant's naïvete in requesting a
guarantee of two terms.[9] The main bout at the gathering
centered around the Vice-Presidential candidates—almost a
dozen in number. The lack of unity in the Curtin delegation
from the Keystone state was uncovered when a member from
Allegheny seconded the nomination of Schuyler Colfax and
promised a majority of 10,000 votes in his county for that
genial gentleman.[10]

Curtin fared badly at the convention. Forney, whom the
Harrisburg *Telegraph* named as head of the delegation,
presented Curtin for the Vice-Presidential nomination. A
nomination for William D. Kelley of Philadelphia by a
delegate from Alabama evoked partial applause and boisterous laughter. On the first ballot Curtin won 51 votes, the
maximum he was to receive. Forty-eight of these came from
Pennsylvania, with Georgia, West Virginia, and Wisconsin
contributing one each. Benjamin Wade was out in front with
147; and Fenton, Wilson, and Colfax each had over 100
votes. After Curtin's poor showing of 40 on the third ballot,
McClure presented a letter from Curtin withdrawing his
name. Cameron's organ, the Harrisburg *Telegraph,* had predicted a solid change to Wade by the Pennsylvania delegation, but fewer than half the group voted for him on the fifth
ballot; and then the entire delegation swung to Colfax, who
received the nomination. McClure believed that Cameron's
influential connections with neighboring senators had much
to do with Curtin's defeat; and the Reading *Eagle* reported
the taking of Curtin's scalp by Cameron at Chicago.[11] Pennsylvania had lost its usual bargaining position at the convention because the state was solid for Grant, while Indiana,

[9] *Notes,* II, 216.
[10] McClure stated that he had practically a solid delegation but
Blaine (*Twenty Years,* II, 390) reported 14 anti-Curtin delegates.
[11] May 21, 1868.

Colfax's state, was not. Before adjourning, the party changed its name to the National Union Republican Party and adopted a platform silent on the tariff. Henry C. Carey, the state's premier economist, was much perturbed by the omission, which he interpreted as a sign of weakness.[12] In Harrisburg, Bergner of the *Telegraph* organized a "ratifying" mass meeting and persuaded the group to thank Cameron publicly for having voted "guilty" on Johnson's bill of impeachment.[13]

Early in 1868, state Democratic leaders were busy trying to find a man capable of matching Grant's popularity. The fast-declining Buchanan did not share the general optimism prevailing within the ranks of the Democracy and believed that victory depended upon the character of the nominee. The former President requested William Bigler to have a private conversation with General W. T. Sherman, the one man Buchanan believed could beat Grant. However, neither Buchanan nor Bigler preferred a military candidate, and the latter wrote Samuel J. Tilden on the subject of Governor Seymour's availability.[14] Shortly before the meeting of the state convention, Bigler received word via Judge Bartley that Sherman disliked Grant, Stanton, and the Democratic leaders alike. This special message from the Republican general placed a quietus on the Sherman movement.

The Democratic state convention meeting in early March nominated C. E. Boyle of Fayette County for auditor general, General W. H. Ent for surveyor general, and elected four delegates-at-large to the national convention. Radical

---

[12] Carey to Forney, May 25, 1868, Carey MSS, HSP. On National Union Convention see Coleman, *Election of 1868;* Harrisburg *Telegraph,* May 20, 22, 23, 1868.
[13] *Ibid,* June 22, 1868.
[14] Buchanan to Bigler, Feb. 15, 1868, Tilden to Bigler, Feb. 28, 1868, Bigler MSS, HSP; Bigler to Buchanan, Feb. 21, 1868, Buchanan MSS, HSP.

legislation, concluded the delegates, was the only barrier to "prompt restoration of [the] states and enjoyment of rights and functions in the Union." The clause on the currency requested an early return to a "specie paying basis" because it was "essential" to the welfare of the nation. Congress was accused of usurping executive prerogatives and of attempts to destroy the independence of the national judiciary. President Johnson was defended for his stand on the Tenure of Office Act, and the impending trial of the impeachment charges was characterized as a "gross and reckless abuse of partisan power, without justification of party purpose." The convention failed to agree on supporting General Hancock, George H. Pendleton, or Asa Packer for the Presidency.[15]

But the Democratic National Convention meeting later in Tammany Hall, New York City, found a harmonious Pennsylvania delegation. Judge George W. Woodward had lately visited the Blairs at Silver Spring in hope of establishing a Packer-Blair ticket.[16] It was probably due to Woodward's influence that the state's delegation had decided to back a favorite son, Asa Packer, millionaire railroad magnate of Carbon County. Woodward's nominating speech was the longest offered at the convention. When the judge finally placed Asa Packer's name in nomination, a bored delegate yawned, turned to a fellow sufferer and asked: "Who in the hell is Packer?" For 14 ballots Pennsylvania's delegation cast its 26 votes solidly for Packer. On the next ballot, the delegation switched to Hancock, another Pennsylvanian, who received a high of $144\frac{1}{2}$ votes on the eighteenth ballot. At this juncture, when it looked as if Hancock was assured of the nomination, Horatio

---

[15] Harrisburg *Telegraph,* March 5, 1868; Clearfield *Raftsman's Journal,* March 11, 1868.

[16] Smith, *Blair Family,* II, 404.

Seymour forced an adjournment. The New Yorkers were determined not to allow Hancock's nomination. That same night such worthies as Abram Hewitt, Samuel J. Tilden, and Seymour, meeting at the Manhattan Club, chose Chief Justice Chase for the prize; but, ironically, the Ohioans outmaneuvered the New Yorkers by stampeding the convention from their son, Chase, to that of New York's Horatio Seymour, and the Democracy lost its best chance to defeat Grant by taking Hancock. The General's wife attributed his defeat to his refusal to make bargains.[17]

The first official action of the state Republicans following their convention was a resolution by their State Central Committee, based upon the "unanimous and earnest convictions of the faithful people of Pennsylvania," demanding the removal of Andrew Johnson.[18] This perfectly timed action occurred on May 12, only four days before the Senate vote on the eleventh article of impeachment. With the excitement of the impeachment proceedings behind them, the Republicans settled down to carry the state for Grant, to maintain their overwhelming majority in Congress, and to win the state offices and legislature. With Grant, the party had a national hero around which it could rally, and Johnson Republicans were generally back in the fold. In Pennsylvania there was no division within the ranks; both the Cameron and Curtin factions were heartily supporting Grant.

The Republican campaign was carried on by prominent party orators, clubs, the Union League, party organs, and the State Central Committee under Galusha Grow. The Committee took the lead in waving the effective bloody shirt: "No thanks to that [Democratic] party that today we have

---

[17] See Coleman, *Election of 1868*, 196-238; Mrs. W. S. Hancock, *Reminiscences of Hancock*, 135-37; Nevins, *Hewitt*, 265-66; Stanwood, *Presidency*, I, 321-25; Harrisburg *Patriot*, July 3, 5, 6, 8, 1868.
[18] Harrisburg *Telegraph*, May 13, 1868.

a country to love or a constitution to revere. It did all in its power to destroy both . . . [and] rejoiced at every Union defeat and mourned over every Union victory." Republican organs tried to frighten the disabled veteran into believing that his pension depended upon a Republican victory. One sample read: "Remember wounded soldier, the Democratic leaders have but one step more, to insure repudiation of your pension."[19] Tanners' clubs named in honor of Grant, the original tanner, were organized to tan Copperhead hides and solicit votes. Officials of the Union League were "fully aware of the evil consequences to the country which would follow the return of the Democratic party to power," and expressed the League's determination to spare no effort to secure a Republican victory in Pennsylvania.[20] The powerful new veterans' organization, the Grand Army of the Republic, was likewise supporting Republican candidates. Curtin, working faithfully to secure Grant's election, sent out invitations for a reunion of the loyal war governors (except Seymour) in conjunction with a veterans' reunion in Philadelphia. Governor Geary, Alexander McClure, General Fisher, and Thomas Marshall also assisted in the state campaign. The Harrisburg *Telegraph* omitted Curtin's name from the list of prominent men taking an active part in the campaign.[21]

The state Democracy based its campaign upon the successful slogans of the preceding year, criticisms of Republican policies, and the prevailing economic discontent of the time. "Let your rallying cries," advised the state committee, "be a government of white men, equal taxation, one currency for all." The Democratic press warned the Demo-

[19] Clearfield *Raftsman's Journal*, Oct. 7, 1868.
[20] Perkins to Wade, Sept. 8, 1868, Papers of Benjamin F. Wade, LC.
[21] Harrisburg *Telegraph*, Sept. 26, 1868.

cratic veteran to beware of the G.A.R. the tool of Radical
politicians.[22] The Democracy, capitalizing on the discontent
of the laborer cursed by unemployment, high prices, and
high taxes, charged that these taxes would go to support
"Radicalism, the Freedman's Bureau and a vast standing
army in time of peace."[23] William H. Sylvis, head of the
National Iron Molders Union and the recognized leader
of labor in the state, aided the Democracy in its attempt to
wean away the laboring men. He wrote: "I have frequently
said there was no hope for the [iron] industry in the Republican Party [because] Wall Street runs the whole concern."
The Chicago platform, charged Sylvis, was an insult to
every workingman in the country, because the great land and
labor reform questions were ignored.[24]

Some prominent Democratic leaders making speeches
within the state were George H. Pendleton, Hiester Clymer,
and Montgomery Blair, the last-named an ostracized Johnson
Republican. The party standard bearer, Seymour, found
time to deliver addresses at Philadelphia, Pittsburgh, Reading, and Harrisburg. General Hancock refused to participate
actively in the campaign allegedly because of his service
wound and his position as an active army officer; but he
could have given a better reason if he wished—the shabby
treatment meted out to him at the national convention by
Seymour's New York coterie.

Both parties worked desperately raising campaign funds
to carry Pennsylvania because of its doubtful status and its
early state elections. Montgomery Blair appealed to New
York bankers and Seymour was asked for funds enough to
procure 12,000 additional votes.[25] Jay Cooke of Philadelphia

[22] Reading *Daily Eagle*, Feb. 8, 1868.
[23] Harrisburg *Patriot*, Oct. 9, 1868.
[24] Erie *Observer*, July 2, 1868.
[25] Coleman, *Election of 1868*, 366.

reported himself to have bled freely for the Republican Party in Pennsylvania. Zachariah Chandler saw the necessity of sending $40,000 of the Republican National Committee's fund into the state.[26] It was reported to John Covode, who was assisting Cameron in taking care of state assessments, that no one was paying less than $250 and most were contributing $500.[27] James G. Blaine of Maine gave $100 to support Covode's congressional candidacy[28] which had assumed national significance because of his prominent connection with Johnson's impeachment. John Covode was having trouble meeting the increased subsidies for votes which his competition was able to pay. For example, there was the case of Ambrose Brown of Blairsville who was taking care of 45 men for Covode and paying their board besides; but the Democrats had outbid Brown by offering to pay $30 per man plus board for each vote against Covode. Ambrose put the proposition squarely to "Honest John," his patron. "So if you want my vote you must come with the money by Saturday . . . if [you] don't there will be forty-six votes short so Goodbye."[29]

Various pre-election devices added credence to the Republican prediction of victory. A straw vote taken on a Lancaster train showed a preference of two to one for Grant over Seymour, while a like poll on Cameron's line, the Northern Central, showed Grant ahead five to one. The Harrisburg *Telegraph* interpreted these polls to mean that Grant had the business man's backing. The large majorities of up to 20,000 forecast by Cameron did not materialize in the state elections held October 13. Both Republican candidates for

---

[26] Ellis P. Oberholtzer, *Jay Cooke* (Boston, 1904), II, 71.
[27] J. R. McAfee to Covode, Sept. 2, 1868, Covode MSS, HSWP.
[28] Blaine to Covode, Oct. 1, 1868, *ibid.*
[29] A. Brown to Covode, Sept. 6, 1868, *ibid.*

state office, Hartranft and Campbell, attained majorities of approximately 9,000 votes. Hartranft received 331,416 votes, or 50.7 per cent of the total cast. Campbell's percentage was slightly less. In the state legislature the Democrats lost their gains of the preceding year. They did increase their number in the state senate by one member, but they lost 14 seats in the lower house. The joint Republican majority had increased from 13 to 25.

At first, the results of the congressional elections could not be determined because of three contested seats. When Governor Geary issued his proclamation of November 17, 1868, naming the congressmen elected, he said no returns had been received from the Twenty-first district (Covode's) that would authorize him, under the election laws, to proclaim any person's name.[30] When the contested seats were finally decided the Democrats received 9 and the Republicans 15, a gain of three seats for the Democracy in the new Congress. Evidently the Democratic Party was not as weak as it had been in 1866, but it had receded slightly from the high water mark of 1867.

In the national election on November 3, Grant's Pennsylvania vote of 342,280 to 313,382 for Seymour gave him a sweeping state majority of 28,898.[31] In view of the fact that 2,507 more votes were cast for the presidential candidate than were given to the leading state candidates, one might conclude that about 8,000 Democratic voters had switched to Grant. In other words, Grant was stronger than his own party in Pennsylvania, and his triumph could be looked upon chiefly as a personal one. The Radical press emphasized the importance of Grant's victory. The Pottsville *Miners' Journal* proclaimed the redemption of the nation:

---

[30] *Papers of the Governors,* 1867-1871, 931.
[31] Smull's *Legislative Handbook,* 1873, 273.

"It seems as if the Creator had flung the banner of his smile over our redeemed head . . . . The third of November will now take its place by the side of the Fourth of July, 1776."[32] The Clearfield *Raftsman's Journal* congratulated the Republican voters on defeating the enemies of the Union—"traitors, rebels, copperheads all";[33] and the Beaver *Argus* chose for its headline the wonderful news that "The Country [Is] Saved —Grant Elected."[34]

The year 1868 saw the passing of three great names in national and Pennsylvania history—David Wilmot, James Buchanan, and Thaddeus Stevens. Had it not been for his famous proviso, probably most schoolboys would never have heard of David Wilmot. During the closing chapters of his career the free-soiler was forced to swallow his pride and follow in the train of Simon Cameron. Serving his fifth year as a judge of the Court of Claims, Wilmot was stricken with "congestion of the brain" and died at his home in Towanda, Bradford County, on March 16.[35] Buchanan, who had taken an interest in politics to the last, was next to follow. One of America's great legalists, "Wedded to the constitution," and insistent upon maintaining an equilibrium of power in our Federal system, he had found legal procedures inadequate for solution of the nation's ills. Nevertheless, he found his niche as a man of "high character, unimpeachable honesty, patriotism and considerable ability."[36] Concerned with posterity's verdict, he died with no regrets for any public acts of his long career, and consoled with the knowledge that

---

[32] Nov. 7, 1868.

[33] Nov. 11, 1868.

[34] Nov. 14, 1868.

[35] Going, *David Wilmot*, 635.

[36] George E. Mowry, "James Buchanan," Collier's *Encyclopedia* (1952), IV, 167.

he had "discharged every public duty . . . conscientiously."[37] Although 20,000 citizens of the Lancaster area turned out to honor the deceased, he appeared as a prophet with honor only in his own land. The Lewistown *Gazette* devoted three lines to Buchanan's obituary, exactly the same space alloted to an aged Negro woman. John Oakford offered Simon Cameron a summary of Buchanan's character in atrocious unrhymed verse:

> Regarded his friends like chess pieces.
> Like Falstaff was ashamed of his soldiers, and
> their commander, Forney
> Could not discriminate men's characters
> Urged J. Clancy Jones as minister to England
> Leaned on Black's judgment
> Had surrendered to southern politicians.

On the back of the page, Cameron wrote the notation, "How true."[38]

Stevens had been clinging on to life, it seemed, with only one earthly goal in view—that of removing Johnson from office. During the anxious impeachment period an angry organ of the Democracy had written:

> Old Thad lies upon his bed
> And thus he doth lament
> My days on earth are nearly o'er
> My hours are nearly spent
>
> . . . . .
>
> Where can I go? Now thats the rub
> I'm sorry I was born
> For Satan will not take me in
> When Gabriel blows his horn

---

[37] Philip Shriver Klein, *President James Buchanan* (University Park, 1962), 427-28.
[38] Oakford to Cameron, June 5, 1868, Cameron MSS, LC.

So I must start a shop myself
Outside the devil's yard
With Butler and some other thieves
To act as picket guard.[39]

On a hot midsummer Washington night, this sinister figure in American history suffered himself to be baptized by Sister Loretta and on the stroke of midnight forthwith gave up the ghost.

The period between Grant's election and his inauguration was one of anxious speculation regarding the complexion of the new Cabinet. In the face of determined efforts by political leaders to elicit specific Cabinet committments from him the President-elect maintained absolute silence on the subject. A committee of Pennsylvania congressmen, sharing the feeling prevailing among the Commonwealth's political leaders, called on Grant who assured them of their state's representation in his Cabinet. Curtin's friends began advancing him for a Cabinet post, which, according to McClure, he did not desire because of probable conflicts with Cameron over control of the patronage.[40]

There was much speculation in the press over reported interviews between A. K. McClure and Grant. In a letter to the Philadelphia *Bulletin* and later in his *Notes* McClure denied calling on Grant for the purpose of urging an appointment for Curtin.[41] According to McClure's version of the story, Judge John M. Read requested McClure to deliver a letter to Grant. McClure, in ignorance of the letter's significance, was on the point of terminating his interview when Grant informed him of the letter's contents and of his deter-

---

[39] Erie *Observer,* March 5, 1868.
[40] *Notes,* II, 221.
[41] *Ibid.,* 221-22; *Bulletin,* quoted in Harrisburg *Patriot,* March 1, 1869.

mination to appoint Cabinet members "entirely in conformity with his personal wishes." McClure, divining Grant's intentions to appoint Adolph Borie, suggested the appointment of a statesman with administrative experience.[42] According to the contemporary press, McClure expected George H. Stuart to receive the appointment because Grant had expressed no objections to him.[43] Possibly McClure, with thirty-five years hindsight, did insert Borie's name instead of Stuart's when he wrote his *Notes.* One reliable source states that Grant, on advice from Cameron, at first offered a post to Stuart, who declined.[44]

McClure's open letter to the Philadelphia *Bulletin,* containing a statement from Grant that he had not received a letter from "—— on the cabinet" compelled Governor Geary to speak on the subject. Geary hastened to correct any illusion regarding his endorsement of Curtin. His telegram to Grant read: "I have never written or telegraphed to you or any other person one word in favor of or against anyone for that position.[45] Actually Geary, who hoped to see Jay Cooke selected for a Cabinet position, was vexed at Grant's disregard of the Philadelphia financier and determined to give the President a piece of his mind.[46] Others believed that Jay Cooke must be Grant's choice. After moving into his $50,000 home, a gift made possible by voluntary contributions in Philadelphia, Grant became practically a citizen of the city, often rode with Henry Cooke, and was a frequent visitor to his home. Moreover, the Cookes

[42] *Notes,* II, 221-22.
[43] Philadelphia *Bulletin,* quoted in Harrisburg *Patriot,* Feb. 26, 1869.
[44] Oberholtzer, *Jay Cooke,* II, 79.
[45] Philadelphia *Press,* Feb. 27, 1869.
[46] Henry Cooke to Jay Cooke, March 10, 1869, Oberholtzer, *Jay Cooke,* II, 79.

had contributed heavily to the Republican campaign chest; but significantly the heaviest contributor to Grant's new residence was Adolph Borie.

On March 4, 1869, shortly after the "sun of peace burst brightly forth" from a cloudy sky, the Union hero was sworn into office. Henry Adams went to the Capitol to hear Grant's Cabinet nominations which "had the singular effect of making the hearer ashamed, not so much of Grant, as of himself."[47] When Adolph Borie's name was read for the Navy post, the question, "Who is Borie?" buzzed around the chamber. Only one senator, it was said, had ever heard of him.[48] At last Pennsylvania's representative in the new Cabinet stood revealed, and the Harrisburg *Patriot* soberly bestowed merit upon the new President for his ability to discover Borie without the aid of McClure, Cameron, or Curtin. The Democratic press stood in general accord with the verdict of the Lancaster *Intelligencer* that never in the history of any nation were such nobodies called to exercise the office of state;[49] and the editor of the Democratic *Watchman* ran the risk of besmirching the good name of Bellefonte when he compared the potential efficiency of Grant's Cabinet to that of his home town council.[50]

The new unknown Secretary of the Navy was the son of a French immigrant who had gained success in his chosen city of Philadelphia. Adolph, his eldest child, secured a fine education, traveled abroad, and then settled down to assist his father. The firm's trade centered in the two areas of the Caribbean and the Far East. Though probably he never heard of the term "dollar diplomacy," Borie understood how to manipulate channels to his firm's advantage. He at first

---

[47] Henry Adams, *Education of Henry Adams* (Boston, 1927), 262.
[48] McCulloch, *Men and Measures*, 350.
[49] March 12, 1869.
[50] March 12, 1869.

considered himself a protectionist Whig and then turned to
Lincoln's party in 1860. Here was a successful business man
turned Republican in the natural course of events. The neat,
modest Borie was just as much surprised over his appointment as was Henry Adams or any other American citizen.

Borie, immediately recognizing his subservience to
Admiral David Porter, the actual head, determined to bow
out as gracefully as possible.[51] On June 25 Borie resigned,
listing reasons of a personal nature and his initial intention
of not remaining long in office.[52] Grant regretted sincerely
Borie's departure and hoped the quiet of the Secretary's
retirement would restore him to perfect health.[53] So departed
the small, dignified Borie, who "took office with a sigh and
gave it up with a laugh";[54] but the Grant-Borie friendship
lasted until death. Grant frequently invited Borie to bring
A. J. Drexel or George Childs along for a friendly game.
Before leaving on his European tour in 1877, Grant used
Borie's residence as a depot to stock such necessities as
champagne for the use of his party in crossing the ocean.

To Simon Cameron, the coming of the Grant Administration signified simplification of the patronage problem. The
obnoxious Andrew Johnson had finally vacated the presidential chair and two bona fide Republican senators now
represented the interests of the Keystone state. Furthermore,
members of the fast disappearing Curtin faction were no
longer in position to demand a share of the spoils. Grant's
Pennsylvania's appointments began about the middle of
March, The juiciest political plum in the state, the Collectorship of the Port of Philadelphia, went to the venerable Henry

[51] George S. Boutwell, *Reminiscences of Sixty Years in Public Affairs*, II, 212.
[52] Borie to Grant, June 25, 1869, Borie Family Papers, HSP.
[53] Grant to Borie, June 25, 1869, *ibid*.
[54] Forney, *Anecdotes*, II. 194.

D. Moore, an old Cameron lieutenant in that area. Grant, in ignorance of the accepted niceties of Federal appointments, nominated Ferdinand Cox of Philadelphia for a consulship but withdrew it when Cameron protested. When the President nominated A. L. Russell, a former Curtin adherent, for an insignificant mission to Ecuador, both Cameron and his junior colleague, John Scott, opposed the appointment and his name was withdrawn.[55] If this test case meant anything, Curtin's followers were definitely outside the pale of Federal patronage and were likely to remain so.

Curtin had received assurances both from Grant and Elihu B. Washburne, the President's confidant, that he would in some manner be rewarded for his services to the party. At the beginning of the presidential campaign in 1868, Curtin had hoped not to be called into active party service because of his poor health and work, but his friends insisted that his help was needed to insure Grant the state. The ex-governor, succumbing to these entreaties, assured Washburne of his aid through a tour then being arranged by the Republican State Central Committee.[56] Following Grant's election, Curtin, fearful of committing publicly a political *faux pas,* called upon his old friend William M. Meredith to advise him concerning an address he expected to deliver at a Philadelphia banquet in January, 1869.[57] Only two days before Grant's inaugural, McClure wrote to Washburne requesting an immediate interview and emphasizing his intention of not talking about the cabinet.[58] McClure, knowing Curtin had no chance of entering the President's official family, very likely desired a last minute assurance of a foreign mission for him. Although McClure denied ever having visited Grant after

---

[55] West Chester *American Republican,* April 27, 1869.
[56] Curtin to Washburne, Aug. 30, 1868, Washburne MSS, LC.
[57] Curtin to Meredith, Jan. 3, 1869, William Meredith Papers, HSP.
[58] McClure to Washburne, March 2, 1869, Washburne MSS, LC.

the embarrassing February interview,[59] the Philadelphia *Press* recorded a "cordial interview" between the pair about a week after the inauguration.[60]

In middle April, Grant nominated Curtin Minister to Russia, and the Senate Foreign Relations Committee followed with an unanimous favorable report. It is hard to determine exactly what happened when the nomination was discussed in executive session of the Senate behind closed doors. Forney's Philadelphia *Press,* which usually had access to such information, reported only one speech in opposition to Curtin's confirmation—a bitter philippic delivered by Simon Cameron. Reputedly, John Scott, the state's new senator, defended Curtin in reviewing his public services.[61] On the same day the Democratic Reading *Eagle* also reported a severe attack by Cameron upon Curtin's nomination. It seems very unlikely that the same correspondent reported both accounts. McClure substantiated the story of Cameron's opposition and according to one of Grant's biographers, Curtin's nomination was accepted only after wrangling.[62]

The voice of Matthew S. Quay, the Beaver *Argus,* branded the account of Cameron's opposition as a "Cock and Bull Story." The weekly published an "authorized account" of Cameron's comments: " . . . while Mr. Curtin was not recommended by the Representatives of his State, and in his [Cameron's] opinion was not the choice of the Republican party of the state, he would not oppose it because he had been nominated by the president."[63] In 1863, when Curtin felt his health would not allow a second term as governor,

---

[59] *Notes,* II, 223.
[60] April 16, 1869.
[61] April 17, 1867.
[62] Hesseltine, *Ulysses S. Grant,* 155.
[63] April 28, 1869,

Cameron had cooperated with McClure and Forney in securing a promise of a foreign mission, because Cameron at that time felt "Curtin should be got rid of."[64] Cameron had served a short time of "exile" in 1862 and realized what prolonged absence could do to a personal political machine. Cameron's opposition to Curtin's going abroad in 1869 indicated that he considered himself in fullness of power, Curtin impotent, and no longer a hazard to be feared at home.

For Andrew G. Curtin there was little choice. As long as he retained the Russian mission, he was in a position commanding respect and prestige. At home he was a private citizen with a famous past, but no future. His former followers found themselves barred from political advancement by the machine Cameron had forged and which gave every indication of remaining in power. Ambitious, able young men like Matthew Quay must either obey the new master's voice or leave the party, while young neophytes in the Republican camp could easily be molded to play their part. Curtin realized fully his precarious position and took the only opportunity for political office which presented itself.

As the time neared for his departure abroad, Curtin's stock rose. Daniel Fox, mayor of Philadelphia, acting on a resolution of the city council, offered Curtin an official farewell to take place at Independence Hall. The reception was held on Saturday, June 12. Such a vast multitude turned out to greet the former governor that he found it impossible to shake hands with all. Over five hundred guests attended the banquet in the Academy of Music. The vast and brilliant room was gorgeously decorated and Hassler's celebrated orchestra, in the parlance of the day, "discoursed delightful

---

[64] McClure, *Lincoln and Men of War Times,* 262-63.

music." Various sentiments were proposed by Curtin, John Scott, Count Bodisco, Francis Jordan, Cyrus Field, and James Pollock. Other notables present were John Cessna, Judge Sharswood, F. Carroll Brewster, A. K. McClure, and William B. Mann. Letters expressing regret for non-attendance were read from Grant, Geary, Hamilton Fish, Borie, Sherman, Meade, Greeley, Forney, and others.[65]

Secretary of State Fish had become unduly exercised over rumors of a coming address from Curtin on the delicate subject of the Alabama claims against Britain; but Curtin relieved the Secretary on that score: "I have made up my mind to say nothing on any subject relating to the foreign policy of the government."[66]

Following another dinner with the Union League, Curtin left June 16 for New York. Accompanying him were his wife, two daughters, and two secretaries. Like other diplomats of the era, Curtin proceeded to his new post in a leisurely fashion. In Germany, he rested and notified Cassius Marcellus Clay, the retiring minister, of his intended arrival. Clay, who held Curtin in much higher esteem than he did Cameron, prepared to receive the new envoy graciously. Clay ventured to predict Curtin's future immediately upon his arrival: "You will not stay long at this court. Why? Because you are too honest a man to favor the Perkins swindle; and as the Immortal Fish comes in under Seward's influence, you will have to go for blackmail or lose your peace."[67] But Curtin remained in Russia three years, although during the trying Catacazy affair it looked as if he might have to come home.

From his frigid Russian retreat, Curtin could not refrain

---

[65] *Honors to Andrew Gregg Curtin* (Philadelphia, 1869).

[66] Curtin to Fish, June 9, 1869, Hamilton Fish Papers, LC.

[67] Cassius M. Clay, *The Life of Cassius Marcellus Clay, Memoirs, Writings and Speeches* (Cincinnati, 1886), I, 452.

from shooting a final shaft at his archenemy, Simon
Cameron. To Washburne he wrote: "I am a little disturbed
by the announcement that Congress will take the usual
Christmas recess and fear your red hot colleague may make
another raid on Bellefonte as he knows the morality of the
village is without the protection of my presence."[68]

The year 1869 not only inaugurated the new Radical
regime of Grant in Washington but also witnessed the end
of Pennsylvania's Democratic voice in the Senate of United
States. Charles R. Buckalew, renowned for his narrow
triumph over Cameron in 1863, would retire, and the ample
joint majority scored by the Republicans in the legislative
elections of 1868 insured the selection of a new Union-
Republican senator. The contest for the senatorship in 1869,
it was easily seen, would lack the striking feature of the
struggle of 1867. There would be no Curtin-Cameron contest,
and it remained to be seen whether any new combination
could challenge Cameron's power or thwart his desire to
select a hand-picked colleague to serve with him in the
Senate. On the surface it looked as if no candidate would
have factional backing. Since, apparently, neither Curtin,
Cameron, nor Geary were showing any interest in the outcome, a fresh crop of aspirants including John Scott, Thomas
Marshall, Glenni Scofield, Chief Justice Thompson, and the
hardy perennials, J. K. Moorhead, B. H. Brewster, and
Galusha A. Grow, all joined in what looked like a free-for-all.

Actually, two powerful interest groups were busy at work
behind the scenes. One of these forces was the Quay-Kemble
combination, known simply as the "Ring," which hoped to
elect Kemble; the other was the Pennsylvania Railroad–
Cameron combination which had decided to back the railroad's able attorney, John Scott of Huntingdon. The Quay-

[68] Curtin to Washburne, Dec. 15, 1869, Washburne, MSS, LC.

Kemble combination was managed by William H. Kemble of Philadelphia and Matthew Stanley Quay of Beaver.

Kemble owed his first entrance into office to a logrolling arrangement between A. K. McClure's Republicans and Kemble's Philadelphia coterie. In order to secure legislative relief for the citizens of Chambersburg lately impoverished by Confederate raids, McClure's friends assisted in electing Kemble state treasurer. Kemble used the state money at his disposal for purposes of private investments and reputedly accumulated a fortune. Quay, who was head of the Ring in western Pennsylvania, had cut himself loose from the impotent Curtin after the latter's defeat for the senatorship in 1867, and began looking for a new luminary to which he might hitch his star. J. Donald Cameron, director of his father's faction, learned of the Kemble plan in the fall of 1868 and warned his local lieutenants of the move. One of them responded: "God forbid that Pennsylvania should be so misrepresented. What is the reason that every villain in Philadelphia pops up like 'Jack in the box' everytime there is a vacant chair."[69]

Cameron was playing the same cagey game he used to procure Cowan's election in 1861. J. K. Moorhead of Allegheny, reluctant to announce his candidacy unless he could get a promise of support from Cameron, wrote of his backing from the Cameron Allegheny men. Cameron, believing it expedient not to antagonize the powerful Pittsburgh chieftain at that time,[70] penned a friendly reply in which he promised nothing definite. In his next communication Moorhead warned Cameron that the Kemble Ring had so effectually "occupied the ground" that it would

[69] W. H. Cobb to Cameron, Oct. 22, 1868, Cameron MSS, LC.
[70] J. K. Moorhead to Cameron, Aug. 24, 1868, *ibid.*; H. Cooke to J. Cooke, Dec. 16, 1868, Crippen Note.

require the combined efforts of all to defeat him. The Pittsburgh magnate was willing to withdraw if Cameron would present a name stronger than his own.[71]

How Kemble was checkmated apparently is not known, but existing evidence points to two figures—J. Donald Cameron and Quay, the minor partner in the Kemble Ring. In late December, 1868, the following comment on J. Donald Cameron appeared in Quay's new journalistic venture, the Beaver *Radical*.

The power he exerts in the politics of Pennsylvania is truly wonderful. His office was constantly crowded, while we were in Harrisburg, with politicians from all parts of the state, and he will have [as] much to do with the election of U.S. Senator this winter as any man in the state, the editor of the *Radical* not excepted.[72]

Certainly this was a strange comment from the professed leader of the Kemble forces. It looked as if Quay might have secretly been received into the communion of the Cameron faction. At the time of Curtin's defeat for the caucus nomination in 1867, Quay had moved the unanimous nomination of Cameron after he was assured of it. This was an extraordinary gesture of friendship for one who had served long as Curtin's private secretary. For the next year Quay had gone his own way, taking time to study the omens. Quay realized that political advancement could best be found within the Cameron fold, and his prominence in the powerful Kemble faction now gave him the opportunity he was seeking—a position in which to bargain successfully with the Camerons. Simon Cameron and his son J. Donald could hardly fail to recognize Quay's talents, and here was an opportunity to pull the props out from under Kemble by

[71] Moorhead to Cameron, Oct. 31, 1868, Cameron MSS, LC.
[72] Beaver *Radical,* quoted in the *Argus,* Dec. 23, 1868.

accepting Quay as a partner. According to McClure, the hostility between Quay and Cameron had disappeared by the end of 1867. Quay's ability to procure the election of his neighbor, W. W. Irwin, to the state treasurership in 1868 proved two things—his unusual political sagacity and Cameron's tolerance of his activities.

On December 18, 1868, Cameron received congratulations on "stopping the Ring" and placing himself in position to name the new senator.[73] A few days later, the Beaver *Argus* reported Kemble's prospects as being "nipped in the bud."[74] This interesting inside information emanating from remote Beaver County was revealed at the same time Quay returned from observing J. Donald Cameron's busy office in Harrisburg. It must be kept in mind that definite information is lacking to prove Quay sold out his partner, Kemble, but the former's sudden appearance as a full-fledged Cameron lieutenant can hardly be explained in any other fashion. Apparently, this was the first forging of the notorious Cameron-Quay machine which was destined to dominate the state's Republican organization for another four decades.

In 1867, if Cameron had not decided to take the senatorship for himself he would likely have supported his friend Benjamin Harrison Brewster of Philadelphia. While in Russia he had promised to support Brewster and then hastened back home to try for the prize himself. The time had arrived, felt Brewster, when Cameron could no longer withhold his support. On the eve of the legislature's reorganization, Brewster made a long pathetic last appeal to the all-powerful: ". . . you can make me senator. The people hold back to know your wish. When they see your

[73] Cobb to Cameron, Dec. 18, 1868, Cameron MSS, LC.
[74] Dec. 23, 1868.

followers lead off for me they will follow." Brewster reminded Cameron of his past (doglike) devotion and concluded: "Do not fail me and give me a wound I can never recover from and your enemies the delight of knowing that you surrendered."[75] Cameron was publicly maintaining silence, but by the end of the year his lieutenants must have received the signal to begin a whispering campaign for John Scott. Cameron had decided to strengthen his already powerful position by establishing an alliance with the fast growing titan of the post-bellum age, the railroad interests, in preference to forcing the candidacy of a friend who was personally obnoxious to many prominent Republicans.

On New Year's Day, 1869, when the advanced guard of legislators began to arrive in Harrisburg, the political atmosphere at the Keystone capital was rife with abounding rumors. James Thompson, the chief justice, who had lately engaged in friendly correspondence with Cameron, was a favored dark horse. Grow's followers and Glenni Scofield, a prominent Radical with no following, were likewise hopeful of last-minute support from the Cameron faction. Both Kemble and Grow were on the scene early pushing their friends for the speakership of the House. The election of a speaker was expected to reveal the relative strength of the various candidates.[76]

The election of John Clark to the speakership on January 4 contributed little toward lifting the fog surrounding the senatorial question. Clark, a Philadelphian, had served as an engineer in the army building roads in Virginia and Tennessee, and had later contracted for the building of portions of the Central and Northern Central Railroads. Cameron had known this quiet man well from the time he

---

[75] Brewster to Cameron, Jan. 1, 1869, Cameron MSS, LC.
[76] Philadelphia *Telegraph*, Jan. 4, 1869.

had worked for the railroads, but few persons were aware of his former connections with Cameron. For the uninformed and the naïve, word was circulated of Clark's neutral position. Even Russell Errett of the Pittsburgh *Gazette* was in *ignorance* of the situation, and Forney's *Press* considered J. K. Moorhead a favorite until the day of the Republican caucus.[77] But according to A. K. McClure, "it was very early discovered by all that the position was irrevocably disposed of before the Legislature met."[78] That the senatorship was decided before the legislature met is a fact not to be disputed, but surely it was known by very few. Benjamin Harrison Brewster did not know the truth and Governor Geary's mouthpiece, the Harrisburg *State Guard,* proclaimed on January 14 Cameron's disinterestedness. One of Cameron's correspondents, E. B. Moore, editor of the West Chester *American Republican,* correctly grasped the situation and listed Grow, Moorhead, Kemble, Thompson, Scofield, and Marshall as the ones who would *not* receive the nomination. Simple subtraction gave his readers the answer —John Scott.

After adjournment of the state House of Representatives on January 6, the Republican caucus consumed only fifteen minutes in selecting its senatorial candidate. General Fisher, an old Stevens man, nominated John Scott. Morrow B. Lowry of Crawford County then nominated Benjamin H. Brewster. Lowry was angry at Cameron because of the recent coup executed against his friend General W. W. Irwin, who had just lost renomination for state treasurer to Robert W. Mackey. Scott was nominated by acclamation, with no requests from the chair for the "Nays."[79] According

---

[77] *Ibid.,* Jan. 5, 1869.
[78] *Notes,* II, 224.
[79] Lancaster *Intelligencer* quoted in Erie *Observer,* Jan. 14, 1869.

to a behind-the-scenes account Scofield and Grow withdrew from the race the night before the caucus immediately following a conference with Simon Cameron, his son J. Donald, and John Scott. The following morning J. K. Moorhead withdrew and announced his support of Scott. But "the real caucus," wrote G. Eyster ". . . was held in a room in Phila., not far from the Penna. R. R. Office, this night one week. Mr. S[cott] was present by request. He had an important interview in Harrisburg with one of its citizens *by request* three weeks ago in which he refused to assist in the organization that was proposed."[80]

It requires little imagination to picture what occurred in the room near the Pennsylvania Railroad office. One of the Camerons, probably J. Donald, acting as agent for the railroad wizard Thomas Scott, had first contacted John Scott in Harrisburg and made arrangements to have him conclude the "bargain" secretly with Thomas Scott in Philadelphia. Eyster's conclusion that John Scott's show of independence[81] won him the support of Cameron and the Pennsylvania Railroad interests, can hardly, under the known circumstances, be taken seriously. McClure, perhaps wishing to minimize Cameron's part in the affair, "revealed" many years later that Thomas Scott, "alone," had accomplished John Scott's election.[82] Gideon Welles, on the other hand, credited Cameron with a complete triumph over the railroad interests: "The railroad controls Pennsylvania, and Cameron has had the adroitness to secure it."[83] And finally, Cameron's

---

[80] [G. Eyster] to William McPherson, Jan. 8, 1869, McPherson MSS, LC. The signature was deleted but the handwriting is undoubtedly Eyster's. John Scott was married to Ann Eyster.
[81] *Ibid.*
[82] *Notes,* II, 225.
[83] Welles, *Diary,* III, 505.

accomplishment in liquidating the Kemble threat before the legislature convened must be recognized.

Certainly Attorney John Scott suited admirably the requirements of the railroad barons. He could, because of long contact with railroad interests, be counted upon to foster favorable railroad subsidies and legislation at Washington; but at the same time he was ostensibly free from political entanglements, with a reputation above reproach. The railroad men, Scott, and Cameron were all interested in national expansion. Had political veterans like Grow or Moorhead been elected, they would likely have insisted upon their fair share of patronage, but John Scott, possessing no clientele, was likely to allow Cameron complete control of the state's patronage. Seemingly, unwittingly or not, the conspirators had made a fine choice, and the press generally agreed on the wisdom of the selection. The Democratic Harrisburg *Patriot* published opinions culled from the press:[84] "An excellent character. If one man controls the legislature it matters little who the man be"— Philadelphia *Bulletin;* "A Conscientious Statesman"—Philadelphia *Press;* "Struck dumb and the editor went fishing"— Pittsburgh *Gazette.* If a pure man could be found among the Republicans, concluded the *Patriot,* his name was John Scott. Other Democratic organs praised Scott on personal ground; but deprecated his subservience in his role as the railroad-Cameron candidate.[85]

The general tone of friendliness exhibited in the Republican caucus contrasted sharply with that reigning in the Democratic ranks. In view of the fact that the Democracy stood no chance of electing its candidate, one would have

---

[84] Jan. 9, 1869.

[85] Bedford *Inquirer,* quoted in Hollidaysburg *Register,* Jan. 13, 1869 ; Lancaster *Intelligencer,* Jan. 13, 1869.

thought it mattered little who should receive the empty compliment. William Wallace, leader of the state party, had taken exactly that attitude in January, 1867, when the nomination was bestowed upon Edgar Cowan; but Wallace knew that Cowan, the renegade, could never exercise control of the state Democracy. The case of the retiring popular senator, Charles R. Buckalew, who had served his party well, was different. To award Buckalew another nomination meant to Wallace a loss of prestige. Besides, the elections of 1867 and 1868 placed Pennsylvania in the "critical" state column, and conceivably, the Keystone state might in the not too distant future switch to the Democratic column. The determination of Wallace to take the recognition for himself led to a bitter fight between the two leaders and split the Democracy into two factions. Wallace's organization was too strong in the caucus for the retiring Senator Buckalew, whom he defeated 31 to 18.[86] The great Democratic schism was to be widened in 1875 when Wallace again sought the nomination.

On January 19, John Scott achieved the senatorship by practically a straight party vote, 78 to 51. This relatively unknown lawyer had gained the high honors strangely predicted for him by Forney almost three years earlier.[87] The new senator, a native of Huntingdon County, was born at Alexandria, July 24, 1824. His Scotch-Irish great-grandfather migrated to Adams County about the year 1740. Scott's father, a shoemaker and tanner by trade, rose to rank of major in the War of 1812, and served in both the state and national legislatures. His son John attended the local elementary school, the Alexandria Academy, and secured additional instruction in the classics from his Presbyterian

---

[86] Philadelphia *Press,* Jan. 21, 1869.
[87] *Ibid.,* March 5, 1866.

pastor. The ambitious John Scott, an apprenticed tanner, preferred a different career and went to Franklin County to study law under Judge Alexander Thompson of Chambersburg. After admission to the bar in 1846, Scott decided to practice law at his county seat, Huntingdon, only a few miles from his home. Four years later he married Anne E. Eyster, who bore him ten children.

Scott first made political headlines when he drew up a formal protest against Buchanan's presidential candidacy in 1852 and presented it to the Democratic state convention. After spending a vacation in Europe for his health, Scott made his first bid for the state legislature in 1854 as the "citizens" candidate but was beaten by the Know-Nothings. In 1860, Scott supported Douglas for the Presidency. The following year he was elected to the state legislature with the support of both major parties. Although classed as a War Democrat, he stumped for Curtin in 1863. His point of departure from Democratic ranks properly began with his support of Lincoln in 1864. Scott gave his delegates to Geary at the state convention of 1866 and actively campaigned for the General. Geary would have taken Scott, who was also the choice of Stevens and Forney, into his cabinet had it not been for Cameron's influence on behalf of Brewster.[88] In 1868 Scott easily cleared the Radical-protectionist bar when he said: "American labor must be protected against the competition of low-priced foreign labor; our Domestic industries properly encouraged. The power of Congress to impose terms upon rebellious states before their readmission . . . must be maintained."[89]

On March 4, 1869, John Scott took his seat in the Senate chamber next to Hannibal Hamlin. Two weeks later his

[88] L. Kauffman to Stevens, Jan. 4, 1867, Stevens MSS, LC.
[89] Lewistown *Gazette,* Aug. 26, 1868.

maiden speech argued against the constitutionality of the Tenure of Office Act.[90] He early showed his independence by moving an amendment to a railroad bill in opposition to Cameron's wishes.[91] McClure's observation that Scott's election left all the Federal patronage to Cameron, seems an overstatement. Several letters in Cameron manuscripts indicate that Scott was sharing in the patronage, though to what extent it is impossible to say. After two years, Scott wrote of a pending appointment not favored by Grant: ". . . we must agree on another, and don't commit Forney until I see you." His correspondence does not smack of servility but rather of collaboration. Scott performed his most notable work in the Senate as chairman of a special committee created to investigate Klan outrages. He supported his committee's report with a powerful speech in favor of a bill to prolong the President's authority to suspend the writ of *habeas corpus*. Of his work, Blaine wrote: "No man wrought so effectively in exposing to the condemnation of public opinion the evil work of the Ku Klux organizations in the South."[92]

With the installation in the Senate of a stalwart friend of Pennsylvania's business interests, the Railroad-Cameron Ring next directed its activities in the direction of Washington, having as its aim the capture of the new Chief Executive. It would be the goal of the Radical leaders to mold the malleable Grant into one of their own stamp. Simon Cameron determined to repeat his accomplishment under Lincoln—recognition of himself as the President's man in

---

[90] Harrisburg *Patriot,* March 25, 1869.

[91] *Cong. Globe,* 41 Cong., I Sess., 473.

[92] Blaine, *Twenty Years,* II, 446-47. On Scott see Jordan, *Encyclopaedia of Pennsylvania Biography,* I, 156-57; Milton S. Lytle, *History of Huntington County,* 207-13; Hollidaysburg *Register,* Jan. 13, 1869,

Pennsylvania. The gullible novice in politics, U. S. Grant, fell an easy prey to the artifices of Cameron. The home of the colorful General Thomas L. Kane in the great northern wood was selected as the ideal spot for establishing a comrade-like relationship between the pair. In mid-June, 1869, Kane was expecting Grant to join him and his only "invited guest," Simon Cameron, but the President wasn't able to make the trip until August.[93] J. Donald Cameron skillfully expedited the Cameron-Grant liaison by furnishing gratis a special excursion car for the President's pleasure during his jaunt through Penn's woods: and the following February, the name of J. D. Cameron appeared on the White House guest list.[94]

In approximately a year, Cameron had completed his conquest of the President. In June, 1870, occurred the famous fishing trip when Cameron took "Jolly Jack" Hiestand and Grant with him to the headwaters of the Susquehanna River in Cameron County. According to current press reports, not a single aquatic craniate vertebrate had been lifted from the waters, but old Simon, the consummate fisher of men, had caught the biggest fish of all— President Grant.[95] And so Pennsylvania's premier politico became a part of the trinity of Chandler, Conkling, and Cameron, which largely dominated the President's thinking with its sophistries.

Cameron assisted Grant in purging his Cabinet of undesirable reformers who would not countenance the orgy of "law jobbery." Attorney General Hoar's removal was

---

[93] Kane to Cameron, June 15, 1869, Cameron MSS, LC; Pittsburgh *Gazette,* Aug. 16, 1869.

[94] Lancaster *Intelligencer,* Feb. 23, 1870.

[95] New York *World,* June 20, 1870. Hiestand of the Lancaster *Examiner,* through Cameron's influence, was appointed naval officer in Philadelphia.

first planned through an appointment to the Supreme Court; but the honest Secretary had affronted too many patronage seeking politicians and the Senate rejected his nomination. Gloated Cameron: "What could you expect for a man who had snubbed seventy senators."[96] Six months later Hoar was subjected to outright dismissal. Secretary Cox, who had organized his department on the merit system and consequently was anathema to the bosses, was next to go. The Interior Secretary was practically forced to resign when the President gave him no support in opposing questionable mining transactions. "Cameron had Cox driven from the cabinet," charged the Harrisburg *Patriot,* because he would not allow the clerks in his department to be assessed for political contributions. Zachariah Chandler assisted Cameron in bringing about Cox's dismissal.[97]

The fall of Charles Sumner before the Grant ax had the effect of further promoting Cameron's prestige under the national administration. The Senate Foreign Relations Committee had reported unfavorably on Grant's plan to annex Santo Domingo. Cameron, a member of the committee, signed the unfavorable report but left a loophole through which he could escape the Grant wrath—"under certain circumstances he would vote for annexation." Not long after Cameron's son-in-law was appointed minister to Turkey, Cameron voted for the President's treaty of annexation in the executive session of the Senate. The following March, through Grant's influence, Sumner was deposed as chairman of the Senate Foreign Relations Committee, and Cameron, the second-ranking Republican on the committee, inherited Sumner's place. Apparently Cameron had no desire to succeed his friend Sumner. "On Sumner's last day in the Senate they parted with a mutual 'God Bless You.' "[98] A Philadelphia paper compared Cameron's new chairmanship to Caligula's promotion of his horse to consul;[99] and a competent historian agreed that "Cameron was badly equipped for the place,"[100] but nevertheless on May 30, 1871, Hamilton Fish thanked Cameron for his efficient chairmanship.[101]

In matters of Federal patronage Cameron was doing very well, but Grant's hasty appointment of Cameron's son-in-law to the Porte brought mostly grief to the father-in-law. Wayne MacVeagh, a former Curtin supporter, had married Jennie Cameron shortly after the war. In the spring of 1870, MacVeagh decided on a European tour in hope of restoring his broken health. Suddenly, on June 1, a fortnight before sailing date, Grant ordered his appointment as minister to Turkey. He received the mission on Friday, the Senate approved on Saturday, and MacVeagh sailed on schedule, with an additional $10,000 in government gold added to the itinerary budget. After a leisurely and enjoyable tour through Scotland, France, Germany, and Italy at the American taxpayers' expense, MacVeagh arrived in Constantinople in October; thereupon, aping his father-in-law's Russian mission, he immediately requested a furlough home. MacVeagh's unabashed proposal to convert his Turkish mission into an European jaunt aroused a storm of protest and under proddings from his father-in-law, the errant diplomat decided to remain until spring.[102]

[98] Edward L. Pierce, ed., *Memoirs and Letters of Charles Sumner* (Boston, 1893), IV, 476.
[99] Hesseltine, *Grant,* 254.
[100] Nevins, *Fish,* 463.
[101] Fish to Cameron, May 30, 1871, Cameron MSS, LC.
[102] Hollidaysburg *Register,* Nov. 30, 1870 ; MacVeagh to Cameron, Dec. 23, 26, 1870, Cameron MSS, LC.

Cameron could hardly say no to Grant's appointment of John W. Forney to the collectorship of Philadelphia. True, Forney's *Press* had spewed its venom upon Cameron in 1867 when the editor headed a coalition designed to block Cameron's candidacy for the senatorship. After a time, passions cooled, Forney began making overtures for a renewal of their periodic friendships, and the editor gave much favorable notice and publicity to Cameron's public services in his *Press*. In doubt as to whether Cameron might be reading his organ, Forney called Cameron's attention to his flattering articles. Forney pretended to accept the collectorship reluctantly and wrote Cameron a letter of appreciation for the "kind consideration," the senator had manifested in securing his confirmation for the collectorship.[103] As long as Forney retained the lucrative Philadelphia post, it looked as if Cameron had nothing to fear from one of the most powerful newspaper editors in the nation. Over a quarter of a century had passed since Forney had wailed: "Simon Cameron's the Senator! God save the Commonwealth."[104]

Cameron was now approaching the acme of his power, prestige, and personal direction of his powerful political-business combination. Having passed the biblical alloted time of three score years and ten, and busy with senatorial and business burdens, he increasingly relied upon the recognized skill of his two leading lieutenants, J. Donald Cameron and Matthew Quay, for the proper functioning and maintenance of the powerful machine he had fashioned over the years. He had succeeded in barring members of the Curtin coterie from the advantage of the patronage and

---

[103] Forney to Cameron, Dec. 29, 1869; March 26, 1871, *ibid.*
[104] Forney to Morton McMichael, March 14, 1845, Forney MSS, LC.

positions of trust. His man Russell Errett was now chairman of the Republican State Central Committee. The only person who stood in the way of Cameron's complete control of the state was Governor Geary, who declared his independence after his re-election. With his success in maintaining great influence over Grant, he not only controlled his own state, but had extended his clientele beyond the borders of Pennsylvania. His "benign" influence was everywhere heard of and recognized. Over two hundred persons in Washington owed their positions to Cameron, stated the Cincinnati *Times.* The reason for the existence of this amazing empire, in the opinion of its beneficiaries, was extremely simple. Here was a man who would make more personal exertions to oblige his "friends" than perhaps any man who ever occupied a seat in the Senate of United States.[105]

---

[105] Cincinnati *Times,* quoted in Lewistown *Gazette,* Nov. 16, 1870.

IX

The Witches' Brew of the Geary Regime

THE ERA OF John White Geary, extending from 1867 to 1873, was characterized by those features found in the postwar age throughout the nation. There was much comment and discussion in the Commonwealth's press of treasury "rings," legislative corruption, the activities of special interests, especially that of the Pennsylvania Railroad, and of corrupt special legislation. The strength of political leaders of the Commonwealth has been emphasized by writers, but little has been heard of the economic power behind the scenes which in alliance with political groups was successful in fostering legislation, for a price, favorable to its interest. The story of the interplay between the representatives of special interest and of the political representatives and officers of the citizenry is one requiring separate study and writing, but since it is interwoven with the political life of the time requires more than passing notice. A special feature of the Geary administration was the subject of executive pardons and the evils thereof.

Not long after Geary's induction into office complaints against the governor's alleged abuse of the pardoning power for political purposes appeared in the Democratic organs. Early in his administration he established a series of pardon regulations which he ordered to be rigidly followed. One of the best features was the publicity attached to each application for pardon. Notice of every application had to appear in the press of the same county in which the conviction was secured, and both the judge and prosecuting district attorney concerned with the case had to be notified.[1] Geary also called attention to the pardoning power which was being dispensed in Philadelphia where a court of quarter sessions altered and remitted fines after the prisoners had begun serving their sentences. Within a period of one year, charged the angry governor, as many convicts were set free from one Philadelphia prison as were pardoned by him in the entire state.[2] The practice of remitting the sentences and fines of convicted criminals after commitment to prison was tantamount to a wholesale dispensation of pardons.

The Democratic press publicized the activities of the pardon brokers in Philadelphia and accused William B. Mann, the city's powerful district attorney, of participation in the nefarious trade. For a fee from those convicted criminals able to pay, the brokers made arrangements with the equally criminal judges. In addition to the evils connected with this practice, there was the constitutional aspect of having the judicial branch of government usurp a prerogative of the state executive. Geary's attorney general brought suit against Philadelphia prison keepers for the purpose of restraining them from carrying out the orders of the Philadelphia courts. Pennsylvania's supreme court gave a verdict in favor of the Commonwealth, holding that a sentence could be changed only in the same term of court in which it was pronounced.[3]

The major source of complaint against Geary's use of executive clemency arose from a law of 1866 disfranchising

---

[1] *Geary and Williams,* Pamphlet Collection, PSL.
[2] *Papers of the Governors, 1857-1871,* 877.
[3] Commonwealth vs. Mayloy and Keating, *Pennsylvania State Reports,* LVIII (1869), 7 Smith, 291-92.

all deserters in the state.[4] According to an estimate made by the Radical Philadelphia *Press,* the state contained 30,000 deserters, "nearly all" of whom were Democrats. Republican judges of elections, allegedly ignoring the miscreants of their own stripe, made it a point to prevent Democratic deserters from voting. During the war, men recruited from the same locale often saw service side by side with their neighbors; and consequently, in local districts a soldier's desertion was often common knowledge although no one possessed proof. When an alleged deserter was refused his vote, he often sued the judge of election, and because that official could not prove his allegation he was found guilty of denying a qualified voter his franchise.[5] In a speech at Bradford, Geary admitted his sympathy for election judges who were being fined $700 or $800 simply for enforcing a law of the legislature. Many of the election judges were veterans willing to go to jail rather than allow the deserters a vote. Geary pardoned election judges whom he considered guilty only of enforcing the laws.

Geary received numerous petitions from convicted election judges in Westmoreland, Clinton, Columbia, Schuylkill, and Lycoming counties praying for executive clemency.[6] The petitions usually stated that the suppliants had rejected the vote of an allegedly qualified voter whom they knew or believed to be a deserter. In the case of Daniel Tarr of Greensburg, the convicted election official stated that the deserter had served with him in Knapp's Battery. Mention of this particular battery, once a part of the governor's old Twenty-eighth Regiment, was certain to strike a responsive

---

[4] Philadelphia *Press,* June 5, 1866.
[5] *Ibid.*
[6] Executive Minutes of Governor Geary, 1867-1868, PHMC.

chord within the proud war hero, Geary. Tarr was pardoned before he began serving his sentence.[7]

The pardon case of Daniel and J. S. Kuhns, who were found guilty of selling liquor to minors in Centre County, commands special attention because it was pleaded on purely political considerations. According to attorney Edmund Blanchard of Bellefonte, many prominent Republicans desired a license system for legal liquor, and a dissatisfied group were on the verge of deserting to the Democratic camp which wanted liquor. One of the Kuhns was an active influential Republican with a large following; consequently the party in Centre County could not afford his loss. Besides, the Democrats had sealed their own lips when they signed the Kuhn petition. The persistent Blanchard, accompanied by G. M. Young, failed to secure an interview with Geary, went back home, and later came back for another try.[8] Among the prominent names on the petition were an ex-governor and a future governor, Andrew G. Curtin and James Beaver, respectively. Geary granted the pardon on December 11, 1867.

The pardon case of I. Robby Dunglison, convicted of assault and battery upon a legislator who had offered $100 to Dunglison if the latter would engage him in personal combat, well illustrated the position of the governor. Geary was so wary of the petitioner that he refused to interview Dunglison except in the presence of his secretary of the Commonwealth, Francis Jordan. A well-known honest legislator wrote: "I hope you may not delay in befriending Mr. Dunglison. He is entitled to our sympathy and friendship." From the headquarters of the Republican state com-

---

[7] Pardon Papers of Governor Geary, PHMC.
[8] Blanchard to Geary, Nov. 7, 1867; Yocum to Jordan, Nov. 22, 1867, *ibid.*

mittee came a letter expressing surprise at Geary's hesitancy. Dunglison was pardoned the same day he was sentenced to sixty days imprisonment.[9]

The reform mayor of Pittsburgh, James Blackmore, was a frequent signer of petitions from Allegheny County. He seemed to take a special interest in the speedy rehabilitation of madams convicted of operating bawdy houses. The prominent Jay Cooke joined with twelve clergymen in asking for the pardon of two Philadelphia burglars whom Judge Allison had labeled hardened criminals. Geary's pardon list for 1868 included at least seven for murder, ten for burglary, eleven for larceny, four for keeping bawdy houses, and two for horse stealing. Geary found on his hands one convicted murderer who had been waiting for death for sixteen years.[10] These few cases illustrate the tremendous pressure brought to bear upon the governor. About 1,500 applications came in each year, most of them accompanied with requests for clemency from the leading men of the state.

Geary deserved neither condemnation nor praise for his pardon record. Certainly, he did not deserve the credit for originating the idea of a pardon board in Pennsylvania. Early in March, 1867, A. K. McClure was advocating such a plan in his *Repository*. "No single individual," argued McClure, "should be intrusted with the pardoning power. Let a bureau of pardon be created, and let the officers in charge be a few lawyers [and] one or two judges with the governor."[11] In 1869 the Philadelphia *Evening Telegraph* was advocating a pardon board and cited New Jersey's use

---

[9] Billingfelt to Geary, Aug. 30, 1869 ; J. S. Graham to Geary, Sept. 3, 1869 ; Owen to Geary, Aug. 23, 1869, *ibid.*

[10] Owen to Geary, Aug. 23, 1869, *ibid.; Papers of the Governors, 1857-1871,* 809.

[11] Chambersburg *Franklin Repository,* quoted in Altoona *Tribune,* March 6, 1867,

of one.[12] Geary issued only a few pardons for purely political reasons. Democratic editors branded Geary's pardon of election judges as partisan, but from the governor's point of view the convicted judges were guilty only of carrying out a patriotic legal duty in refusing the franchise to known deserters. Certainly the governor was not working in conjunction with any pardon brokers of the Philadelphia stripe.

The postwar legislative body of Pennsylvania vied with that in Albany for the notoriety of being the most corrupt in the nation. Seeking for definite proof is almost like searching for the proverbial pot of gold at the end of the rainbow. The research historian cannot expect to find signed receipts for paid legislative votes in the papers of public men of the period; yet the evidence of such corrupt transactions is so overwhelming that one must accept it as a fact. Pamphlets of the period bear such titles as "The Degradation of our Representative System and its Reform," and "An Inquiry into the Causes and Cost of Corrupt State Legislation." The secretary of the Commonwealth, Francis Jordan, during the course of his arguments against the passage of special legislation, linked with it another "giant evil," the practice of "buying and selling" legislative votes.[13] To the respected John Hickman, it seemed impossible for a legislator to return from Harrisburg with an unsullied reputation.[14] A survey conducted by the Harrisburg *State Guard* during the legislative session of 1869 found 22 honest legislators out of a total of 133.[15] "Bad as Albany was, men agreed if she should be destroyed by fire from heaven, Harrisburg might well fear the same fate."[16]

---

[12] April 6, 1869.
[13] "Information prepared for the Constitutional Convention," Pamphlet Collection, PSL.
[14] Erie *Observer,* Oct. 3, 1867.
[15] Quoted by Lancaster *Intelligencer,* May 12, 1869.
[16] Allen Nevins, *Emergence of Modern America,* 180-81,

The following extracts are offered as evidence of Pennsylvania's legislative corruption:

In both houses there was enough wrangling for ten taverns. Never before have we seen so squalid array of low brows grouped together in any legislative chamber, not even in Albany. Solid Pennsylvanians say freely . . . that the present legislature is the most corrupt that ever preyed upon that bleeding Commonwealth.[17]

We suppose that we may take it for granted that our state Capital is an Augean stable which needs cleansing. If any of our readers visited Harrisburg they will well remember the mysterious beckoning into the corners, the whispered questions as to what he wants 'put through' and the assurance that it can be done "if he will only make it all right."[18]

The manner in which legislation was carried on at Harrisburg had become a source of public scandal. Every year new codes of laws were enacted, affecting all manner of vested interests and entailing great confusion. . . . Citizens and corporations were often led to resort to the most demoralizing means of controlling votes in the Legislature, as their only defense against ruthless spoilation.

[The legislators] often proposed statutes for the simple purpose of alarming capital and levying upon it a gigantic blackmail . . .; while those who wished to gain special favors by law did not hesitate to avail themselves of means so easily purchasable.[19]

[At the Constitutional Convention] delegate followed delegate in stating that the legislature had been corrupt and the convention must try to better its reputation. Harry White said a friend of his, a senator visited the Connecticut legislature. He was told "Sir, in Connecticut the reputation of a member of the Pennsylvania Legislature is not very high." John Broomall said he had

---

[17] Beaver *Argus*, April 21, 1869, quoting Theodore Tilton.
[18] Philadelphia *Evening Telegraph*, Feb. 13, 1867.
[19] Lathrop, *History of the Union League*, 104-05.

been placed where "I would not acknowledge that I had been a member of a Pennsylvania legislature unless closely pressed upon the question."[20]

How to put a stop to legislative corruption is now the question of the day. It has come that few bills are passed on their intrinsic merit, but men expect an equivalent in dollars and cents for their votes on the plainest matters of public justice and public expediency.

Pay them well, and they will stickle at nothing in ministering to the rapacity of corporations or the ambition of political aspirants.[21]

After reading the foregoing testimony one would have to be skeptical indeed to doubt the general character of the state's legislature. The two common ways which the corrupt legislators used to sell their votes were on the passage of special legislation, and the election of two public officers, United States senator and state treasurer. In the senatorial elections of 1857 and 1867 there was little doubt of the use of money to procure votes, and the one of 1863 had a narrow escape from the same influence. In the postwar years the office of state treasurer was looked upon as the most profitable in the state. At the beginning of each legislative session the members were immediately besieged by emissaries of the candidates for office. ". . . it is notorious," reported Secretary Francis Jordan, "that the legislators are bought and sold."[22] In one of his annual messages Governor Geary had likewise noted that few poor men had failed to emerge from the treasurership rich. Certainly, thought the chief executive, there must exist great advantage, unknown to the

---

[20] William A. Russ, "Origin of the Ban on Special Legislation in the Constitution of 1873," *Pennsylvania History*, XI (October, 1944), 260-75.

[21] Titusville *Morning Herald*, April 18, 1867.

[22] Jordan, "Information Prepared," PSL.

public, which accounted for the "disgraceful scramble" to acquire the office.[23]

Out of this unseemly scramble for the opportunity to manipulate the taxpayers' money for personal gain there emerged the Quay-Mackey Treasury Ring. When Matthew Quay presented Robert W. Mackey, an unknown Allegheny County banker, for the high position of state treasurer in 1869 he could hardly have realized that he was selecting the man who for a decade was to share with him an honored and favored position in the Cameron machine. If General W. W. Irwin of Beaver, the incumbent, and Matthew Quay had been able to agree, Mackey might not have emerged from obscurity. According to press rumors, Quay recommended deposits of state funds in Cameron "pet banks" and Irwin refused. Cameron, it will be recalled, had tolerated Quay's management of Irwin to the office following Curtin's defeat for the senatorship. Quay, irked at Irwin's seemingly lack of gratitude and his unmanageability, set to work to unseat him.

Quay was not a rich man and could not afford the money it would now take to unhorse Irwin, but Mackey found a powerful sponsor in the person of General George W. Cass, president of the Pittsburgh, Fort Wayne and Chicago Railroad. This Democratic leader of western Pennsylvania had already advanced Mackey to the cashiership of the Allegheny National Bank. The prospective "pet banks," it was alleged, contributed $75,000,[24] and this amount, together with Cass's funds and Quay's "pulling of the strings," provided Mackey's election. Because members seldom bolted the party ticket, the purchase of the majority party caucus

---

[23] *Papers of the Governors, 1857-1871,* 1009.
[24] Lancaster *Intelligencer,* quoted in Bellefonte *Democratic Watchman,* Jan. 15, 1869.

usually insured election. Contrary to press expectations, Mackey defeated Irwin in the majority Republican caucus, and also the Democratic candidate, Charles W. Cooper, 76 votes to 51, but three honest disgusted Republicans, Lowry, Billingfelt, and Fisher, expressed their disapproval of the Cass-Quay deal by refusing to vote for Mackey.[25] These men were the forerunners of the full-scale Liberal revolt which took place in 1872.

The following year when Mackey sought re-election the new treasury combine suffered a temporary reverse. Irwin's supporters offered to bolt Mackey's caucus nomination if they could get Democratic support. Irwin gave Wallace, the Democratic leader, a list of Republicans pledged to vote for him, and the Democracy was so anxious to secure Mackey's defeat that they accepted the deal and Irwin was elected when 15 Republicans failed to support Mackey.[26] Thomas Scott, much disturbed over the Republican schism, interviewed J. Donald Cameron with the idea of smoothing out the complications, but found when *"personal enmities"* entered into such a contest as existed between Mackey and Irwin, men were deaf to reason.[27] The following year Mackey was easily elected with the support of Cameron and the railroad interests. The former bolters with few exceptions were meek as lambs and back in the regular Republican fold. McClure related: "[Mackey] not only defeated Irwin with ease, but held his organization in the hollow of his hand from that time until his death some ten years later." The Quay-Mackey Treasury Ring was back to stay.

---

[25] For a sketch of Robert W. Mackey, see McClure, *Notes,* II, 255-68.

[26] McClure labeled these insurgents old Curtin men, but Billingfelt and the Lancaster group were old Stevens men, and Lowry, the leader of the insurgents had not voted for Curtin in 1867.

[27] Scott to Cameron, Jan. 11, 1870, Cameron MSS, LC.

In his "Information" prepared for the proposed Constitutional Convention of 1873, Francis Jordan could have gone on to say that Mackey and his Treasury Ring were forced to pay blackmail annually to remain in power. The Ring could afford the blackmail only because the treasurer used the huge state funds in the same manner an individual might manipulate his own private accounts. The profits derived from the use of approximately one and one-half million of the Commonwealth's fund yielded over $100,000 annually to the Ring, charged the Harrisburg *Patriot*.[28] In his annual message of January 6, 1869, Governor Geary stated: "I regret to state that the last Legislature, although fully forewarned in regard to the insecurity and want of proper . . . guards for the safekeeping of the money . . . failed to determine upon any mode by which the Treasury may be effectually guarded."[29]

The greatest contributor to the special legislation evil was the absence of general laws to cover a general subject, although not infrequently the legislature passed legislation for the benefit of special interests in full knowledge of general legislation already on the statute books. If general laws were effective to cover the chartering of different types of corporations, no legislative action would have been necessary, and applications would pass only through the courts. As long as a specific act had to be passed for each incorporation, the legislators were in a position to demand pay. Moreover, one favored corporation could buy special privileges which another of the same type did not possess. In an address before the Social Science Association of Philadelphia, Francis Jordan branded special legislation "one of the great-

---

[28] Sept. 15, 1871.
[29] *Papers of the Governors, 1857-1871*, 938.

est evils of the days";[30] and Governor Geary repeatedly emphasized this evil. "Social and special legislation is one of the serious evils of the times"; warned the chief executive, "and I regard it as part of my duty to discourage it in every honorable way."[31] In 1871 when the legislature passed bills for the relief from taxation of two Philadelphia banks, Geary vetoed them. On a saving of $55,000, the amount owed the state, the banks could well afford such legislation.

The governor often suffered abuse for the pernicious practice of the legislature in passing special legislation. Out of a total of 6,710 private bills, Geary vetoed 268 of them in four years but still they kept coming. In addition to the use of general legislation, both Jordan and McClure advocated an increase in the size of the legislature. In the small Senate, three or four votes often decided the passage of a bill, consquently senators commanded a much higher price for their votes. McClure's plan of increasing the number of senators to 100 and the representatives to 500, thought the Harrisburg *Patriot* would merely reduce the price of votes. One has only to read Geary's messages and study his vetoes to realize that the Governor was honestly trying to check the evil. In spite of his vigilance, "snakes" would occasionally slide through. During the declining hours of a legislative session, bills were piled by the hundreds upon Geary's desk and it was almost impossible to detect all bills granting special privileges. One such "snake" was the Allegheny Railroad Bill which the governor signed on March 8, 1867. The bill granted the road power to execute bonds . . . to an amount sufficient to meet the *necessary* outlay upon any branch road or roads, to be hereafter constructed." Although Geary requested the legislature to repeal the act, the Lan-

---

[30] "Constitutional Reform," Pamphlet Collection, PSL.
[31] Executive Minutes of Governor Geary, 1867, PHMC,

caster *Intelligencer* sneered at the governor's doltish policy
of signing bills without reading them.[32]

Geary tried to make it clear that he was not the enemy of
railroad development, but rather the opponent of any corporation seeking special privileges. Because he especially
feared the powerful Pennsylvania Railroad, the governor
would sometimes sign bills granting favors to the small entrepreneur. For example, Thaddeus Stevens had reason to feel
pleased over the bill favoring his notorious "tapeworm." "I
think the bill quite liberal indeed," wrote a Stevens supporter; "so much so that we can go where we wish. Governor
Geary told me that we might need something additional and
if so now is the time."[33]

Early in his administration Geary let the Pennsylvania
Railroad know what to expect from him. When an act of
March 21, 1866, supplemental to its incorporation, was
presented for repeal, Geary vetoed it. In an unusually long
veto message, the governor reviewed the history of the
Pennsylvania Railroad. The original act of incorporation
had set the stock at $7\frac{1}{2}$ million with permission to reach not
over $10 million, and the legislature had permitted five
successive increases to a maximum of $30 million in 1866. In
addition, the tonnage tax, one of the conditions of the
charter, had been repealed and the accumulated tax released.
The new law would increase the stock over 130 per cent,
increasing the indebtedness from $26 to $46 million. Moreover, the directors were given unlimited privileges to
extend the stock. Geary speculated how one was to know in
what branch of business the railroad would be "confined

[32] *Papers of the Governors, 1857-1871,* 827 ; *Intelligencer,* March 27, 1867.
[33] L. Kauffman to Stevens, Feb. 14, 1867, Stevens MSS, LC.

[and] to what may it not be extended?" Where was the power to keep it within its "legitimate functions"?[34]

Geary's veto of the "Big Steal," or "$9½ million railroad swindle," created the biggest stir of all. When the Pennsylvania Railroad bought the state works of Pennsylvania, the Commonwealth received in exchange $9½ million worth of Pennsylvania Railroad bonds, of which about one-third were exchanged for Allegheny Railroad bonds guaranteed by the Pennsylvania road. It was proposed in the bill to take these bonds and distribute them among four new railroads in order to "facilitate" their construction. Under the long title of the bill one would surmise its purpose to be as laudable as some proposed under the New Deal. Driven to its logical conclusions, the bill would have released the Pennsylvania Railroad Company from almost $10 million worth of obligations because it was no longer required to guarantee the bonds. Geary, who must have been working on his veto before the bill was sent to him, presented his long veto message the day after receiving it. The omnibus nature of the legislation made it unconstitutional, said the governor; and again it was unconstitutional because the bonds were part of the sinking fund which must not be applied for any purpose other than reduction of the debt, unless the debt sank below $5 million.[35] The governor had previously recommended the sale of the Commonwealth's non-interest-bearing railroads bonds to the highest bidder, the proceeds to be applied to the reduction of the debt.[36]

As a tribune of the people Geary had asked for elimination of special privilege, the checking of monopolistic growth, the honest exercise of the franchise, and an end to

[34] *Papers of the Governors, 1857-1871*, 818-25.
[35] *Ibid.*, 1103-13.
[36] Philadelphia *Telegraph*, Jan. 6, 1869.

the bartering of public offices by state legislators. He had pointed out the Pennsylvania Railroad's "pre-occupancy of nearly every possible railroad route" in the state and had vetoed legislation designed to relieve that road of its obligations to the Commonwealth. A large part of the Democratic press agreed with the Erie *Observer* that Geary's veto of the "Big Steal" was a "rare act of honesty and independence."[37] But did Geary's vetoes and the passage of a free railroad bill in 1868 mean that the Pennsylvania Railroad was blocked in its aim to control the lines and rolling stock within the state? Actually, by 1871, the huge octopus had already achieved its main purpose within the state.

In spite of the complaints of its lobbyists, the Pennsylvania line showed consistent gains in expansion and profits. In 1867, the payment of dividends upon original investment was equal to 46 per cent above the legal rate of interest. The company had gained this strong position by "aiding the completion and extension of other railroads where private capital would not incur the risks."[38] The system then had an unbroken line from Columbus, Erie, and Pittsburgh to Philadelphia and Baltimore. Relief from the tonnage tax made possible the construction of double lines and aid to the western auxillaries. By 1870 the total annual profits of the Pennsylvania Railroad, counting its subsidiaries, amounted to over $13 million, a gigantic sum for that day and age.[39] It is little wonder that the powerful New York lines were looking with apprehension upon this monster to the south. Under a reorganization plan, J. Donald Cameron gave up the presidency of the Northern Central, a line running from

---

[37] April 14, 1870.

[38] Twentieth *Annual Report* of the Board of Directors of the Pennsylvania Railroad Company.

[39] See various annual reports of the Pennsylvania Railroad Company.

Baltimore, via Sunbury to Buffalo, New York, to Thomas Scott, the president of the Pennsylvania Railroad.

The guiding spirit of the Pennsylvania Railroad for twenty years was that *entrepreneur extraordinary* Thomas A. Scott, the dynamo in breeches, who finished his productive life at the early age of fifty-five. Station Agent Scott, beginning his meteoric career in Duncansville, in two years attained the assistant superintendency of the newly completed Pittsburgh division of the Pennsylvania Railroad and in 1858 was made its general superintendent. Another two years found him, at the age of thirty-six, first vice-president of the Pennsylvania Railroad. His work during the war years won him acclaim as one of the master organizers of the day. In his capacity of assistant in the War Department, he rescued Cameron's office from almost hopeless chaos.

Scott, realizing from the beginning the value of powerful political connections, decided to cast his lot with Cameron and the Unionists. In 1860 Scott furnished Cameron's Pennsylvania delegation with passes to Chicago. In Congress, Cameron had tried to get the government to build a bridge across the Ohio River, allegedly as part of the Federal system of post roads, but actually so Scott's railroad would have easy passage into Ohio. During these years, Cameron was capturing the Northern Central Railroad and operating it in coordination with the Pennsylvania. Scott's management of the repeal of the tonnage tax established his standing as the master lobbyist of the state. From 1861 onward Scott usually got what he wanted and after 1866 only Geary's alliance with the Radical Progressives made him tread cautiously. In 1867 Scott saw his friend returned to the Senate and two years later he secured another railroad man, John Scott, as Cameron's junior colleague.

In 1861 Thomas Scott had started his drive for the

supremacy of the Pennsylvania Railroad in the state by
persuading the legislature, through very questionable
methods, to lift the tonnage tax. Further lobbying produced
special legislation of a favorable nature culminating in the
acts of 1870 which gave the Pennsylvania line virtually a free
hand within the state. The other goal, monopoly of the oil
transportation, was achieved with the defeat of the Atlantic
and Great Western Railroad, and the creation of Scott's
companies engaged in pipeline transportation. In a decade,
Scott had achieved mastery of the Commonwealth's
transportation.[40] Working toward transcontinental control,
he held the Union Pacific in 1871 long enough to
get himself elected its president. The same year, Scott,
probably with Cameron's help, secured the last choice
picking the government granted to railroads—the Texas
Pacific Railroad grant of 13,000,000 acres. By 1876, Scott
was president of fifteen different corporations including the
Pennsylvania Railroad and the Texas and Pacific Railway.
Two years later the master builder was a paralytic invalid.
He never fully recovered and died in 1881.[41]

In the midst of public discussion on the new Grant
Administration, "rings," legislative corruption, activities of
the Pennsylvania Railroad, and Geary's pardons, the time
arrived to select candidates for another gubernatorial contest. Geary's attempt at renomination was taken for granted,
but the big question, his strength, remained to be determined.
The weakened Curtin faction, remembering the part Geary

[40] For a complete discussion of this subject see Rolland H. Maybee, *Railroad Competition and the Oil Trade, 1855-1873* (Mount Pleasant, Michigan, 1940).

[41] On Scott's career see Samuel H. Church, "Thomas A. Scott", *Dictionary of American Biography*, XVI, 500-501 ; Thomas S. Fernon, "Thomas A. Scott as a Pledge-Breaker and Salary Grabber," HSP ; Forney, *Anecdotes*, 100: Samuel R. Kamm, *Civil War Career of Thomas A. Scott ;* Philadelphia *Press*, May 31, 1881.

had played in bringing about Curtin's defeat for the senatorship, wished to block the governor's renomination. Shortly
before the convention, Matthew Quay, Simon Cameron's
new man wrote: "We will support him [Geary] . . . unless
satisfied that his nomination will result in defeat of our
ticket."[42] Evidently the Cameron men were pursuing a
"waiting" policy. Geary was popular with the working class,
and most of the papers, especially the rural weeklies, supported him; but the big dailies like the Philadelphia *Press*
and Pittsburgh *Gazette* gave Geary no endorsement. The
neutral Philadelphia *Telegraph* commented upon the many
enemies Geary had made and his lack of friends.[43]

Geary had begun his first administration free of the Curtin
faction; before its end, he determined to free himself from
the Cameron forces which had procured his nomination in
1866. McClure wrote that Geary "had the active support of
Cameron" in his fight for renomination,[44] but there seems to
be no evidence to substantiate this. At the end of three years
the governor felt strong enough to bring about his own candidacy. With the aid of the workers, the drys, and especially
the Radical wing which supported his progressive program
and had opposed corporate interests, the proud Geary hoped
to make himself the acknowledged head of the Republican
Party in the state. To accomplish this, he must secure the
renomination in his own right and then go forward to victory
over the Democracy. Next would come the senatorship or,
perchance, a direct step to the Presidency. A visit from
President Grant, only a few days before Pennsylvania's
Republican state convention opened, promoted rumors that
Geary was seeking Grant's assistance.

[42] Beaver *Radical,* quoted in Greenville *Argus,* June 16, 1869.
[43] Feb. 19, 1869.
[44] *Notes,* II, 268. Geary's biographer supported McClure's view.
See Harry M. Tinkcom, *John White Geary* (Philadelphia, 1940), 127.

Cameron understood fully the reason for Geary's independence and decided to allow him to fry in his own fat in order to teach him a lesson. The attack by Geary's mouthpiece upon Russell Errett is proof of a Cameron-Geary break. Of Cameron's lieutenants, none were dearer to his heart than Errett, the Pittsburgh editor. Errett was one of the few newspaper men to praise Cameron's rejected "report" for 1861, when he was Secretary of War, and he defended Cameron when Lincoln steered him from his Cabinet. Furthermore, the Pittsburgh *Gazette,* Cameron's paper, announced that the Federal officeholders in Philadelphia were against Geary and would "doubtless prove a mischievous agency in the coming convention."[45] One can be sure that if Cameron was for Geary, the Federal officeholders in Philadelphia would not be working against him.

The Republican state convention met in Philadelphia, June 23, 1869, in Concert Hall. Forney's *Press,* which had been silent on the gubernatorial question for a week, now confirmed Geary's strength. The night before the convention opened the anti-Geary men held a caucus for the purpose of planning their strategy. The same day the Lancaster *Intelligencer* reported that the majority of the delegates were for Geary, but it remained to be seen whether Cameron could defeat the instructions of the people.[46] An opportunity for Cameron's newest lieutenant, Matthew Quay, to display his position in an ostentatious manner had presented itself and he made the most of it. Before a temporary chairman could be elected, Quay moved that the nomination be made by acclamation, and again he moved the nomination prior to the adoption of a platform. Quay first nominated George V. Lawrence for governor, withdrew his name, and then

---

[45] Pittsburgh *Gazette,* June 21, 1869.
[46] June 23, 1869.

moved Geary's nomination by acclamation—a motion he knew in advance that the convention would not accept. Geary won easily on the first ballot—122 votes to 11, distributed among C. M. Lilley, General Meade, and Horace Porter. Rather than expose the weakness of the Cameron faction, Quay had withdrawn its candidate, Lawrence. Geary had accomplished what none of the leaders thought he was capable of doing—he secured a majority of the convention delegates without assistance from the bigwigs of any faction. Most of the delegates received instructions in their local districts to support Geary, and naturally voted for him when the majority could not agree on any other candidate. Here was an unusual accomplishment—a gubernatorial candidate nominated by the grass roots of the party.

The remaining duties of the convention were performed without delay. Henry W. Williams was declared the party's candidate for supreme judge by acclamation. The light note of the convention was struck when delegate Lauman was asked whether his candidate for supreme judge, General Horace Porter, was a citizen of Pennsylvania. Lauman replied that Porter lived with Grant, who spent most of his time in Philadelphia. The gathering endorsed the new fifteenth amendment, a protective tariff, the governor's past administration, and the recent rejection of the proposed Johnson-Clarendon Treaty. Before adjourning, the group heard Geary's acceptance speech: "You, the chosen representatives of the people, confer the nomination and confer upon me the plaudit, 'well done, good and faithful servant.' I certainly need no better, no higher, no stronger verdict."[47] Taking a slap at both the Cameron and Curtin groups, Geary announced the policy of nonrecognition of all factions. The

---

[47] "Geary and Williams," Pamphlet Collection, PSL.

governor was pointing the way to a new era of party harmony under his leadership.

Few doubted the reasons for the conceited governor's victory. Both the Greenville *Argus* and the Pittsburgh *Gazette* attributed it directly to the people.[48] The West Chester *American Republican* admitted Geary's strength with the people but grudgingly added: "Geary was *not* our first choice." At first glance this announcement by a rural weekly appeared of little import, but when it is noted that the editor, E. B. Moore, was one of Cameron's leading correspondents and confidants, the statement took on added significance. When Geary wrote the exciting story of his re-election to his brother Edward, he boasted: "I had to contend with the Curtin, and Cameron factions combined at my nomination . . . and in that I distanced them both."[49] It is hard to escape the conclusion that Geary's convention victory was due largely to his own efforts. If Cameron "actively" supported Geary for the nomination, the people, the press, Cameron's lieutenants, and Geary himself were ignorant of the fact.

The struggle for the Democratic gubernatorial nomination began as a three-cornered fight among Asa Packer, General George W. Cass, and the supporters of General Winfield Scott Hancock. The year before, Hancock had come within an ace of capturing the presidential nomination and this very popular soldier would have made a very formidable candidate in opposition to Geary; but he made no attempt to grab the prize. In early February Cass's chances were reported best,[50] and when the state convention opened in middle July the situation remained unchanged. Charles

---

[48] *Argus,* June 25, 1869; *Gazette,* June 24, 1869.
[49] Geary to Edward Geary, Jan. 7, 1870, Geary MSS, PHMC.
[50] Lewistown, *Gazette,* Feb. 24, 1869.

Buckalew's opening address denounced Geary's administration, his failure to check the flow of private bills, the payment of more interest on the debt, and high state government expenses. Before the balloting began, William Wallace read a letter from Hancock declining a nomination because of his military status. But in 1868 under similar conditions Hancock had presented no objections to the Democratic National Convention when his candidacy was advanced.

The first ballot revealed that something had changed the relative strength of the gubernatorial contestants. Packer's 59 votes led Cass by a plurality of 11 with Hancock and McCandless sharing 26 votes. On the third ballot Packer received the nomination, 95 votes to Cass's 37. Cyrus L. Pershing of Cambria won the nomination for Supreme Court Judge. The platform opposed the "imposition" of Negro suffrage upon the people. The Republican controlled legislature was condemned for not submitting the proposed fifteenth amendment to popular vote. The internal revenue tax was termed grossly unjust, and equal rights were asked for native and foreign citizens.[51]

Concerning this Democratic struggle for the nomination, A. K. McClure later told a strange tale of events behind the scenes:

Mackey ascertained that a number of commercial delegates in Philadelphia could control the nomination and give it to Cass, and without communicating with Cass or any of his friends, he made a deal with these delegates to support Cass, and put up his own checks for $12,000. "Tom" Collins, as he was familiarly named, found that the Philadelphians were in the market, ascertained the price, and a few hours before the ballot, he gathered up $13,000 in spot cash, paid it to the contracting leader, and nominated Packer. Neither Cass nor Packer had any knowledge

---

[51] Harrisburg *Patriot,* July 15, 1869; Philadelphia *Press,* July 15, 1869; Reading *Eagle,* July 15, 1869.

of the efforts to purchase delegates in their interests, and Collins never informed Packer of the expenditure he had made to secure his acceptance as a Democratic candidate. I have heard Mackey refer to this incident as an evidence that in an emergency spot cash will beat checks.[52]

The press had some inkling of what had happened. The Cass men, according to the Harrisburg *Telegraph,* counting on 80 votes, "only awoke to the *sell* when it was too late . . . Cass's men were met at every point by the irresistible argument in words and coins." "A mob of blackguards from Philadelphia," reported the Pittsburgh *Gazette,* had secured Packer's nomination at the last moment by a "rush."[53]

Horatio Alger could not have conceived of a better character for one of his success stories than Asa Packer. As a youth of seventeen, this itinerant from the Nutmeg state entered the Commonwealth to try for fame and fortune. His experience as a carpenter's apprentice fitted him for his job of building a canal boat—his first floating stock. Careful savings earned with his coal boat permitted him to make further investments in coal lands, and increasing capital allowed him to become a storekeeper and contractor on the Lehigh Canal. He risked all to complete his dream—the Lehigh Valley Railroad. The venture proved so profitable that at the end of twenty years Packer had amassed a fortune estimated at $20 million, reputedly the largest in the state. Billy Sunday, the famed evangelist, once referred to Packer as an example of a rare combination—a man possessed of both wealth and fairness. The Democratic candidate had served in the state legislature and in Congress. An associate judgeship of a county court gave him his title "Judge

---

[52] *Notes,* II, 263-64.
[53] *Telegraph,* quoted in Pittsburgh *Gazette,* July 31, 1869 ; Gazette, July 30, 1869.

Packer." At the Democratic National Convention of 1868, Packer was a favorite-son candidate.[54]

Packer, because of his lack of forensic talents, indicated that his campaign would be of the dignified front-porch variety. In his acceptance speech Packer had promised to work for reduced state expenses, internal improvements, maintainance of state credit, and a "cautious" use of the pardon power. Packer tried to contain the assault which he knew would come to any wealthy candidate by urging the government to give careful consideration to the interests of labor, and by emphasizing his early laboring years.[55] His friends pictured the magnate as a Christian patriot, an enterprising business man, the friend of industry, and a prime product of our free institutions. His election would mean reform and overthrow of the corruption at Harrisburg.[56] Even Cameron's Harrisburg mouthpiece admitted that there was much in Packer's character—"his industry, integrity, enterprise, and liberality."[57]

Compared to the gubernatorial campaign of 1866, the one of 1869 was tame indeed. In 1866, great crowds gathered to hear the oratory of McClure, Marshall, Curtin, Grow, Clymer, and Cowan, But in 1869, the campaign dragged along in a perfunctory manner. Packer refused to canvass, and Geary lacked ability as a stumper. The press compensated partly for the lack of activity on the part of the main performers. An inquiring voter could find plenty of reasons in the dailies and weeklies of the period why he should, or should not, vote for one or the other candidates.

The Republicans prepared to use popular prejudice

---

[54] On Asa Packer see Milton C. Stuart, *Asa Packer* (Princeton, 1938).
[55] Pittsburgh *Gazette,* July 31, 1869.
[56] Erie *Observer,* Aug. 12, 1869 ; Harrisburg *Patriot,* Sept. 22, 1869.
[57] Harrisburg *Telegraph* quoted in Erie *Observer,* July 29, 1869.

against vast wealth to their advantage. The partisan *New York Times* compared the gubernatorial struggle to a battle of dollars, age, and imbecility against brains, patriotism, and activity.[58] Packer's Lehigh Valley Railroad, charged Forney's *Press,* was "instinctively anti- Pennsylvania" and was engaged in subordinating the interests of the Keystone state to that of New York. Packer had allegedly fraternized with Copperhead Vallandigham, paid his poor workmen in 40 per cent company script, and oppressed his river boatmen.[59] The Republican state committee found Packer "impregnated with all the abominable heresies of the Copperhead and Free Trader," and favorable only to big business.[60]

The Democracy attacked Geary's pardons, his legislative record, the rampant corruption centered at the state capital, the high cost of state government, and the whole Republican regime since the Civil War. Geary's signing of the "Calamity Act," under which railroad companies could not be held liable for the loss of limb of a carrier's main agents, aroused some public indignation. Another piece of questionable legislation was the Partisan Registry Law which, according to McClure, the governor signed in fear of his defeat for re-election. A third piece of legislation for which Geary was criticized was the "Peter Herdic Act," which eliminated a judicial district. This act was "condemned" by the state supreme court.[61] In 1868 the state executive department was costing twice what it did in 1860 and the Senate was spending over three times as much. The cost of public printing had jumped from $30,000 to $135,000 and the average expenses of state government had increased 65 per cent. All knew

---

[58] *New York Times* quoted in Harrisburg *Patriot,* July 24, 1869.
[59] Philadelphia *Press,* July 15, Sept. 6, Pittsburgh *Gazette,* Aug. 6, 1869.
[60] Pittsburgh *Gazette,* Sept. 28, 1869.
[61] Reading *Eagle,* July 22, 1869.

that the legislature was responsible for this waste and fraud, but every beneficiary pointed his finger to the adjoining member of the "Ring," and justly or not, the governor found himself shouldering a share of the blame.

Geary defended his pardon record vigorously and cited his establishment of safeguards. The Registry Law, which gave Republicans an advantage at the polls in Philadelphia, the governor characterized in his annual message of 1869 as a safeguard against fraudulent voting. The supreme court of the state declared the act constitutional.[62]

The Republicans opened their state campaign at Pittsburgh in early September where the chief attraction, Senator Morton of Indiana, warned that a victory for Packer would pave the way for a Democratic victory in national politics. Although convinced that Philadelphia was lost if drastic steps were not taken, John Covode, the Republican state chairman, publicly announced his confidence in Geary's re-election. At Bradford, in one of his few public appearances, Geary placed the blame for special legislation entirely upon the legislature. In an impromptu address at Greensburg, while visiting his brother-in-law, Geary noted that the railroads, banks, corporations, and special privilege were now paying the tax formerly contributed by real estate. An amusing feature of Geary's campaign was his "water wagon." He was a confirmed dry, and had boasted at the State Temperance Convention that he had not touched liquor for years. But during the 1866 campaign he had met a group of Germans in a saloon at Erie. The beer was flowing, and the candidate had taken a draught for purposes of sociability. By 1869, the governor's one stein had risen to a baker's dozen, and many German-Americans considered Geary's pledge a direct repudiation of the sacred bonds of comrade-

---

[62] *Papers of the Governors, 1857-1871,* 947.

ship forged in the Erie saloon. Geary finished his tour of the western part of the state by September 23, and then started east. Geary received aid from Senator John Scott who spoke in Pittsburgh, Erie, and Lancaster.[63]

Apparently, Cameron took no active part in the campaign. Geary had won his own renomination, and Cameron determined to maintain a hands-off policy. If the proud Geary wished support from Cameron he would have to humiliate himself to procure it. The state chairman, Covode, fearful of defeat for the Republican ticket, was crying for help from the Curtin men, and now Geary and his friends, fearful of defeat, turned to Cameron. On September 14 Geary and Cameron were observed taking a ride together in the park at Reading.[64] Five days later the elder Blair wrote to Cameron: "I am right glad to hear that Geary's friends are obliged to cry to you, 'help me captain or I sink.' You may do your best for him and yet Packer may send him packing. If you don't help him, it is very certain this would be the case."[65] Whether Cameron came to Geary's aid is a moot question. There seems to be no evidence in Cameron's private papers or in the press that he did so. A. K. McClure gave himself and William B. Mann the major credit for rescuing Geary.

Geary's sacrifice of his attorney general, Benjamin Harrison Brewster, to the Curtin remnant enlivened what was otherwise a dull campaign. Geary and Covode could see nothing but defeat for the governor unless the aid of William B. Mann, an old Curtin man, could be enlisted. Mann, Republican boss of Philadelphia, possessed a power-

---

[63] Pittsburgh *Gazette,* Aug. 20, Sept. 3, Sept. 13, 1869.

[64] *Ibid.,* Sept. 24, 1869.

[65] Philadelphia *Press,* quoted in Harrisburg *Patriot,* Oct. 4, 1869. Public release of this letter, if genuine, could have for its purpose only the embarrassment of Geary.

ful organization capable of getting out the city's Republican vote. According to McClure, who at the time had close associations with Mann in Philadelphia, Covode, acting as intermediary, visited Mann and McClure for the purpose of working out a *rapprochement* between the Geary and Mann forces. Mann and McClure declined because the Curtin men had been denied patronage, and the latter was particularly bitter against Geary's attorney general who had heaped "systematic defamation" upon him. The two were not interested in bargaining as long as Brewster remained in office. At the conclusion of several parleys, Geary capitulated to the Mann-McClure terms—Brewster's dismissal with the privilege of the pair to name Brewster's successor.

Brewster's first intimation of Geary's decision to offer him up as a sacrifice was procured from the text of a public letter appearing in a Philadelphia paper dated July 30, 1869, bearing the signature of John Covode, the state chairman. In it Brewster was informed that Covode, in consultation with his "political associates," who were desirous of bringing about Geary's re-election, believed that Brewster's resignation would "go a long way" toward healing existing dissensions. The request, stated Covode, had the authorization of the governor.[66] Geary sent Brewster a special message assuring him that Covode's letter was unauthorized by him; but when the governor failed publicly to repudiate Covode's open letter, Brewster suffered a "sense of wrong at Geary's silence."[67] Brewster refused to resign at Covode's request, and it was not until two months later, after his re-election, that Geary in accordance with his bargain asked for his attorney general's resignation. Brewster hotly replied: "I

---

[66] Philadelphia *Sunday Republic,* quoted in Harrisburg *Patriot,* Aug. 10, 1869.

[67] Savidge, *Life of Brewster,* 104.

will not submit. I will not permit you, at the instance of a class that you denounced to me as corrupt factionists . . . thus to evict me from a place I never sought."[68] But Brewster was compelled to submit when, on October 23, Geary appointed another in his place.

Brewster's successor was his unrecognized half brother, F. Carroll Brewster, one of the leaders of the Philadelphia bar. Mann and McClure, with carefully planned malice aforethought, had selected him in order to compel B. J. Brewster to suffer the ultimate in galling humiliation. Joseph M. McClure, Geary's new deputy attorney-general, was reputedly a relative of A. K. McClure. If so, McClure received a bonus which he did not mention in his *Notes*.[69] There seems no explanations for McClure's falsification of the time of Brewster's dismissal. He dated it "immediately," which meant August. Perhaps his memory slipped him, or he could not resist the temptation to magnify his importance in the episode. And contrary to McClure's version, Brewster knew that he was being prepared for the sacrifice several months before Geary asked for his resignation.

An important question remained to be answered in connection with the Brewster episode. Why did Cameron not intercede in Brewster's behalf? Would not his dismissal be considered a direct slap in the face for the man who had brought about his entrance into the Geary cabinet? Nine months had scarcely passed since Brewster had openly expressed his wrath at Cameron's failure to support him for the senatorship,[70] and consented to allow John Scott the prize. Brewster's remarks had led to a rupture with Cameron, but after publication of Covode's open letter asking for his

[68] *Ibid.*, 105 ; Harrisburg *Patriot*, Oct. 27, 1869.
[69] *Notes*, II, 270-73.
[70] Philadelphia *Press*, Jan. 7, 1869 ; [G. Eyster] to McPherson, Jan. 8, 1869, McPherson MSS, LC.

resignation, Brewster sought hastily to rehabilitate himself
with his former chief. Cameron acknowledged his regret for
the break in their long friendship,[71] the election went by,
Brewster suffered dismissal, and the misunderstanding
between the two remained;[72] but the answer was clear.
Cameron would not have come to the relief of a man who
had publicly repudiated him and whose "repentance" came
about under such compelling circumstances. What Geary
would have done had Cameron insisted upon Brewster's
retention in the cabinet is problematical.

On October 12, 1869, Geary won his fluke victory. The
campaign had created little interest, the weather was
inclement on Election Day, and the returns were unusually
light; twenty thousand fewer votes being cast than in 1866.
Geary's official vote was 290,552 to Packer's 285,956,[73] a
majority of less than 4,600 votes. To Geary's way of thinking, he had scored a "grand victory," the "Lookout Mountain" of his political career. He regarded his own position in
the state as being stronger than ever before, with his
influence acknowledged by all; "the formidable and malignant combinations" which had opposed him were now "laid
out cold," groveling suppliants at his feet. Packer had spent
about one million dollars and used every denunciation within
his power, reported Geary, in an exaggerated vein, but the
governor had fought squarely and compelled Packer and his
"tallies [to] wince at every turn." In addition, complained
the boastful Geary, he had been forced to bear the sins of
both the state and national governments.[74]

A. K. McClure took quite a different view of Geary's

[71] Cameron to B. H. Brewster (copy), Aug. 20, 1869, Cameron
MSS, LC.
[72] General Kane to Grant (copy), Oct. 29, 1869, *ibid.*
[73] Smull's *Legislative Handbook,* 1873, 277.
[74] Geary to Edward Geary, Jan. 7, 1870, Geary MSS, PHMC.

"grand victory." Geary had simply capitalized on district attorney Mann's iron grip on Philadelphia elections which he had secured through the Registry Law. The Brewster sacrifice called for Mann's help, and Cameron's ancient enemy was in position to use unscrupulous methods to accomplish his part of the contract. Although McClure was party to a bargain which admittedly resulted in a fraudulent majority for Geary in Philadelphia, McClure thoughtfully impressed one fact upon his readers—that Mann controlled the city machinery and had therefore perpetrated the fraud. McClure viewed himself as an innocent bystander.

Knowing McClure's intense dislike for Geary, one might conclude that he deliberately falsified the situation when he wrote: "I speak advisedly when I say that the leaders who managed Republican affairs in the city more than doubted Geary's honest election, and he was the only Governor of Pennsylvania who entered . . . with a clouded mission."[75] But all evidence points to the truth of McClure's charges. Outside Philadelphia, Geary's majority for the state was a scant 200 votes. In 1866, Philadelphia contributed almost 30 per cent of Geary's majority; in 1869 it counted 95 per cent of it. In the state elections of 1867 and 1868 Philadelphia had gone Democratic and had elected a Democratic mayor. Many conservative Republicans, taking a dim view of the democratic proclivities displayed by Geary during his first term, probably failed to cast a vote for any gubernatorial candidate. Williams, the Republican candidate for supreme judge, received a higher vote than Geary.[76] It is inconceivable under the circumstances that a city which for the preceding two years went Democratic should contribute 95 per cent of

---

[75] *Notes,* II, 274.
[76] Harrisburg *Patriot,* Oct. 20, 1869.

a statewide Republican victory to a candidate who was weaker than his party.

Geary, the lone wolf, entered his second administration independent, it is true, but held in contempt by the conservatives and by both the Curtin and Cameron factions of this party. The governor's sympathy for the Radical program of Southern reconstruction, then in fullness of power under the benevolent supervision of President Grant, insured full cooperation by the Keystone state's administration of the military steps taken in the prostrate South to insure supremacy of the Republican Party through disqualification of a majority of the whites and the enfranchisement of hordes of illiterate Negroes. But the Radical onslaught within the state was ebbing. Geary, the Radical overlord, possessed no power outside his limited personal demesne and there were no prospects that he could enlarge it at the expense of the Cameronian-corporate empire.

X

Voices of Protest

THE PERIOD 1869–1871 furnished the immediate background for the great political eruption of 1872—the Liberal Republican movement. Rumors and proof of the corruption emanating from the state legislators, the Treasury Ring, Mann's regime in Philadelphia, and many other sources within the Commonwealth, provoked symptoms of revolt from honest-minded citizens, who set up local reform tickets and, in a few cases, scored victories. Among the voices of protest heard was that of Governor Geary, but the chief executive could exert little strength except in a negative fashion. In early 1871, proponents of reform were apprehensive that the movement was dying; but before the year had passed, renewed rumblings of protest were louder than ever. With genuine signs of revolt in the air, the old guard gave way and the reformers scored one triumph—the promise of a new constitution.

Eighteen-seventy marked the flood tide of the state Democracy in the postbellum age. At no time following 1862 did the party make a better showing. No state executive offices were at stake; the remarkable gains were accomplished only in congressional and state legislative elections. The mass of citizenry, eager for information about the exciting struggle in Europe between Bismarck's Prussia and Napoleon III's new French empire, paid scant attention to the few political items which journalists consigned to obscure niches in their

357

sheets; and at home, Fenian activities along the Canadian border commanded much public interest.

In lieu of a state convention (there was no need for one) the Republican State Central Committee, under John Covode's leadership, met tardily at Altoona in September for the purposes of formulating the official party "line" of the campaign. The Committee's "Address" denounced the Democracy for having obstructed the march of civilization, of being wedded to slavery, and of almost destroying the integrity of the Union.[1] With the Fifteenth Amendment now in effect, a man could not be denied the franchise because of his color, and the party hoped to capitalize on the appearance of the Negro voters.

The Democrats on their part were working very actively and using their organizations efficiently throughout the state and nation.[2] Samuel J. Randall, Chairman of the Democratic Congressional Committee, felt the need for financial aid so urgent that he appealed to former President Johnson for funds.[3]

Following the state elections neither party was in position to do much boasting. Pennsylvania's new congressional representation would consist of thirteen Republicans and eleven Democrats, a gain of two seats for the latter. Three narrow Democratic victors were Leonard Myers, R. Milton Speer, and Henry Sherwood, whose total majority was only fifty-three votes. The Democrats had not forgotten Cessna's renegade activities and especially rejoiced over his defeat. Concerning Speer's victory over D. J. Morrell in a normal Republican district, a Huntingdon historian recorded: "The defeat of the latter [Morrell] was not regarded as possible

[1] West Chester *American Republican,* Oct. 4, 1870.
[2] McClure, Notes, II, 282-283.
[3] Randall to Johnson, July 15, 1870, Johnson MSS, LC.

during the campaign and was a complete surprise to his party and friends."[4] The new legislature would seat seventeen Democratic senators to the Republican's sixteen; but in the House the Republicans outnumbered their opponents 55 to 45. The total vote cast in the state was only 525,000 or 165,000 below that of 1868. The advent of Negro suffrage may have caused some members of both parties to remain away from the polls. "Colored Suffrage," wrote McClure, was perhaps the only obstacle to Republican success in 1870.[5]

In Philadelphia, where the Republicans had executed an excellent job of gerrymandering, the Democrats were able to elect only one congressman, the hardy perennial Samuel J. Randall, although their total city vote was only 317 less than that of the victors. The surprise election of John V. Creely, an Independent Republican, over Charles O'Neill, the regular candidate, created a stir. Policing of the city polls by troops sent by Grant for the purpose of enforcing the election laws had the effect of hurting the Republicans. It was the turning away of Republican repeaters which brought about the unexpected election of Colonel Robert Dechert to the state Senate and gave the Democrats their majority of one in that body.

In 1871 the Republicans determined to capitalize on the veteran's popularity. Listing of their caucus nominations for state offices resembled a roster of officers at a command post—General Harrison Allen, Colonel David Stanton, Colonel Francis C. Hooten, and Colonel Robert Beath. The last-named, a gallant officer who had lost his leg at New Market, was nominated for surveyor general, and Colonel Stanton easily gained the nomination for auditor general. It

[4] Milton S. Lytle, *History of Huntingdon County*, 216,
[5] McClure, *Notes*, II.

was common knowledge that Stanton, a rural physician from Beaver County, owed his nomination to Matthew Quay. In fact the Democratic press had hailed the coming Republican state convention on May 17 a Quay conclave where Cameron's henchmen would "issue decress," manipulate the Treasury Ring, and "master spirit" the convention.[6] Quay's success in persuading the convention to permit the permanent chairman and the two candidates for state office to appoint the chairman of the Republican State Central Committee led to the selection of Cameron's western Pennsylvania press agent, Russell Errett, to succeed the late John Covode.

The Republican state convention, belatedly sensitive to the voices of protest against current corruption in governmental and political circles, called for reforms. A constitutional convention was requested; all state officers were to be elected by the people; special legislation was to be prohibited; and, an "adequate" civil service system was recommended. The tariff received its usual endorsement together with a call for a gradual reduction in taxes. Although complaints were heard everywhere about the Republican waste at Harrisburg, the "reform convention" (surely with tongue in cheek) blandly resolved that "the return of the Democrats to power in either state or nation must inevitably be attended with a return to extravagance in expenditure."[7]

The Democracy held its state convention in late May. Taking a note from the Republican's success formula, the party likewise nominated soldier candidates: General William McCandless for auditor general and Captain James H. Cooper for surveyor general. Convention debate centered around the "new departure" resolution. Passed by a vote of

[6] Bellefonte *Democratic Watchman,* May 19, 1871 ; Erie *Observer,* May 25, 1871 ; Harrisburg *Patriot,* Jan. 2, 1871,

[7] Beaver *Argus,* May 24, 1871.

76-53, this formal expression recognized the "binding obligations of all provisions of the constitution . . . as they now exist." The new departure, simply an acceptance of a *fait accompli,* the Fifteenth Amendment, meant that the state party no longer considered Negro suffrage a political issue. Other resolutions condemned the oppressive tariff, the income tax, and the Republicans for refusing to modify the Registry Act. The convention called attention to a speech of Senator Carl Schurz, the independent Republican from Missouri, which it characterized as containing "well known and frequently announced Democratic doctrine." The "Address" of the Democratic State Central Committee denounced Grant's Administration and the militant Radical policy of reconstruction.[8]

In spite of the Evans scandal which was supposed to hurt Republican chances, the party defeated the Democrats in both state and legislative elections. According to A. K. McClure the Democrats had no hope of carrying Philadelphia where the registry law placed the whole election machinery in the hands of William B. Mann. Stanton defeated McCandless by a majority of 15,000, and Colonel Beath's majority over Cooper was almost 30,000. Over 90 per cent of Stanton's majority came from Philadelphia, where the Negro vote was delivered to the Republicans "in a package."[9] The legislative elections reversed the situation in the state Senate where seventeen Republicans would now outvote sixteen Democrats. The Republican victories in the lower house were crushing—only 36 Democrats were elected to 72 for the Republicans. One independent was elected and

---

[8] Appleton's *Annual Encyclopaedia,* 1871, 621 ; Harrisburg *Patriot,* May 25, 1871 ; Erie *Observer,* June 29, 1871.

[9] McClure, *Notes,* II, 283. Dr. David Stanton died before assuming the office of auditor general and by direction of the legislature John F. Hartranft continued in office until December, 1872.

one seat remained vacant. The Republican joint majority of 27 was now the largest since 1867. The electorate of the state overwhelmingly endorsed the proposed Constitutional Convention, 328,354 to 70,205. Most of the negative votes came from Democratic strongholds like Berks, where 10,905 votes were cast against it. But in Philadelphia only one vote in thirty was negative.[10]

Through the years 1870 and 1871, the orgy of corruption and scandal continued unabated. Senator James A. Rutan's resolution to inquire into alleged corrupt practices of the Pennsylvanian Railroad officials in connection with legislative practices was interpreted merely as a move to blackmail the railroad.[11] In Harrisburg, 38 men were employed at a cost of $30,000 annually to fold and wrap public documents although the same work could have been done by contract for $4,000. Members of the legislature were getting a dollar a day for stationery bills although they were supposedly limited to $25 for each session. Bergner, Cameron's editor of the Harrisburg *Telegraph*, was receiving $25,000 for public printing, "his honest share of the patronage."[12] In Pittsburgh, the city hall scandal was rocking the Iron City. The new hall was expected to cost $350,000, but over $600,000 had already been spent and the end was not in sight. All the "heavy contractors," reported the strongly Republican *Gazette*, were "out and out Democrats."[13] In Philadelphia Charles Yerkes, broker for the city treasurer, was held in $50,000 bond on charges of larceny, and William T. Forbes, pension agent, was arrested on charges of embezzlement.[14]

---

[10] Smull's *Legislative Handbook, 1873*, 282-83.
[11] Harrisburg *Patriot*, Jan. 3, 1870.
[12] Reading *Times*, quoted in Bellefonte *Democratic Watchman*, March 13, 1870.
[13] Evans, *Henry W. Oliver*, 57.
[14] *Public Ledger Almanac*, 1871, 54.

Of all the alleged frauds, none created as much stir as the George Evans "Scandal." During the war the Commonwealth had accumulated claims against the national government, some of which were still in arrears two years after Lee's surrender. A joint resolution of the legislature provided for the appointment of a special agent empowered to solicit collection of the suspended claims. Geary appointed George O. Evans special agent on May 22, 1867, the same day the resolution passed. Compensation for the grant was not to exceed 10 per cent of the amount collected, and he would receive no pay if he failed to make any collections. Although the amount of claims was known to be over $2,000,000, it was believed that only a fraction could be collected. But the enterprising agent exceeded all expectations; Evans even discovered additional claims and by July, 1871, had collected almost $3,000,000. The bond agreement which Geary had signed provided that the agent should "pay over . . . all moneys [collected] less the commission allowed." Evans, allowing himself the maximum 10 per cent, retained $291,000, and paid the remainder of his collections.

When the amount of Evans' commission became known, a storm of protest spread through the press. To the general public, almost $300,000 seemed an exorbitant fee for the agent's services. The legislature, it was pointed out, had never established the exact rate of commission and Evans was bound to pay over the whole amount collected. Although Geary viewed the affair "a matter for congratulation, not [for] complaint," public opinion forced action. A warrant sworn out through State Treasurer Mackey read: "George Evans did wholly neglect fail and refuse to account for the said several sums of money collected."[15] Evans was arrested but a judge ordered his release because the defend-

---

[15] "Correspondence between the joint legislative committee to

ant had retained his commission of 10 per cent in good faith.

The Cameron and McClure factions joined in accusing Governor Geary of complicity in a plot to appropriate fraudulently public funds for his own use. The admission of Geary's Auditor General Hartranft to the "borrowing" of $7,000 from Evans added credence to the accusations. "There is no escape from the conviction," charged Cameron's West Chester *American,* "that he [Geary] was not only party to but was altogether responsible for the embezzlement."[16] When Geary's enemy, Alexander K. McClure, entered the state Senate in January, 1873, he pushed through a resolution to investigate the Evans transaction. He had "obtained positive and indisputable information where $52,000 of the Evans $300,000 had been received by a prominent man, where he had invested it and how the securities were held."[17] McClure, "[carrying] his head as high as ever and nervously [twitching] his cane" announced to the press that "somebody [would] be hurt before the end of the session."[18] The committee met, collected information, and issued subpoenas. Continued McClure: "The Senate adjourned on Friday [February 7?] until the following Monday and on Saturday morning the person against whom the investigation was specially directed suddenly dropped dead in his home."

McClure introduced his resolution on January 14, 1873. Three weeks later, ex-Governor Geary dropped dead at his home on Saturday morning, February 8. McClure used six key phrases or words in his *Notes,* all of which fit Geary perfectly: *viz.,* "prominent man," "dropped dead," "home," "morning," and "Saturday." A scanning of the leading

investigate the settlement of the Pennsylvania war claims, by George O. Evans and Governor John W. Geary," Pamphlet Collection, PSL.
[16] Sept. 12, 1871.
[17] *Notes,* II, 342.
[18] Harrisburg *Telegraph,* Jan. 18, 1873.

papers of the Commonwealth does not seem to reveal any
prominent person except Geary that would fill these requirements. Moreover, between January 14 and March 7, there
were only two week-ends when the state senate adjourned
from Friday to Monday; and February 8 included one of
these. The prominent person whom McClure was accusing
of accepting $52,000 from Evans may have been John White
Geary.

The notorious Registry Law, which applied only to
Philadelphia, gave that city the doubtful reputation of being
the most corrupt in the state. It was passed April 19, 1869,
and, as already noted, was William Mann's instrument in
carrying out his bargain with Geary and Covode. "This
law," wrote McClure, "provided for registration entirely
under the control of the Republican organization, and only
those registered with their approval could vote."[19] No citizen
could vote unless his name appeared on the Board of
Canvassers' list. The canvassers for each election district
were hand picked by the Republican-controlled Board of
Aldermen, which also selected election officers. Democratic
judges of election were selected on the basis of their willingness to be controlled. Democratic districts were carried by
the simple method of having gangs of repeaters make their
rounds. One may wonder why William B. Mann, a strong
Curtin supporter, was not struck down by the Cameron
organization, but the answer is obvious—Mann had achieved
personal control of the municipal Republican machine and,
consequently, was in an excellent position to bargain. As long
as he and his registry law produced respectable Republican
majorities in the great city of Philadelphia, the state organization could not afford to overthrow its best guarantee of
carrying the state in a close election.

---

[19] *Notes*, 11, 237.

High on the list of names protesting the activities of the Treasury Ring and political corruption in general was that of the Morrow B. Lowry of Crawford County. Hoping to silence him the state Republican organization procured for him the consulship at Honolulu, but Lowry refused it.[20] In August 1870, Lowry announced his intention of running for the state Senate as an Independent. The Erie Democrats failed to nominate a candidate with the idea of leaving the field open to Lowry.[21] Later, Lowry announced his candidacy for Congress against the Republican candidate, Scofield, provided the Democrats made no nomination. The hesitant Democrats named a candidate only one month preceding election, and Lowry immediately withdrew.

Like tactics were used on two other Republican reformers, McClure and General Fisher of Lancaster. The latter, a hero of Gettysburg fame, accepted a Federal judgeship in Montana and was removed from the scene in April, 1871.[22] McClure, the former publisher of the well-known Chambersburg *Franklin Repository*, had moved to Philadelphia where he established a lucrative law practice as a railroad attorney. Adolph Borie, on authorization from President Grant, tendered McClure the office of United States District Attorney, but according to McClure, he refused the offer.[23] Grant, angered at McClure's rebuff of his attempt to "harmonize" the Republican Party in the Keystone state, sought his revenge on McClure the following year.

In Allegheny County the proponents of reform appeared in force. An entire ticket for Congress and the state legis-

[20] Harrisburg *Patriot*, Aug. 11, 1870.

[21] *Ibid.*, Aug. 18, 1870.

[22] Alexander Harris, *Biographical History of Lancaster County* (Lancaster, 1872), 206.

[23] McClure, *Notes*, II, 328-29.

lature was selected in July, 1870.[24] The Beaver *Argus* considered this true Republican slate a good one and attached a great political significance to the movement.[25] On the other hand, Quay's Beaver *Radical* expressed great disgust at the rebellion in Republican ranks, and called upon Cameron and John Scott to interfere. Mackey visited J. Donald Cameron, enjoying his waters at Bedford Springs, to confer on the subject of halting the "progress of reform" in Allegheny County.[26] Nothing came of the reform movement in Allegheny in 1870, but the following year, the Democrats, Reformers, and the Workingmen's parties combined to elect the mayor of Pittsburgh. James Blackmore, known generally as the Reform candidate, defeated the Republican organization candidate by 1,400 votes. In former years, Republican municipal candidates in Pittsburgh usually won by 2,000 votes.[27] Blackmore's election, claimed the Erie *Observer*, was a protest against rings.[28]

In Philadelphia reform movements created a stir in political circles through the summer of 1870. A group of Independent Republicans from the fourth congressional district bolted William D. Kelley's nomination and asked Colonel William B. Thomas to accept their support. Thomas, an old officeholder under Lincoln, was expelled from the Union League for accepting the honor.[29] Dr. E. D. Gazzam announced himself as the Reform candidate from the fifteenth legislative district and Colonel Christopher Kleinz did likewise in the fourth legislative district. On August 17,

---

[24] Pittsburgh *Commercial* quoted in Harrisburg *Patriot,* July 9, 1870.

[25] Beaver *Argus,* July 13, 1870.

[26] Beaver *Radical,* quoted plus comments in Harrisburg *Patriot,* July 31, 1870.

[27] Beaver *Argus,* Dec. 13, 1871.

[28] December 14, 1871.

[29] Harrisburg *Patriot,* July 30, 1870.

1870, a small group of citizens met at the Wetherill House for the purpose of organizing a Reform Party. Resolutions were adopted calling for the "formation of reform clubs and the election of delegates to the Convention to be held September 1st for the nomination of a reform ticket."[30] A much larger group meeting twelve days later called for revision of the state constitution, longer legislative sessions, and approved the proceedings of the Labor Reform Congress of August, 1869. On August 31, only eleven friends of Reform attended its meeting and little more was heard of the Reform Party except an announcement in the press that it *had not* died.

The case of John V. Creeley proved there was some strength in the Independent Republican movement in 1870. Creeley, failing to get the regular Republican nomination for Congress in a Philadelphia district, charged fraud, and appealed to the State Central Committee. When the nomination was awarded to Charles O'Neill, the incumbent, Creeley announced his candidacy on an Independent ticket. The Democrats supported Creeley and he was elected over O'Neill by a vote of 11,059 to 10,131.[31] At the same time, Independent candidates for Congress ran in four other districts in the state.

The voices of protest included those of women's rights, temperance, and labor reform. In May, 1870, the Pennsylvania Anti-Slavery Society held its last meeting. The members, having seen their goal accomplished, now decided to advance the cause of women's suffrage. Agitation produced few results for the "ladies" except admittance to some

---

[30] Philadelphia *Inquirer,* Aug. 17, 1870.

[31] Smull's *Legislative Handbook,* 1873, 179, listed Creeley simply as "Republican."

political meetings. On the other hand the temperance movement showed considerable strength. The twenty-seventh annual session of the Sons of Temperance of Pennsylvania reported an appropriation of $5,000 for the use of the Committee on Lectures and Public Meetings for 1871, and the distribution of over 20,000 tracts and temperance papers. Early in 1871, General William Patton and others began a movement to organize a political temperance party. James Black, the state's leading advocate of temperance, strongly endorsed political action: "Your [Patton's] very strong and forcible letters on the subject of independent temperance political action were very welcome and gave our friends great satisfaction. I enclose you a call for a convention to organize."[32] Organization of a Temperance Party, commented the Pottsville *Miners' Journal,* could have the effect only of weakening the Republican Party because most Republicans favored temperance while 80 per cent of the Democrats were against it.[33] The Temperance Party completed its organization, ran a slate of candidates for state offices, but succeeded in polling only a few thousand votes. Both Governor Geary and Senator John Scott were prominent temperance men.

Besides assisting the temperance movement Geary was active in supporting general reforms. When a labor reform meeting was held in Harrisburg, Geary appeared on the platform. Not to be outdone, the Democrats sent a representative in the person of Richard Haldeman, Simon Cameron's son-in-law. Geary's annual message in 1871, in contrast to that of 1870 which emphasized national affairs, called for reforms. The governor advocated a revision of the state constitution, increased minority representation, a larger

---

[32] Philadelphia *Inquirer,* May 3, 7; October 4, 1870; Black to Patton, Jan. 25, 1871, New York Public Library Miscellaneous Collection on Pennsylvania, microfilm, PHMC,

[33] July 1, 1871.

legislature, popular election of the state treasurer and super-intendent of public schools, and creation of the office of lieutenant governor. He re-emphasized the evils of special legislation, lack of security for state funds, and the dangers of powerful corporations.[34] Rather significantly, the leading Democratic organs applauded the governor's message while the powerful Conservative Republican press had little comment.[35]

That the spirit of revolt was in the air, there could be little doubt, and its proponents were not restricted to one group or party. The majority of the people, believed the Ridgway *Elk County Advocate,* hoped to see radical reforms carried out under the Republican banner.[36] Thousands of rank-and-file Republicans, agreed the neutral Philadelphia *Telegraph,* were ripe for revolt, but under the circumstances, it was best to vote for an honest Democrat.[37] Speaking of the political situation in the fall of 1871, McClure wrote: "Revolt was exhibited in every part of Pennsylvania, and especially in Philadelphia where opposition to ring rule had been intensified to the uttermost by the violent fall election of 1871."[38] True, the people of the Commonwealth had already expressed a mandate for a revision of their constitution, but would this suffice? Would either major party take steps toward appeasing the voices of protest?

Pennsylvania was not the only state where protests were being registered against the existing regimes and the corruption accompanying them. At the beginning of 1872, Republican leaders elsewhere were looking with alarm upon the

---

[34] Harrisburg *Patriot,* Jan. 6, 1871 ; Lancaster *Intelligencer,* Jan. 11, 1871.

[35] *Ibid.,* Bellefonte *Democratic Watchman,* Jan. 6, 1871.

[36] May 11, 1871.

[37] Quoted in Erie *Republican,* June 8, 1871.

[38] *Notes,* II, 291.

record of the Grant Administration. To them there seemed little excuse for the militant vindictive policy still being pursued in parts of the South. The abuses arising under the spoils system and the general corruption emanating from its fountain head at Washington, seemingly without any note of protest from the President, set thinking men within the Republican ranks to wondering whether the party could survive. Apparently, the next four years would see no change of policy; Grant had surrendered himself to a clique of machine bosses who were exponents of the existing evils. Moreover there was no question of Grant's renomination for a second term.

Out of Missouri came the Liberal call for unified Republican action against "Grantism." At first little notice was taken of the invitation to convene at Cincinnati for the purpose of nominating a Liberal national ticket, but suddenly, like wildfire, one state after another responded to the call. If a response came from Pennsylvania it was most likely to originate from the Independent Republicans of Philadelphia who were putting on a reform fight of their own under the leadership of A. K. McClure. But participation in the coming Liberal convention at Cincinnati was likely to create as many problems as could be settled there. Would acceptance of the invitation mean breaking all ties with the old party? Was there any prospect of success without support from the Democracy? If the two groups did coalesce would the Liberals turn out to be a Jonah and the Democracy a whale? And who could be expected to support the movement within the Keystone state? Surely it could not be the supporters of the Cameron machine who were enjoying the benefits of the current regime and who were anxious to maintain the status quo. Was the mass of citizenry really interested in reform or change? And finally, was there a sufficient number of able men that enjoyed the public confidence available to conduct a successful revolt? Andrew G. Curtin, Cameronism's greatest foe, was absent in Russia. Would he be willing to return and assist in breaking the bonds which sent him into exile? These were the questions which the Liberal movement would set in motion, and which remained to be answered.

Alexander K. McClure unwittingly became a forerunner of the Liberal Republican movement in Pennsylvania. It all started in October, 1871, by "an act of God"—the death of George Connell, state senator-elect from a Philadelphia district. Thomas Scott, William Kemble, William G. Moorhead, and Jay Cooke, representing powerful railroad and corporate interests, requested McClure to accept the Republican nomination for the vacant seat. McClure, an able railroad attorney, could well represent the business interest in the Senate. Certainly this was no invitation to start a reform movement. Suddenly the organization broke off negotiations; and later both Moorhead and Scott notified McClure that neither could openly support him because of the opposition from Washington. Clearly the powerful opposition to McClure's candidacy stemmed from the Cameron-Grant coalition.[39] Both Grant and Cameron had reasons to defeat McClure's candidacy; the latter because McClure had opposed him even more vehemently than Curtin; and Grant, because McClure had declined a Federal appointment and later refused an invitation to confer with the President on the subject of a Cabinet vacancy.

According to McClure, Grant's insolence in dictating a

---

[39] Curtin, in far-off Russia, was given the inside information by one who served as his "private————————at Harrisburg." Evidently Matthew Quay could not resist the temptation to acquaint his old friend with the interesting battle behind the scenes. See Curtin to Washburne, March 1, 1872. Washburne MSS, LC.

candidacy for legislative office provoked him to announce himself as an Independent Republican candidate in opposition to the regular organization choice, Henry C. Gray, only ten days before the special election scheduled for January 30, 1872.[40] The district Democrats made no nominations and threw their support to McClure, the pronounced foe of the detested Registry Law, and proponent of reforms desired by the Democrats.[41]

A most interesting feature of McClure's campaign was concealment of his true motives for running. Almost one thousand citizens in the district had requested his candidacy in the name of reform; and consequently in the eyes of the public, McClure was a valiant warrior in the battle against corruption, willing to sacrifice all to rid the city of its vicious ring, of which William B. Mann, McClure's friend, was the master. Actually, McClure was impelled by a consuming passion to triumph over Grant and Cameron, and a performance of commendable public service in the process was to him only a desirable by-product. In an appearance before the Citizens Reform Association, McClure protested his devotion to Republicanism and pointed to his past record as proof. McClure, sensitive to his constituents' desire to see Grant renominated, placed the onus of blame for corruption upon others whose "crowning shame . . . is their effort to fling the name of President Grant into the contest." But significantly McClure warned his listeners that no reforms would be started during a presidential election year.[42] Some of the city's Republican papers supported McClure, but the conservative *North American* called on Grant to assist in his defeat. John W. Forney maintained a benevolent neutrality,

---

[40] *Notes,* II, 295. McClure gave a complete story of this episode in his *Notes,* II, 290-314.

[41] Harrisburg *Patriot,* Jan. 22, 1872.

[42] Philadelphia *Press,* Jan. 30, 1872.

which was the best McClure could expect while the *Press*'s editor was enjoying the Grant-Cameron patronage.

The Republican election repeaters did their work well and McClure, the Republican reformer, was apparently defeated by a majority of 891 votes. But one of the leaders of the repeaters secretly gave McClure all the details of the frauds, so it was not difficult for him to produce the evidence he needed in order to contest the election. In his *Notes,* McClure told a long story of how the ring exhausted its efforts to prevent his case from being presented before the Senate. Had it not been for the efforts of three Republican Senators, McClure would not have been heard. The Senate special committee examined about a thousand witnesses for McClure and eight hundred for Gray. Four members of the committee, all Democrats, branded the Gray returns false and fraudulent. McClure was declared elected by a majority of 224 votes, and Gray vacated his seat.[43]

As early as 1870, John W. Forney privately expressed his disgust with the evil influences surrounding President Grant. It looked as if the whole South would be lost in 1872 because the Republican party was going to the dogs, cried the editor, who confessed his own state of despair.[44] Now Forney believed that party managers ought to take warning from the Gray contest in the light of Republican losses.[45] Forney's resignation from his lucrative collectorship, concurrently with McClure's post-election contest with Gray, looked like a move to support McClure; but to Forney it was merely relief from a painful situation, and he was now free to "serve the public and cooperate in the great work of reform within the lines of the Republican Party."[46] The editor was

[43] Appleton's *Annual Encyclopaedia, 1872,* 663.
[44] Forney to H. Carey, May 25, 1870, Carey MSS, HSP.
[45] Philadelphia *Press,* Feb. 2, 1872.
[46] *Ibid.,* Feb. 13, 1872.

working himself into an untenable position from which he never succeeded in extricating himself during the exciting campaign of 1872. In defiance of obvious logic, Forney chose to support the forces of reform while at the same time refusing to recognize their anti-Grant character. He would assist in severing the corrupt body of this monster of perdition but maintain the head inviolate.

The reform movement within the Republican Party in Philadelphia did not end with McClure's exciting campaign of ten days. Two prominent Republicans, Benjamin H. Brewster and E. Joy Morris, delivered addresses before a reform audience on February 7, 1872. At a later meeting called March 30 to institute reforms within the party, the reformers charged "bad men" with having seized control of the party in the city, of disgracing the party name, and of making the elective franchise a mere mockery. The reformers pledged their support to only "good, true and faithful Republicans." They expressed "unlimited" confidence in Grant and hoped to see the party saved through reorganization.[47]

Up to this point, the reformers of Pennsylvania had signified no intention of joining a third-party movement or organizing a revolt against "Grantism"; and not once had they called themselves Liberal Republicans. The reform movement in Philadelphia had grown out of the abuses suffered in municipal government and reached a climax in the disgraceful frauds surrounding Gray's election. McClure had spoken in general terms of reforms outside the state but had made no specific mention of the movement which had shaken Missouri. Nevertheless, McClure, the reform candidate, privately fighting for revenge against Cameron and Grant,

---

[47] *Ibid.,* April 1, 1872,

had publicly become the champion of righteousness against the forces of evil.

The Liberal Republican movement initiated under the leadership of Carl Schurz and B. Gratz Brown in Missouri was designed to remove political disabilities suffered by Southern sympathizers. This crusade then came to include men like Senators Lyman Trumbull and Charles Sumner, who charged Grant with having concentrated power in his own hands, with destroying the government of states, and with having surrendered himself to the influence of men of the Conkling-Cameron-Chandler stripe.[48] The Missouri Liberal platform of January 24, 1872, largely the work of Schurz, called for equal suffrage (for Southern whites), complete amnesty, tariff reform, and no Supreme Court "packing."[49] Essentially this is what the Democracy had been demanding for several years, and the Greenville *Argus* branded the movement a "new rebellion by which, through the combined votes of renegade Republicans and sham Democrats, Grant is to be defeated and the old rebel party returned to power—if they have good luck."[50] At the January mass meeting of the Liberal Republicans at Jefferson City, an invitation was extended to all Liberals who opposed Grant's re-election to attend a national convention at Cincinnati on May 1.

The New York editor Horace Greeley, one of the first to respond to the summons, called on McClure in Philadelphia to enlist his aid. Apparently McClure had given little attention to the movement until Greeley visited him. It was perfectly logical that Greeley should appeal first to the leader of the Philadelphia reformers. McClure, cautiously preferring

---

[48] Harrisburg *Patriot,* Feb. 27, 1872.
[49] McPherson, *Handbook of Politics, 1872,* 165-66.
[50] Feb. 2, 1872.

to measure anti-Grant sentiment before making any commitments to Greeley, "was utterly surprised to find how
serious was the defection against Grant among . . . influential Republican leaders." Former Speaker Galusha A.
Grow and two prominent Pittsburghers, J. K. Moorhead and
Thomas A. Marshall, were on the list of those giving favorable responses to McClure's inquiries.[51]

Forty-one men signed the Liberal Republican call which
appeared in the press throughout the state; but the names of
Marshall, Moorhead, and Grow did not appear on the list.[52]
Perhaps the first two privately agreed with McClure but did
not have sufficient courage to take the step, and Grow was
conveniently absent from the state. Neither can one find the
names of William Meredith and Benjamin H. Brewster, who
were willing to go along with reform as long as it remained
within the party. And where was editor John W. Forney?—
the man who the critics said had resigned his collectorship
for the purpose of fighting Grant. The most prominent man
on the list, John Hickman, had his political career behind
him. No prominent Cameron men responded to the call, and
only one state officer prominently associated with Geary, his
deputy attorney general, signed it.

McClure and his followers, it should be kept in mind,
were sponsoring a revolutionary movement in opposition to
the Republican state organization. If the insurgents succeeded, they would not necessarily bring about the downfall
of the party; but on the other hand, if they failed, the partici-
pants would find themselves in the dilemma of men without
a party. Bolting the party caucus was sometimes forgiven,
but party desertion was something different, and therefore
these renegades were literally signing their political death

---

[51] For McClure's prominent part see *Old Time Notes*, II, 327-33.
[52] Harrisburg *Patriot*, April 20, 1872.

warrants as bona fide members of the Republican Party. The Liberal summons invited all "Republican brethren" of the Commonwealth who believed that "the party should have a nobler destiny than mere subordination to personal purposes" to join the national group at Cincinnati. The state Liberal platform read:

We believe . . . that all taxes imposed should be with a view to revenue, and so adjusted as to protect the industrial interests of the whole country; that the special legislation in the interest of capital against labor should be reprobated; that the military rule in time of peace, and military interference with popular elections are in conflict with the whole spirit and genius of our free institutions; that local self government should be reasserted with all the majesty of the sovereign people against the encroachments of Federal power, and that the civil service reform is imperatively demanded to protect the freedom of political action from the now common controlling influence of official patronage.[53]

The state Liberal platform was ingeniously devised to please both the protectionist and the antiprotectionist. In contrast, the revised Missouri platform of April had called for a reduction in the tariff together with a revision of the state constitution favorable to the ex-Confederates.[54]

Under the leadership of A. K. McClure, their leading apologist, the state Liberals made haste to prepare for the coming national convention. At a "convention" of the Liberal Republicans on April 20, 1872, a state executive committee and various subcommittees were created to take care of the necessary details. A reporter for the Harrisburg *Patriot* found the majority of the "delegates" in favor of Andrew Curtin for president, William McClellan for gov-

---

[53] Bellefonte *Democratic Watchman*, April 26, 1872.
[54] Charles H. Hoppes, "The Liberal Republican Movement in Pennsylvania," MS, Pennsylvania State University, 1934.

ernor, and William McCandless for auditor general; but no
steps were taken to create a state Liberal ticket. In a public
letter to the Philadelphia *Evening Bulletin,* McClure listed
his reasons for joining the movement against Grant. The
President could have been forgiven for his "personal [and]
malignant hostility" against reform, wrote McClure, on the
basis of deception; but Grant's efforts to abet corrupt election returns in Philadelphia could not be excused. "The
command came from the President that there must be no
investigation." The reformer made no mention of Grant's
hostility to his senatorial nomination, the actual basis of the
feud. He was now opposing Grant's renomination, concluded
McClure, because the president "was the foe of every principle of reform" and because in his opinion, the majority of
the Republicans of Philadelphia desired another candidate.[55]

Proclaiming the slogan, "On to Cincinnati," the Pennsylvania Liberals joined those of other states in a mass invasion
of the Queen City of the West for the National Liberal Convention held in early May. At Pittsburgh the Eastern group
joined the Northwestern Liberals led by M. B. Lowry and
the colorful General Kane. The members to be seated could
not be designated until after the arrival of the state's
unwieldy delegation, but Hickman, Lowry, Kane, and
McClure, it was believed, would constitute the state's
delegates-at-large.[56] The top newspaper men of the day,
Murat Halstead, Samuel Bowles, Whitelaw Reed, and Henry
Watterson constituted the "Quadrilateral," the purpose of
which was first to break David Davis, the leading presidential
prospect, and then swing the convention to the man of their
choice. The center of attraction at the motley convention

---

[55] Philadelphia *Evening Bulletin,* quoted in Bellefonte *Democratic
Watchman,* April 26, 1872.
[56] Harrisburg *Patriot,* April 30, 1872.

was the imposing, egotistical Alexander K. McClure—"The Jupiter Tonans of reform," commented Watterson, who "looked like a god" when he entered the room and proceeded to best Schurz, Halstead, and Watterson in dinner conversation.[57] Forney agreed that McClure was "among the most talked about [at the Convention]; in the prime of life, about forty three, of herculean frame, at least six foot two, winning address, and great power of endurance."[58]

David Davis, the outstanding contender for the Liberal presidential nomination, had assisted in managing the Lincoln campaign of 1860 and later the President appointed him to the Supreme Court with Cameron's blessing.[59] Other leading aspirants were Charles Francis Adams, Horace Greeley, and Lyman Trumbull. The day before the convention opened, believed McClure, all plans were completed for a Davis-Greeley ticket; but overnight the situation changed. The Quadrilateral successfully completed the first portion of its scheme to break Davis but failed to stampede the convention to Adams.[60]

When the balloting began, the crafty McClure, without authority to do so, allowed the Pennsylvania delegation to cast its first ballot for Curtin, who was in Europe unaware of the political situation in United States.[61] Through this unauthorized premature strategy, McClure forestalled any advantage Curtin might have held at the regular Republican convention and precipitated the great war governor's name into the Liberal camp before Curtin could state his position.

---

[57] Henry Watterson, *"Marse Henry"* (New York, 1919), I, 249-50.
[58] Forney, *Anecdotes,* I, 326.
[59] Harry E. Pratt, "David Davis," MS, University of Illinois, 1930, 122.
[60] H. D. Moore writing from St. Petersburg to Republican headquarters, Harrisburg *State Journal,* Aug. 10, 1872, quoted in Hoppes, "Liberal Republican Movement in Pennsylvania," 40.
[61] Curtin to Washburne, June 2, 1872, Washburne MSS, LC.

Before the second ballot could be cast, Pennsylvania's delegation withdrew Curtin's name, retired for consultation, and then contributed most of its strength to Adams where it remained until the stampede began for Greeley on the sixth ballot. After the various delegations had changed their votes Greeley had 502 to 187 for Adams. Greeley's nomination was made unanimous and B. Gratz Brown received second place on the ticket.[62] A Pennsylvania delegate contributed the only light touch of the convention with his resolution, carried amid great merriment, "that it was expedient . . . to nominate a candidate for President, who is afflicted by a large circle of friends."

The Liberal platform called for immediate removal of all Confederate disabilities, local self-government, impartial suffrage, the supremacy of the civil over the military authority, and one term for President. The civil service was termed a scandal and reproach to free institutions. An end to grants for railroads or other corporation and a speedy return to specie payment was demanded. Turning its back on the sensitive tariff question, the convention returned the problem "to the people in their congressional districts and the decision of Congress thereon."[63] The convention did not neglect to issue a powerful denunciation of the leading exponent of "Grantism," the President himself.

The greatest and most crucial question yet remained unanswered. Would these Liberal Republican voices of protest be joined by those of the Democracy for the purpose of engaging in a general crusade against the evils of a corrupt era and the continued vindictive policy of a militant Radical regime in the beaten South. Could the Democracy swallow a nauseating humble pie with Horace Greeley constituting the

---

[62] Stanwood, *History of the Presidency,* I, 344.
[63] *Ibid.,* 341-42.

main ingredient? McClure had returned homeward from the convention in a state of mortification and despair. Evidently the Liberals had not the strength alone to triumph over Grant, and McClure could not envision Democratic acceptance of Greeley.[64]

The immediate reaction of the Democratic press in Pennsylvania to Greeley was generally negative. Edgar Cowan's brother claimed for his paper the honor of being the first to urge adoption of the Greeley-Brown ticket.[65] The Lancaster *Intelligencer,* a leading Democratic weekly, in a survey of 55 Democratic journals of the state, found only the Titusville *Courier* and the Indiana *Democrat* favorably disposed toward Greeley. However, the Lancaster sheet regarded a combination of the Democrats with the Liberal Republicans and Labor Reformers a golden opportunity.[66] The prominent Reading *Eagle,* though it believed Greeley's nomination by the Democracy would "strike terror" in the Grant camp, held back from advocating an alliance with the Liberals.[67] The influential Harrisburg *Patriot* merely found Greeley a new liability of the Liberal protectionists; but the rabid editor of the Bellefonte *Democratic-Watchman* launched a vicious attack upon Greeley, the "Consistent, determined, inveterate [and] malignant enemy" of Democracy.[68] Pennsylvania's great Democratic jurist, Jeremiah Black, in an open letter to the York *Gazette,* charged: "the violent temper of the Cincinnati movement is breaking the democracy to pieces, there are thousands of men in the party who will refuse to be dragooned or bullied into the support of the ticket."[69]

---

[64] *Notes,* II, 336.
[65] Greensburg *Frank Cowan's Paper,* July 17, 1872.
[66] May 15, 1872.
[67] Reading *Eagle* quoted in *ibid.,* May 7, 1872.
[68] May 10, 1872.
[69] Black to editor of *Gazette,* May 20, 1872, Black MSS, LC.

The Democratic state convention, which was held three weeks after the Cincinnati gathering, very carefully left the road open to either acceptance or rejection of Greeley at the national convention. The Democracy followed a most unusual procedure in failing to endorse a well-known favorite son or to express its opinion on the question of amalgamation with the Liberals. The majority of delegates favored the strongly backed candidate of Jeremiah Black and J. Glancey Jones, General W. S. Hancock, and would have preferred a "straight party" nomination at the coming national convention in Baltimore.[70] Certainly if the question had been left to the decision of Pennsylvania's Democracy, Greeley would have received scant support. The Keystone state was numbered among the four highest opposed to the acceptance of the Liberal candidate.[71]

The National Democratic Convention met at Baltimore, July 9, 1872. At an early night session held for the purpose of uniting Pennsylvania's uninstructed delegation, Samuel J. Randall of Philadelphia argued for Greeley's acceptance in opposition to J. Lawrence Getz, leader of the anti-Greeley men from Berks. Greeley could not carry the Democratic stronghold of Berks, argued Getz, and therefore there was little hope he could carry the state. Following a decision to allow each delegate to vote his own choice, a stormy session was held the next morning where efforts were made to compel the state's delegation to vote as a unit. A trial delegation vote gave Greeley 35 votes to 12 for Chief Justice Thompson, with the remainder of the ballots scattered.[72] A

---

[70] Greenville *Argus ;* Earle D. Ross, *Liberal Republican Movement* (New York, 1919), 137.

[71] *Ibid.,* 133. The other three were New York, New Jersey and Delaware.

[72] Harrisburg *Patriot,* July 10, 1872.

second ballot revealed no additional strength for Greeley
and it was agreed that the chairman of the Pennsylvania
delegation would move the unanimous nomination of
Greeley if he should receive two-thirds of the convention's
vote.

Both the Liberals and the regular Republicans from
Pennsylvania had "wire pullers" busy in Baltimore.
McClure's Liberal coterie was working for Greeley while a
special emissary of Cameron, Democratic delegate A. L.
Noyes, was aiming to block Greeley's nomination. Cameron,
who feared that a Liberal-Democratic coalition was strong
enough to overthrow Grant, requested the help of Noyes, a
candidate for the Democratic gubernatorial nomination.
Noyes, who preferred to "keep quiet for a while," believed
that Greeley's nomination would actually assist Grant's
re-election.[73]

The convention nominated Greeley on the first ballot; the
only opposition coming from the states of Pennsylvania and
Delaware, which gave support to Black and Bayard,
respectively. According to the prearranged plan, William
Wallace then moved the unanimous nomination of Greeley.
The convention had decided to unite with the Liberals in an
attack upon the "military despotism of Grant, Caesarism,
and centralization," to "discard all consideration of party
tradition," and to select a "good and wise man" who offered
better chance of success. The Democracy accepted the
Liberals' platform along with their candidate. When the
secretary began reading the proposed platform from the
convention floor, his voice was deafened with the applause. A
member from Delaware rose to protest against acceptance
of a platform without debate and Pennsylvania sustained his

[73] Noyes to Cameron, May 21, July 5, 1872, Cameron MSS, LC.

motion; but on the vote only 7 of Pennsylvania's 58 votes were cast against its adoption.[74]

Acceptance of Greeley by the Democratic national organization forced the reluctant state Democrats to pay lip service to the coalition candidate, and presumably to aid the Liberal Republicans in their efforts to overthrow Grantism. But to many of the state's Liberals it seemed that one strong potential remained to be added to the voices of protest which would insure victory. This administrator of the *coup de grace* to the Grant-Cameron combination they saw in the person of Andrew G. Curtin. Friends and enemies alike overestimated the former governor's hold on the people of the Commonwealth. Hardly had the Liberal Republican movement begun when current rumor had it that Curtin, the great question mark, was homeward bound to participate in it. During the late winter months, Curtin had been vacationing in sunny climes far from his frigid post at St. Petersburg and his travels had prevented him from gaining much information concerning the Liberal upsurge. Alarmed over his poor state of health, Curtin had written to the Secretary of State from Nice in late February concerning his resignation. At that time the Republican reformers had attained no national significance, and the movement had no organization in Pennsylvania. Evidently Curtin was not proposing his return for political purposes.

Curtin's ministry to Russia had created a fine impression at the Czar's court and newspapers at home had not entirely forgotten the "Soldiers' Friend." Prince Alexander Gortchakov, Russian Chancellor, considered Curtin the second

[74] On Democratic National Convention see Harrisburg *Patriot,* July 9-12, 1872 ; Ross, *Liberal Republican Movement,* 141 ; Charles H. Jones, Life and *Public Services of J. Glancey Jones* (Philadelphia, 1910), II, 153-54 ; Stanwood, *History of the Presidency,* I, 349.

ablest man in the whole foreign diplomatic corps at St. Petersburg.[75] Occasionally, newspaper articles concerning Curtin's activities in far-off Russia appeared in the press, and there were frequent demands for his return. Curtin's absence, it seemed to the Harrisburg *Patriot,* had allowed Cameron to assume the undisputed Radical leadership of the Commonwealth.

By spring Curtin's future status was still undecided. He had received no answers from Secretary Hamilton Fish concerning his resignation. He knew of Buckalew's nomination on the Democratic gubernatorial ticket and believed it strong. Curtin could not see how John F. Hartranft, the strongest Republican contender for gubernatorial honors, could be chosen because of his connections with the Treasury Ring and he expected a weaker man to receive the nomination. At this point Curtin was still definitely a regular Republican, but at home the press was busily arguing and predicting the former governor's future course. The Greenville *Argus,* which considered Curtin's influence over the people as paramount, believed him too shrewd to commit political suicide by casting his lot with the Liberals.[76] The conservative wing of the Republican press continued to assure the public of Curtin's allegiance to the party. The ex-governor, reported the Harrisburg *State Journal,* was "as true a Republican as Grant."[77] Even Cameron's Harrisburg *Telegraph,* much in contrast to the remarks it made about Curtin on his departure to Russia, struck the following conciliatory note: "We do not think Governor Curtin will prove weak enough to join such a reckless, hopeless and treacherous movement against the Republican party." Such a move,

[75] Titian J. Coffey, "Curtin as Minister to Russia," Egle (ed.), *Curtin,* 428-38.

[76] March 30, 1872.

[77] Quoted in Lewistown *Democratic Sentinel,* April 12, 1872,

warned the *Telegraph,* would lead only to political suicide for him.[78]

The news of Curtin's departure from St. Petersburg for London unloosed a new chain of speculation and spurred the Grant forces into efforts to prevent his return. As a member of the diplomatic corps, Curtin could not, with propriety, make a public statement of his intentions; and apparently Grant assigned his friend Washburne to the task of persuading Curtin to remain in Europe. Following his arrival at London about July 15, Curtin backtracked his steps to visit Washburne at Paris.[79] The Grant Administration did everything in its power to keep Curtin in Europe. "He was met in Paris by a man of national prominence," wrote McClure, "who stated to Curtin that he was distinctly authorized to offer him his choice of either the French or English missions if he would remain in the diplomatic service." Upon his return to London he was urged to accept the English mission.[80] During the heat of the campaign in September, McClure charged the Grant Administration with having "pursued" Curtin in Europe and offering him any position within the gift of the government.[81]

Although Grant failed to keep Curtin in Europe, the Administration did not give up hope of making an eleventh-hour deal with him after his arrival in the United States. Judge John M. Read, the Commonwealth's incoming chief justice, informed Secretary Fish of the approximate date when Curtin was expected to arrive and of "what he wants." In full agreement with Read on the question of Curtin's

[78] April 25, 1872.
[79] Curtin to Washburne, June 21, July 15, Aug. 6, 1872, Washburne MSS, LC.
[80] *Notes,* II, 328.
[81] Harrisburg *Patriot,* Sept. 16, 1872 ; Huntingdon *Globe,* Sept. 17, 1872.

importance in the contest, Grant's Secretary of State for-
warded Read's letter to the President with the advice to see
Curtin, "secure him,"[82] and make certain of his support, "for
conquest of the state in October will make easy work
throughout the country in November."[83] The day following
Curtin's arrival in New York, Grant wrote Read of his
personal belief that Curtin's defection would likely cause
the Republicans to lose the significant early state elections
in October.[84] Curtin did not see Grant; the latter went on
vacation to Long Beach, and Curtin, after spending several
days under his physician's care in New York, departed to
Saratoga for a rest.

Although Curtin publicly maintained silence for almost
a month, he apparently informed McClure of his intentions
at the end of a fortnight. In his Columbia speech of September 16, McClure assured his audience of Curtin's adherence
to the Liberal Republican movement. Cameron likewise
expressed the opinion that Curtin would support Greeley.
Possessing no longer any political status in the Republican
Party, cracked the irate Cameron, there was nothing else
for his ancient enemy to do except join the Liberals.[85]
Although not fully recovered, Curtin left Saratoga for his
home at Bellefonte where a crowd estimated at six thousand
received him with a tremendous ovation. Special trains from
Lock Haven, Clearfield, Altoona, Tyrone, and Philipsburg
brought admiring crowds to welcome their war leader.
Radicalism was something which he had left behind him at
the war's end, confessed Curtin to his huge audience. Curtin

---

[82] Fish to Grant, Aug. 19, 1872; Fish to Read, Aug. 19, 1872,
Fish MSS, LC.
[83] Nevins, *Hamilton Fish*, 608.
[84] Grant to Read, Aug. 26, 1872; Ross, *Liberal Republican Movement*, 181.
[85] Philadelphia *Press*, Aug. 31, 1872.

had determined to fight for clean government; it was not right that the people of Pennsylvania could not "purify their own government" free from outside interferences [the Grant-Cameron coalition]."[86]

Before leaving Saratoga, Curtin had addressed a letter to McClure for public consumption. The bitterness which Cameron's victory over Curtin in the senatorial contest of 1867 had engendered in Curtin's heart now stood revealed. A short extract read:

The bad rule that has wholly compassed the channels of political administrative authority in Pennsylvania is not of recent creation. It was the tireless but impotent power that confronted the action of the government, state and national, during the dark days of the civil war, and steadily struggled to gather advancement and gain from the bitter sorrows of the people. Six years ago it attained control of our state; how it was achieved is remembered in humiliation by all . . . . The republican organization that has made its name illustrious in maintaining the unity of the states and redeeming a continent to freedom was seized in contempt of the will of the people and its victories perverted to licensed wrong.[87]

Curtin's charge that Simon Cameron through a period of national crisis had used his office of Secretary of War and his later association with Lincoln for the purpose of personal profit at the expense of the "bitter sorrow of the people," was a serious indictment indeed.

Curtin had crossed his Rubicon never to return. He had chosen to assist the opposition Democratic camp in an attempt to destroy a state political dynasty which he could never hope to shake while remaining within the ranks of the party he had assisted in building and sustaining. The enraged editor of Curtin's hometown Republican paper read the ex-

[86] Bellefonte *Democratic Watchman*, Sept. 27, 1872.
[87] *Ibid*.

governor out of his old party three days prior to his arrival in Bellefonte. In a choleric vein highly reminiscent of the medieval papacy, editor Brown thundered his anathema: "He has gone over to the Rebels and Traitors, and let him go and be Damned! Damned! Damned! ay, doubly, trebly Damned! and let the Democrats receive him when he comes home!"[88]

The council of the voices of protest was now virtually complete. In Pennsylvania, the separated, feeble segments arrayed against the potent political and economic evils of the era had, in combination with reform-minded Republicans, the Democracy, and the Curtin anti-Cameron coterie, grown into a mighty force capable, it seemed, even to the devotees of Grantism, of overthrowing the old established regime. But the battle remained to be won.

---

[88] Bellefonte *Republican*, quoted in Bellefonte *Democratic Watchman*, Sept. 27, 1872.

XI

The Triumph of Reaction

THE DEMOCRACY was the first to raise its state standard in the titanic struggle of 1872. As already noted, the Keystone Democrats, confronted with the question of a future coalition with the Liberals on a national level, solved their dilemma by shifting the entire responsibility upon the National Democratic Convention. On the other hand, the Liberal Republicans had as yet given no indication of selecting a ticket for state offices, and their probable support of the Democracy would likely prove of little value in its attempt to defeat the regular Republican candidates. The difficult problem of the Democratic state convention would be to choose a gubernatorial candidate and platform not likely to be obnoxious to the state's Liberal Republicans and at the same time not to bid openly for Liberal support until the National Convention had made its decision.

The state Democracy met in convention at Reading on May 30, 1872. The quality of its members, observed Richard Vaux, was not above the level of those in the memorable session of 1869 when Tom Collins' bank roll outmaneuvered treasurer Mackey's checks—they were worshipers of the American god, cash.[1] The leading candidates were former United States Senator Charles R. Buckalew; A. L. Noyes of Westport, a close friend of Simon Cameron; General McCalmont, a popular war figure; and Mackey's candidate of 1869, General Cass, who was the favorite. The hostility

---

[1] Vaux to Bigler, Feb. 2, 1872. Bigler MSS, HSP.

between Buckalew and Wallace initiated during their senatorial caucus struggle of 1869 was not apparent at the convention. In event of a state Democratic victory in 1872, with
Buckalew installed in the governor's chair, Wallace would
suffer no difficulty in securing a caucus nomination for
United States Senate. It appeared, however, that Buckalew
stood little chance of capturing the prize when, on the first
ballot, Cass jumped far ahead of any of his competitors. At
the end of seven ballots with Buckalew then in the lead with
60 votes to 45 and 17 for Cass and Noyes respectively, the
delegates stampeded to Buckalew. Other state nominations
were William Hartley for auditor general and James
Thompson for supreme judge.

Other tasks of the convention were to choose the candidates for congressmen-at-large, to name delegates to the State
constitutional convention, and to prepare a suitable platform
—a particularly delicate task because of the necessity of
making it palatable to the Liberals. The platform appealed
to the people of the Commonwealth to elect a Democratic
governor in order to insure "at once a correction of existing
wrongs," and to remove "every taint of political corruption"
for the good of a public whose confidence had suffered
abuse through a "long period of official mismanagement,
waste, and fraud . . . ." Grants made by the legislature to
questionable corporations such as the South Improvement
Company called for special condemnation. Although no
mention was made of the Liberal Cincinnati resolutions,
their kinship to those of the Democracy was easily
discernible.[2]

Buckalew's nomination received support from the Democratic state press. Not one of the seven strong Buckalew

[2] On Democratic State Convention see Harrisburg *Patriot*, June
1, 3, 1872 ; McPherson, *Handbook of Politics*, 174-75,

CHARLES ROLLIN BUCKALEW: Minister Resident to Ecuador, 1858-1861; United States Senator, 1863-1869; Democratic Gubernatorial Candidate, 1872; Congressman, 1887-1891. *Courtesy of Pennsylvania Historical and Museum Commission.*

organs listed by the Harrisburg *Patriot* hinted that the
Democratic candidate might receive any assistance from the
Liberals; all expressed confidence in their man's ability to
defeat the Republican choice for governor.[3] The Democratic
candidate would command a large share of the Republican
vote, irrespective of the Liberals, predicted the *Patriot*,
because he was of the conservative school of politics.[4]
Greeley's New York *Tribune*, characterizing Buckalew as a
man of "stainless integrity," promised him (with doubtful
propriety, it seemed) the support of the Liberals. A rumor
circulated by the Harrisburg *Telegraph* that the Republican
Philadelphia *Press* would support Buckalew brought a quick
denial from its editor. An unworthy Ring candidate, protested Forney, should not be supported for the gubernatorial
office.

The Democracy's candidate for governor, Charles R.
Buckalew, was born on a farm in Columbia County on
December 28, 1821. Now long after graduating from Hart-
ford Academy he took up the study of law, becoming prosecuting attorney at the age of twenty-four and a state senator
at thirty. A Democrat of the strict constructionist school, he
adhered to those principles throughout his career. In the
state senate he had served ably on a commission assigned
the task of revising the state's penal code. He left the legislature for almost three years of diplomatic service in
Ecuador and upon his return in 1861 was re-elected to the
state senate. He had already worked his way to top recognition in the state Democratic organization and in 1861 was
accepted as the senate minority leader. When the Democrats
were able to command a majority of one vote on joint ballot
of the general assembly in January, 1863, Charles Buckalew

---

[3] June 3, 1873.
[4] June 5, 1873.

realized that his big moment had come. If he could win the Democratic caucus nomination and party lines held, there was a chance to enter the Senate of United States. This he accomplished with the defeat of Simon Cameron in one of the state's most exciting elections.[5]

Buckalew served in the Senate during the depressing period of President Johnson's impeachment. In defense of the Chief Executive he delivered a powerful address on the President's power of removal, showing that the power to remove was executive in nature, and supporting his argument with a reference to an act of 1789.[6] On the question of Johnson's guilt, Buckalew voted in the negative while his colleague, Simon Cameron, with unseemly haste, answered guilty before the clerk had time to finish his question.[7] Possessing little organizing ability or knowledge of political strategy, Buckalew nevertheless was one of the ablest Democratic leaders of his day. "He won his position in the party," wrote McClure, "solely by the great ability he possessed, his practical efficiency in legislation and the absolute purity of his character."[8] To the radical George W. Julian, Buckalew appeared as a man of sterling qualities, modest, and "only appreciated by those who knew him intimately."[9] But to Simon Cameron, who had suffered a galling defeat in 1863, Buckalew was an "artful fellow and with great bitterness hidden under a very meek manner."[10]

The Democratic-Liberal Republican coalition was not the

[5] For a sketch of Buckalew see article by Witt Bowden, *Dictionary of American Biography,* III, 225-26.
[6] *Cong. Globe,* 39 Cong., 2 Sess., 407, 438-40, 461-63 ; *Supplement,* 40 Cong., 2 Sess., 510.
[7] DeWitt, *Impeachment and Trial of Andrew Johnson,* 551.
[8] *Notes,* II, 39.
[9] George W. Julian, *Political Recollections* (Chicago, 1889), 358.
[10] Cameron to J. A. J. Creswell, June 2, 1873, Creswell Papers (Crippen Note).

only force working ostensibly for reform in 1872. Both the newly organized Labor Reform and Temperance parties had acquired a considerable following within the state and the latter had selected a slate of candidates for state office in 1871. In addition to being the first to get into the presidential field in 1872, the Labor Reformers ran a ticket for state offices, something the Liberals did not chose to do.

Ambitious Governor John White Geary had struck out for himself at the end of his first term, and his efforts to garner support even from the lesser groups, labor and prohibition, was interpreted to mean that he possessed presidential ambitions.[11] The governor naturally wished to become the candidate of some group more powerful than the Labor Reformers but as it happened he nearly became their choice. Geary's address of May, 1871, acknowledged the National Labor Union's claim as a new party in the political arena. The governor, claimed the Harrisburg *Patriot,* was attempting to divorce himself from the so-called Republican Party.[12] His benevolent attitude toward labor was so well known outside his own state that early in 1871 a Tennessee paper was predicting Geary's candidacy on the Labor Reform ticket of 1872.[13]

The National Labor Reform Party held its national convention at Columbus in late February. On an early informal presidential ballot, Pennsylvania's governor received 60 votes, but when Geary polled only 45 votes on the first formal ballot he was considered out of the running, and Judge David Davis was nominated.[14] The party's lengthy platform of sixteen resolutions called for modification of

---

[11] *Notes,* II, 276.
[12] May 9, 1871.
[13] Nashville *Union,* quoted in Greenville *Argus,* Feb. 1, 1871.
[14] The official accounts differ. McPherson gave Geary 45 votes on the first formal ballot, but Stanwood recorded none.

the tariff, civil service reform, increased governmental regulations over railroads, "immediate restoration" of the Union,
only one term for President, debarring of Chinese laborers,
and an end to the sale of public land." Editor J. W. Forney
charged that the Labor Reform Convention, having been
manipulated in favor of the Democracy, was "definitely
anti-Republican" and labeled its candidate, David Davis, a
"dissatisfied Republican."[16]

On call from Thomas Greevy and John Siney, the Pennsylvania Labor Reform state convention met at Williamsport
on May 7. This unique "state convention" seated 57 delegates representing eight states outside the Commonwealth.
Almost all of Pennsylvania's delegates lived in the anthracite
region. John Siney, the president, proudly opened the
Commonwealth's first Labor Reform Convention where
"representatives of the working masses had come to protest
against the rule of monopoly and concentration of wealth."
In addition to adopting the lengthy Columbus platform en
masse, the convention passed several resolutions of its own
calling for absolute purity of the election franchise, legislation for control of gigantic monopolies, and elimination of
the system of political patronage. One delegate created a
furor by insisting upon a policy of national protection to
American industry. W. P. Schell, of Bedford, was nominated
for governor on the first ballot. Other state nominations were
James Thompson for supreme judge and Esaias Billingfelt
for auditor general. Billingfelt was a Liberal Republican,
and the other two were Democrats. The Labor Reformers
had expressed no faith in the Republican old guard. Before
adjournment the chagrined Labor Reformers learned of

---

[15] Stanwood, *History of the Presidency,* I, 336-38.
[16] Philadelphia *Press,* Feb. 27, 1872.

Davis' withdrawal, called another national convention, and nominated Charles O'Conor of New York.[17]

The Prohibition Party held its national convention at Columbus concurrently with the Labor Reformers. Its platform demanded prohibition of liquors, the franchise for women, and an end to discrimination by the government against labor in favor of capital. James Black of Pennsylvania was nominated for the Presidency. The Keystone state's lone presidential nominee of 1872 was born at Lewisburg in 1823, studied law at his home academy, and was admitted to the bar in 1846. While a youth he joined the temperance movement, having conceived a "strong dislike to the fashionable habit of dram drinking." At first a Democrat, he was among the first to join the new Republican Party in 1854. His "sincerity, honesty and boldness of purpose had gained him his recognition."[18]

As usual the Republicans found plenty of names in 1872 from which to choose their candidate for governor. Although Geary was retiring from office with apparently a creditable record, he had failed in his efforts to build a political machine and exerted little voice in choosing his successor. Neither did the Curtin men possess enough strength to exercise any influence in the selection of a gubernatorial candidate. With the Cameron-Quay-Mackey combination in control of the Republican state political organization, no one could hope to receive the nomination without its blessing. Besides General Hartranft, the names most frequently mentioned for the honor were Harry White, Francis Jordan, and W. W. Ketcham. White and Hartranft were deserters from the

---

[17] On State Labor Reform Convention see McPherson, *Handbook of Politics,* 1872, 175, 211 ; Pottsville *Miners' Journal,* March 30, 1872 ; Williamsport *Gazette and Bulletin,* May 7, 8, 1872.

[18] Alexander Harris, *Biographical Sketch of Lancaster County,* 47-48.

Curtin camp. Before disclosure of Hartranft's connection with the Evans Scandal his nomination had been considered almost certain.[19] Francis Jordan, secretary of the Commonwealth, was able to secure the delegates from only two counties, Bedford and Huntingdon. White had some strength in the western Pennsylvania and Philadelphia areas.

Meeting of the delegates for the Republican state convention at Harrisburg in early April found Hartranft still leading the field. An early pre-convention poll revealed 68 delegates favorable to Hartranft, and at this juncture John W. Forney began his press campaign to block the "veterans' candidate." Despite the editor's rumors of Cameron's coolness and the "growing weakness" of Hartranft, the auditor general captured the nomination on the first ballot, 87 votes to 45 for Ketcham.[20] Other work of the group included the nomination of Harrison Allen for auditor general and the naming of delegates to the national and constitutional conventions. Russell Errett's gag resolution called for the nomination of national convention delegates by a special committee named by the presiding officer of the convention. The platform lauded the accomplishments of the Grant Administration, complimented the Commonwealth's citizens for calling a constitutional convention, and pleaded for protection of American industry.[21]

Unlike the Democracy, the Republicans of the state were not united in acceptance of their party's gubernatorial candidate. The Scranton *Republican*, Pittsburgh *Chronicle*, Lancaster *Express*, and Pittsburgh *Dispatch* doubted the wisdom

---

[19] Erie *Observer*, Aug. 3, 1871 ; Greenville *Argus*, Dec. 8, 1871.

[20] West Chester *Republican*, Jan. 23, 1872 ; Philadelphia *Press*, April 8, 9, 1872.

[21] McPherson, *Handbook of Politics*, 1872, 173-74 ; Harrisburg *Patriot*, April 10, 11, 1872 ; Philadelphia *Press*, April 9-11, 1872.

of Hartranft's nomination; and the Pittsburgh *Post* questioned the candidate's fitness for high office.[22] It is possible that Cameron doubted the wisdom of Hartranft's nomination at the time, but did not deem it advisable to override the opinions of his trusted lieutenants. Cameron's confidant, E. B. Moore, claimed that at no time did Cameron personally favor Hartranft's candidacy;[23] nevertheless the Cameron organization had secured his nomination. Naturally the Democratic press had a field day in calling the public's attention to Hartranft's connections with the Evans Scandal. The Republicans, it seemed to the Reading *Eagle*, were actually making a strong bid for defeat.[24]

Immediately after Hartranft's nomination, a movement was initiated to have him shelved in favor of another candidate. Both Grant and Hartranft looked askance upon each other's nomination. Reportedly, emissaries of the Republican state committee met with Forney to ascertain if he might be appeased; but the volatile editor would be satisfied with nothing less than an entirely new state ticket.[25] After biding his time over a period of six weeks, the editor of the *Press* launched a full-scale attack on the gubernatorial candidate in middle June. Forney also declared war on Cameron and his machine charging that the men responsible for Hartranft's nomination had secured it for the purpose of associating his name with Grant, thereby securing his election and a perpetuation of their own rule.[26] Less than a month had

---

[22] Quoted in Bellefonte *Democratic Watchman*, April 19, 1872: *Post* quoted in Williamsport *Gazette*, April 23, 1872.

[23] West Chester *American* quoted in Pottsville *Miners' Journal*, June 1, 1872.

[24] Quoted in Bellefonte *Democratic Watchman*, April 19, 1872.

[25] Hoppes, "Liberal Republican Movement," 30; Harrisburg *Patriot*, April 23, 1872.

[26] Philadelphia *Press*, June 15, 1872.

passed by since Forney had invited Cameron to dinner enclosing a laudable admonition, "Let us have peace."[27]

Hartranft now became the gubernatorial storm center. No results came from Forney's early proddings, and the editor renewed his assault in early July: "It is manifest now that the Republican State Central Committee do not intend to bring about a modification of the ticket. They become aiders and abetters of the conspiracy to continue in existence the present rapacious state treasury ring." More than twenty influential Republican organs, claimed the *Press,* were opposed to the state ticket.[28] Finally, under tremendous pressure, the Committee met behind barred doors to consider the matter of Hartranft's recall. Only one member, William B. Mann, urged a change, and the group, protesting lack of power to take action unless Hartranft resigned, did nothing. Cameron, afraid of the consequences of a state defeat in the early October election, was understandably much concerned about the matter. In view of Geary's fluke victory in 1869 and the Liberals' support of Buckalew, the situation looked critical indeed. Following a request for guidance from friends, Cameron assembled a private conclave but his son, J. Donald saved the day for Hartranft, declaring that the "party could save itself only by assuming the aggressive and standing by its state ticket."[29] To call another state convention would certainly be to invite new hazards; in view of the temper of the times it could conceivably have gotten out of hands. The state ticket would stand or fall with Hartranft.

The subject of the storm center, John F. Hartranft, like Geary, was a famous soldier, and also like most of the

[27] Forney to Cameron, May 21, 1872, Cameron MSS, LC.

[28] *Press,* quoted in Harrisburg *Patriot,* July 3, 1872.

[29] Delano to Cameron, Aug. 14, 1872, Cameron MSS, LC; McClure *Notes,* II, 346.

Commonwealth's preceding governors, of German descent.[30] He was born in Montgomery County on December 16, 1830. Passing from the hands of private tutors he entered Marshall College preparatory school at Mercersburg, transferred to Union College at Schenectady, and graduated near the top of his class in the field of civil engineering. Next he turned to politics, serving two terms as deputy sheriff of his native county. He had used his spare time to study law and, after a period of apprenticeship in a local law office, he passed the bar examination and was admitted in 1859. On the outbreak of the war, Hartranft, then a colonel of Montgomery County's militia, led his men into service as ninety-day volunteers. His command had the doubtful reputation of being the worst-clothed militiamen in the state, first going into the service in civilian regalia and then changing into something worse—the first full issue of shoddy. On the eve of Bull Run his regiment departed en masse for home and Hartranft served on General Franklin's staff during the battle. In the fall of 1861 he organized a new regiment and saw service the remainder of the war. His actions at Spotsylvania Court House and Fort Stedman earned him two promotions, and he emerged from the war a major general of volunteers. His duties (special provost marshal) at the execution of Mrs. Surratt, earned him unpleasant publicity in 1872 as the hangman of an innocent woman.[31]

Hartranft entered the state political field at the end of the war. At the Union state convention of 1865, the Curtin men combined with Stevens' coterie to give Hartranft the nomination for auditor general over Cameron's choice, Hiestand.

[30] Seven preceding governors were of German descent. They were Synder, Hiester, Shulze, Wolf, Ritner, Shunk, and Bigler. Hartranft was the fourth governor born in Montgomery County.
[31] Armor, *Lives of the Governors of Pennsylvania*, 491-12; *Pennsylvania German Magazine*, VIII, 475-77.

Hoping to become Curtin's choice for governor in 1866, Hartranft was reluctant to accept. But the next year he made no attempt to capture the gubernatorial nomination, was re-elected in 1868, and remained in office through 1872. Cameron realized that Hartranft, a popular soldier and well-known public officer, was a likely prospect to succeed Geary. In 1869 Cameron catered to Hartranft in the matter of patronage, allowing him to control his home county, Montgomery. Regarding Hartranft's reaction to this friendly gesture, E. B. Moore of West Chester wrote: ". . . [He] is pleased with the manner in which he has been treated. You can rely on him as a friend hereafter, which is also a matter of importance."[32]

The last important political gathering of the 1872 campaign was that of the Republicans who held their national convention at Philadelphia on June 5. This assemblage could hardly be called a nominating convention, if by that term is meant a body deliberating for the purpose of selecting a presidential candidate. The meeting merely ratified a selection already made; in this particular instance the person of General U. S. Grant, the incumbent. This being the case, the chief subject of discussion centered around the Vice-Presidency. Andrew D. White recorded that "the most noteworthy features . . . were the speeches of sundry delegates [fifty Negroes] from the South."[33] The *Nation's* reporter scored the boring eloquence of the Negro delegates, "who having an inch given them, took an ell." Before the Liberal Republican movement got under headway there had been some sentiment to support Curtin for Vice-President. Francis P. Blair, Jr., believed that Curtin's supporters included at

---

[32] Moore to Cameron, April 7, 1869, Cameron MSS, LC.
[33] Andrew D. White, *Autobiography of Andrew Dickson White* (New York, 1905), I, 172.

least two senators.[34] But the unauthorized use of Curtin's name at Cincinnati had killed what little chance he might have had at Philadelphia.

There is hardly any doubt that Simon Cameron played the decisive role in substituting Henry Wilson for Vice-President Colfax on the Grant ticket. Cameron's first choice for the honor was his own son J. Donald, and two papers announced that the state delegation had endorsed him;[35] but when no further interest was shown in him at the convention, Cameron wisely decided not to present his name. Cameron owed a debt to Henry Wilson. The senator from Massachusetts had defended Cameron in the Senate when his name had been presented for the Russian mission; and again after Lincoln's death, Wilson supported the Secretary's contention that he had not suffered dismissal from the Cabinet, but had resigned. Cameron was aided in his drive to defeat Colfax by the Washington press which had taken a dislike to the Vice-President. Regarding Cameron's powerful influence at the convention, the head of the Indiana delegation wrote: "In my own mind I gave up the contest on Tuesday when Cameron failed to give us any assurance of support."[36] In the opinion of William D. Foulke, the refusal of Cameron and his delegation to support Colfax was "decisive" and brought Wilson's nomination on the first ballot.[37]

Because of Pennsylvania's importance in the early October elections, a reporter for the *Nation* paid particular attention to the opinions of the state's delegates at the national convention. One experienced Pennsylvania politico discounted

[34] Smith, *Blair Family,* II, 499.
[35] Philadelphia *Press,* July 9, 1872 ; Harrisburg *Patriot,* June 6, 1872.
[36] Orando J. Hollister, *Life of Schuyler Colfax* (New York, 1866), 373.
[37] William D. Foulke, *Life of Oliver P. Morton,* II, 257.

Forney's defection and expected it to cause no serious split in the party. According to another delegate, the Philadelphia men "didn't give a damn who was elected," and they intended to go along with Hartranft. Mingling with the delegates was Henry W. Oliver, the iron magnate from Pittsburgh, who participated in preparing the party plank and saw to it that his industry received recognition along with the candidates, Grant and Wilson. The resolutions commended Grant for his "modest patriotism . . . sound judgment, practical wisdom . . . and incorruptible integrity."[38] But the *Nation's* reporter left the convention with the feeling that the Democrats would carry the state in October.[39] The Republican Old Guard had discovered no fault in its own tenets of "Grantism"; nor had it found any cause to modify the militant policy of the party in the newly reconstructed South—a vindictive program designed to ensure future Radical supremacy through maintenance of puppet "black and tan" government.

At first glance the battle lines of the 1872 campaign within Pennsylvania seemed fairly simple to grasp. The Democracy had endorsed Greeley, the Liberal Republican presidential candidate against Grantism. On the other hand, the Liberals, having failed to establish a ticket for state offices, were expected to reciprocate by supporting the Democratic candidates for state office. But there was another small Republican group under the leadership of John W. Forney that threw its support to Grant while at the same time savagely attacking Ring control of the state. Conveniently using gubernatorial candidate Hartranft as a medium of attack, Forney was engaging in the fray with a bent toward un-

---

[38] McPherson, *Handbook of Politics*, 1872, 205 ; Tweedy, *Conventions*, 125.
[39] *Nation*, June 13, 1872.

loosening the iron grip of the Cameron machine upon the Commonwealth. In this one respect he was aligned with the Liberals.

A. K. McClure assumed leadership of the state's Liberal Republicans. He used the tactics of attacking Grantism when addressing audiences outside the Commonwealth and of fighting the "Ring" when speaking within. His first address of the campaign delivered in New York on June 3 was intended to persuade the Democrats of the need for their endorsement of Greeley at their national convention. Reviewing in detail Grant's first administration, McClure began with a condemnation of the President for his vindictive Southern policy and his "prostitution of power," and concluded with a panegyric on Greeley.[40] McClure was chief author of the "Bugle Call," a broadside containing the text of the state's Liberal Republican program. The "Bugle Call" revealed little evidence of a fight against Grantism—it was a clear call to overthrow Simon Cameron:

The present political rule in Pennsylvania must be overthrown. It is a living libel upon Republicanism and a blistering blot upon the Commonwealth . . . its prostitution of power and traffic in federal, state, and municipal favors, have driven competent and upright men from public service, and its complete subordination to the interests of Simon Cameron makes every path leading from it point to public purity and individual manhood.

This battle for reform must be fought in our State contest. In vain will the leaders of misrule plead to escape the trial before the people by hiding their deformities under a national standard . . . . The election of an honest legislature will restore the government of Philadelphia to control of her own citizens. If the discharge of this plain and imperative duty by the people in October shall defeat or endanger either Greeley or Grant in

---

[40] Harrisburg *Patriot*, June 4, 1872.

November, in this State, there can be no argument or apology offered for their success.[41]

To McClure's way of thinking, partial victory could be achieved by defeating Grant and Hartranft, but *complete victory* could be secured only through control of the legislature, the body that had the power to defeat or return Simon Cameron to the Senate of United States. All who desired removal of the evil Cameron-Mackey Republican ring, advised McClure, should vote for Buckalew and a Democratic state legislature.[42] McClure next began a tour of North Carolina and other states, reserving Pennsylvania as the battleground for the final days of the campaign.

Able out-of-state speakers led by Horace Greeley and Carl Schurz toured the Commonwealth assisting local orators. Schurz delivered addresses at the larger cities of Pittsburgh, Philadelphia, Lancaster, Pottsville, Scranton, and Erie. Greeley, attired in his familiar white coat and hat, followed mostly the line of the Pennsylvania Railroad speaking on the subjects of his personal success and national affairs. Physical exhaustion compelled him to cancel a portion of his appearances.[43] On his return from the Indiana State Fair, Greeley spoke at Erie, Sunbury, and a few other towns. John Frazier continued the main theme of the state Liberals—the unhorsing of Cameron and the members of his ring. "Gentleman, be not deceived," warned Frazier, "the question . . . is not whether Greeley or Grant shall be president; it is whether the corrupt cabal, Cameron, Hartranft, and Mackey shall continue to exercise imperial power in Pennsylvania." The election of Hartranft to the gubernatorial office, continued Frazier, would be followed by the

---

[41] *Ibid.*, July 12, 1872, quoting "Bugle Call."
[42] *Ibid.*, July 22, 1872.
[43] *Ibid.*, Sept. 20, 1872 ; Erie *Observer*, Sept. 19, 1872.

return of Cameron to the Senate ". . . a man who has done more to debauch the public morals of this state and nation than perhaps any other living person.""

Curtin's broken health prevented him from taking much part in the contest. Arrangements were made to have him speak at Concert Hall in Philadelphia where a vast crowd estimated at 5,000 listened to a stirring oration directed against the Ring and the corruption surrounding it. No mention was made of Grant or Greeley, not even of Cameron; but the former governor's audience well knew against whom his invectives were directed. On his way back to Bellefonte, Curtin delivered a brief address at Altoona. Curtin's struggle was not against Grant, but his archenemy Simon Cameron.

Following the National Democratic Convention's endorsement of Greeley, the Liberal Republicans received several Republican notables into their lists. In Allegheny County, J. K. Moorhead, Thomas Marshall, and John Riddle, a former Republican candidate for mayor of Pittsburgh, announced themselves as Liberals and found places on the Liberal Republican State Committee. The Liberals made much ado over the addition of Galusha A. Grow to their number. The former national speaker, twice blocked in his efforts to secure a Republican nomination to Congress, had become president of a Texas railway company. Although Grow announced his support of Greeley, he remained in Texas, took no part in the campaign, and made no statement of opposition to his home state's Republican ticket; consequently the author of the Homestead Act can hardly be included in the Commonwealth's Liberals." The last man of note to announce himself for the Liberal Republicans was

---

⁴⁴ Bellefonte *Democratic Watchman,* Sept. 20, 1872.
⁴⁵ DuBois and Matthews, *Galusha A. Grow,* 273-74.

E. Joy Morris, a cultured diplomat and local political leader of many years service.

That the Liberal Republicans of the Commonwealth were putting up a knock-down-and-drag-out fight can scarcely be questioned. Their leaders were men of outstanding ability. But they could not determine whether Pennsylvania's voters really wish to exchange Ring control of the state—corrupt though it might be—for a curious political monstrosity whose Liberal head had no control over its Democratic body and tail. Were the fruits of four years of bloodletting now to be sacrificed with the termination of a Radical militant policy which continued "Grantism" would insure?

The most interesting sidelight of the campaign was John W. Forney's personal war on Simon Cameron. In fact a casual reader unacquainted with the political issues of the day might have picked up an issue of the Philadelphia *Press* and put it down with the idea that Cameron was running for governor. The large circulation of his Philadelphia organ made Forney's anti-Cameron campaign comparatively simple. In addition, the articles appearing in the *Press* were widely copied by Democratic journals and by the Republican weeklies opposed to Hartranft. Following Forney's resignation from the Philadelphia collectorship, he signified his willingness to come to terms with Cameron, but no understanding was reached.[46] When Cameron insisted upon the dismissal of the Forney men enjoying Federal patronage, he placed President Grant in a distressing dilemma. Grant's private secretary explained to Cameron the necessity for allowing Forney a share of the patronage.[47] Grant had gotten his fingers burned when he tried pulling Cameron's chestnuts out of the fire in the McClure-Gray contest, and did not

---

[46] Cameron to Forney, May 21, 1872, Cameron MSS, LC.
[47] Babcock to Cameron, Aug. 16, 1872, Cameron MSS, LC.

relish the thought of extracting from under himself one of the best props in the Commonwealth—the Philadelphia *Press.* So there continued to exist during the remainder of the contest the anomalous situation of Forney praising the fountainhead of his source of enmity. Forney's position, aptly commented a Bellefonte editor, was comparable to that of the devil busily engaged in saving souls within the gates of hell.[48]

There is some evidence to show that Forney's attacks forced Cameron to bargain with his nemesis. In July, stated D. C. Forney, Cameron offered to remove Allen, the candidate for auditor general, from the ticket, and allow J. W. Forney to name his successor if only the *Press* would cease its attacks upon Hartranft. Reputedly, at a dinner, Cameron had stated that he could have knocked "hell into both Grant and Curtin," if the latter had been chosen as the vice-presidential candidate; and moreover "no man should be recognized politically *in his state* without his consent; that he . . . could, if he desired, transmit the same power to posterity."[49] Succeeding years were to bear evidence that Simon Cameron was no idle boaster.

Forney's last move against Cameron revealed him a master strategist. The ingenious editor traveled to the state library, secured Hartranft's books for the years 1866-1871; and after a week's hard work, publicly revealed his figures. Out of $618,000 owed the state in taxes over a six-year period, Cameron's Northern Central Railroad had paid only $158,000, leaving in arrears $460,000 due the Commonwealth. Surely, it seemed, Hartranft had proved to be Cameron's dream auditor.[50]

[48] Bellefonte *Democratic Watchman,* Sept. 20, 1872.
[49] Open letter of D. C. Forney to New York *Herald* quoted in Huntingdon *Globe,* Aug. 6, 1872.
[50] Philadelphia *Press,* Oct. 1, 1872,

The first wave of Liberal Republicanism in Pennsylvania had evinced some strength in itself; and added to the might of the Democracy, and other reform elements, the movement could have appeared irresistible. Sensing in the conflict a kinship to the late Johnson-Republican struggle of 1866, Edgar Cowan, Johnson's old lieutenant, emerged from retirement. The Democracy, believed Cowan, could nominate Greeley only because of the necessity for liberating the South and breaking the plundering rings.[51] Greeley was engaged in leading a revolt against wickedness, admitted Jeremiah Black, and therefore must be supported as the lesser of two evils.[52] Not without justification the Liberals were optimistic, and the forces of Greeley and Buckalew were riding high during the summer months. The accusations directed against Hartranft would ordinarily have been sufficient in themselves to have brought defeat to any gubernatorial candidate. At first Whitelaw Reid thought Pennsylvania was safely in the Democratic-Liberal column.[53] Many assumed, because the leaders and the press had accepted the strange union between Greeley and the Democrats, that the great mass of voters was prepared to do the same.

The main line of attack directed by the Republicans against Charles Buckalew, the gubernatorial candidate, was identical with that used against all Democratic candidates of the period. Allegedly he had opposed every measure tending to aid in suppressing the rebellion and had hindered in every possible way the work of congressional reconstruction in the South. In addition he was opposed to "wholesome financial measures," and had voted uniformly against protection to American industry, thus "striking at the vital inter-

<hr/>

[51] Greensburg *Frank Cowan's Paper,* July 17, 1872.
[52] Black to William Welsh, Aug. 3, 1872, Black MSS, LC.
[53] Royal Cortissoz, *Life of Whitelaw Reid* (New York, 1921), I, 224.

ests of Pennsylvania." In rebuttal, a Democratic organ compared Buckalew's record to that of a War Democrat and insisted upon his friendliness to a tariff, "if it were well regulated."[54] To the strongly protectionist Pottsville *Miners' Journal,* Buckalew, the cultivated aristocrat, was an enemy of labor.[55]

Buckalew vigorously defended his record on the stump. In his Lancaster speech of August 20, the Democratic candidate accused Russell Errett of attempting to revive the passions of war, and pointed proudly to his own legislative record which proved his willingness to prosecute the late war. His vote against the bill for pay increase of colored troops he defended on the basis of its retroactive features. At Erie, Buckalew commented upon his visit to the Republican state convention which, he found, had for its purpose the re-election of Cameron and Mackey, and the elevation of Hartranft to a higher station where he could further the schemes of the Ring. Significantly the Democratic gubernatorial standard bearer made no reference to national issues, the case for Greeley, or against "Grantism."

Up to this time Hartranft had remained publicly silent; neither could Governor Geary be drawn actively in the contest. Nevertheless, the Republican machine was working efficiently and silently; and if not with words, such as they had—silver and gold. The Republican National Committee, convinced of the necessity of carrying Hartranft in the October elections in order to insure Grant's election, sent $75,000 into the Commonwealth, totally exhausting their resources in the process. As usual the firm of Jay Cooke and Company was "milked" for all it was worth with a

---

[54] Erie *Dispatch* quoted in Erie *Observer,* Aug. 29, 1872 ; Erie *Observer,* Aug. 29, 1872.

[55] September 28, 1872.

contribution of $30,000 for the cause of Grantism. Additional funds were raised by Cooke's good friends and by forced contributions from the Federal clientele who were assessed what the traffic would bear.[56]

Tremendous pressure was brought upon Governor Geary to pardon the Philadelphia brokers, Yerkes and Mercer, who had sworn that Hartranft, the auditor general had received a "cut" from the profits of the Evans deal. The disreputable pair promised, in exchange for a pardon, to retract their sworn statement of Hartranft's implication in the scandal. Cameron, Hartranft, Mackey, and President Grant assembled in Philadelphia, dispatched a special agent to Harrisburg to secure a pardon from Geary, and effected the immediate release of Yerkes and Mercer from the Philadelphia penitentiary. Intelligent citizens doubted the efficacy of a retraction performed under such compelling circumstances. As a protective measure, the governor published a list of 133 names, all "respectable members of the Philadelphia bar" who had signed the pardon petition. Among them was the name of Alexander K. McClure.[57]

As the time approached for the Pennsylvania October elections, reaction in favor of Hartranft and Grant allowed the Cameron forces to regain confidence. By the last of August, both Simon Cameron and his son Donald were satisfied that Hartranft would be elected.[58] From New York State Roscoe Conkling wrote of his rejoicing over Simon Cameron's assurances.[59] The two Camerons could have added that Philadelphia, with approximately one-sixth of

[56] Oberholtzer, *Jay Cooke,* II, 355-57.

[57] Harrisburg *Patriot,* Sept. 30, 1872. For McClure's account see *Notes,* II, 347.

[58] J. D. Cameron to McPherson, Aug. 21, 1872 ; McPherson MSS, LC.

[59] Conkling to Cameron, Aug. 24, 1872, Cameron MSS, LC.

the state vote, would prove an insurmountable problem to the Liberals and Democrats. Boss William B. Mann could have his repeaters vote as many times as it seemed necessary, and just in case that did not prove sufficient, election judges could adjust the figures. McClure related the amusing story of Nick English, the election judge, who altered the returns so that a coterie of gamblers would not lose their bets that Hartranft would carry the city by 20,000 votes.[60] The "official" returns gave the Republican candidate a majority of 20,437, but Allen, his running mate, recorded a majority of 19,999. Likely, the same gamblers had bet that Allen would not attain a 20,000 majority. Gambling friends of Simon Cameron had dispatched last-minute telegrams to him requesting the odds on Hartranft's election.[61]

The state elections of October 9 gave Hartranft 353,387 votes to Buckalew's 317,760. The city of Philadelphia, the liberal use of campaign money, loyalty to the Union tradition, public indifference to political corruption, and Hartranft's "proven innocence," provide the best answers to his 35,000 majority over Buckalew. Philadelphia with 17 per cent of the state vote contributed 57 per cent of the Republican majority. Hartranft's majority in the three counties of Philadelphia, Allegheny, and Lancaster equaled his total majority in the state.[62] The Republicans carried only three more counties than they had in 1871. Evidently, great exertions had been made to call out the electorate, because the total number voting was almost 100,000 more than the figures of 1869.

If the Keystone Liberals and Democrats could not beat

---

[60] *Notes,* II, 347.

[61] Cameron MSS, LC.

[62] *Smull's Legislative Handbook,* 1873, 289-91. Allen the Republican candidate for auditor general won over Hartley, 352,568 votes to 315,788.

the discredited Hartranft, there was little chance of accomplishing Grant's defeat. With the nation on the verge of a financial collapse, Jay Cooke and associates were working desperately to sustain the market,[63] and business men were experiencing nightmares in apprehension of what might result if the erratic Greeley should succeed to the Presidency. McClure recorded the fear of prominent business Democrats and their liberal contributions to the Republican campaign chest in Philadelphia. These measures were hardly necessary because over 100,000 Democrats in the state could not accept Greeley and failed to vote, although protectionists were popular with many Democrats. Democracy's editors had ordered their menu of "boiled crow" in vain. When the Liberal Cincinnati convention nominated Horace Greeley, it in effect elected Grant. Pennsylvania's returns gave 349,689 votes to Grant and 211,961 to Greeley.[64] A Commonwealth vote of 170,000 less than in the state elections indicated that Hartranft, the Cameron ring candidate, was more popular than Grant. Hartranft's plurality of 4,000 over Grant seemed to defy logic, in view of Forney's strong support of Grant and his bitter opposition to Hartranft, the Cameron candidate. Apparently, about 100,000 Democrats who had voted for Buckalew shunned the polls on presidential Election Day.

The congressional and state legislative returns were equally crushing to the Democracy. Only five Democrats were elected to Congress while the Republicans returned nineteen representatives from congressional districts and three at large for a total of twenty-two. This was fewer than the Democracy had after the elections of 1866. The Democrats won only three of the eleven state Senate seats, and

[63] Oberholtzer, *Jay Cooke*, II, 355.
[64] Smull's *Legislative Handbook*, 1873, 285.

thirty-nine of the one hundred House seats. The new legislature of 1873 would consist of 78 Republicans, 53 Democrats, 1 Independent, and 1 Liberal Republican.[65] The next United States senator was certain to be a Republican. Strangely, the combined forces of the Liberal Republicans and the Democrats had proved weaker than the Democracy alone.

The results wrecked the political futures within the Republican Party of Pennsylvania's two leading Liberals, Andrew G. Curtin and A. K. McClure. Reporters of the Philadelphia *Press* found the latter apparently undisturbed over the results, because, stated McClure, he expected Philadelphia to return 10,000 fraudulent votes. About 20,000 Democrats, charged McClure, had not voted their own ticket and probably 15,000 failed to vote; and stranger indeed was the fact that hourly returns showed Hartranft running behind his ticket but the final tally placed him far ahead. If the proud ex-governor could find no solace in the returns neither did he suffer any remorse: "For my course in the election I have no regrets. To have acted otherwise would have been personal degradation."[66] Upon the occasion of Curtin's death in 1894, *Harper's Weekly* commented: "Governor Curtin shared in the blindness and terrific downfall of the so-called 'Liberal Movement' of 1872. He never sought to extricate himself from the ruins of that unstable party edifice. He remained in the ranks of that uncongenial [Democratic] minority party . . . whither his revolt had driven him."[67]

Secretary Fish, the President's helpmeet, pronounced to

---

[65] *Ibid.*, 516, 530. Grant's Pennsylvania majority was over two and one-half times that of New York.

[66] Curtin to Carey, Oct. 15, 1872, Carey MSS, HSP.

[67] October 20, 1894.

Cameron the bizarre benediction: "The expurgated Republican Party is stronger on account of those who have gone out from it. Let the 'Curtain fall.' "[68]

The Liberal Republican movement presents many interesting problems and puzzling aspects to the student interested in an analysis of this post-bellum political upheaval within the Keystone state. To arrive at a completely satisfactory answer would be to fathom the inner thoughts of men long since dead. The crusade of 1872 appealed to men with a great variety of motives and likely few responded from the urge of a single stimulus. Were these few properly reformers, or were they a motley collection of soreheads, "have-nots," and political opportunists masquerading in the crusade against the political corruption of the era. Certainly, notwithstanding all the fanfare and furor created within the Commonwealth, only a small percentage of the rank and file responded. If its leaders were many, its followers were few.

One wing of the leading Liberal Republicans may be designated simply as Curtin men. Heading the list was Curtin himself, along with A. K. McClure, Thomas Marshall, Eli Slifer, Joseph M. McClure, and William Lewis. Slifer had served Curtin faithfully for six years as secretary of the Commonwealth. Marshall was an old Curtin man who had exhausted his abusive vocabulary upon Cameron in 1860, later repented of his actions, and now was back in his original fold. All these men had a direct interest in smashing the Cameron machine. The Commonwealth was not big enough for these hostile factions within the Republican Party and one must go. William Lewis, a one-time War Democrat, was publisher of the Huntingdon *Globe*. He seems not to have had any particular ax to grind and was simply a

---

[68] Fish to Cameron, Oct. 9, 1872, Cameron MSS, HSP.

Curtin supporter. His paper was one of the few journals of the state to call itself a "Liberal' 'organ.

Another group of Liberals, J. K. Moorhead, Henry L. Cake, David Barclay, William Stewart, and John Hickman were former congressmen. Not one of these men had served in the outgoing Congress or the preceding Forty-first Congress except Cake. John Hickman, a leading congressman during the Buchanan era, could view his political career only in retrospect. J. K. Moorhead, a wealthy industrialist from Pittsburgh, had served in Congress from 1859 to 1869, and once was regarded the party leader in Allegheny County. Although in a sense a free-lance politician, he had generally followed Simon Cameron. He had hoped to secure the nomination for governor or senator in 1869 and became embittered when he found Cameron had put him off with "fair words." Moorhead's motive could have been revenge. Henry L. Cake of Schuylkill County, an anthracite operator by profession, who served in Congress from 1867 to 1871, was a reputable, fair-minded, progressive citizen. In 1870, when Cake graciously granted a wage increase to his coal miners, he was blacklisted as a dishonorable coal operator by the Anthracite Board of Trade.

A survey of the 1872 General Assembly indicates an amazing indifference to the Liberal movement. Only two regular Republicans, Senator Billingfelt, an honest German of Lancaster, and Representative Bomburger of Harrisburg, a rich banker who had a personal grudge against Cameron, joined it.[69] Billingfelt had secured the regular Republican congressional nomination in 1872 and then resigned because he could not endure Hartranft and Allen. He had served in

---

[69] McClure had been elected in a special election as an Independent Republican, but the next year's directory listed him Liberal Republican.

the State Senate from 1867 to 1872 where he had opposed the Treasury Ring. Here was a man sincerely fighting for reform. Former Senators Benson, Mason, and Coray also supported the movement. Coray had been a leading bolter against Mackey in 1870, and the following year again refused to succumb to the ring.

Two other well known Liberals were Morrow B. Lowry, an old friend of John Brown, and E. Joy Morris, an eleventh-hour convert. Lowry, the son of a Presbyterian Covenanter, drove his cattle to market and knew how to drive a sharp bargain. His somewhat erratic nature is illustrated in his desire to see banks mustered out with the troops at the end of the war. He was known widely for his charitable work on behalf of orphans and abandoned children. Mackey's replacement of Lowry's friend Irwin in the state treasury post partly accounted for his enmity toward the Cameron-supported Ring. E. Joy Morris, on Cameron's insistence, had received the mission to Turkey in 1861 from Lincoln. He served at the Porte until his sudden recall by Grant to make room for Wayne MacVeagh, Cameron's son-in-law. Before returning home he reminded Cameron that he would never forget what his benefactor had done for him. He did accept an independent [Liberal] nomination for Congress in 1872 but did not discuss campaign issues in public and ended with a vote for Grant.[70]

One could not close a review of the state's leading Liberal Republicans without mention of the colorful eccentric Thomas L. Kane, McKean County. This striking "pint-size" promoter of the Philadelphia and Erie Railroad was the only close friend of Cameron to desert to the Liberal camp. Before the war an abolitionist, state free-soil leader, and agent of the

---

[70] Carman and Luthin, *Lincoln and the Patronage*, 88 ; Morris to Cameron, June 10, 1870, Oct. 16, 1873, Cameron MSS, LC.

Underground Railroad, Kane had in 1861 organized his renowned "Bucktail" regiment. During the course of the conflict he was wounded and captured, participated in the conflict at Gettysburg although too weak to mount his horse, and emerged a brevet major general. In the post-bellum era he had divided his time between his business duties at Philadelphia and his mansion in the great northern forest, the rendezvous selected for the Grant-Cameron liaison. On his way to the Cincinnati Liberal conclave he had dispatched a pathetic farewell message to Simon Cameron. Perhaps his political action in 1872 can be explained partly as the workings of an eccentric mind.[71]

In addition to these leaders of the Liberal movement in the Commonwealth, many more of lesser note could be named. Almost without exception they were the "have-nots," who occupied no positions of public trust in 1872. Republican Liberalism had little appeal to members of the General Assembly or to beneficiaries of patronage; it attracted rather those who had nothing to lose. The state Liberal leaders had concentrated their attack almost entirely upon Cameron and his "Ring." At the moment, the evils evident in the national government and Southern relief appeared remote and the fall of Grantism was only an incidental goal in the campaign. Their chief objective, reform within Pennsylvania, was synonymous with the fall of the Cameron-Quay-Mackey machine.

The ingredients of Pennsylvania's Liberal Republican revolt constituted a multiplicity of motives. Certainly the Curtin group *was* interested in reform. McClure's attack on his friend Mann, an old Curtin supporter, proved that he pulled no punches. Curtin and his followers—the soreheads

---

[71] See Diary of Charles A. Ashburner, entry of July 16, 1876, PHMC.

and reformers in one—maintained the double objective of removing their enemy, Simon Cameron, and corruption in government. Revenge, reforming zeal, and political considerations all played their part in the Liberal movement. The struggle which had ostensibly started as an independent reform movement in Philadelphia retained its original objective—the fall of Cameronism after its merger with the national Liberal-Democratic groups. McClure had made "Cameronism the issue from the beginning to the close of the campaign."[72] Actually, there was little relationship between the movement which came out of Missouri and that which materialized in Pennsylvania. The scene was now set for the curtain to fall on the final act of the Andrew G. Curtin political tragedy. Had Hartranft been defeated, it is believed that Simon Cameron would have retired from political life, because the state gubernatorial struggle was looked upon as Cameron's fight.[73] During the course of the campaign Cameron had given no inkling of his intention to run for re-election to the Senate. Not many men in political life would care to run for an office from which they would emerge an octogenarian. But immediately after Grant's re-election inquiries began to pour in regarding his intentions. One enthusiastic supporter wrote: "Nothing can beat you. You are invincible."[74]

On January 3, 1873, the remote Beaver *Radical* announced that it was "generally understood" that Matthew Quay would serve as Hartranft's new secretary of state, and that Simon Cameron, in the absence of any competition for the Republican caucus nomination, was a "walk over" for the United States Senate. Quay's little weekly, the *Radical*,

[72] McClure, *Notes,* II, 348-349.
[73] Erie *Dispatch,* quoted in Erie *Observer,* Jan 3, 1873.
[74] H. B. Anthony to Cameron, Oct. 9, 1872, Cameron MSS, LC.

released the latest political scoops and everyone knew the reason why. Five days later, only twenty-four hours after the tired Republican legislators arrived at the state capital, the faithful were called into party caucus. There was a general desire among the legislators to get the matter over as quickly as possible. A motion was made to nominate Simon Cameron by acclamation for the Senate of United States. But another nomination followed and time was wasted with a vote. The results tallied 65 for Cameron, 4 for W. D. Kelley and 2 for Wickersham.[75]

Until the very day of the Republican caucus it was believed that Charlemagne Tower, a gentleman reputedly unknown to fame if not to fortune, would oppose Cameron for the nomination.[76] Legislative blackmailers, grieved at the prospects of witnessing an important election like the senatorship go by the board without any returns for their nefarious trade, encouraged the Pottsville magnate to run for the office with the prize presumably going to the highest bidder. Admittedly, few men could afford to bid against Simon Cameron, now a millionaire, but Tower had the resources to do it. McClure took upon himself chief credit for spiking the blackmailers' plot. Curtin's lieutenant, the recent leading exponent of honest elections within the Commonwealth, could hardly support any other kind at the moment; nevertheless he could not support Cameron, the caucus nominee.

The election for United States senator was held on January 21, 1873. Simon Cameron was elected easily over

---

[75] On senatorial election see Beaver *Radical,* January 17, 24, 1873 ; Harrisburg *Patriot,* Jan. 8, 22, 1873.

[76] Tower, a highly respected gentleman, was a descendant of John Tower, an emigrant into the Bay Colony in 1637. His son, Charlemagne Tower, made a brilliant record for himself in the diplomatic service of United States.

the Democratic candidate, William Wallace, 75 to 48. For the first time in his life, Cameron was elected without a contest in either the caucus or the legislature. Thirty years later McClure believed that he had cast his vote for William D. Kelley, but the official record showed that he voted for Thomas Marshall of Pittsburgh.[77]

The following day John L. Hartranft was inaugurated governor of Pennsylvania, and a week later John White Geary wrote to his brother in faraway Oregon: "All's well that ends well"; but less than a fortnight later the proud Geary lay in eternal sleep only a few blocks from the capitol.[78]

It would be difficult indeed to improve upon the following exposition of Simon Cameron's position in January, 1873: "He is the undisputed master of Pennsylvania. Every department of the State government is at his feet. He is the fountain of all political honors and preferments, and the signs are that he will be able to transmit his rule."[79] But in 1886, the mellowed Cameron, tottering on the brink of the grave, was asking for a benevolent verdict from posterity: "I have made enemies because I had opinions and the courage to assert and defend them. I am an old man now, who has lived through the most wonderful days of our history, and when I am gone all I ask is that people may say that I did the best I could and was never untrue to a friend."[80]

In 1873, for the first time in its history of two decades, the Republican Party of Pennsylvania was without powerful opposition factions. Cameron had disposed of his two most powerful opponents, Curtin and Forney. Curtin's endorsement of the Democratic gubernatorial candidate, Charles

---

[77] *Notes*, II, 349; *Journal of the Senate*, 1873, 134.
[78] Geary to Edward Geary, Feb. 1, 1873, Geary MSS, PHMC.
[79] Harrisburg *Patriot*, Jan. 29, 1873.
[80] Savidge, *Life of Brewster*, 218.

Buckalew, together with his acceptance of a Democratic seat in the constitutional convention of 1873, gave him no alternative except to join the Democratic ranks. John W. Forney likewise found his way back to his first love, the Democracy. The independent governor, John White Geary, was now supplanted by a loyal Cameron man, Hartranft, and Russell Errett's elevation to the chairmanship of the Republican State Central Committee was an added guarantee of Cameron's undisputed place in the party. Such was Cameron's strength after 1872, that when he chose to lay aside his titular honors in 1877, he, easily and quietly, passed the scepter of power unchallenged to his son and Matthew Quay.

The re-election of Grant was a triumph for the spoilsmen, the corporate interests, and the continuance of the policy of militant Republicanism—the program which Pennsylvania's leaders like Thaddeus Stevens and Simon Cameron had assisted in initiating. The Commonwealth's Republican Party purged of its idealism, and with the progressive Radicals now impotent, was fully dedicated to the forces of conservatism. The kindred spirits of Grantism and Cameronism, united and strengthened in victory were prepared anew to furnish comfort and aid on a reciprocal basis. In parts of the South the militant Radical policy still supported by Federal bayonets, was intended to guarantee the fruits of a victory achieved through a tragic outpouring of blood. To militant Republicans these compensating rewards could be maintained only if the party remained triumphant throughout the nation.

*Appendixes**

* Statistics for appendix are found in Smull's *Legislative Handbook* for 1868, 1869, 1870, 1873; Pennsylvania *Legislative Documents* for 1861, Document 21; *Tribune Almanac* for 1861; Ziegler's *Legislative Manual* for 1866.

APPENDIX I

Vote for President, 1860

Counties	Lincoln	Fusion	Douglas	Bell
Adams	2,724	2,644	36	38
Allegheny	16,725	6,725	523	570
Armstrong	3,355	2,108	5	50
Beaver	2,824	1,621	4	58
Bedford	2,505	2,224	14	86
Berks	6,709	8,846	420	136
Blair	3,050	1,275	239	397
Bradford	7,091	2,188	9	22
Bucks	6,443	5,174	487	95
Butler	3,640	2,332	13	22
Cambria	2,277	1,643	110	124
Cameron	—	—	—	—
Carbon	1,758	1,301	369	21
Centre	3,021	2,423	26	16
Chester	7,771	5,008	263	202
Clarion	1,829	2,078	—	12
Clearfield	1,702	1,836	—	23
Clinton	1,736	1,244	72	—
Columbia	1,873	2,366	86	14
Crawford	5,779	2,961	62	22

Cumberland	3,593	3,183	26	147
Dauphin	4,531	2,392	195	169
Delaware	3,181	1,500	152	288
Elk	407	523	—	—
Erie	6,160	2,531	17	90
Fayette	3,454	3,308	24	147
Forest	107	47	—	—
Franklin	4,151	2,515	622	76
Fulton	788	911	1	49
Greene	1,614	2,665	26	17
Huntingdon	3,089	1,622	55	22
Indiana	3,910	1,347	—	22
Jefferson	1,704	1,134	6	5
Juniata	1,494	1,147	2	62
Lancaster	13,352	5,135	728	441
Lawrence	2,937	788	16	31
Lebanon	3,868	1,917	10	103
Lehigh	4,170	4,094	145	52
Luzerne	7,300	6,803	—	—
Lycoming	3,494	2,402	187	91
McKean	1,077	591	—	2
Mercer	3,855	2,546	2	49
Mifflin	1,701	1,189	83	36
Monroe	844	1,262	291	—
Montgomery	5,826	5,590	509	690
Montour	1,043	786	311	4
Northampton	3,839	4,597	115	171
Northumberland	2,422	2,306	97	72
Perry	2,371	1,743	8	38
Philadelphia	39,223	21,619	9,274	7,131
Pike	381	831	—	1
Potter	1,545	521	—	—
Schuylkill	7,568	4,968	422	139
Snyder	1,678	910	60	5
Somerset	3,218	1,175	1	10

Sullivan	429	497	—	1
Susquehanna	4,470	2,548	2	6
Tioga	4,754	1,277	11	9
Union	1,824	812	28	6
Venangol	2,680	1,932	6	6
Warren	2,284	1,087	4	—
Washington	4,724	3,975	8	91
Wayne	2,857	2,618	—	2
Westmoreland	4,887	4,796	13	13
Wyoming	1,286	1,237	8	—
York	5,128	5,497	562	574
Total	268,030	178,871	16,765	12,776

APPENDIX II
Vote for Governor, 1860

Counties	Curtin	Foster
Adams	2,773	2,849
Allegheny	15,879	9,190
Armstrong	3,474	2,698
Beaver	2,682	1,715
Bedford	2,464	2,561
Berks	6,833	10,318
Blair	3,051	2,172
Bradford	6,664	2,328
Bucks	6,383	6,330
Butler	3,526	2,548
Cambria	2,177	2,583
Carbon	1,722	1,930
Centre	3,165	2,824
Chester	7,540	5,913
Clarion	1,795	2,297
Clearfield	1,755	2,040
Clinton	1,750	1,703
Columbia	1,848	2,586
Crawford	5,277	3,178
Cumberland	3,625	3,716
Dauphin	4,555	3,302
Delaware	3,183	1,996
Elk	421	633
Erie	5,613	2,469
Fayette	3,382	3,556
Franklin	4,053	3,379
Fulton	828	957
Forest	129	69
Greene	1,529	2,669
Huntingdon	3,070	2,114
Indiana	3,672	1,886
Jefferson	1,886	1,493

APPENDIX III
Vote for Governor, 1863

Counties	Curtin	Woodward
Adams	2,689	2,917
Allegheny	17,708	10,053
Armstrong	3,146	2,977
Beaver	3,037	2,056
Bedford	2,430	2,704
Berks	6,005	12,627
Blair	3,283	2,386
Bradford	6,722	2,954
Bucks	6,266	6,836
Butler	3,328	3,054
Cambria	2,164	3,000
Cameron	318	216
Carbon	1,542	2,119
Centre	2,714	3,058
Chester	7,988	5,498
Clarion	1,618	2,598
Clearfield	1,531	2,483
Clinton	1,607	1,911
Columbia	1,801	3,342
Crawford	6,141	4,236
Cumberland	3,434	4,075
Dauphin	5,075	3,875
Delaware	3,462	1,789
Elk	336	722
Erie	6,259	3,260
Fayette	3,091	3,791
Franklin	3,876	3,710
Fulton	761	1,022
Forest	91	58
Greene	1,484	2,960
Huntingdon	3,260	2,167
Indiana	3,961	1,955
Jefferson	1,754	1,698

County			County		
Juniata	1,503	1,465	Juniata	1,456	1,737
Lancaster	13,012	7,153	Lancaster	13,341	7,650
Lawrence	2,645	959	Lawrence	3,063	1,251
Lebanon	3,847	2,234	Lebanon	3,658	2,653
Lehigh	4,166	4,556	Lehigh	3,696	5,526
Luzerne	6,662	6,916	Luzerne	7,022	9,808
Lycoming	3,615	3,034	Lycoming	3,414	3,865
Montour	983	1,220	McKean	727	622
McKean	1,098	700	Mercer	3,907	3,408
Mercer	3,624	2,794	Mifflin	1,709	1,626
Mifflin	1,723	1,490	Monroe	684	2,712
Monroe	822	2,163	Montgomery	6,238	7,489
Montgomery	5,812	7,392	Montour	1,119	1,447
Northampton	3,507	5,249	Northampton	3,465	6,538
Northumberland	2,429	2,955	Northumberland	2,649	3,356
Perry	2,416	2,128	Perry	2,328	2,296
Pike	324	843	Philadelphia	44,274	37,193
Philadelphia	40,233	42,119	Pike	270	1,184
Potter	1,410	615	Potter	1,470	619
Schuylkill	7,301	7,067	Schuylkill	6,506	8,547
Somerset	2,977	1,372	Somerset	3,064	1,738
Snyder	1,704	1,134	Snyder	1,758	1,231
Sullivan	394	543	Sullivan	359	713
Susquehanna	4,110	2,456	Susquehanna	4,134	2,932
Tioga	4,147	1,331	Tioga	4,504	1,617
Union	1,820	1,019	Union	2,024	1,250
Venango	2,581	2,132	Venango	3,295	2,979
Warren	2,112	1,172	Warren	2,274	1,386
Washington	4,768	4,206	Washington	4,627	4,371
Wayne	2,610	2,537	Wayne	2,211	3,152
Westmoreland	4,830	5,276	Westmoreland	4,404	5,581
Wyoming	1,192	1,366	Wyoming	1,379	1,418
York	5,322	6,665	York	5,512	8,069
Total	262,397	230,269	Total	269,506	254,171

APPENDIX IV
Vote for President, 1864

APPENDIX V
Vote for Governor, 1866

Counties	Lincoln	McClellan	Counties	Geary	Clymer
Adams	2,612	3,016	Adams	2,910	3,126
Allegheny	21,519	12,414	Allegheny	20,511	12,795
Armstrong	3,526	3,211	Armstrong	3,758	3,078
Beaver	3,237	2,304	Beaver	3,310	2,385
Bedford	2,336	2,752	Bedford	2,591	2,835
Berks	6,710	13,266	Berks	7,121	13,288
Blair	3,292	2,686	Blair	3,520	2,768
Bradford	6,865	3,007	Bradford	7,134	3,091
Bucks	6,436	7,335	Bucks	6,805	7,399
Butler	3,475	2,947	Butler	3,544	3,661
Cambria	2,244	3,036	Cambria	2,643	3,295
Cameron	325	232	Cameron	374	303
Carbon	1,721	2,251	Carbon	1,906	2,339
Centre	2,817	3,399	Centre	3,094	3,565
Chester	8,446	5,987	Chester	8,500	6,221
Clarion	1,780	2,833	Clarion	1,776	2,813
Clearfield	1,516	2,801	Clearfield	1,650	2,786
Clinton	1,666	2,135	Clinton	1,754	2,337
Columbia	1,914	3,467	Columbia	1,965	3,583
Crawford	6,441	4,526	Crawford	6,714	4,969
Cumberland	3,604	4,354	Cumberland	4,030	4,567
Dauphin	5,444	4,220	Dauphin	5,691	4,301
Delaware	3,664	2,145	Delaware	3,647	2,262
Elk	348	835	Elk	376	916
Erie	6,911	3,722	Erie	7,237	3,957
Fayette	3,221	4,126	Fayette	3,569	4,359
Forest	85	62	Forest	100	76
Franklin	3,862	3,821	Franklin	4,299	4,106
Fulton	694	906	Fulton	775	1,055
Greene	1,583	3,074	Greene	1,699	3,230
Huntingdon	3,321	2,477	Huntingdon	3,248	2,239
Indiana	4,320	2,197	Indiana	4,458	2,109

County			County		
Jefferson	1,820	1,877	Jefferson	2,015	1,912
Juniata	1,437	1,753	Juniata	1,516	1,814
Lancaster	14,469	8,488	Lancaster	14,592	8,592
Lawrence	3,408	1,389	Lawrence	3,560	1,410
Lebanon	3,780	2,779	Lebanon	4,194	2,696
Lehigh	3,908	5,920	Lehigh	4,159	5,731
Luzerne	7,645	10,145	Luzerne	8,733	12,387
Lycoming	3,401	4,207	Lycoming	3,871	4,448
McKean	767	652	McKean	877	714
Mercer	4,220	3,569	Mercer	4,416	3,757
Mifflin	1,643	1,718	Mifflin	1,725	1,835
Monroe	685	2,698	Monroe	705	2,699
Montgomery	6,872	7,943	Montgomery	7,286	8,342
Montour	1,130	1,496	Montour	1,130	1,523
Northampton	3,726	6,944	Northampton	3,859	6,870
Northumberland	2,915	3,608	Northumberland	3,361	3,829
Perry	2,406	2,446	Perry	2,581	2,495
Philadelphia	55,797	44,032	Philadelphia	54,205	48,817
Pike	260	1,180	Pike	360	1,084
Potter	1,390	680	Potter	1,346	620
Schuylkill	7,851	9,540	Schuylkill	8,793	10,514
Snyder	1,679	1,368	Snyder	1,792	1,326
Somerset	2,788	1,719	Somerset	3,062	1,759
Sullivan	369	660	Sullivan	436	761
Susquehanna	4,203	2,959	Susquehanna	4,429	2,981
Tioga	4,673	1,584	Tioga	4,791	1,628
Union	1,945	1,352	Union	1,991	1,287
Venango	3,849	3,341	Venango	4,409	3,492
Warren	2,541	1,505	Warren	2,687	1,572
Washington	4,951	4,579	Washington	4,977	4,712
Wayne	2,274	3,989	Wayne	2,357	2,883
Westmoreland	4,650	5,977	Westmoreland	5,046	6,113
Wyoming	1,337	1,402	Wyoming	1,408	1,499
York	5,568	8,500	York	5,896	8,780
Total	296,391	276,316	Total	307,274	290,096

APPENDIX VI			APPENDIX VII		
Vote for Governor, 1869			Vote for Governor, 1872		
Counties	Geary	Packer	Counties	Hartranft	Buckalew
Adams	2,622	3,009	Adams	2,765	3,038
Allegheny	17,858	13,301	Allegheny	25,771	16,490
Armstrong	3,439	3,079	Armstrong	4,434	3,469
Beaver	3,096	2,402	Beaver	3,685	2,882
Bedford	2,845	2,832	Bedford	2,973	2,977
Berks	6,971	13,531	Berks	7,898	13,947
Blair	3,484	2,773	Blair	4,263	3,244
Bradford	6,653	3,686	Bradford	7,443	4,434
Bucks	6,505	7,061	Bucks	7,278	7,658
Butler	3,250	2,994	Butler	3,985	3,440
Cambria	2,539	3,187	Cambria	2,823	3,530
Cameron	474	423	Cameron	572	531
Carbon	1,940	2,625	Carbon	2,444	2,533
Centre	3,102	3,464	Centre	3,292	3,712
Chester	8,230	6,146	Chester	9,386	6,510
Clarion	1,785	2,831	Clarion	2,727	3,583
Clearfield	1,799	3,015	Clearfield	1,995	3,432
Clinton	1,830	2,509	Clinton	2,018	2,632
Columbia	1,845	3,714	Columbia	2,110	3,826
Crawford	6,107	4,865	Crawford	7,031	6,473
Cumberland	3,514	4,408	Cumberland	4,176	4,614
Dauphin	5,660	4,328	Dauphin	7,450	5,113
Delaware	3,532	2,295	Delaware	4,339	2,638
Elk	475	968	Elk	628	1,193
Erie	6,498	4,338	Erie	7,467	5,271
Fayette	3,340	4,229	Fayette	3,954	4,631
Forest	365	293	Forest	418	340
Franklin	3,698	4,006	Franklin	4,505	4,182
Fulton	680	1,006	Fulton	797	1,125
Greene	1,542	2,992	Greene	1,795	3,450
Huntingdon	2,825	2,368	Huntingdon	3,249	2,690
Indiana	4,003	2,070	Indiana	4,472	2,146

Jefferson	1,967	2,039	Jefferson	2,407	2,247
Juniata	1,254	1,642	Juniata	1,352	1,739
Lancaster	13,804	8,316	Lancaster	13,774	9,064
Lawrence	3,217	1,492	Lawrence	3,426	1,705
Lebanon	4,027	2,696	Lebanon	4,285	2,824
Lehigh	4,555	6,133	Lehigh	5,355	6,895
Luzerne	8,690	9,696	Luzerne	12,341	14,433
Lycoming	4,053	4,587	Lycoming	4,639	5,056
M'Kean	880	696	M'Kean	1,025	950
Mercer	4,529	3,785	Mercer	5,573	4,598
Mifflin	1,640	1,702	Mifflin	1,786	1,765
Monroe	659	2,692	Monroe	658	2,839
Montgomery	7,363	8,447	Montgomery	8,454	8,463
Montour	1,066	1,555	Montour	1,378	1,623
Northampton	4,023	7,449	Northampton	4,880	8,121
Northumberland	3,497	4,000	Northumberland	4,314	4,363
Perry	2,439	2,408	Perry	2,752	2,514
Philadelphia	51,202	46,802	Philadelphia	69,278	48,841
Pike	315	1,054	Pike	246	1,134
Potter	1,334	708	Potter	1,466	1,042
Schuylkill	7,902	8,901	Schuylkill	8,980	9,378
Snyder	1,719	1,315	Snyder	1,906	1,372
Somerset	2,940	1,700	Somerset	3,430	1,802
Sullivan	406	759	Sullivan	431	744
Susquehanna	4,064	2,982	Susquehanna	4,333	3,403
Tioga	4,535	1,825	Tioga	5,504	2,376
Union	1,788	1,207	Union	2,069	1,374
Venango	3,508	3,241	Venango	5,071	4,415
Warren	2,430	1,679	Warren	3,176	2,333
Washington	4,476	4,632	Washington	5,294	4,992
Wayne	2,275	2,715	Wayne	2,119	3,030
Westmoreland	4,853	6,195	Westmoreland	5,581	6,475
Wyoming	1,452	1,772	Wyoming	1,561	1,791
York	5,545	8,326	York	6,400	8,388
Total	290,552	285,956	Total	353,387	317,760

APPENDIX VIII

Vote for President, 1868

Counties	Grant	Seymour
Adams	2,917	3,170
Allegheny	25,487	14,671
Armstrong	4,082	3,412
Beaver	3,648	2,624
Bedford	2,687	2,898
Berks	7,917	13,973
Blair	3,986	3,066
Bradford	7,768	3,538
Bucks	7,085	7,613
Butler	3,803	3,256
Cambria	2,935	3,558
Cameron	508	394
Carbon	2,188	2,745
Centre	3,429	3,646
Chester	9,178	6,490
Clarion	1,998	2,928
Clearfield	1,974	3,096
Clinton	2,056	2,532
Columbia	2,143	4,022
Crawford	7,322	5,455
Cumberland	4,171	4,594
Dauphin	6,507	4,397
Delaware	4,166	2,616
Elk	568	1,119
Erie	8,007	4,555
Fayette	3,792	4,608
Forest	355	294
Franklin	4,451	4,171
Fulton	802	1,107
Greene	1,809	3,301
Huntingdon	3,417	2,179
Indiana	4,809	2,223

APPENDIX IX

Vote for President, 1872

Counties	Grant	Greeley
Adams	2,735	2,580
Allegheny	25,846	9,055
Armstrong	4,297	2,078
Beaver	3,517	1,798
Bedford	2,901	2,165
Berks	7,741	10,201
Blair	4,251	2,183
Bradford	7,452	3,564
Bucks	6,613	5,445
Butler	4,015	2,534
Cambria	2,841	2,544
Cameron	554	340
Carbon	2,452	1,946
Centre	3,142	2,695
Chester	9,249	3,802
Clarion	2,558	2,304
Clearfield	1,970	2,329
Clinton	2,003	1,758
Columbia	2,009	3,001
Crawford	6,938	4,887
Cumberland	3,895	3,557
Dauphin	6,954	3,331
Delaware	4,231	1,166
Elk	679	753
Erie	7,502	4,787
Fayette	3,881	2,663
Franklin	4,301	3,136
Fulton	737	807
Forest	360	155
Greene	1,852	2,829
Huntingdon	3,099	1,805
Indiana	4,386	1,266

Jefferson	2,147	2,068	Jefferson	2,253	1,156
Juniata	1,473	1,753	Juniata	1,306	1,265
Lancaster	15,792	8,513	Lancaster	14,288	5,717
Lawrence	3,789	1,647	Lawrence	3,429	945
Lebanon	4,345	2,858	Lebanon	4,171	2,076
Lehigh	5,004	6,321	Lehigh	5,342	5,622
Luzerne	10,723	14,303	Luzerne	12,966	10,904
Lycoming	4,713	4,839	Lycoming	4,423	3,837
McKean	1,028	730	McKean	1,040	618
Mercer	4,979	4,078	Mercer	5,517	3,411
Mifflin	1,846	1,807	Mifflin	1,685	1,127
Monroe	812	2,915	Monroe	787	2,205
Montgomery	8,083	8,803	Montgomery	8,080	5,113
Montour	1,269	1,697	Montour	1,384	1,333
Northampton	4,791	7,762	Northampton	4,841	6,155
Northumberland	3,825	4,240	Northumberland	4,271	3,356
Perry	2,664	2,416	Perry	2,563	1,744
Philadelphia	60,985	55,173	Philadelphia	68,792	23,407
Pike	370	1,313	Pike	339	797
Potter	1,703	693	Potter	1,463	554
Schuylkill	8,707	9,428	Schuylkill	8,657	6,983
Snyder	1,925	1,318	Snyder	1,803	915
Somerset	3,261	1,778	Somerset	3,495	1,383
Sullivan	473	851	Sullivan	440	571
Susquehanna	4,882	3,392	Susquehanna	4,536	2,907
Tioga	5,549	1,951	Tioga	5,730	1,777
Union	2,081	1,277	Union	1,997	916
Venango	4,759	3,774	Venango	4,780	2,986
Warren	3,620	1,757	Warren	3,090	1,538
Washington	5,051	4,867	Washington	5,134	3,223
Wayne	2,909	3,539	Wayne	2,463	2,152
Westmoreland	5,285	6,360	Westmoreland	5,412	4,719
Wyoming	1,623	1,766	Wyoming	1,552	1,399
York	6,449	9,094	York	6,299	6,753
Total	342,280	313,382	Total	349,689	211,961

Bibliography

MANUSCRIPTS

Dauphin County Historical Society, Harrisburg
    Correspondence and Papers of Simon Cameron
Dickinson College Library, Carlisle
    Slifer-Dill Manuscripts
Historical Society of Pennsylvania, Philadelphia
    William Bigler Papers
    Borie Family Papers
    Papers of James Buchanan
    Henry C. Carey Papers
    Salmon P. Chase Papers
    Lewis S. Coryell Papers
    Gilpin Papers
    Governors of Pennsylvania Manuscript Collection
    Scrapbooks of the Governors of Pennsylvania
    Simon Gratz Collection
    Diary of Francis Jordan, 1846-1877
    Joseph A. Kneass Scrapbook
    William F. Lutz Collection, 1785-1874
    William Meredith Papers
    Collection of the Historical Society of Pennsylvania
Historical Society of Western Pennsylvania, Pittsburgh
    Papers of John Covode
Library of Congress, Washington
    Jeremiah Black Papers
    Papers of James Buchanan
    Simon Cameron Papers
    Salmon P. Chase Papers
    Papers of John Covode

Hamilton Fish Papers
John Wien Forney Papers
Andrew Johnson Papers
Robert Todd Lincoln Collection
Edward McPherson Papers
Papers of John G. Nicolay
Edwin M. Stanton Papers
Papers of Thaddeus Stevens
Papers of Benjamin F. Wade
Elihu Washburne Papers
Lincoln Memorial University, Harrogate
Cassius M. Clay Manuscripts
Pennsylvania Historical and Museum Commission, Harrisburg
Diary of Charles A. Ashburner
Executive Correspondence of Andrew G. Curtin
Executive Minutes of John White Geary
Geary Letters (on loan from Oregon Historical Society)
Pardon Papers of John White Geary
Sylvester K. Stevens Checklist of Pennsylvania Newspapers
Wyoming Historical and Geological Society, Wilkes-Barre
Hendrick B. Wright Papers

PRIVATE COLLECTION

Notes of the late Lee F. Crippen taken from the James M. Cameron Papers, in possession of the author through the courtesy of Cathell C. Crippen.

NEWSPAPERS

The newspapers, including microfilm reproductions, with the exceptions listed in parenthesis after the place of publication, are located in the Library of Congress; Historical Society of Pennsylvania; Pennsylvania Historical and Museum Commission; Pennsylvania State Library; and the Pennsylvania State University Library.

Altoona, Pennsylvania, (Blair County Historical Society)
  Tribune, 1860-1868
Beaver, Pennsylvania
  Argus, 1865-1873 (microfilm)
  Radical, 1872-1873 (microfilm)
Bedford, Pennsylvania
  Climber, 1866
  Gazette, 1858-1862; 1864-1865 (microfilm); 1867-1870
Bellefonte, Pennsylvania
  Central Press, 1859-60; 1866
  Democratic Watchman, 1860-1873
  Republican, 1870, 1872
Bloody Run (Everett), Pennsylvania
  Bedford County Press, 1868
Bradford, Pennsylvania
  Reporter, 1864-1866 (microfilm)
Chambersburg, Pennsylvania
  Franklin Repository, 1864-1865
Clearfield, Pennsylvania
  Raftsman's Journal, 1867-69
Erie, Pennsylvania
  Observer, 1857-1873 (microfilm)
  Weekly Observer, 1857-1860; 1863 (microfilm)
Greensburg, Pennsylvania
  Frank Cowan's Paper, 1872-73
  Herald, 1868-1870
Greenville, Pennsylvania
  Advance, 1871-1873 (microfilm)
  Argus, 1869-1873 (microfilm)
Harrisburg, Pennsylvania
  Daily Patriot, 1871-1872
  Patriot and Union, 1866-1867
  Morning Patriot, 1868-1870
  Weekly Patriot and Union, 1865
  Telegraph, 1860-1862; 1868-1869

Hollidaysburg, Pennsylvania (Blair County Historical Society)
  Register, 1868-1873
Huntingdon, Pennsylvania (Juniata College Library)
  Globe, 1866-67, 1872
  Journal, 1867, 1871-72
Lancaster, Pennsylvania (Lancaster Newspapers, Inc.)
  Intelligencer, 1863-1873
Lewistown, Pennsylvania
  Democratic Sentinel, 1871-1873
  Gazette, 1868-1871
Lock Haven, Pennsylvania
  Clinton Democrat, 1864
Meadville, Pennsylvania
  Crawford Democrat, 1865-1867 (microfilm)
Newcastle, Pennsylvania
  Lawrence Journal, 1859
New York, New York
  Times, 1878
  Tribune, 1878
Philadelphia, Pennsylvania
  Age, 1863-1864, 1866
  Evening Bulletin, 1862-1864
  Evening Telegraph, 1862, 1866-1867, 1869
  Inquirer, 1861
  North American, 1855, 1863, 1866-1867
  Press, 1861-1863, 1866-1867, 1869, 1872
  Public Ledger, 1855, 1860, 1863, 1867
Pittsburgh, Pennsylvania
  Gazette, 1863-1864, 1866-1869 (microfilm)
Pottsville, Pennsylvania
  Miners' Journal, 1866-1872, 1873
Reading, Pennsylvania
  Daily Eagle, 1868-1870 (microfilm)
Ridgeway, Pennsylvania
  Elk County Advocate, 1871-1873

Washington, D.C.
   Post, 1889
West Chester, Pennsylvania
   American Republican, 1869-1872
Williamsburg, Pennsylvania
   Temperance Vindicator, 1868
Williamsport, Pennsylvania
   Gazette and Bulletin, 1871-1872 (microfilm)
   Lycoming Gazette, 1867-1868 (microfilm)
   West Branch Bulletin, 1866-1867 (microfilm)

OFFICIAL DOCUMENTS

Pennsylvania

   Journal of the House of Representatives, 1860-1873
   Journal of the Senate, 1860-1873
   Laws of the General Assembly of the Commonwealth of Pennsylvania, 1860-1872
   Legislative Record, 1864-1872
   Pennsylvania Archives, Fourth Series, Papers of the Governors, VIII, (1858-1871); IX (1871-1883), Harrisburg, 1902
   Pennsylvania Legislative Manual, 1858
   Pennsylvania State Reports, Vol. 58, Philadelphia, 1869
   Smull, John A., *Pennsylvania Legislative Handbook,* 1873
   Ziegler, Jacob, *Manual for Government . . . of the Commonwealth of Pennsylvania,* Harrisburg, 1864

United States Government

   A Compendium of the Ninth Census, Washington, 1872
   Congressional Globe, 39 Congress, 1 Session—42 Congress, 2 Session.
   McPherson, Edward, *A Hand-Book of Politics,* Washington City, 1872
   Papers Relating to Foreign Affairs, 1861-1862, Two Parts, Washington, 1862

Richardson, James D. (ed.), *A Compilation of the Messages and Papers of the Presidents, 1789-1897,* 1899

United States Census Bureau (compiler), *Manufactures of United States in 1860* (from 8th Census), Washington, 1865

United States Census Bureau (compiler), *Statistics of United States in 1860,* Washington, 1866

War of the Rebellion: . . . Official Records of the Union and Confederate Armies, 130 vols., Washington, 1880-1901

ALMANACS AND PRINTED DIARIES, MEMOIRS, REMINISCENCES, "WORKS," AND CORRESPONDENCE

Adams, Henry, *The Education of Henry Adams,* Boston, 1927

American Annual Cyclopaedia, 1866-1872

Annual Report of the Board of Directors of the Pennsylvania Railroad Company, 1867-1873, Philadelphia.

Basler, Roy P. (ed.), *The Collected Works of Abraham Lincoln,* 9 vols., New Brunswick, 1933-1953

Beale, H. K. (ed.), "Diary of Edward Bates, 1859-1866," American Historical Association *Annual Report,* 1930, IV, Washington, 1932

Bigelow, John, *Retrospections of an Active Life,* 5 vols., New York, 1909

Black, Chauncey F., *Essays and Speeches of Jeremiah S. Black,* New York 1885

Blaine, James G., *Twenty Years of Congress,* 2 vols., Norwich, 1884-1886

Boutwell, George S., *Reminiscences of Sixty Years in Public Affairs,* 2 vols., New York, 1902

Butler, Benjamin F., *Butler's Book,* Boston: A. M. Thayer & Co., 1892

———, *Private and Official Correspondence of General Benjamin F. Butler During the Period of the Civil War,* 5 vols., Norwood, 1917

Chase, Salmon P., "Diary and Correspondence of Salmon P. Chase," American Historical Association *Annual Report,* 1902, II, Washington, 1903

Childs, George W., *Recollections,* Philadelphia, 1890

Chittenden, L. E., *Recollections of President Lincoln and His Administration,* New York, 1891

Clay, Cassius M., *The Life of Cassius Marcellus Clay, Memoirs, Writings, and Speeches,* 2 vols., Cincinnati, 1886

Ford, Worthington C., *Letters of Henry Adams,* Boston, 1930

Forney, John W., *Anecdotes of Public Men,* New York, 1873

Hancock, Mrs. W. S., *Reminiscences of Winfield Scott Hancock,* New York, 1887

Hoar, George F., *Autobiography of Seventy Years,* 2 vols., New York, 1903

Howe, M. A. DeWolfe (ed.), *Home Letters of General Sherman,* New York, 1909

Julian, George W., *Political Recollections,* Chicago, 1884

Lamon, Dorothy (ed.), *Recollections of Abraham Lincoln, 1847-1865,* by Ward Hill Lamon, Chicago, 1895

McClure, Alexander K., *Abraham Lincoln and Men of War Times,* Philadelphia, 1892

———, *Old Time Notes of Pennsylvania,* 2 vols., Philadelphia, 1905

———, *Recollections of Half A Century,* Salem, 1902

McCormack, Thomas J. (ed.), *Memoirs of Gustave Koerner,* 2 vols., Cedar Rapids, 1909

McCulloch, Hugh, *Men and Measures of Half a Century,* New York, 1888

Moore, John Bassett (ed.), *The Works of James Buchanan,* 12 vols., Philadelphia, 1908-1911

Nicolay, John G., and Hay, John (eds.), *Complete Works of Abraham Lincoln,* 12 vols., n.p. (Published by Lincoln Memorial University) 1929

Pease, Theodore, and Randall, J. G. (eds.), "The Diary of Orville Hickman Browning," 2 vols., *Illinois Historical Collection,* XX, XXII, Springfield, 1925, 1933

Pierce, Edward L. (ed.), *Memoir and Letters of Charles Sumner*, 4 vols., Boston, 1893

Poore, Ben: Perley, *Sixty Years Reminiscences*, 2 volumes in one, Cincinnati, 1886

Public Ledger Almanac, Philadelphia, 1870-1873

Riddle, Albert G., *Recollections of War Times*, New York, 1895

Seward, Frederick W., *Reminiscences of a War-Time Statesman and Diplomat, 1830-1915*, New York, 1916

Sherman, John, *Recollections of Forty Years*, 2 vols., Chicago, 1895

Tribune Almanac, II, 1855-1868, New York, 1868

Watterson, Henry, *"Marse Henry."* 2 vols., New York, 1919

Welles, Gideon., *Diary of Gideon Welles*, 3 vols., Boston, 1911

Whig Almanac, 1855

Wilson, Rufus Rockwell, *Intimate Memories of Lincoln*, Elmira, 1945

PAMPHLETS AND OFFICIAL POLITICAL PROCEEDINGS

(Arranged by subject or abbreviated title) All pamphlets listed are in Pennsylvania State Library unless otherwise noted.

CAMERON: "Life and Public Services of General Simon Cameron," by Edward B. Moore, n.d.

CLYMER and GEARY: "Record of Heister Clymer and Historical Parallel between him and Major-General John W. Geary," n.d.

CURTIN: "Life and Services of Andrew G. Curtin," an address by A. K. McClure, January 20, 1895

COVODE: "Memorial Addresses on Hon. John Covode," Washington, 1871

DEGRADATION AND REFORM: "The Degradation of our Representative System and its Reform," by Joshua Francis Fisher, Philadelphia, 1863

DEMOCRATIC PARTY: "Record of the Democratic Party, 1860-65," n.p., n.d.

————: *Proceedings* of the National Democratic Convention at Charleston, Washington, 1860

————: *Official Proceedings* of the National Democratic Convention at Baltimore, 1860, Cleveland, 1860

————: *Official Proceedings* of the Democratic National Convention, 1864, Chicago, 1864

EVANS FRAUDS: "Correspondence between the joint legislative committee to investigate the settlement of the Pennsylvania war claims, by George O. Evans and Governor John W. Geary," Harrisburg, 1872

EVANS FRAUDS: "Pennsylvania Frauds: What Dr. Paine Knows of the Frauds of the Pennsylvania War Claims," n.d., n.p.

GEARY: "A Sketch of the Early Life and of the Civil and Military Services of Maj. Gen. John W. Geary," Philadelphia, 1866

GEARY and WILLIAMS: "Geary and Williams," Philadelphia, n.d.

LABOR: "Tract No. 1 issued by the Workingmen's Club of Philadelphia," n.p., n.d.

RAILROAD EXTORTION: "Report of the Committee on the Judiciary of the Senate of Pennsylvania relative to alleged Extortionate charges by the Railroad Companies of the State," Harrisburg, 1868

REFORM: "Constitutional Reform," by Francis Jordan, Philadelphia, 1872

REPUBLICAN PARTY: *Official Proceedings* of the Republican Convention, 1856, Pittsburgh, 1856

————: *Proceedings* of the First Three Republican Conventions of 1856, 1860, and 1864, Minneapolis, n.d.

SCOTT: "Thomas A. Scott as a Pledge-Breaker and Salary Grabber," by Thomas S. Fernon, Philadelphia, 1878, HSP.

SENATORIAL ELECTION FRAUD: Report of the Select Committee of the House of Representatives on the Subject of the Alleged Frauds in the election of United States Senator," Harrisburg, 1863

STATISTICS FOR CONVENTION: "Statistical and Other Information prepared for the Constitutional Convention of Pennsylvania," by Francis Jordan, Harrisburg, 1872.

UNION LEAGUE: "The Union League and the Political Situation in Philadelphia," Philadelphia, 1873

GENERAL WORKS AND MONOGRAPHS

Albert, George Dallas, *History of County of Westmoreland* . . ., Philadelphia, 1882

Barclay, Thomas S., *Liberal Republican Movement in Missouri, 1865-1871*, Columbia, 1926

Beard, Charles A. and Mary, *Rise of American Civilization: The Industrial Era*, New York, 1927

Boucher, John N., *History of Westmoreland County*, 2 vols., New York, 1906

Bowen, Eli, *A Pictorial Sketch-Book of Pennsylvania*, Philadelphia, 1852

Burgess, John W., *Reconstruction and the Constitution, 1866-1876*, New York, 1909

Cale, Edgar B., *The Organization of Labor in Philadelphia, 1850-1870*, Philadelphia, 1940

Carman, Harry J., and Reinhard H. Luthin, *Lincoln and the Patronage*, New York, 1943

Coleman, Charles H., *The Election of 1868*, New York, 1933

Curti, Merle, *The Growth of American Thought*, New York, 1943

Cushing, Thomas, *et al.*, *History of Allegheny County*, Chicago, 1889

Davis, Stanton Ling, *Pennsylvania Politics, 1860-1863*, Cleveland, 1935

Dewey, David R., *Financial History of the United States*, Eighth Edition, New York, 1922

Dewitt, David M., *Impeachment and Trial of Andrew Johnson*, New York, 1903

Dumond, Dwight L., *The Secession Movement, 1860-61*, New York, 1931

Dunaway, Wayland F., *History of Pennsylvania*, New York, 1946

Egle, William H., *An Illustrated History of the Commonwealth of Pennsylvania*, Revised Edition, Philadelphia, 1880

Eiselen, Malcolm R., *Rise of Pennsylvania Protectionism*, Philadelphia, 1932

Fryer, Benjamin A., *Congressional History of Berks [Pennsylvania] District*, Reading, 1939

Geary, Sister M. Theopane, *History of Third Parties in Pennsylvania, 1840-1860*, Washington, 1938

Halstead, Murat, *Caucuses of 1860*, Columbus, 1860

Haynes, Fred E., *Third Party Movements Since the Civil War*, Iowa City, 1916

Hesseltine, William B., *Lincoln and the War Governors*, New York, 1955

Hoppes, Charles H., "The Liberal Republican Movement in Pennsylvania," MS, Pennsylvania State University, 1934

Josephson, Matthew, *The Robber Barons*, New York, 1934

Koontz, William H. (ed.), *History of Bedford and Somerset Counties*, 2 vols., New York, 1906

Lathrop, George P., *History of the Union League of Philadelphia*, Philadelphia, 1884

Logan, John A., *The Great Conspiracy*, New York, 1886

Luthin, Reinhard N., *First Lincoln Campaign*, Cambridge, 1944

Lytle, Milton S., *History of Huntingdon County*, Lancaster, 1876

Macartnay, Clarence E., *Lincoln and His Cabinet*, New York, 1931

McCabe, James D. (E. W. Martin), *Behind the Scenes in Washington*, n.p., 1873

McLaurin, John J., *Sketches in Crude-Oil*, Harrisburg, 1896

Martin, Asa E., and Shenk, Hiram H. (eds.), *Pennsylvania History Told By Contemporaries*, New York, 1925

Maybee, Rolland H., *Railroad Competition and the Oil Trade, 1855-1873*, Mount Pleasant, 1940

Milton, George F., *Abraham Lincoln and the Fifth Column*, New York, 1942

Moore, Frank (ed.), *The Rebellion Record*, 11 vols., New York, 1861-68

Mueller, Henry R., *The Whig Party in Pennsylvania*, New York, 1922

Myers, C. Maxwell. "The Rise of the Republican Party in Pennsylvania, 1854-1860," MS, University of Pittsburgh, 1940

Nevins, Allen, *Emergence of Lincoln*, 2 vols., New York, 1950

———, *Emergence of Modern America*, 1865-1878, New York, 1927

———, *Ordeal of the Union*, 2 vols., New York, 1947

Nichols, Roy F. (new introduction by), *Battles and Leaders of the Civil War*, 4 vols., New York, 1956

———, *Disruption of American Democracy*, New York, 1948

Oberholtzer, Ellis P., *History of the United States Since the Civil War*, 5 vols., New York, 1937

Page, Elwin L., *Cameron for Lincoln's Cabinet*, Boston, 1954

Parrington, Vernon L., *Main Currents in American Thought*, 2 vols., New York, 1930

Pike, James S., *First Blows of the Civil War*, New York, 1879

Pitkin, Thomas M. "The Tariff and the Early Republican Party," MS, Western Reserve University, 1935

Rhodes, James F., *History of United States, 1850-1877*, 7 vols., New York, 1899

Robinson, Elwyn B. "The Public Press of Philadelphia During the Civil War," MS, Western Reserve University, 1936

Ross, Earle D., *Liberal Republican Movement*, New York, 1919

Shannon, Fred A., *The Organization and Administration of the Union Army, 1861-1865*, 2 vols., Cleveland, 1928

Smith, William E., *The Francis Preston Blair Family in Politics*, 2 vols., New York, 1933

Snyder, Charles M., *The Jacksonian Heritage: Pennsylvania Politics, 1833-1848*, Harrisburg, 1958

Stanwood, Edward, *A History of the Presidency from 1788 to 1897*, Boston, 1898

Taussig, Frank W., *The Tariff History of United States*, Fifth Edition, New York, 1910

Todes, Charlotte, *William H. Sylvis and the National Labor Union*, New York, 1942

Tweedy, John, *History of the Republican Conventions, 1856-1908*. Danbury, 1910

Usher, John P., *President Lincoln's Cabinet*, Omaha, 1925
Weeden, William B., *War Government in Massachusetts, New York, Pennsylvania and Indiana*, Boston, 1906
Wilson, William B., *History of the Pennsylvania Railroad*, 2 vols., Philadelphia, 1895

BIOGRAPHICAL

Armor, William C., *Lives of the Governors of Pennsylvania*, Norwich, 1874
Barnes, Thurlow W., *Life of Thurlow Weed, II, Memoir*, 1884
Biographical Directory of the American Congress, 1774-1927, Washington, 1928
Biographical Encyclopaedia of Pennsylvania of Nineteenth Century, Philadelphia, 1874
Brigance, William N., *Jeremiah S. Black*, Philadelphia, 1934
Cortissez, Royal, *Life of Whitelaw Reid*, 2 vols., New York, 1921
Crippen, Lee F., *Simon Cameron*, Oxford, 1942
[Curtin], *Honors to Andrew Gregg Curtin*, Philadelphia, 1869
Deacon, Charles R. (manager), *A Biographical Album of Prominent Pennsylvanians*, Philadelphia, 1890
Dubois, James T., *et al.*, *Galusha A. Grow*, Boston, 1917
Egle, William H. (ed.), *Andrew Gregg Curtin: His Life and Services*, Philadelphia, 1895
Foulke, William D., *Life of Oliver P. Morton*, 2 vols., Kansas City, 1899
[Geary], *Memorial Addresses on the death of Governor John W. Geary*, Harrisburg, 1873
Going, Charles B., *David Wilmot: Free Soiler*, New York, 1924
Green, Arnold W., *Henry Charles Carey: Nineteenth-Century Sociologist*, Philadelphia, 1951
Hamlin, Charles E., *The Life and Times of Hannibal Hamlin*, Cambridge, 1889
Harris, Alexander, *A Biographical History of Lancaster County*, Lancaster, 1872
Hesseltine, William B., *Ulysses S. Grant: Politician*, New York, 1935

Jones, Charles W., *Life and Public Services of J. Glancy Jones*, 2 vols., Philadelphia, 1910

Jordan, John W., *Encyclopaedia of Pennsylvania Biography*, 3 vols., New York, 1941

Kamm, Samuel R., *The Civil War Career of Thomas A. Scott*, Philadelphia, 1940

Klein, Philip S., *President James Buchanan*, University Park, 1962

Konkle, Burton A., *Life and Speeches of Thomas Williams*, 2 vols., Philadelphia, 1905

McClure, Alexander K., *Life and Services of Andrew G. Curtin*, Harrisburg, 1895

Meade, George G. (ed.), *The Life and Letters of George Gordon Meade*, New York, 1913

Nevins, Allen, *Abram S. Hewitt*, New York, 1935

———, *Hamilton Fish*, New York, 1937

Oberholtzer, Ellis P., *Jay Cooke*, 2 vols., Philadelphia, 1907

Pearson, Henry G., *The Life of John A. Andrew*, 2 vols., Boston, 1904

Pratt, Harry E., "David Davis," MS, University of Illinois, 1930

Randall, James G., *Lincoln the President*, 2 vols., New York, 1946

Russell, William A., "A Biography of Alexander K. McClure," MS, University of Wisconsin, 1953

Sandburg, Carl, *Abraham Lincoln: The War Years*, 4 vols., New York, 1939

Savidge, Eugene C., *Life of Benjamin Harrison Brewster*, Philadelphia, 1891

Smith, William Ernest, *The Francis Preston Blair Family in Politics*, 2 vols., New York, 1933

Stuart, Milton C., *Asa Packer*, Princeton, 1938

Tinkcom, Harry M., *John White Geary*, Philadelphia, 1940

White, Andrew D., *Autobiography of Andrew Dickson White*, 2 vols., New York, 1905

White, Horace T., *The Life of Lyman Trumbull*, Boston, 1913

Woodburn, James A., *Life of Thaddeus Stevens*, Indianapolis, 1913

HISTORICAL ARTICLES

(anon), "The Political Campaign of 1872," *North American Review*, CXV (1872), 401-22

Ashhurst, Richard L., "William Morris Meredith," *American Law Register*, LV (1907), 201-43

Beale, Howard K., "The Tariff and Reconstruction," *American Historical Review*, XXXV (January 1930), 276-94

Blankenburg, Rudolph, "Forty Years in the Wilderness; or, Masters and Rulers of 'The Freemen' of Pennsylvania," *The Arena*, XXXIII (1905), 1-10, 113-27

Boucher, John N., "Edgar Cowan: United States Senator from Pennsylvania during the Civil War," *Americana* (1932), 247-260

Carr, Clarke, "Why Lincoln Was Not Nominated by Acclamation," *Century*, LIV (1907), 503-506

Conlin, Sister, Frances L. "The Democratic Party in Pennsylvania from 1856-1865." American Catholic Historical Society *Records*, XLVII (1936), 132-83

Cox, Jacob D., "How Judge Hoar ceased to be Attorney-General," *Atlantic Monthly*, LXXVI (1895), 162

Dickson, Samuel, "George Sharswood—Teacher and Friend," *American Law Register*, LV (1907), 401-27

Dodds, A. John, "Honest John Covode," *Western Pennsylvania Historical Magazine*, XVI (1933), 175-82

Oliver, John W., "Matthew Stanley Quay," *Western Pennsylvania Historical Magazine* (1934), 1-12

Pershing, B. F., "Senator Edgar A. Cowan," *ibid.*, IV (1921), 224-33

Pratt, Harry E., "Simon Cameron's Fight for a Place in Lincoln's Cabinet," Abraham Lincoln Association *Bulletin*, No. 49 (1937), 3-11

Robinson, Elwyn B., "The North American," *Pennsylvania Magazine of History and Biography*, LXIV (1940), 345-55

———, "The Press: President Lincoln's Philadelphia Organ," *ibid.,* LXV (1941), 157-70

Russ, William A., "The Origin of the Ban on Special Legislation in the Constitution of 1873," *Pennsylvania History,* XI (1944), 260-75

Worthington, T. K., "Historical Sketch of the Finances of Pennsylvania," American Economic Association *Publications,* II (May 1887), 14-106

Index

466   *The Triumph of Militant Republicanism*

Trumbull, Lyman, attacks Cameron, 187

Union League, 205, 239, 295, 308, 367 ; organization, 174-75 : endorses Lincoln, 198
Union Party, *see* Republican Party
United States, House of Representatives, 27, 129 ; contest for speakership, 97-98 ; censures Cameron, 183 ; Senate, 108, 187, 242, 278, 306

Vallandigham, Clement L., 161, 238
Van Buren, Martin, 31, 34
Vaux, Richard, 79, 260-61, 391

Waddell, William B., 215
Wade, Benjamin F., 97, 197, 233, 278-79, 290, 291
Walborn, Cornelius A., 194, 232
Wallace, William, 247, 281, 384 ; party leadership, 214 ; blocks move to replace Clymer, 272 ; rejects judgeship nomination, 280 ; factional fight for senatorial nomination, 317 ; senatorial nominee (1875), 419
War Democrats, 142
Washburne, Elihu, 305 ; and Curtin conference, 387
Washington Peace Convention, 109-110
Watterson, Henry, on Liberal Republican convention, 380
Weir, Hugh H., 248
Welles, Gideon, 185, 219-20, 315
Welsh, William H., 89 ; senatorial candidate, 1861, 125
West Chester *American,* accusations against Geary, 364
Whig Party, in Pennsylvania, 29, 40 ; endorsement of Fillmore, 41
White, Andrew D., 402
White, Harry, 199, 262, 398
Wickersham, James P., 421
"Wide-Awakes," 86-87
Williams, Henry, nominated for state supreme court, 1867, 282 ; in 1869, 344 ; sketch of, 282-83
Williams, Thomas, 211, 290
Williamson, Passmore, 42
Williamsport, Labor Reform Convention of 1872, 396
Wilmot, David, 29, 31, 42, 44, 114 ; his proviso, 29, 39 ; candidate for governor, 46-47 ; at Peace Convention, 110 ; defeated for caucus nomination (1861), 120-23 ; elected Senator for short term (1861), 125 ; tries for senatorial renomination, 190-91 ; death of, 299
Wilson, Henry, 185, 187 ; and Vice-Presidency, 403
Wilson, William Bender, 129
Winnebago Indians, 36
Witte, William H., 71, 161